Russia

49509

RUSSIA

EIGHTH EDITION

A Historical Introduction from Kievan Rus' to the Present

John M. Thompson
and Christopher J. Ward

WESTVIEW
PRESS

Westview Press
Hachette Book Group
1290 Avenue of the Americas
New York, NY 10104
www.westviewpress.com

Eighth Edition: July 2017

Published by Westview Press, an imprint of Perseus Books, LLC, a subsidiary of Hachette Book Group, Inc.

The Hachette Speakers Bureau provides a wide range of authors for speaking events. To find out more, go to www.hachettespeakersbureau.com or call (866) 376-6591.

The publisher is not responsible for websites (or their content) that are not owned by the publisher.

Print book interior design by Jack Lenzo

Library of Congress Cataloging-in-Publication Data has been applied for.
ISBNs: 978-0-8133-4985-5 (paperback), 978-0-8133-5077-6 (ebook)

CONTENTS

ACKNOWLEDGMENTS

I would like to recognize a number of individuals and institutions for their assistance to me over the years and during my involvement with this project.

My first thanks go to Professor Martha Cooley of Guilford College, who was my undergraduate Russian history instructor and who encouraged me to pursue my studies at the graduate level.

Second, I wish to acknowledge my first graduate-level Russian history professor, the late David MacKenzie of the University of North Carolina at Greensboro. As the author of several important works on Russian and Balkan history as well in his mentorship of me, Dr. MacKenzie provided essential training and encouragement that has benefitted me throughout my career.

Of all the influences in my professional life, Professor Donald Raleigh of the University of North Carolina at Chapel Hill deserves my deepest appreciation. As my advisor at UNC, Dr. Raleigh played the leading role in the development of my scholarship and training as an educator. Since I met Don over twenty-five years ago, he has given me his unyielding support both as a graduate student and as a colleague. I am indebted to him for his tireless advocacy of me.

I am also grateful to Clayton State University, Koninklijke Brill, and the staff at Westview Press and Perseus Books, in particular Holly Birchfield and Katharine Moore, for their assistance.

In addition, I am profoundly honored that the late Professor Thompson agreed to allow me to serve as coauthor of this new edition of his textbook, which I have relied on many times in the past in my own teaching and with which I am now proud to be involved.

Finally, I am most thankful for the support and encouragement provided by my wife, Heidi, my son, Neil, and my parents, Jim and Carol, throughout my career.

My thanks to you all.

CHRISTOPHER J. WARD
ATLANTA, APRIL 2017

PREFACE

After Putin's brazen annexation of Crimea and his fomenting of anti-Ukraine separatism in eastern Ukraine, it became clear that a new edition of this short history was needed. Fortunately, Christopher J. Ward, an experienced and able colleague, agreed to undertake the bulk of the revision. He greatly improved earlier chapters, thoroughly updated the suggested readings, and wrote an excellent and objective last chapter on the Putin era. The first impetus for a revised edition came from Katharine Moore at Westview Press, and she has been a constant guide and valuable resource throughout. Once again I hope that this account of Russia's past will provide students and general readers with a clear and balanced look at the struggles and triumphs of the Russian people, who have endured a great deal, contributed much to world culture, and surely deserve a secure and fruitful future.

JOHN M. THOMPSON
PHIPPSBURG, MAINE
OCTOBER 2016

PREFACE TO THE FIRST EDITION

This book grew out of dissatisfaction my students and I experienced with longer, more detailed histories of Russia at the University of Hawaii in spring 1983, when I taught a survey course treating the entire history of Russia in one semester. Such a course, difficult under the best of circumstances, becomes almost impossible for both instructor and students when the latter must try to master in fourteen weeks the complex material of a six-hundred-page textbook designed for a two-semester course. In my view, there is no up-to-date, clear, short history of Russia that gives approximately equal attention to earlier Russian history and to the modern period since 1801. I hope this book will fill a need for teachers and students at the upper secondary and college levels.

At the same time, I have become aware of the interest in Russia and its past on the part of many individuals not enrolled in courses in Russian history, those in other fields or with a general curiosity about foreign cultures or international affairs. Friends of my children, acquaintances, audience members at public lectures I give, and others frequently ask me, "I would like to learn something about Russia and its history. Is there a good short book I can start with?" Unfortunately, I cannot recommend any single book as an introduction to the subject. Consequently, although I have written this volume primarily for students, I have also had in mind general readers, with the goal that this brief account might both provide them basic information and whet their appetites for further reading and study of Russian history.

To some extent, this book is also the outgrowth of my career as a student and teacher of Russian history for almost forty years. The story of the Russian people—their tribulations and courage, their tragedies and triumphs, and their remarkable contribution to world culture—remains just as fascinating to me today as when I first encountered it in 1946 in the undergraduate classroom of Professor E. Dwight Salmon of Amherst College. I hope that readers can glimpse the personalities, excitement, and drama of Russian history even in this introductory account.

A work of this circumscribed compass has obvious limitations. In this preface and throughout the book, I occasionally use the terms "Russia" or "Russian" to refer to the whole territory and collection of peoples in the tsarist empire or the Soviet Union. The reader needs to keep in mind that this terminology is for brevity and convenience, that, in fact, Russia is only part of a much larger state and Russians comprise barely half the population of the Soviet Union. Although the book tries to make clear that the tsarist empire was multinational from at least the 1600s and that non-Russians made important contributions to Russian and Soviet history, a longer volume would be needed to give adequate treatment to the non-Russian aspects of this story.

Similarly, I could deal only cursorily with a number of significant topics, such as religious history, and no subject could receive full and definitive treatment. Moreover, many questions in Russian history are still matters of lively historiographic debate. Although I have tried to note the most significant of these disputes, lack of space made it infeasible to present contending positions in detail or to take account of the Marxist views of Soviet historians as fully as is probably warranted.

The book is designed for the introductory survey course that treats Russian history from Kiev to the present in one semester. Since the chapters are short, averaging about twenty-five pages, the instructor can require corollary reading as well. The book can also be used in two-semester survey courses in which the instructor wants students to acquire a basic chronological structure and framework of information from a textbook but also seeks to expand their acquaintance with Russian history and culture by asking them to read primary sources, selected articles, contemporary documents, or fiction (poetry, short stories, novels, plays). To assist both students and general readers who wish to delve more deeply into a topic that interests them, a brief list of recommended readings in English follows each chapter. Maps and illustrations have been chosen to relate directly to the text.

This history is predominantly a straightforward narrative. It aims to give the reader a logically organized, lucid, unembellished account of the main events and developments in the history of Russia from its origins to today. No particular theory about the evolution of Russia is espoused; no special or novel interpretations are advanced. Within the limits of space, the chapters analyze why important events happened, and readers are challenged to think through their own answers to certain questions. Whenever a conclusion is put forward that is not widely accepted among Western scholars or that represents a new point of view, I have noted it as my own.

DATES AND NAMES

Beginning in 1700 and continuing until February 1918, dates in Russia were calculated according to the Julian calendar, or in the Old Style. In the eighteenth century, that calendar was eleven days behind the Gregorian calendar (New Style) used in the West; in the nineteenth century, it was twelve days behind; and in the twentieth century, thirteen days. Because students are familiar with Western dates, we have given all dates in the New Style, or according to the Gregorian calendar.

Since some Russian names are familiar to Western readers (e.g., Nicholas for the last tsar, Leo Tolstoy for the novelist), transliterating all names according to strictly followed rules would create confusion. We have tried to use common sense, seeking clarity while at the same time avoiding excessive anglicization.

ACKNOWLEDGMENTS

I am indebted to my first graduate-level teachers of Russian history, Professors Philip E. Mosely and Geroid T. Robinson, for providing the enthusiasm and insights on which I began to build my own understanding of Russia and the Soviet Union. My students at the University of Hawaii and my colleagues there, Professors Don Raleigh and Rex Wade, empathized with my complaints about the difficulty of the course I was teaching and the lack of suitable text material for it, and all of them strongly encouraged me when I was seized by a determination to try to write the book I needed. My employer, the Universities Field Staff International, generously released me half-time between May and September 1984 so that I could begin this book. My first editor, Alex Holzman, reacted enthusiastically when I first suggested this volume and assisted me with heartening support in the initial stages of planning and writing it.

Invaluable help was furnished by Professor John T. Alexander of the University of Kansas, a distinguished scholar of seventeenth- and eighteenth-century Russia, who acted as my consultant and meticulous first reader. He not only caught many errors and awkward expressions but was willing to discuss with me points of befuddlement and interpretation. I am most grateful for his cheerful assistance. Needless to say, he is in no way responsible for whatever mistakes and infelicities remain.

This book was written at home, and I thank my wife warmly for her constant support and understanding.

J. M. T.
SEPTEMBER 1985

CHAPTER 1

INTRODUCTION: ANCIENT RUSSIA AND KIEVAN RUS'

THE GEOGRAPHY OF RUSSIA AND THE FORMER SOVIET UNION

Most Westerners find it difficult to comprehend the vast expanse of territory encompassed by Russia and the other fourteen states of the former Soviet Union,[1] which existed as the Union of Soviet Socialist Republics (USSR) from 1917 to 1991. In order to comprehend the enormity of this space, we should be aware of a couple of impressive facts: that this gigantic region covers one-sixth of the land surface of the entire earth, across Eurasia from the Pacific Ocean in the east to the Baltic Sea (an arm of the Atlantic Ocean) in the west (see Map 1.1). But it requires a specific experience to make concrete the great sweep of the Russian and neighboring lands.

For John M. Thompson, the coauthor of this book, this realization came one evening in the 1960s, when he boarded a train to travel from Kiev, the capital of what was then the Soviet republic of Ukraine, to Moscow, the capital of the Soviet Union and now of Russia. Thompson found himself occupying a compartment with his fellow passengers and what seemed like a hundred suitcases, bundles, packages, and even a small trunk. A conversation between Thompson and one female passenger soon revealed that her husband was a colonel in the Soviet Air Force stationed in Vladivostok, a main port and base on the Pacific Ocean. She had been home visiting relatives in Ukraine and had stocked up on a few supplies to make her life on the distant frontier of the Soviet Far East a bit more comfortable. As he tried to wedge himself in among the boxes and bags, Thompson asked her how long a trip she would have. When she replied "eight nights and seven days," his jaw dropped. Seeing his surprise, she admonished

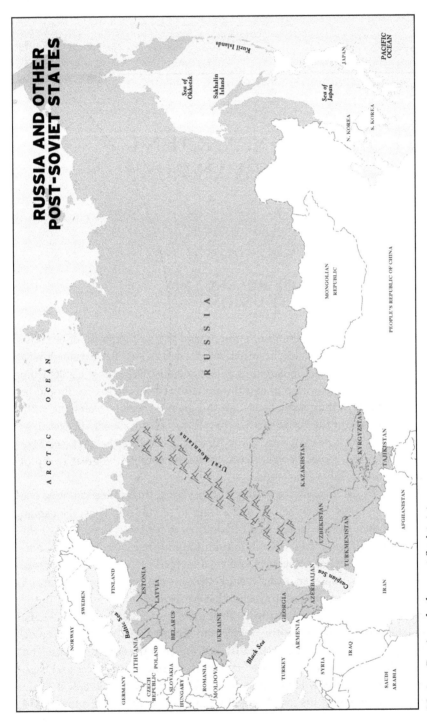

MAP 1.1. Russia and other post-Soviet states

Professor Thompson: "Yes, it is a big country, much bigger than yours." In fact, the former USSR was larger than the United States and Canada combined. Today, the contemporary Russian Federation is the largest nation in the world and occupies nearly 11 percent of the total land area of our planet.

For Christopher J. Ward, the other coauthor, who traveled along the Trans-Siberian Railway between Moscow and the Siberian city of Irkutsk in 2000 and again in 2010, the enormity of Russia was also striking as he passed from European Russia east into Siberia and the Russian Far East. While conducting research for his dissertation and later his first book, Ward witnessed firsthand the great expanses of the Russian countryside as well as the dynamism of Russia's two largest cities, the "Northern Capital" and former imperial capital of St. Petersburg (known from 1924 to 1991 as Leningrad) and Moscow, which is one of the world's largest cities with a population of over sixteen million people. While the Russian Federation experienced by Ward had changed greatly from the Soviet state visited by Thompson, the profound size and impact of the Russian and post-Soviet lands remained.

Six thousand miles and eleven time zones from east to west, three thousand miles from north to south, with the world's longest coastline (much of it along the Arctic Ocean), the expanse of the Russian Empire, the former Soviet Union, and the fifteen post-Soviet states contains every sort of terrain: deserts, semitropical beaches and fruit groves, inland seas, sweeping semiarid plains, rugged mountains, treeless grasslands known as steppe, thick forests, long rivers, and the icebound tundra of the far north.

The size of Russia and the other states of the former Soviet Union creates special challenges for the people living there. How can such a huge territory be managed and its riches extracted and used efficiently? How can its inhabitants stay in touch with one another and develop a sense of common identity and purpose? How can power be exercised and the state administered over such vast distances? What should be the balance between control from the center and local decision making? Should new industry be developed where a majority of the people live but where there are few resources, or where there exist large quantities of raw materials but few inhabitants?

In addition, the great extent of the region's landmass produced important strategic consequences over the centuries. Paradoxically, the area was both hard to conquer and hard to defend. The peoples living in the region at various times have coped with enemies on three, four, and occasionally even five fronts. Thus, the governments of the area have had to allocate much of their effort and resources to defending large territories. However, the opponents of Russia and neighboring lands often had trouble invading and occupying the region. Although the Mongols succeeded in conquering and ruling much of what is now Russia and the other post-Soviet states from the 1200s to the 1400s, the Poles, the Swedes, the Turks, the French under Napoleon, and the Germans twice in the twentieth century had less luck, turned back in part by the enormous distances to be traversed.

In assessing the influence of the region's natural environment on its history, we find that its location is as important as its size. For example, if you lived in Washington, DC, and were suddenly transported by magic to a city in the former Soviet Union with a comparable latitude, where do you think you would end up? In Moscow? Kiev? Not at all. You would miss the area entirely because it lies within latitudes parallel to those of Canada and Alaska. St. Petersburg, for example, is just a bit farther north than Juneau, Alaska.

This northerly position on the earth's surface causes recurring hardships for the citizens of Russia and many of the other post-Soviet states. In many areas, winters are long and cold, and the growing season for food is short. Also, much of the land is so far north that it cannot be farmed, and living there is difficult. Consequently, imperial Russia and the Soviet Union were never rich agriculturally, despite their huge size.

Although situated in the northern part of the great Eurasian landmass, the Russian Empire and the former Soviet Union stretched south, east, and west so that they touched most of continental Asia, the Middle East, and Europe (see Map 1.1). As a result, the region has always been a crossroads of cultures and ideas. Russia and many of the other post-Soviet states were affected by European, Asian, and Islamic civilizations and absorbed aspects of all of them. In turn, and increasingly in the past two centuries, the Russian Empire, the former Soviet Union, and today's Russia and other post-Soviet states have influenced (and on occasion dominated) their neighbors.

In particular, Russia's central location in Eurasia has contributed strongly to its mix of cultures and values today and to its important role in contemporary world affairs. Although linked to both Asia and the West, Russian and neighboring societies have evolved in distinct and complex ways. They need not be characterized as exotic, Asian, or merely offshoots of Western civilization. Their unique history has produced modern societies unlike any others. As such, the region must be understood on its own terms.

Partly because of its northerly location and partly because it is situated far from the major oceans, Russia has a forbidding climate in most regions: very hot and dry in the summer, bitterly cold in the winter, with a spring marked by deep mud that makes travel on unpaved roads almost impossible. Since most of the rain comes across Europe from the Atlantic Ocean, it peters out as it moves over the Russian agricultural plain from west to east. Some of the best soil receives insufficient rainfall, and almost all the farming in central Asia requires irrigation. As a result, less than 15 percent of Russia's land is used for growing food, another feature that limits the country's agricultural potential and strength.

In some ways, the Russian Empire and Soviet Union in particular were well protected, especially by the frozen expanse of the Arctic Ocean to the north and by some of the highest mountains in the world to the southeast (see Map 1.1). Yet along their borders in the east, the southwest, and the west, Russia and neighboring states had virtually no natural defenses and at different times suffered invasions from all these points of the compass.

Moreover, the heart of the Russian Empire and Soviet Union was one vast plain, broken only by the Ural Mountains, which are not very high and, in any case, do not reach all the way to the Caspian Sea. The impact of this plain on the area's development was double-edged. Russia and adjacent lands often lay open to attack across this terrain, but the extent of the plain made it easy for the Russian state to expand and bring surrounding nationalities under its rule. One can easily visualize horsemen, traders, and modern armies moving back and forth across these flat expanses.

But Russians and other peoples who lived in the region traveled as much by water as by land. Although the Russian Empire was largely landlocked and had limited access to the sea—the Arctic shore opens primarily on ice, and the Baltic and Black Seas and the Sea of Japan in the far east lead to the Atlantic and Pacific Oceans only through narrow straits—much of Russia and neighboring lands possesses a widespread system of interconnecting rivers, "the roads that run," as folk wisdom puts it. Until about one hundred and fifty years ago, when railroads, motor vehicles, and planes appeared, Russians and other peoples moved extensively by boat, up and down the rivers, which generally flow in a north-south or south-north direction, or on the tributaries that touch each other along an east-west axis. Thus, the earliest inhabitants, using river routes, traveled to and traded with Europeans and Vikings to the northwest, Byzantine Greek Christians to the southwest, and Asian merchants and artisans to the south. Later, the Russian Empire's expansion across Siberia, led by fur trappers and traders, was carried out primarily by water. Even in modern times, river transport plays an important role in moving goods and people throughout the region (see Figure 1.1).

Modern Russia and the former Soviet Union possess rich natural resources, but much of this wealth, such as oil, natural gas, and other abundant minerals, was exploited only recently. For most of its history, the peoples of Russia and surrounding areas were quite poor, and they struggled to survive and improve their way of life while supporting, with limited resources, a government-organized

FIGURE 1.1. Barge traffic in the 1890s on the Volga River, an important commercial artery in the region from the earliest times. (Courtesy of the Library of Congress, LC-DIG-prok-02445)

defense against recurrent enemies. Unfortunately, carrying the burden of the state and the army often meant that people lived in harsh poverty. Since World War II, there has been progress in raising the quality of life, and the resources exist for citizens of the region to live more comfortably in the future.

THE PEOPLES OF RUSSIA AND THE FORMER SOVIET UNION

The most striking fact about the population of the states of the former Soviet Union is their great diversity: some 125 national groups, of which over 20 included more than one million people, inhabit the area. During the Soviet period, school textbooks were printed in over fifty languages, and today a wide

FIGURE 1.2. A typical non-Russian citizen of the former Soviet Union: Kazakh visitor from Central Asia in Red Square in front of the Kremlin. (UN Photo / Marvin Bolotsky)

variety of religions and cultures coexist within the borders of Russia and the other post-Soviet states. Jews generally spoke Russian and intermixed with the rest of the population throughout European Russia (the modern states of Russia, Ukraine, and Belarus). The other large, non-Slavic nationalities spoke their own languages, lived in geographically separate regions, had their own republics within the federal state of the USSR, and formed independent states after 1991. In the twentieth century, non-Russian groups developed a sense of ethnic identity and growing nationalist aspirations, which created the pressures that contributed to the collapse of the Soviet Union and the birth of fifteen post-Soviet states.

Of the approximately 290 million people living in the fifteen states of the former Soviet Union today, the largest ethnic groups have the following characteristics:

Russians:[2] 131 million
  81 percent of the population in Russia
  27 percent of the population in Latvia
  25 percent of the population in Estonia
  24 percent of the population in Kazakhstan
  17 percent of the population in Ukraine
  8 percent of the population in Belarus
Turkic and Tatar peoples: 89 million
  Azerbaijanis: 32 million (92 percent of the population in Azerbaijan)
  Bashkirs: 2 million
  Kazakhs: 15 million (64 percent of the population in Kazakhstan)
  Tatars: 8 million
  Turkmens: 6 million (85 percent of the population in Turkmenistan)
  Uzbeks: 26 million (81 percent of the population in Uzbekistan)
Ukrainians:[2] 45 million (78 percent of the population in Ukraine)
Belarusians:[2] 10 million (88 percent of the population in Belarus)
Caucasian peoples: 10 million
  Armenians: 5 million (98 percent of the population in Armenia)
  Georgians: 4 million (87 percent of the population in Georgia)
Baltic peoples: 6 million
  Latvians: 1.3 million (62 percent of the population in Latvia)
  Lithuanians: 2.6 million (87 percent of the population in Lithuania)
Finno-Ugric peoples: 1.1 million
  Estonians: 910,000 (69 percent of the population in Estonia)
Jews: 1.7 million

As this short overview indicates, geographic and demographic factors influenced the development of society in Russia and the former Soviet Union. A word of caution is in order, however. History is made by individuals in a society interacting with each other and their neighbors. Thus, it would be a misleading oversimplification to conclude that primarily Russian institutions, such as a centralized authoritarian government, or traditional Russian values, such as a concern for the group rather than the individual, resulted primarily from the harsh conditions of the region's natural environment.

THE FORMATION OF KIEVAN RUS'

Kievan Rus' emerged in the late 800s or early 900s. Briefly centered in the city of Novgorod in what is now northern Russia and then for several hundred

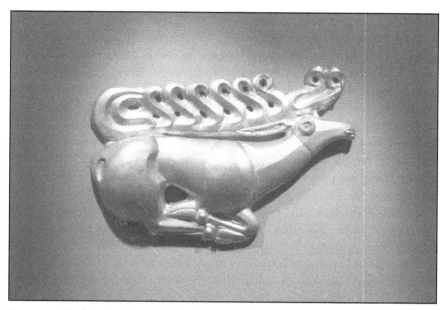

FIGURE 1.3. Scythian jewelers crafted a dynamic gold stag. (Courtesy of Dr. Daniel Wood)

years in the city Kiev on the Dnieper River in what is now the state of Ukraine, Kievan Rus' was a loose confederation whose origin remains unclear. During the late 700s and 800s, traders and warriors known as *Rus'* (the term from which the word "Russia" derives) participated in commercial activity in northern Russia and along the upper Volga River. Most likely, the Rus' were Swedish Vikings, but they intermingled and interacted with local groups of Finns, Balts, Volga Bulgars, and Slavs. They sought silver and luxury goods from the east, for which they traded furs and even slaves. In 860, an expedition of Rus' reached Constantinople, but regular contact with the Byzantine Greek civilization based in that city developed only later.

The most detailed historical source, *The Primary Chronicle*, compiled by monks in the eleventh century, recounts that since there was no order among the Slavic tribes in the 800s, they invited a Varangian (a term for Swedish Viking) named Riurik and his two brothers to come and rule over them. But this chronicle was written several hundred years later, partly for the purpose of legitimizing Riurik's alleged descendants' claims to power, making the story suspect in itself. In addition, a growing body of archeological and other evidence suggests that the role of the Varangians in Russia was a good deal more complex than the picture *The Primary Chronicle* paints.

As long-distance traders, the Varangians were well acquainted with the trading routes from Scandinavia to the east and to the Byzantine capital at

Constantinople that passed through today's Russia and Ukraine, primarily down the Dnieper River and across the Black Sea. Thus, the Varangians, though occasionally plundering and conquering as they did in Western Europe a short time later, entered the region primarily as traders and mercenaries. It seems logical to assume that in these roles they worked closely with local Slavic leaders to increase order and security, to protect trade routes, and to encourage regular payment of tribute by rural peoples to the commercial and military leaders of the towns in the area. Thus, although in certain times and places Slavs and Varangians undoubtedly clashed, and on occasion the Varangians may even have attempted to assert political control over Slavic groups, the Varangians and local leaders probably cooperated much more often in pursuit of common objectives. The most sensible conclusion is that the Varangians worked with Slavic chieftains to create a loose confederation of local states known as Kievan Rus'.

This first civilization is important to an understanding of Russian civilization for several reasons. In Kievan Rus', the fundamental characteristics of Russian culture and religion took root. Kievan Rus' also introduced basic and lasting political ideas and social institutions. Finally, it created the tradition of the region as a force in international affairs and as a linkage point between Europe and Asia.

HOW DID THE PEOPLES OF KIEVAN RUS' MAKE A LIVING?

Kievan Rus' lasted from the late 800s to the early 1200s. At its largest, the Kievan confederation was long and skinny. In the eleventh century, it stretched for thousands of miles from the Baltic Sea in the north to the Black Sea in the south, including a band of territory of varying width both east and west of its main axis on the Dnieper River (see Map 1.2). Educated guesses put its maximum population at about seven or eight million, of whom fewer than a million lived in towns and cities. The largest cities, like Kiev, probably contained tens of thousands of people, but in most of the over two hundred fortified centers that have been identified, the population was undoubtedly less than five thousand.

Over 85 percent of the people lived on the land as farmers, hunters and trappers, beekeepers, and herdsmen. Most of the farming was small in scale and used primitive implements, such as wooden plows and harrows, though some iron plows existed. Most of what people produced, they ate. But some of the output was delivered or seized as tribute or taxes to political and

MAP 1.2. Kievan Rus', circa 1100.

military leaders, first representing clans or tribes and later based in towns within Kievan Rus'. Besides crops used to feed soldiers and townspeople, the goods included furs, honey, hides, and wax, all of which could then be traded to outsiders, primarily the Byzantine Empire. Since there were frequent military campaigns to collect tribute and recurring wars with outsiders, captives were taken and often sold or traded as slaves, a convenient commodity since they could walk to market.

Because individual farmers, or even farming families, of the sort that existed later could not muster sufficient labor power to grow crops in the difficult conditions and with the poor methods of that era, most rural people in Kievan Rus' banded together in communes. A farming commune, known in Russian as *obshchina* (pronounced "ohbshcheena"), usually consisted of several extended families, although some apparently included individuals who were not near relatives. Members of both the collective farm and the obshchina pooled labor and tools to accomplish heavy agricultural tasks. They shared not only the work but the products of their labor. Throughout much of the area's history, these institutions, dominated by patriarchal elders, embodied joint responsibility for taxes and military recruits. They also fostered attitudes of egalitarianism and collectivism that influenced society.

Feudalism has sparked historiographic controversy about Kievan Rus', so it is useful to note several aspects of Kievan Rus' society related to feudalism that had an impact on later history. In the first place, the system of tribute (and later taxes) led to continuing obligations on the part of peasant farmers to various sorts of social, religious, and political overlords. Although in the Kievan Rus' period these obligations were neither usually in the form of labor nor tied to land ownership (obshchinas generally possessed their own land), they later took the form of service to a particular lord in return for certain use rights to land. Thus, in Kievan Rus' a pattern of obligation developed that in later centuries and under different economic and political conditions would help turn essentially free peasants into serfs.

Second, Kievan Rus' incorporated concepts of service that resembled some aspects of the relationship between lord and vassal in Western Europe. In particular, fighting men in Kiev, who came to be known as boyars, served particular princes, although the terms and duties of such service are rather unclear. This service concept later reappeared as a major principle at the time of the development of the Muscovite state, commonly known as Muscovy.

Finally, a key ingredient of European feudalism was largely lacking in Kievan society: the idea of mutuality. In the European relationship between lord and vassal, the lord had definite responsibilities to his subordinate vassals; in return, the vassals had obligations to the lord. Some writers have argued that this sense of a contract, of a mutual responsibility, is a crucial element in the development of representative government and civil rights in Western civilization. Whether they are right or not, the principle of mutual obligation hardly existed in Kievan Rus', and this may have contributed later to the ease with which the tsars of the Russian Empire asserted unlimited authority over all the people, lords and peasants alike.

Historians have also argued whether agriculture or trade predominated in the Kievan Rus' economy. The most likely answer is that, although most of the people farmed, producing agricultural and forest goods, trade and commercial activity also played an important role, especially in the life of the towns. Their location favored the peoples of Kievan Rus' in this regard. Situated between northern Europe and Constantinople and midway between central Europe and Asia, they could carry on a lively commerce in several directions.

There were, of course, risks. Small nomadic groups, such as the Cumans and Pechenegs, often attacked trading parties, particularly at rapids, where boats and goods had to be portaged. Terms of trade with the Byzantine Empire were not always favorable, and Kievan Rus' sent several military expeditions against Constantinople to compel the opening of better trading opportunities and contracts. Thus, military activity, including the collection of tribute, and trade went hand in hand. As a result, warriors and merchants (often the same persons) ranked high on the Kievan Rus' social scale.

The importance of trade to Kievan Rus' society was not only due to its economic benefits. Because the Kievan Rus' traded with neighbors on all sides, in Constantinople and in Asia, they were exposed to a wide range of ideas, technologies, and cultural influences. Kievan Rus' was not a "closed" society in any way but interacted effectively with Christian Europe, with the Hellenic empire of Byzantium, and with the Islamic civilization of the Arabs.

THE SOCIETIES OF KIEVAN RUS'

No evidence exists to tell us when class differentiation began in Kievan Rus', but by the time of the first law codes, compiled in the eleventh and twelfth centuries, the lines were sharply drawn. Depending on how one defines a distinct class, there were as many as eleven classes stipulated by Kievan Rus' law. But these can be allocated among seven main categories: princes, boyars (nobles), merchants, artisans, *smerdy* (peasants), semifree persons, and slaves. At the top of the ladder were the princely families. Allegedly descendants of Riurik and his brothers, they exercised military, judicial, and administrative power over most Kievan Rus' towns and territories. Relations among the princes were complicated, and their struggles for political preeminence led to civil war and greatly weakened the Kievan Rus' confederation.

At first, each prince had his own band of military servitors, of whom many in the beginning were probably Vikings. But soon they merged with already existing groups of Slavic warriors, and by the 1000s, a Slavicized upper class of lords, the boyars, had formed. Their numbers were always small, but their role was crucial since they carried out military service on behalf of prince, town, and state and also assumed administrative and governing responsibilities. Some of them certainly engaged in commerce as well.

In this role, they blended with a separate merchant class, the origins of which undoubtedly predate the formation of Kievan Rus'. The merchants, though of lower rank than that of the princely families and boyars, had considerable influence because of their importance to the economy of Kievan Rus' and because, in some towns, they also exercised political power. The merchants were among the chief consumers of the goods they imported from Asia and Byzantium: silks, spices, wines, fruits, metals, and jewelry.

Most people in towns fell into a broad group of artisans and workers. Their equivalent in the countryside, the peasants, bore the colorful designation *smerdy* ("the stinkers"). Some were dependent on princes or boyars, but apparently most were free. Through debt or other circumstances, both artisans and peasants could fall into the semifree class comprising people who were bound to another through some sort of obligation.

At the bottom of the social ladder were slaves. How important they were to the Kievan Rus' economy is not clear. Some may have been semifree individuals who fell into complete bondage, but a majority were apparently captured in war, and many were therefore not Slavic. In the earlier years of Kievan Rus' rule, slaves formed an important trade commodity.

RELIGION AND CULTURE IN KIEVAN RUS'

The single most important event in the history of Kievan Rus' was its official adoption of Christianity in 988. Although pagan beliefs and practices as well as earlier cultural attributes of Kievan Rus' society persisted long afterward, the acceptance of Christian religion fundamentally altered Russian civilization. Adopting Christianity affected not just religious beliefs and practices but also law, education, literature, the arts, attitudes and feelings, and even the political system.

An extremely significant aspect of Kievan Rus' conversion was that Christianity came to the area from the Byzantine Empire, which practiced what is today called Eastern, or Orthodox, Christianity. When the Kievan Rus' were converted, the Christian church was still united, although there were already considerable differences between its western wing based in Rome and its eastern wing centered in Constantinople. A short time later, in 1054, these divisions became irreconcilable, and the church split in two, forming the Latin (Roman Catholic) Church, which dominated in Western Europe, and the Greek (Eastern Orthodox) Church, which was prevalent in the Balkans, the Middle East, and the Eastern Slavic lands, including much of contemporary Belarus, Russia, and Ukraine.

This separation had three important consequences. First, the development of Christianity took quite a different form in the Eastern Slavic lands from that in Western Europe. Second, as the hostility between the two main branches of Christianity heightened, Kievan Rus' was put at odds with its nearest neighbors to the west: Poles, Lithuanians, and later German settlers along the shores of the Baltic Sea, all of whom were Roman Catholic. Finally, the region's intellectual and cultural contacts with Western European societies were curtailed for five or six hundred years, almost into modern times, when religious differences became much less important. It is true that the Mongol conquest of the area in the 1200s also acted to sever its ties with central and Western Europe, but religious difference was a formidable barrier and a source of suspicion and hostility.

In the year 955, the first woman ruler of Kievan Rus', Olga (one of the few women who appears in the sources from this period), chose Christianity for herself, but another three decades elapsed before Vladimir, one of Kievan Rus' ablest princes, decided to adopt Christianity as the official religion for the whole state and all its subjects. To make sure everyone got the message, he had the pagan idols smashed and arranged a mass baptism in the Dnieper River for all the inhabitants of the city of Kiev, at least according to *The Primary Chronicle*.

We do not know Vladimir's reasons for choosing Eastern Christianity, but can surmise fairly safely that the close commercial and political ties that Kievan Rus' had developed with Constantinople over the preceding hundred years were an important factor. Vladimir, who was later made a saint in recognition of his decision, was likely influenced by the fact that two Christian monks, Saints Cyril and Methodius, had developed a written language that, though based on Greek, transcribed the spoken Slavic language quite well. This new literary language meant that people did not need to learn Greek or Latin to become Christians, and the average person could understand the Mass and other church services. Today, Belarusian, Russian, Ukrainian, and other languages are written in the Cyrillic alphabet, named in honor of Saint Cyril.

Finally, geographic and political factors undoubtedly weighed heavily in Vladimir's choice. If he selected Judaism, its nearest adherents, the Khazars, were some distance away to the southeast, and their power was already in decline. If he chose Islam, the Arabs were even farther away, and he would be drawn into wars against their continuing enemy, the Byzantine Empire. Latin Christianity had spread only recently to northern Europe and must have seemed quite insignificant to Vladimir in comparison to the nearby might and magnificence of Orthodox Christianity, with its seat at Constantinople.

The Christianity Vladimir adopted had several important characteristics that were reinforced by local conditions and later differentiated it sharply from Western Christianity, particularly after the Latin Church split in the 1500s into

Protestant and Catholic branches. One was the almost mystical concern in Orthodox Christianity with the collective spirit of the whole congregation. In the religious service itself and in the spiritual outlook of the faithful, the focus is on the group of believers rather than on individual souls and their salvation. This attitude, called *sobornost'*, meaning "spirit of the congregation," fit well with the collective sense of the community that had already been developed among the Eastern Slavs through the peasant institution of the obshchina.

Orthodox Christianity also strongly emphasized outward forms of religion: the church buildings and decorations, the icons (paintings on wood of holy figures and saints), and the structure and ritual of the Mass itself. To stress these visible signs of devotion made it easier to wean the Eastern Slavs away from pagan idols and customs and to convert an illiterate population; together with the concept of sobornost', however, it encouraged a rather routine and passive practice of the new religion rather than engaging individuals directly in the process and stimulating personal commitments of faith and belief. Later, in Western Christianity, particularly after the Protestant Reformation, individualism in religion (and later in other matters) gained ground, while collectivism continued to predominate in Russian Orthodox Christianity.

Finally, Byzantine Christianity was quite otherworldly, stressing asceticism, the importance of a communal monastic life, and the rewards of the hereafter. Again, this tendency was strengthened in its transplantation to Kievan Rus', and later it worked against the Orthodox Church's taking an active role in everyday life as a force for social betterment.

For a long time, Christianity was only thinly superimposed on the basic animistic beliefs and customs of the Slavic population of Kievan Rus'. Many old pagan rites and practices were continued or even adapted to the new religion. As a result, some historians say, many peoples of Kievan Rus' never fully understood the new faith and accepted it only superficially. Only the educated few in the upper classes of society were fully committed to Christianity.

At the same time, there is no doubt that the introduction of Christianity raised the general level of culture, learning, and artistic expression in Kievan Rus'. Well-educated monks and priests entered the area, monasteries were established, churches were built, and artisans were trained. By the middle of the eleventh century, Kievan Rus' civilization, though modeled on Byzantine achievements in most fields, had reached a height of cultural and artistic splendor that was not to be equaled in the area again until some five hundred years later.

The introduction of a written language, Old Church Slavonic, meant that books were produced and circulated. To be sure, only a tiny fraction of the population was literate, but this upper crust was quite sophisticated, aware of intellectual currents and developments in both Byzantium and Europe. In addition, Constantinople masters taught Kievan Rus' the art of painting icons and introduced them to church music. A magnificent cathedral in Byzantine style, Saint Sophia, named after the main church in Constantinople (also known as Hagia Sophia), was built in Kiev and decorated by local craftsmen. Kievan Rus' artisans, who had developed great skill in working with indigenous materials, particularly wood, modified Byzantine forms into a distinctive and charming style. Unfortunately, because almost all the buildings they erected were made of wood and were subsequently destroyed in the frequent fires that plagued Kievan Rus' towns, we have only a few descriptions or examples of these striking architectural achievements.

Education, scholarship, art, architecture, and music were all predominantly religious in motivation and theme. Naturally, all these aspects of cultural life followed Byzantine precepts and models. But Kievan Rus' artists soon introduced local subjects and techniques, and before long, they had surpassed their Byzantine masters in icon painting, creating some of the most moving and beautiful religious paintings in the world.

Nonreligious, primarily folk art also developed, particularly in songs and stories. The first secular piece of literature, *The Tale of the Host of Igor*, is a stirring pagan saga of the adventures of a Kievan Rus' prince and his followers in fighting an array of enemies to defend their homeland. In the words of the tale:

Igor leads his warriors to the Don.
The birds in oak trees portend his misfortunes
The wolves howl of the menace in the ravines
The eagles with their clatter summon beasts to a bony feast
The foxes yelp at the crimson shield.
O Russian land! You are so far behind the mountains. . . .
With their shields the Russians have divided the great field
Seeking honor for themselves and glory for their prince.[3]

Considered as a whole, Kievan Rus' culture and civilization in the 1000s and 1100s was probably at a higher level than Western European civilization at the same time. Moreover, the upper classes in Kievan Rus' society interacted with the elite of central and Western Europe. In addition to the contacts between and travels of Kievan Rus' and European merchants, the princely families in Kievan Rus' intermarried with noble and royal families in the German states and Scandinavia.

POWER AND POLITICS IN KIEVAN RUS'

The impact of Byzantine civilization was felt not only in religion and culture, but also in thought, values, and attitudes. These influences were made tangible in the Kievan Rus' law codes of the eleventh and twelfth centuries and the political order. Yet in politics, Byzantine ideas could never quite overcome more traditional concepts and institutions; they had their greatest impact later during the Muscovite period.

For example, the Byzantine state was a clearly defined geographic area over which the emperor and his administration exercised control. But the concept of state and sovereignty in the Kievan Rus' system was much less clear. Authority derived originally from the person of the prince, and his jurisdiction ran along trade routes, over scattered areas that paid him tribute, and in certain fortified centers rather than over a specific contiguous territory.

Moreover, although eventually it was recognized that the prince at Kiev was the senior prince and therefore head of the confederation, princes in other towns had rights of their own. They also felt free to contest for leadership with the Kievan prince. Certain towns, particularly the important northern trading and administrative center of Novgorod, also had autonomous rights. The princes at Kiev possessed little centralized authority or direct administrative and political control, but rather led a fluid confederation of towns and tribes.

In the middle of the Kievan Rus' period, Iaroslav (1019–1054), one of the ablest princes, tried to set up a system of rotating rulership under which younger brothers to the prince of Kiev held power in towns designated according to their seniority. When the ruler at Kiev died, everyone moved up one notch. This system was designed to avert the bitter and bloody struggles for succession that had plagued the politics of Kievan Rus' over the preceding hundred years. But such a complicated system, requiring great self-restraint by all the players, soon broke down in practice, and the succession to the princedom at Kiev continued to be settled on most occasions by force and strife.

This meant that Kievan Rus' princes had to spend a good part of their reigns fighting off rival claimants to the throne. In addition, princes had to defend the confederation from external enemies on all sides and, particularly, to protect the trade routes to Byzantium from nomadic attacks originating in the southeast. A further major military obligation was to keep sufficient pressure on the Byzantine emperors so that they would grant political concessions and favorable commercial privileges to the prince, his warriors, and his merchants. As if all this were not enough, the prince was frequently called upon to wage military campaigns against recalcitrant subjects or neighboring tribes who refused to pay taxes or deliver tribute.

It is little wonder that a good part of a prince's life was spent in warfare. One of the most successful military leaders of Kievan Rus', Sviatoslav, who ruled from 962 to 972, is described in *The Primary Chronicle* as follows:

> Stepping light as a leopard, he undertook many campaigns. Upon his expeditions he carried with him neither wagons nor kettles, and boiled no meat, but cut off small strips of horseflesh, game, or beef, and ate it after roasting it on the coals. Nor did he have a tent, but he spread out a horse blanket under him, and set his saddle under his head; and all his retinue did likewise.[4]

When the princes were at home, they faced other obstacles to their rule. Two political-administrative institutions existed in Kievan Rus' to represent the interests of the upper classes: the boyar *duma* and the *veche*. The duma was a body of the highest-ranking nobles who in theory advised the prince, though it remains unclear how much power it had or how regularly princes consulted it. Before major military campaigns and during succession struggles over title to the head principality at Kiev, it behooved the prince to garner as much support from the boyars as possible, and he probably used the duma for that purpose.

The veche, a town council dominated by merchants, had considerable influence, particularly in towns in the north, where it had a stronger and longer tradition. In a few places, such as Novgorod, the veche on occasion exercised full political authority and administered the town and surrounding territory. But in other towns, it had only a minor advisory role.

As with any series of rulers, the princes of Kievan Rus' varied greatly in ability, persistence, and success. The first few were Vikings, though they were quite Slavicized; all the rest for over two hundred years were ethnic Slavs. Although the legendary credit goes to Riurik, Prince Oleg was the actual founder of Kievan Rus'. A Varangian from Novgorod, he saw the advantages of linking as many towns as possible along the main trade route from the Baltic to the Black Seas, and he united Novgorod and Kiev by force. Moving his base to Kiev around 880, he established the primacy of that city, "the mother of Rus' towns," which lasted until 1132. In 907, Oleg attacked Constantinople. As a result of his victories, he was able to negotiate an effective commercial treaty with Byzantium in 911. Oleg also merged his Viking and Slavic warriors into a single upper class and established greater control over the Slavic tribes along both sides of the Dnieper River.

Almost a hundred years after Oleg had established and begun to consolidate the state, Vladimir, who ruled from 980 to 1015, made remarkable strides in extending its authority east, south, and west and in raising the Kievan Rus' level of culture and sophistication, in part by adopting Christianity as the official religion.

Yet Vladimir's sons fought over the succession, and civil war weakened the confederation for two decades. Strong leadership was restored under Iaroslav the Wise, who reigned from 1036 to 1054. He extended Kievan authority over new areas and was able to put an end for some time to the constant, harassing attacks of the Pechenegs in the east. He also supervised the compilation of the first law code and encouraged the building of Saint Sophia and other important churches. Within a few decades of his death, however, inter-princely fighting had again become widespread, and except for a brief resurgence in the first quarter of the twelfth century, Kievan Rus' power and cohesion declined steadily over the next hundred and fifty years.

CONCLUSION

Various reasons have been advanced for the Kievan Rus' decline. As is so often true in explaining major events in history, not one cause but many produced the collapse of the Kievan confederation. Perhaps the most important was its political weakness. Neither effectively centralized nor cohesive, by the late 1100s, under weaker princes, Kievan Rus' increasingly disintegrated into rival princedoms and towns that spent more time fighting each other than their common external enemies. No institutionalized central government existed, and the struggle to become grand prince became increasingly divisive. For example, between 1139 and 1169, the throne changed hands seventeen times. The loose confederation gradually fractured into its component parts.

A second major factor in the Kievan Rus' decline was its loss of economic strength. The goods it traded became less valuable, and at about the same time, Europeans established new trade routes to the Near East and Asia, while the position of the Byzantine Empire weakened. As a result, the trade routes across the region became less important, and the Kievan Rus' economy declined.

However important political, economic, and commercial causes were to the Kievan Rus' demise, in the end, external factors played the decisive role. Throughout its history, Kievan Rus' had struggled, with limited resources, against foreign foes, particularly various nomads from Asia who constantly attacked the state from the southeast. In the 1100s, this effort increasingly became a losing fight, and Kievan Rus' was weakened by recurring battles against the Cumans. These latest nomadic invaders succeeded on various occasions in cutting the trade route to the Black Sea and caused much damage as well as loss of life. In 1169, Andrei Bogoliubskii, prince of Vladimir-Suzdal, an area in the northeast, sacked Kiev and then chose to reign as grand prince at Vladimir instead of Kiev. In the thirteenth century, the Mongols arrived to administer the coup de grâce to the remnants of Kievan Rus'.

Although Kievan Rus' was overrun and conquered, the civilization it created was not. Kievan Rus' left a powerful legacy on which much of the subsequent Russian and Ukrainian civilizations were built. Kievan Rus' had succeeded in drawing together and blending four elements: the ancient indigenous population, the imprint of successive steppe empires, the influence of the Varangians and Vikings, and the powerful impact of Byzantium.

The most significant gift Kievan Rus' bestowed on subsequent generations was Orthodox Christianity. The Orthodox Church and faith played quite a different role in the region than Christianity did in Western history, but its importance in the development of society cannot be denied. After the Bolshevik Revolution of 1917, the Soviet government attempted to eliminate religion, but it failed. More than fifty million Christians were practicing their faith in 1991 when the Soviet Union collapsed. Today, the Orthodox Church plays a major political, social, and religious role in Belarus, Russia, and much of Ukraine.

With Orthodox Christianity came Byzantine culture, learning, and law. Consequently, Kievan Rus' produced from the very beginning a compound of indigenous Slavic values and forms and Byzantine borrowings. The result was quite distinct from Western European civilization. A foundation had been laid, but it was only a beginning. Much more, and much of it traumatic, was to happen to the successors of Kievan Rus' as they struggled to build a unique civilization and future.

FURTHER READING

Barford, P. M. *The Early Slavs: Culture and Society in Early Medieval Eastern Europe*. Ithaca, NY: Cornell University Press, 2001.

Cross, Samuel H., and Olgerd P. Sherbowitz-Wetzer, trans. and eds. *The Russian Primary Chronicle*. Cambridge, MA: Medieval Academy of America, 2012.

Dolukhanov, Pavel M. *The Early Slavs: Eastern Europe from the Initial Settlement to the Kievan Rus*. London: Longman, 1996.

Franklin, Simon, and Jonathan Shepard. *The Emergence of Rus', 750–1200*. London: Longman, 1996.

Hosking, Geoffrey A. *Russia and the Russians: A History*. Cambridge, MA: Belknap Press of Harvard University Press, 2001.

King, Charles. *The Black Sea: A History*. Oxford: Oxford University Press, 2004.

Levin, Eve. *Sex and Society in the World of the Orthodox Slavs, 900–1700.* Ithaca, NY: Cornell University Press, 1989.

Martin, Janet. *Medieval Russia, 980–1584.* 2nd ed. Cambridge, UK: Cambridge University Press, 2007.

Milner-Gulland, Robin. *The Russians.* Oxford: Blackwell, 1997.

Plokhy, Serhii. *The Gates of Europe: A History of Ukraine.* New York: Basic Books, 2015.

———. *The Origins of the Slavic Nations: Premodern Identities in Russia, Ukraine, and Belarus.* Cambridge, UK: Cambridge University Press, 2006.

Pushkareva, Natalia. *Women in Russian History from the Tenth to the Twentieth Century.* Translated and edited by Eve Levin. Armonk, NY: M. E. Sharpe, 1997.

Rybakov, B. *Kievan Rus.* Moscow: Progress Publishers, 1989.

Sawyer, P. H. *Kings and Vikings: Scandinavia and Europe, A.D. 700–1100.* London: Methuen, 1982.

Shchapov, Y. N. *State and Church in Early Russia, 10th–13th Centuries.* New Rochelle, NY: Caratzas, 1995.

CHAPTER 2

KIEVAN RUS' IN CRISIS AND THE MONGOL CONTACT, 1054–1462

In the twelfth century, internal dissension gravely weakened Kievan Rus' civilization. In the thirteenth century, the Mongol arrival transformed it even further. While some features of Kievan Rus' society persisted and were incorporated into the Muscovite state that arose in the fourteenth century, a new civilization emerged beginning in the eleventh century that differed in a number of ways, many of which resulted from the psychological, economic, and political effects of the Mongol contact.

For Russians, other Slavic peoples, and many non-Slavs living in the thirteenth and fourteenth centuries, the overriding need was for security. This was at the very time when Europeans, as they emerged from the Middle Ages, were enjoying increased protection from feudal infighting and external attack as well as benefiting from rising economic well-being provided by improved agriculture and reviving trade. Meanwhile, Russians, Ukrainians, and many others who lived under Mongol control were forced to deliver tribute and sometimes conscripts to the Mongols. Trade and handicraft production languished, and agriculture remained primitive. Consequently, limited resources hampered the regional populations' efforts to protect themselves and to create a stable society. Moreover, the enemies of the Russians and other neighboring peoples maintained continuing pressure on them. The post–Kievan Rus' civilization struggled to overcome the Mongol impact in conditions that were far from ideal.

KIEVAN RUS' AND ITS RIVALS

Despite brief periods of strong, unifying rule by able princes, Kievan Rus' from 1054 to the Mongol invasion in 1237 was characterized primarily by internal dissension and political weakness. This was partly due to the fact that Kievan Rus' was inherently unstable, based as it was on rotating authority among princely families and lacking the concept and practice of a homogeneous, centralized territorial government. It was also due to the relentless pressure of foreign enemies, particularly nomadic tribes to the southeast.

As the Kievan Rus' confederation disintegrated, the average citizen reacted in two ways. Many fled from the open, exposed plains of southern Russia to the thick, protecting forests of the north. A substantial population shift took place in the eleventh through thirteenth centuries, from southern Russia to the northeast in particular.

Second, peoples throughout Russia and neighboring lands sought security from the depredations of outside foes and neighboring princes by placing themselves under the protection of a local boyar, monastery, or prince. This marked a significant step toward the development of a social system characterized by privileges for the upper classes and obligations for the lower classes. But a considerable period of transition occurred before serfdom and the service state emerged.

In political terms, when the senior prince at Kiev could no longer command tribute and allegiance from all the towns and tribes over whom Iaroslav the Wise had ruled, the Kievan Rus' system began to break up, and separate principalities and city-states emerged. At the height of this process of disintegration, the region was divided into dozens of such small units, many of which fought each other. Generally speaking, different forms of government tended to predominate in three main areas:

- the southwest (Volynia and Galicia): aristocratic (rule by boyars)
- the northwest (Pskov and Novgorod): democratic/oligarchic (rule by the veche)
- the northeast (Suzdal and Moscow): monarchic (rule by a prince)

However, there were exceptions to this pattern, and in many principalities, all three institutions—boyar duma, veche, and prince—coexisted, although one was dominant.

The southwest encompassed the territory stretching west and northwest of Kiev to the northern slopes of the Carpathian Mountains and including present-day Belarus. It contained two important principalities, Volynia and Galicia, and was probably the richest area agriculturally. It had excellent prospects for emerging as the center of a revived state, the logical successor to Kievan Rus', with close ties to Europe. Strategically, the principalities of Volynia and Galicia had certain advantages. They were located far enough west to be spared the incursions of the Cumans. They were next door to Poland and Hungary, two strong European states of the time, with which Volynia and Galicia had lively commercial and cultural interactions.

On the other hand, their location created certain disadvantages. Their trading partners, Hungary and Poland (and later Lithuania), were larger and more powerful and soon began to covet the resources of neighboring Volynia and Galicia. Moreover, Hungarians, Poles, and Lithuanians were all Latin Catholics and looked upon the Orthodox Christians to their east as ripe for reconversion into the fold of true Christianity. Finally, these small states were not far enough west to escape the Mongols, who overran and briefly occupied the region in the 1240s.

Another liability to the southwest's potential as the nucleus of a new state was that political power in Volynia and Galicia was quite unstable. Wealthy boyar landholders contended with aspiring princes for political control, and until the 1500s it was the only region in which a boyar had the audacity to claim a princely throne. During the period of Mongol control, boyar power and prestige continued to grow, and it seems likely that Volynia and Galicia would have ultimately had a full-fledged system of aristocratic rule had the two territories not been absorbed by Lithuania and Poland, respectively, in the 1300s.

A second area that could have shaped and led a resurrected state was the northwest. The first towns and organized governments were probably established here, even before the founding of the city of Kiev. Its largest town, calling itself Lord Novgorod the Great, had a population of over thirty thousand and ranked in splendor and culture with the major towns of Europe. Organized as a city-state, Novgorod controlled a considerable hinterland from which it drew forest and agricultural products. It traded extensively with Scandinavia and the northern German towns along the Baltic Sea, exchanging furs, wax, honey, and timber for grains, woolens, wine, metal, and sweets. It also served as a major storage and transshipment point for trade to the south down both the Volga and Dnieper Rivers. At the same time, small manufacturing and craft works were almost as important to Novgorod as commerce. The town was well known for its talented artisans, who created not only practical items like tools and corduroy (log-paved) streets but intricate wooden decorations and tall, elegant churches in a distinctive northern style.

The people of Novgorod were cultured, energetic, and decidedly independent-minded. Despite a number of threats, the Novgorodians preserved their independence for six hundred years, a remarkable record in those times. However, they finally succumbed to the rising state of Moscow after 1470.

It is, of course, an oversimplification to call Novgorod democratic. Like many other societies, Novgorod did not permit women, slaves, and certain other social classes to vote. But most freemen could, so it was a republic in form and provided a considerable degree of representative government. Voters elected both an all-city government and district administrations in five boroughs. For the first few hundred years, there was a prince, though one with strictly limited powers. In 1136, the veche began to elect the prince, who reigned but did not govern. After the 1290s, the post of prince was abolished altogether.

Novgorod possessed a complex and quite enlightened judicial system as well as an autonomous church, whose archbishop was elected by the townspeople (though confirmed by the highest official of the Orthodox Church in the area, the metropolitan of Kiev).

The veche, a town meeting of all freemen, was summoned by the ringing of a special bell. In the 1470s, when Moscow conquered Novgorod, the bell was carried back to Moscow as a symbol of Novgorod's loss of freedom. In the beginning, the veche, besides electing officials, decided major issues of policy. Later, an elected council, or executive committee, acted in its stead on most matters. Also, the wealth, education, and influence of the leading merchants and landowners meant that they increasingly controlled Novgorod's government and affairs. It became more an oligarchy than a democracy.

As in most medieval towns, disease, famine, and fire regularly ravaged Novgorod. Moreover, the veche was supposed to act unanimously, and when there were strongly opposing viewpoints, quarreling in the veche could lead to fisticuffs and brawls. Finally, as the gap between the boyars (upper-class merchants and landowners) and the rest of the population widened, social strife would occasionally erupt, as *The Chronicle of Novgorod* for the year 1418 makes clear:

> And again they [the common people] became enraged like drunkards, against another boyar, Ivan Yevlich . . . and on his account pillaged a great many boyars' houses, as well as the monastery of St. Nikola in the Field, crying out: "Here is the treasure house of the Boyars." And again the same morning they plundered many houses in the Lyudgoshcha Street, calling out: "They are our enemies." . . . And they began to ring throughout the whole town, and armed men began to pour out from both sides as for war, fully armed, to the great bridge. And there was loss of life, too. Some fell by arrows, others by arms . . . and a dread fell on the people on both sides.[1]

At its height, Novgorod controlled a good part of what is today northern Russia, including the satellite town of Pskov as well as colonized territories to the northeast along the shores of the Arctic Ocean. By acknowledging Mongol suzerainty and paying tribute to the Mongol khan, it averted direct Mongol attack or occupation. This strategy permitted Novgorod to fend off enemies to the west, including Sweden, the Teutonic Knights who occupied the area along the eastern shore of the Baltic Sea, and later the Lithuanians. But Novgorod was not a warrior state, and its decentralized system of government made it an unlikely candidate to lead the restoration and unification of the region.

The honor fell instead to the area of the northeast and, ultimately, to a small and obscure principality that was not even founded until the middle of the twelfth century: Moscow. Although the northeast contained old and important cities, such as Suzdal and Rostov, it had fewer resources than either the southwest or Novgorod. The balance of power began to shift there, even before the Mongol invasions, for two reasons. First, it was a relatively secure area, entirely in the forest zone and fairly far removed from the area's western and southeastern foes. Second, it developed a tradition of princely rule that permitted the beginnings of centralized authority and effective government.

Thus, when the tradition that the most powerful prince should be based at Kiev broke down, his seat was moved to Suzdal, then to a newer town in the northeast, Vladimir. Later, the metropolitan, the chief official of the Orthodox Church, also migrated from Kiev to the northeast. In this way, the tradition of unity was preserved in the states of that region, including, eventually, Moscow.

Moreover, as trade declined and land became a more important resource, the princes of the northeast, dependent primarily on agriculture, were better able to mobilize the limited wealth of the country and to establish viable state power. But before they could do so, they had to endure the arrival of the Mongols.

THE ARRIVAL OF THE MONGOLS

In the woods, glades, and towns of today's northeastern Russia, the year 1237 must have seemed like any other year. The seemingly endless winter had at last erupted suddenly into a green and luxuriant spring. The crops had been sown, tended, and harvested; winter pelts and hides were prepared for market; traders had come and gone; and quarrels among the region's princes had been no worse or more harmful than customary. To be sure, people still passed along rumors of a new and ruthless band of nomads who had routed the local army fourteen years earlier southeast of Kiev, but neither hide nor hair of the intruders had been seen since.

The autumn had been spent accumulating food and fuel for winter, repairing houses and town walls, and hunting and trapping. No one was prepared for what suddenly occurred in mid-December, as reported, no doubt with some exaggeration, in chronicles and other early sources:

> With irresistible vigor and astonishing speed, the Mongols made their way through the forests of Penza and Tambov, and appeared before the beautiful city of Riazan. For five days they discharged a ceaseless storm of shot from their ballistae [military catapults] and, having made a breach in the defenses, carried the city by assault on the 21st of December, 1237. The prince, with his mother, wife [and] sons, the boyars and the inhabitants, without regard to age or sex, were slaughtered. . . . Some were impaled, some shot at with arrows for sport, others were flayed or had nails or splinters of wood driven under their fingernails. Priests were roasted alive, and nuns and maidens ravished in the churches before their relatives. No eye remained open to weep for the dead.[2]

Who were these invaders? Today, we know much more about the Mongols than the bewildered and hapless citizens of Riazan in the thirteenth century, although the origins of the Mongols—where they first lived and who their cultural forebears were—remain obscure. In Russia and other East Slavic lands, the Mongols were known as Tartars or Tatars, but term "Tatar" is more accurately used to designate Turkic groups allied with the Mongols who subsequently settled in southeastern Russia and the Crimea. In any case, the Mongols emerged in the 1100s, clearly in the same mold as earlier nomadic horsemen, such as the Scythians and later the Huns, who attacked the main centers of civilization and invaded Europe, trampling over the Slavs north of the Black Sea as they passed westward from inner Asia.

The Mongols, however, differed from their predecessors in two important respects. First, their impact was even more significant both materially—in terms of loss of life as well as the physical destruction of towns, churches, and dwellings—and psychologically in terms of how they terrorized and subjugated their opponents. Second, the Mongols were extremely well organized and disciplined, characteristics that permitted them to establish the largest empire in history. At its height, the realm of the great khan of the Mongols stretched five thousand miles from China in the east to the Adriatic Sea in the west and from Siberia in the north to the Persian Gulf in the south. The Mongols soon withdrew from Europe, and this huge empire, as a unit, did not last very long. Nevertheless, the Mongols conquered and ruled China and Russia, influenced India and Islam, and threatened Western Europe (see Map 2.1). Moreover, they did all this with a relative handful of warriors and administrators: several hundred thousand Mongols held sway over more than one hundred million people in Eurasia.

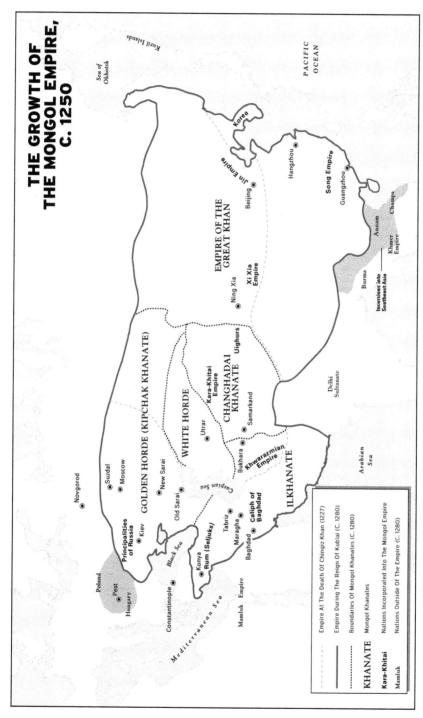

MAP 2.1. The growth of the Mongol Empire, circa 1250.

This astounding achievement was due largely to the impact of one man, Genghis (more accurately, Chingiz) Khan. He was born as Temuchin, around 1165, the son of a minor chieftain among some nomadic tribes living in present-day Mongolia. Reputedly a skilled horseman and archer by age eleven, Temuchin worked unceasingly as a young man to unite the quarreling Mongol tribes. Finally, in 1206, at a solemn conclave of tribal leaders, he was proclaimed "mighty ruler," or Genghis Khan. He apparently believed it his divine mission to rule the world. After subduing neighboring regions, he conquered northern China, almost all of central Asia, and part of Persia (contemporary Iran). After his death in 1227, his three sons and grandson, Batu Khan, extended the empire by overrunning most of the Kievan Rus' principalities, the Caucasus, southwestern Asia, and the rest of China.

The Mongols' dazzling military success depended on four qualities that characterized almost all of their campaigns: surprise, mobility, organization, and discipline. Applied together, these traits permitted the Mongols to

FIGURE 2.1. Genghis Khan, founder of the Mongol Empire. (GL Archive / Alamy Stock Photo)

overrun armies that were often twice as large as their forces. Mongol generals were carefully selected and trained, usually by the great khan himself. They relied on stealth as well as tactical and strategic surprise to catch the enemy unaware and confuse him in battle. The army was organized on a decimal basis into units of ten, one hundred, one thousand, and ten thousand, and strict discipline was enforced from the lowliest soldier to the highest general reporting to the great khan.

Mongol warriors were outstanding horsemen and highly skilled with the bow and arrow. They wore cloth, leather, or metal armor and could travel incredible distances, as this account by Marco Polo, who worked at the court of Kublai Khan, shows:

> [The Mongol soldiers] are also more capable of hardships than other nations; for many a time, if need be, they will go for a month without any supply of food, living only on the milk of their mares and on such game as their bows may win them. Their horses also will subsist entirely on the grass of the plains, so that there is no need to carry store of barley or straw or oats.[3]

Finally, the Mongols were skillful adapters. By the time they invaded Russia and neighboring lands, they had learned from the Chinese how to use catapults and other siege weapons.

Between the attack on Riazan in 1237 and their armies' push through central Europe to the Balkans in 1241–1242, the Mongols overran and destroyed most of the cities in the former Kievan Rus' lands. Those in the northwest were spared direct conquest. A few towns that offered no resistance were bypassed, but the usual pattern was to raze a town's main buildings, to slaughter or enslave up to a quarter of the population, and to demand future subordination to Mongol rule. Princes and boyars who knuckled under were tolerated, as was continuation of the activities of the Orthodox Church. Even after the Mongols converted to Islam in the latter part of the thirteenth century, they made no attempt to force the Eastern Slavs to become Muslims.

After Genghis Khan's death in 1227, his empire was divided among three surviving sons and a grandson. The western territories fell to the grandson, Batu Khan, who planned and executed the invasion of Russia and neighboring territories as far west as Central Europe. In the spring of 1242, his forces unexpectedly withdrew from the Balkans, and he returned to his headquarters at Old Sarai, a town north of the Caspian Sea along the Volga River. It is unclear whether this voluntary withdrawal occurred because Batu believed he was overextended militarily and politically, because he lost interest in Europe,

FIGURE 2.2. Alexander Nevskii. (Heritage Image Partnership Ltd /
Alamy Stock Photo)

not finding anything there to justify permanent Mongol occupation, or because he was anxious to be near the center of Mongol power in Asia so that
he could participate in the selection of a successor to the great khan, his uncle
Ugedei, who had died a few months before. Perhaps all of these considerations
influenced him.

Whatever his reasons, one result of Batu Khan's pulling back was the
consolidation of his authority in a western Mongol state that soon became
virtually independent and was known as the Khanate of the Golden Horde
(apparently called "golden" from the gold-leaf decorations that adorned the
felt tents of Batu Khan and some of his leading lieutenants). Batu Khan and
his successors established a system of indirect rule for the Russian and neighboring lands. Local princes had to recognize the suzerainty of the khan but
were allowed to continue to administer their principalities. For example, Alexander Nevskii, a national hero in Russia because he defeated the German
order of Teutonic Knights, was permitted to rule Novgorod and assume the

title of grand prince as long as he acknowledged Mongol overlordship. The princes had to go regularly to the khan's capital at Sarai to pledge submission and to receive a *yarlyk*, or charter of authority. The Golden Horde collected taxes among the local principalities, based on a crude census of the population that the Mongols carried out. Later, the Mongols permitted Slavic administrators to assess the taxes for them.

Occasionally, the Mongols also demanded recruits for their armies, but such levies were relatively infrequent. The Mongol overlords interfered little in people's daily lives and tolerated the Orthodox Church. If, however, any town or group resisted their dominion, the Mongols, reacting swiftly, wreaked terrible vengeance on the rebels, leveling villages or towns and killing or enslaving the inhabitants.

The Mongols ruled the Russian and many neighboring lands in this fashion for about a hundred forty years. Because of Mongol decline and growing local strength, the Russians in particular, although still obliged to recognize Mongol suzerainty and subject to sporadic depredations by Mongol troops, became increasingly independent after 1380.

THE IMPACT OF THE MONGOLS

Like the Vikings' role in the founding of Kievan Rus', the Mongols' impact on subsequent civilization is a touchy issue. Some writers are anxious to blame those characteristics of Russian and other Eastern Slavic development since the thirteenth century of which they disapprove, such as autocratic government and serfdom, on the poor example and punishing harassment of the Mongols. Otherwise, they claim, the area might have evolved democratically, as the West did.

Some scholars, although eager to discount Mongol influence on the societies of Russia and its neighbors, are nevertheless happy to ascribe their early struggles in Muscovite times and their relative backwardness compared to European civilization to the destructiveness of Mongol rule. Finally, some observers argue that the Mongols simply reinforced and brought out negative traits already inherent in Russian civilization in particular before the thirteenth century: cruelty, repression, militarization, and expansionism.

As is so often the case in historiographic debates, a middle-ground approach seems the most sensible. The Mongols certainly affected the course of Russian and neighboring regional history. It would be difficult to dismiss their devastating invasion and two centuries of domination as counting for naught. But it would be equally foolish to decide that Mongol precepts, values, and institutions completely shaped the Muscovite state that emerged in the fourteenth century. In the first place, Mongol rule was indirect; the Mongols made no effort to mold Russia and other areas exactly in their image. In the second place, the new society grew organically out of the traditions and three-hundred-year experience of the Kievan Rus' confederation and the conditions and challenges of its times. The Muscovite leaders tried not to imitate Mongol society because they thoroughly detested the Mongols for what they had done to their land and because the Mongols were, in the Muscovites' opinion, pagans and infidels.

To see how this middle-of-the-road conclusion about the impact of the Mongols works out in practice, we will examine some of the areas in which the Mongols did have some influence and then note those in which they had almost none. From such a viewpoint, the most important effect of the Mongol conquest was economic. In three key ways, the Mongols' defeat and subjugation of Russia and neighboring areas led to severe economic losses. First, and perhaps least important, was the immediate physical destruction: the leveling of towns and villages, the seizing of goods and crops, and the killing of large numbers of people. This was certainly a setback, but these costs were shortly recouped, and after Mongol dominion was established and acknowledged by most local princes and towns, subsequent physical devastation was not extensive.

Second, the Mongols seriously weakened the productive capacities of local society. In those preindustrial times, most production was agricultural, but there was also a significant output of household goods, clothing, tools, implements, buildings, and other handicrafts by artisans, who, though limited primarily to using human power, displayed a high degree of skill and ingenuity. Most of these goods were consumed locally, in towns and villages, but some were traded regionally and a few internationally. Kievan Rus', like other European and Asian societies, had developed this kind of production to a moderate level. Although the evidence is not clear whether artisan work had already begun to decline before the Mongols' arrival as part of a general weakening of the Kievan Rus' economy, it is evident that the destruction associated with the Mongol invasion was a serious setback to this sector of economic life. Not only were workshops and tools destroyed, but skilled artisans were killed or sent as captives to work at the Mongol capital of Sarai. It was not so easy for society to bounce back from losses of that sort.

Finally, although the Russians and other peoples apparently profited by their secondary participation in the extensive international trade carried on by the Mongols, this was more than offset by the Mongols' expropriation, mainly through a fairly efficient system of taxation, of most of the surplus the local population produced. In colloquial terms, they skimmed the cream off the local economy. This was a serious blow because early agricultural societies had, even in the best of times, little surplus. To have the Mongols take most of it each year left the East Slavs and others struggling to survive, with little opportunity for economic growth.

Even though some studies suggest that trade and economic activity under the Mongols were less curtailed than once believed, the essential point is that, without the Mongol contact, the local economy might have gone through, and indeed formed the easternmost part of, the same economic upsurge that Western Europe experienced in the fourteenth century and that undergirded Europe's commercial revolution and subsequent worldwide expansion. An important part of this economic boom was the accumulation of capital (or surpluses) from the production and trading of agricultural and handicraft goods. This stimulated the growth of towns and a wide range of social and political changes in Western civilization. Yet Slavic and other peoples under the Mongols had limited opportunities to expand production, increase trade, and accumulate capital. Whatever surplus was built up, the Mongols took.

A somewhat less complex, but still quite tangled, issue is the political effects of Mongol rule. Some scholars have argued that the local princes borrowed Mongol political ideas, particularly the concept of the unlimited, unchallengeable authority of the Mongol khan, and melded these into the theory and practice of absolute rule in the Muscovite state. Yet this view is not entirely convincing: the Russians and other nearby peoples had both indigenous and Byzantine models of autocratic power exercised by a single ruler on which to draw. And when they wanted to justify the autocracy, they referred to these.

It has also been suggested, even less convincingly, that the Russians in particular took from the Mongols a goal of establishing a universal world empire, that the messianic mission of Slavic (or, later, Communist) world dominion had its origins in Genghis Khan's belief that he was divinely anointed to conquer the universe. But, again, it is much easier to trace the origins of such ideas to the later concept of a special Christian mission for the Russian people and state rather than to try to find Mongol roots for them.

To be sure, many policies of the early Muscovite princes were a reaction against the Mongol overlordship, designed first to survive and then to overthrow the Mongol yoke. Consequently, in this indirect sense, the Mongols greatly influenced Moscow's political actions and institutions; their direct influence, however, was relatively small.

The Mongols did have a significant psychological effect on Russia and other populations in the region, although such an influence is almost impossible to substantiate. The notion that, because local Slavs and others were forced to submit to the Mongol yoke and their princes had to humble themselves at the court of the khan, they became inherently servile and craved strong rule is, of course, utter rubbish. But that the peoples in the region were shocked, humiliated, and grief stricken by the suddenness, fury, and cruelty of the Mongol onslaught makes excellent sense. And this certainly made them extremely, if not obsessively, concerned with their own safety and that of their society and state. Russians and others had been battling various foes and invaders throughout the previous four hundred years of their recorded history, but the Mongol conquest was experienced on an entirely different, traumatic level. It is no exaggeration to say that the excessive fear of the outside world that some Russians and other peoples have displayed over the past five hundred years can be traced in part to the nightmarish devastation of their society between 1237 and 1241 at the hands of the Mongols.

Finally, it is certainly true that the Mongol contact affected development by making it more difficult for local principalities to stay in close touch with Constantinople and the states of central and Western Europe. Recent research has shown that the area was not as totally cut off and isolated as we once believed, that some trade and cultural contacts persisted throughout the period of the Mongol yoke. But, obviously, personal, intellectual, and commercial ties were much attenuated by Mongol rule at the very time when Europe was beginning to change in a rapid and revolutionary way. The local Orthodox peoples might well have been as suspicious of the culture of Roman Catholic Europe as they were of the culture of the Islamic Golden Horde. Nevertheless, there had been close links between Kievan Rus' and Western Europe in the preceding centuries, and it is logical to assume that the intellectual, social, and economic stirrings and excitement of the High Middle Ages, particularly of the Renaissance, would have had some spillover and impact in Russia and neighboring lands had they not been first under the Mongols' thumb, then bending all their energies to overthrow them.

It is important to note that the Mongol domination accelerated the division of the former Kievan Rus' territories, though perhaps did not cause it. Such a fragmentation would probably have occurred anyway, but the Mongol conquest strengthened the centrifugal tendencies already at work. In what is today Belarus and western Ukraine, where Mongol domination lasted only one hundred years, Volynia and Galicia were absorbed by Lithuania and Poland. This marked a branching of the Eastern Slavic peoples into Belarusians in the west, Ukrainians in the southwest, and Russians in the northeast. At the same time, the Mongol invasion undoubtedly facilitated the occupation of the lands along the Baltic Sea by Germanic knights and later by Swedes so that these territories remained outside Muscovite and Russian imperial control for several hundred years.

The list of areas in which the Mongols' rule had little or no effect is much shorter than that just discussed, but it encompasses important aspects of society. First, because the Mongols governed indirectly through princes, the daily lives of those who survived the first assault and whose princes did not defy the Mongols changed little. Their customs and patterns of living were not affected. Local social and political arrangements and institutions remained basically unaltered. The peasant commune, the village, the town, the principality—all remained much as before.

Most importantly, the beliefs and culture of local peoples persisted. This continuity permitted gradual reestablishment of a distinctly East Slavic society and the emergence of an autonomous and finally independent and expanding Muscovite state. The Orthodox Church, which the Mongols left untouched, was able to preserve and transmit the essentials of earlier civilization through the period of Mongol domination: religion, education, literature, and values all survived. In the hardest times, the people could look to and rally around the church. It carried forward the tradition of unity and uniqueness on which a resurrected civilization could be built. Playing the role of both consoler and protector, the church played an indispensable role in preventing the people from abandoning themselves to despair and in holding the society together. Later, with the prince, the church was able to induce the people to support a new political system that eventually liberated them from the Mongols.

THE DECLINE OF MONGOL POWER

The loose confederation of Kievan Rus' collapsed under the Mongol onslaught in part because it was divided and had no viable state system. In an ironic turnabout, Russians, Ukrainians, and others were finally able to rid themselves of the Mongols because the latter became disunited and failed to build an effective state structure. The huge Eurasian empire put together by Genghis Khan and his successors had split into several parts by the end of the 1200s. And in the 1300s and 1400s, the Khanate of the Golden Horde, the empire's westernmost unit and the local overlord, gradually weakened as a result of power struggles among Batu Khan's descendants and increased internal dissension among its component tribes. As a result, although nominal Mongol suzerainty over the region continued until 1480, Mongol power could be brought to bear only sporadically, and the local principalities gradually acquired autonomy.

One factor undermining Mongol authority was that, although they had developed an organization and system of rule well suited to expansion and conquest, they did not have a well-developed social or religious system that would enable them to hold together disparate peoples and societies. The Mongols constituted a thin overlay on existing cultures, and they did little to fuse their domains into an integrated civilization. Without linguistic, religious, or cultural unity, the Khanate of the Golden Horde could not develop a strong political structure, and the centrifugal tendencies within it gradually began to pull it apart. In the 1400s, separate khanates were established at Kazan and Astrakhan and in the Crimea, a fragmentation that made the task of the local princes striving for independence a good deal easier.

Though divided, the Mongols (or Tatars, as their descendants came to be called) were still formidable foes. Mongol rule did not collapse of its own weight. The Muscovite princes and the Lithuanians worked hard to overturn it and succeeded only after a long struggle.

CONCLUSION

In assessing the Mongol period, it is important neither to dismiss nor to overplay it. Looked at from the broadest perspective, the Mongol era left three significant legacies for future civilization. First, it heightened a deep sense of insecurity among the population and within society. The fear of being overrun and subjugated might eventually have faded from the consciousness of ordinary people and their leaders, except that subsequent events kept those anxieties boiling. Thus, time and again in the history of the region, the people and state struggled, with limited resources, to ward off foreign intruders and to ensure their own safety and security.

Second, the Mongol invasion made unity and cohesiveness a high-priority value in future society and the emerging Muscovite and imperial states. Kievan Rus' had had no chance against the Mongols, in part because it was divided, with each prince and his followers trying to fend for themselves. Out of that experience and the necessity of building a strong state to overthrow the Mongol yoke came an emphasis on the strength to be found in a common religion, Orthodoxy, and a common allegiance to the grand prince (later the tsar). Without the Mongols, a state or empire might eventually have been formed out of the disparate pieces into which Kievan Rus' civilization had separated, but it is at least equally possible that the Russians and other Eastern Slavs would have remained divided and been absorbed by their powerful neighbors: Poles, Lithuanians, and others.

Finally, whatever specific effects the Mongols had in draining the economy and terrorizing the population, a highly significant fundamental outcome of their rule was to spur the divergence of Eastern Slavic civilization from the

West. The area was bound to emerge as a unique society, but at least in Kievan Rus' times, it was developing along a track roughly parallel to that of Western Europe and its Latin Christian civilization. But after the Mongols, the distance between them had perceptibly widened, and society evolved along more distinctly different lines than it had a few centuries earlier. As a result, serfdom emerged in Russia and some adjacent lands just as it was disappearing in Western Europe. Trade and commercial capitalism flourished in Europe but languished in many of the Eastern Slavic lands. While much of Western Europe bubbled over with intellectual ferment and social fluidity, particularly during the Renaissance, thought in much of Russia and neighboring lands remained quite traditional, even stagnant. Local society became increasingly rigid and stratified. The Mongol era made certain that the future Muscovite and Russian imperial civilizations would follow a different course from that traversed by the West.

FURTHER READING

Halperin, Charles J. *Russia and the Golden Horde: The Mongol Impact on Medieval Russian History*. Bloomington: Indiana University Press, 1985.

Kollmann, Nancy Shields. *By Honor Bound: State and Society in Early Modern Russia*. Ithaca, NY: Cornell University Press, 1997.

Martin, Janet. *Medieval Russia, 980–1584*. 2nd ed. Cambridge, UK: Cambridge University Press, 2007.

Morgan, David. *The Mongols*. The Peoples of Europe. Oxford: Blackwell, 1986.

Ostrowski, Donald. *Muscovy and the Mongols: Cross-Cultural Influences on the Steppe Frontier, 1304–1589*. Cambridge, UK: Cambridge University Press, 1998.

Presniakov, A. E. *The Formation of the Great Russian State: A Study of Russian History in the Thirteenth to Fifteenth Centuries*. Translated by A. E. Moorhouse. Chicago: Quadrangle Books, 1970.

Vernadsky, George. *The Mongols and Russia. A History of Russia*, vol. 3. New Haven, CT: Yale University Press, 1953.

CHAPTER 3

THE RISE OF MOSCOW, 1328–1533

In the mid-1300s, four major centers of power and civilization stood in the region under our examination: the Mongols in the southeast; the emerging Lithuanian (and later Polish-Lithuanian) state in the west; Novgorod in the northwest; and two contending princely states in the northeast: Tver and Moscow. Any of these had the potential to become heir to the Kievan Rus' confederation and the unifier of what would become the Russian Empire. Yet by the early 1500s, Moscow, which a hundred fifty years earlier was the smallest and least promising contender, had emerged as the dominant power. In the words of *The Primary Chronicle*, it "gathered the Russian lands" under its rule and established a loosely centralized state. In five generations, Moscow defeated all its nearby rivals, such as Tver and Novgorod, threw off the Mongol yoke, and seized much of the territory of the Lithuanian state, pushing it westward and into an eventual union with Poland.

This remarkable development, almost as sweeping and dramatic as the Mongol contact itself, also had fateful consequences for the future course of the region's history. First, Moscow's expansion set the emerging society on a course of imperial domination of neighboring lands that would make it, five hundred years later, the largest and longest-lasting territorial empire in modern history. The burgeoning Muscovite state included, at an accelerating pace, many non-Slavic ethnic groups, cultures, and religions, making for a diverse and complex society. Second, Moscow's victory meant that the principle of obligatory service to the ruler, a policy that was key to Moscow's success, became a central tenet of local society from that time forward. Third, the triumph of Moscow ensured that of the three political concepts that coexisted in Kievan Rus' times—princely or autocratic rule, republican or democratic government, and boyar or aristocratic domination—the autocratic system would prevail in the new Muscovite and later Russian imperial states. Finally, the rise of Moscow meant that the region would have a strong Orthodox religious orientation. If, for example, the Lithuanian state had won instead, the resulting society would have been Latinized, subjected to Roman Catholic influences, and ruled by an aristocratic system of governance. Thus, the triumph of Moscow set firmly in place characteristics of a Muscovite and later Russian imperial society that would last for more than five centuries, down to 1917.

THE ODDS AGAINST MOSCOW

Among the major power centers in the early 1300s, the tiny principality of Moscow seemed an unlikely winner. Other northeastern princedoms, like Suzdal-Vladimir, Riazan, or Tver, appeared stronger. Moscow's disadvantages were several. It was, to begin with, an upstart. First mentioned in *The Primary Chronicle* in the year 1147, it was fortified in 1156 but remained a minor principality and was then ravaged by the Mongols in 1237. Even in the early 1300s, as its significance began to grow, Moscow was still small and arguably second-class compared to its long-established and more powerful rivals.

In addition, the princes of Moscow had to fight against the dominant principle of post–Kievan Rus' society: the *udel*, or appanage, system. Appanages were princely holdings of land, or territories, from which the prince and his family were expected to draw economic sustenance and over which the prince exercised considerable administrative, judicial, and political rights. In a sense, an appanage was the prince's private property, but he controlled it for public purposes as well. It is important to note that primogeniture, or the inheritance of property by the eldest son, did not operate in post–Kievan Rus' times. Thus, a prince's appanage and title were divided among all his sons, a system that produced more and more princes with smaller and smaller holdings from generation to generation. Moreover, boyars, the princes' aristocratic servitors, who held *votchinas* (pronounced "voht-cheenas")—hereditary estates for which they owed no service—also divided their lands among their heirs. As a result, the overriding tendency during the thirteenth and fourteenth centuries was for territory to be cut up constantly into bits and pieces. The princes of Moscow had to reverse that trend, or at least make it work for them.

Muscovite rulers also had to contend with the Kievan Rus' tradition of senior, or grand, princes and the rotation of people in that office. The princes of Moscow first had to claim and solidify the title of grand prince and then make sure it was passed on only to their eldest sons.

Moreover, the founders of the Muscovite state had extremely limited resources with which to defeat powerful rivals. Theirs was not a particularly rich town, they had little accumulated wealth, and they possessed no tangible assets to give them an advantage over others. Consequently, they had to scrimp and save and then mobilize and manage what little was available to them more efficiently than their competitors.

Finally, the Muscovites' level of technology and culture was certainly no higher, and was perhaps even lower, than their enemies'. To be sure, they had the great spiritual advantage of the Orthodox Church's support; otherwise, they had no great tradition, no well-educated servitors or general population, no special skills or weapons, no knowledgeable and wealthy merchants or intellectuals, and no ideas or precepts, at least in the beginning, that gave them any edge over other contenders for power in the Eastern Slavic lands.

MOSCOW'S ADVANTAGES

Despite its liabilities, Moscow also had a number of assets that help explain its rapid ascent to dominion over the lands that it would acquire. Some of these were circumstances that benefited the Moscow princes but over which they had no control; others resulted from the conscious actions and policies of the princes. We will examine this latter set of advantages for Moscow first.

Security and Internal Order

It is logical to ask how a population could have acquiesced so abjectly in the building of a state and society that was based on absolutism and that soon instituted the oppressive social system of serfdom. Yet if we imagine ourselves back in those times, we can at once see how attractive the policies of the growing Muscovite state were for the inhabitants of the region. For almost three hundred years, the people had been buffeted by civil war, invasions, and finally conquest. Their towns and villages had been overrun and razed many times. Apart from the usual medieval disasters of famine, fire, and disease, their lives were in constant danger, and they were afraid and insecure most of the time.

It is not surprising, therefore, that when the Moscow princes said, "Here you will be safe," people flocked to the territory and willingly served the Muscovite rulers. They were happy to trade freedom for protection. It is true, of course, that the Moscow princes could not absolutely guarantee security and tranquility; for example, the Mongols sacked the city in 1382. Moreover, many Muscovites were engaged in fighting external foes of the principality: rival princedoms, the Mongols, and the Lithuanians. Nevertheless, within the territories controlled by Moscow, a rapidly expanding area, peace and order reigned most of the time. In our view, which is based largely on that of V. O. Kliuchevsky, the leading

Russian historian before the 1917 Revolution, the Moscow princes' ability to provide security for the people was their greatest asset.

Organization and Management

From the evidence we as historians have available, Moscow princes were generally skillful administrators and proprietors of their domain, probably abler in this regard than most of their rivals. Although they did not have much with which to work, they made the most of their limited resources. They encouraged agriculture and helped colonize and develop new lands. They built up the city of Moscow and established other towns. They handled their military campaigns adroitly and succeeded in balancing their fiscal base with their military expenses. They were successful tax collectors and merchants, and they encouraged commerce among the population. One of the first princes, who ruled from 1327 to 1341, was appropriately called Ivan Kalita, or John the Moneybags.

The Moscow princes were also generally successful in avoiding civil war within the princely family. Only once during the two centuries of Moscow's climb to preeminence was there protracted quarreling and strife over the succession to the throne. Finally, they managed to minimize the division of the Muscovite lands among heirs each time a prince died. Although younger sons at times inherited territories of Moscow, every effort was made to ensure that before long these reverted to the larger Moscow state of the senior son, or grand prince.

Diplomatic Skill

Moscow princes displayed remarkable ability in dealing with an array of foreign foes. Toward the Mongols, they were submissive and helpful at those times, particularly in the fourteenth century, when the Mongols were still strong and could easily crush the fledgling Muscovite state. As a reward for their obedience and cooperation, Moscow's rulers were empowered to serve as tax agents for the Mongols and received Mongol assistance against the rival principality of Tver. Yet when Mongol power declined in the latter half of the 1300s, the Moscow princes were quick to seize the opportunity to turn against their masters and to lead a virtual crusade against Mongol domination. Over time, the Muscovite state emerged as a symbol of resistance to Mongol oppression, thus giving it a further advantage in its struggle to unify the lands it sought.

The Moscow princes were also adept in dealing with the Lithuanians, the principality of Tver, and the leaders of Novgorod. On most occasions, the Muscovites outmaneuvered their opponents and thus were able to expand their domain at less military cost than would otherwise have resulted.

Identification with the Orthodox Church

An important advantage for the Moscow princes was their close cooperation with the Orthodox religion and the church. In this way Moscow was able to draw directly on the tradition of Kiev and to act as the logical successor of a great and unified Russian state and civilization.

The Orthodox Church played an increasingly important role in the region at this time. Pagan practices and attitudes persisted, and many still believed in powerful natural forces and spirits. Nevertheless, the church provided a symbol of unity and continuity for the people. When all else was in confusion and upheaval, the church served as a refuge for and consoler of the people. The rituals of the church were familiar and comforting, and its doctrine promised eventual salvation. Moreover, it was a faith and practice that most of the East Slavs living in the region shared, no matter what specific territory they lived in.

The church was also important economically. By the 1500s, one-quarter of all the land in Russia belonged to the church and its monasteries, much of it bequeathed by devout parishioners. The monasteries were often active in establishing outposts and havens in the forested wilderness and in colonizing new territory in the north. Many peasants worked on church land, probably under slightly better conditions than peasants on private or princely estates.

Finally, the church was the main center of artistic and cultural life throughout this period. Under the Mongol occupation, the church attempted to preserve scholarship and education, but only a few people were literate; most of the boyars and even many of the clergy could not read or write. Moreover, Orthodoxy emphasized Masses and rituals rather than intellectual training and rational inquiry. The other strand of church activity, represented in the monasteries and the work of the revered monk Saint Sergius (1322–1392), focused on asceticism and a denial of this world. Consequently, the Orthodox Church did not play the important scholarly, educational, and intellectual role that the Roman Catholic Church did in Western Europe during this same period. Nevertheless, it remained the center of the learning and culture that persisted under Mongol rule.

Almost all the written literature of the time was religious: chronicles of events, lives of saints, sermons. It was quite stylized and traditional, and there were few secular writings to match the lyricism and vigor of the earlier *Tale of the Host of Igor*.

The glory of culture during this period was in religious art and architecture. As we noted earlier, the peoples of Kievan Rus' had learned icon painting from Constantinople but had already begun to develop it in their own style. Because icons are not familiar to many Westerners (icons were banned in the

Latin Church), their significance and beauty are sometimes not fully appreci-
ated. In viewing and understanding an icon, it is important to remember that
each one served two crucial purposes. It was designed to both educate and inspire the illiterate and bowed-down worshipper who gazed upon it (originally
only in churches, though later in most homes). Thus, it had to be clear and articulate on the one hand, conveying a simple but powerful message about the
Bible, the life of Christ, or the lives of saints. On the other hand, it had to dazzle
and uplift so as to provide an important spiritual experience for the humble
churchgoer.

In the 1300s, icon painters began to elevate their work to a plane considerably beyond anything the Byzantine masters had achieved, and in the icons of
Andrei Rublev, who died in 1430, this art form reached its apogee. Rublev's mas-
terpiece, *The Old Testament Trinity* (see Figure 3.1), is one of the world's great
paintings, combining perfect composition and harmony with warm feeling and
exquisite grace. Its rich and soft colors are an important part of the painting, so
a black-and-white reproduction unfortunately cannot do it full justice.

FIGURE 3.1. The beautiful *Old Testament Trinity* icon by
Rublev, painted in the early fifteenth century. (© Sovfoto)

The church made a final, significant contribution to cultural life through architecture. Some of the finest churches were built in this period. Many of them, particularly the wooden churches, have not survived, but those that are still standing impress the observer with their clean, utilitarian, but graceful lines and their superb decorations and cupolas. The major stone churches in Moscow, although built under the supervision of imported Italian architects, remain today as complex, impressive monuments to the creative fusion of Byzantine style with indigenous expression (see Figure 3.2).

Since the church occupied a central position, the Moscow princes associated themselves closely with the church and worked with the Orthodox hierarchy continuously in the monumental task of defending and unifying the lands they controlled and sought to control. The political benefits were enormous, since the Moscow princes could claim not only the mantle of Kievan Rus' and the most glorious ancient traditions but also the blessing of the church leaders and, through them, of God himself. Relations between the princes and the church were at times strained, but overall, Moscow's identification with Orthodoxy helped it to gain power and set the basic tone of the area's civilization for generations to come.

Other advantages that Moscow enjoyed as it grew and expanded were more fortuitous, having relatively little relation to the policies of the princes.

FIGURE 3.2. Interior of the Church of the Assumption in the Moscow Kremlin, showing the icons painted on the pillars before the altar. (SPUTNIK / Alamy Stock Photo)

Moscow's Location

One does not have to accept geographical determinism in history to conclude that Moscow happened to be extremely well situated. The city grew up in the middle of today's northeastern Russia, almost equidistant in every direction from the borders of the traditional Russian lands. This site served it well in two ways: the city was strategically placed, so its ruler could easily move outward to absorb other local principalities, yet it was far enough away from its external enemies, such as the Mongols and the Lithuanians, that they could not easily attack.

Moscow's Commerce

As a corollary to its location, Moscow developed as an important trading center. Two main commercial routes crossed in Moscow: one ran from the northwest to the southeast, that is, from Novgorod to the Black and Caspian Seas via the Don and Volga Rivers, and the other extended from the south up the Dnieper River to the cities northeast of Moscow, such as Rostov and Suzdal. Situated on the Moscow River, the city provided its merchants easy access by tributaries to the three main rivers of European Russia: the Don, the Dnieper, and the Volga. Although earlier historians stressed the agricultural basis of Moscow's economy, and while the importance of trade had certainly declined since Kievan Rus' times, more recent evidence suggests that commerce was well developed in Moscow and contributed notably to its success.

Luck

One of the fascinations of history is that, time and again, the historian comes across a significant incident or factor that can only be ascribed to accident or chance. In this case, the princes of Moscow were just plain lucky. They lived much longer than most of their contemporaries and consequently had long reigns. For example, Ivan III (Ivan the Great) ruled for forty-three years from 1462 to 1505, providing remarkable stability and continuity for the state at a crucial period in its development. Between 1389 and 1584, almost two hundred years, the Muscovite state had only five rulers, an incredible record for the time.

This meant that the uncertainty, and often the civil war, that had customarily marked each succession in Kievan Rus' times recurred infrequently. Moreover, each prince, beginning with Dmitrii in 1359, ruled long enough to consolidate his position and the state's power as well as to carry out a set of consistent policies designed to expand and strengthen the realm. Had the throne been in contention every five or ten years, with new princes struggling to assert their authority, the Muscovite state could hardly have grown and prevailed in the way that it did. Although several of the princes of Moscow took power in their teens, their long reigns are still remarkable in an era of high infant mortality and frequent epidemics. They may have been hardy, but they were also lucky.

MOSCOW'S ASCENT, 1328–1533

To see concretely how the Muscovite princes overcame their liabilities and took advantage of their assets, we will survey briefly the most important events that marked the gathering of the Russian lands. Moscow's rise was both rapid and dramatic, with surprisingly few setbacks along the way. In the first hundred fifty years, from the early fourteenth century to the middle of the fifteenth century, Moscow grew from a tiny principality smaller than the state of Rhode Island to a major state the size of Connecticut and Massachusetts combined.

Founded in the mid-1100s, Moscow was not at first a significant town in the region. Its larger neighbors, boasting princes such as the colorfully named George the Long Arm and Dmitrii Big Eyes, were more powerful and politically influential. In the late 1200s and early 1300s, the princes of tiny Moscow took a first step down the road of expansion by incorporating territory along the Moscow River into their principality. They also began what was to be a bitter, almost two-hundred-year struggle with the older principality of Tver, located northwest of Moscow.

An important prize in this rivalry was the title of senior prince. Traditionally associated with Kiev, the office of senior prince had been transferred to the northeastern town of Vladimir in 1169, when Kiev was much weakened. In the early 1300s, the princes of Moscow and Tver claimed the title at various times, but finally around 1331, Ivan I (Ivan Kalita) of Moscow, who also ruled Vladimir, was recognized as senior prince, and the important title was associated with Moscow from then on.

A second significant event at the same time was the move to Moscow of the metropolitan, the highest official of the Orthodox Church in the region. To some extent, chance favored the Muscovites on this occasion. The seat of the metropolitan, originally in Kiev, had been transferred to the northeast in the twelfth century. In 1326, an extremely popular and talented metropolitan, Peter, died while visiting Moscow. He was later canonized, and Saint Peter's name became associated with Moscow. In 1328, his successor decided to reside in the city. From that time on, the metropolitans of the Orthodox

Church worked closely with the grand princes of Moscow to oppose the Mongols (converted to Islam in the preceding century) and the heretic Lithuanians (predominantly Roman Catholic after 1386) as well as to bring together the principalities in a unified state (see Map 3.1).

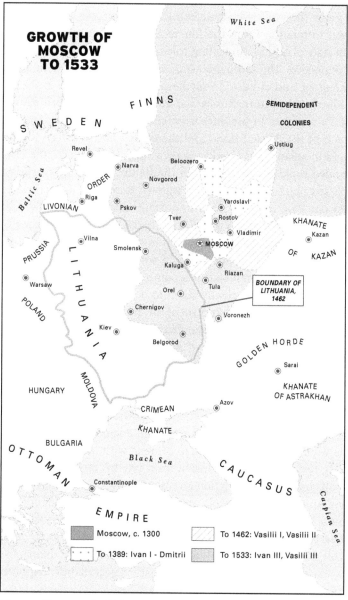

MAP 3.1. The growth of Moscow to 1533.

The reign of Ivan I in the 1300s was important in other ways. An able ruler, he made Moscow more secure, managed its resources effectively, and encouraged commerce. He acted as tax collector for the Mongols and minimized Moscow's tax burden. Finally, he bought up territories adjacent to Moscow as one method of extending his domain.

As it grew, the Muscovite state came into increasing conflict with its regional rival, Lithuania. From the fourteenth to the sixteenth centuries, the Lithuanian state played an important role in regional history, and a few words about it are needed. The Lithuanians are a Baltic people with an ancient and distinct language and culture. In medieval times, they lived in the forests of what is today northwestern Russia and along the southeastern shores of the Baltic Sea. In response to pressure from crusading German knights who occupied much of the Baltic littoral and threatened northwestern Russia in the 1200s, the Lithuanians organized their own state. In the 1300s, the Lithuanian state expanded rapidly southeast from the Baltic, occupying territories until it encompassed much of what is today western Russia. At its farthest advance, the Lithuanian state included such important cities as Kiev, Chernigov, and Smolensk and the territory of Volynia, and reached all the way to the Black Sea.

Because the Lithuanians were few in number, they fused with the local Russian nobility as they expanded. Hence, some historians prefer to call their empire a Lithuanian-Russian state. Its dominant language is known today as Belarusian. This state could clearly claim to be an heir of Kiev and acted as a formidable rival to Moscow for control of the area.

In 1386, the Lithuanian ruler married a Polish princess and began to convert his people to Latin Christianity. As a result of this personal union with Poland, Catholic and Polish influences in Lithuania-Russia grew. The union also strengthened the state, and though checked by Moscow in the east, Lithuania defeated the Germans in the famous Battle of Tannenberg in 1410 and soon extended its suzerainty southwestward toward the Balkans. In 1569, the Union of Lublin formally joined Lithuania and Poland. The resulting state was predominantly Polish and continued to contend with Moscow.

The long reign of Dmitrii Donskoi from 1359 to 1389 was marked by continued expansion and consolidation and by Moscow's recurring struggles with the Lithuanians and the Mongols. Although Dmitrii Donskoi could accomplish no more against the Lithuanians than to check their expansion eastward into the heart of Russia, he did win an important and famous victory over the Mongols at the Battle of Kulikovo Field in 1380. *The Primary Chronicle* has left us a stirring, colorful, and somewhat exaggerated description of that encounter:

There never was such a mighty Russian Army, for all forces combined numbered some 200,000. . . . A week later, on September 6, they reached the River Don. . . . Early Saturday morning, September 8, he told his troops to cross the river and go to the meadow. At first there was a heavy fog but when it later disappeared everyone crossed the Don; there was a real multitude of troops as far as one could see.

At six o'clock in the morning the godless Tatars appeared in the field and faced the Christians . . . and when these two great forces met they covered an area thirteen versts [eight miles] long. And there was a great massacre and bitter warfare and great noise . . . and blood flowed like a heavy rain. . . . At nine o'clock God took mercy on the Christians; many saw an angel and saintly martyrs helping the Christians. . . . Shortly thereafter the godless fled and the Christians pursued them . . . to their camp where they took all of their wealth and their cattle, killing many and trampling others.[1]

This defeat was the beginning of the end for the Mongols, even though two years later they counterattacked and burned Moscow.

Dmitrii's successor, Vasilii I (1389–1425), built up the economic strength of his domain and expanded Moscow's holdings. When he died, a struggle for the throne broke out, and a period of political turmoil ensued. In the fighting, Vasilii's eldest son and the eventual victor, Vasilii II (1425–1462), was blinded. After finally establishing himself securely in power, he ruled successfully and, in 1452, refused to pay any further tribute to the Mongols, although he left it to his son, Ivan III, to formally renounce Mongol suzerainty over Russia in 1480.

During the reign of Vasilii the Blind, the Russian Orthodox Church took an important step toward becoming an independent institution apart from its Armenian, Georgian, Greek, Ukrainian, and other branches. With the Byzantine Empire gravely threatened by the Turks, the Greek Orthodox Church had reached a tentative reconciliation with the Roman Catholic Church in the political hope of ensuring European assistance against Turkish attacks. The majority of the clergy in the Russian Church repudiated this agreement and, in 1443, established a separate church administration. In 1453, the Turks captured Constantinople, and the Russian Orthodox Church was on its own in any case.

In the course of the long reigns of Ivan III (the Great) and Vasilii III from 1462 to 1533, the Muscovite state and system took nearly final form, and many of the basic institutions that characterized local civilization down to the 1700s were firmly established. It was also the period of Moscow's maximum expansion: the city grew from a still relatively small principality in what is today northeastern Russia to a major European power stretching hundreds of miles in every direction from its capital (see Map 3.1). Ivan the Great (1462–1505) in particular brought to their fullest development the four basic methods used by his predecessors to gather the Russian lands: inheritance, colonization of unoccupied areas in the north and east, purchase, and conquest.

Ivan's defeat of the republic of Novgorod in the 1470s brought under Moscow's control Novgorod's vast holdings in the north as well as its trade contacts through the Baltic with Europe and Scandinavia. Novgorod fell at last, after over one hundred years' opposition to Moscow, because it was a badly divided society. The elite looked to Lithuania for help against Muscovite encroachments, but the majority of the people, resenting the boyars and merchants anyway, objected to allying with Catholics and fought Ivan's forces only halfheartedly. The Novgorodians were defeated first in 1471 and then, after further resistance, were completely humiliated in 1478. The veche bell, Novgorod's symbol of freedom, was seized and taken to Moscow, and the city's lands were annexed to the Muscovite state. In 1485, a similar fate befell Moscow's old competitor, Tver. Thus, Ivan the Great both absorbed Moscow's nearest rivals and formally liberated the region from the Mongol yoke. Only Lithuania-Russia remained to challenge Moscow for leadership of the lands of the former Kievan Rus' confederation.

Under Vasilii III (1505–1533), Moscow further extended its sway, particularly westward against Lithuania, and annexed the important cities of Pskov and Smolensk. Vasilii also exerted pressure against Moscow's main enemy to the east, the Khanate of Kazan, ruled by descendants of the Mongols.

Important political and social changes accompanied the extensive expansion under these two influential rulers. Although in many respects the Muscovite princes still ruled the state much as if it were their private domain, state administration became both more complex and more institutionalized. At the same time that the power and authority of the rulers increased, grander and more prestigious symbols and trappings were adopted. One reflection of this was the marriage in 1472 of Ivan III to Zoe Paleologus, a niece of the last Byzantine emperor. At about the same time, the title of grand prince was superseded by the designation *autocrat* or *tsar*, both borrowed from Byzantine practice. The word "autocrat" in its Russian translation literally meant "the self-wielder of power" but was increasingly interpreted as "the holder of unlimited authority." "Tsar" (derived from the Latin *caesar*) also connoted complete and absolute power. Finally, in 1493, Ivan the Great took for himself the appellation *gosudar* (pronounced "ga-soo-dar"), or "sovereign of all the Russian lands."

The new grandeur of titles was complemented by the adoption of a new symbol, the two-headed eagle used by both the Byzantine emperor and the Holy Roman emperor in Europe, which lasted until 1917, and by the development of elaborate court ceremonials, including the formal anointing and coronation of the tsar in a Kremlin cathedral. As a reflection of his new status, Tsar Vasilii III opened diplomatic relations with the Holy Roman emperor and the pope in Europe and with the Turkish sultan in Constantinople.

The most important political development, however, was the growth of the concept of state service. In the past the majority of the prince's warriors, administrators, and servitors had been boyars. Customarily each boyar had his own hereditary estate, or *votchina*, and on it he exercised almost total authority, without interference from the prince or the state. He contracted with the prince to perform specific duties in return for certain rewards and was free to leave the prince's service at any time (and to sign on with another prince if he wished). In short, the prince had relatively little hold over a boyar, except the offer of money, trade, or protection that the boyar could not obtain on his own. During the rise of the Muscovite state and as the princes of Moscow saw their territory grow, they naturally tried to set up a system of land tenure and service over which they would have more control.

Increasingly, they took on servitors who were not boyars (or who were sometimes impoverished or landless boyars) and who, in return for service, received a grant of land to support them. This land, called a *pomestie* (pronounced "pa-mes-tye"), was at first allotted to the servitor only for the duration of his service. Later, the pomestie, like the votchina, became hereditary. Clearly, these men of service were more directly under the thumb of the prince or tsar, and Vasilii III tried to prevent both boyars and servitors from leaving his service. There was even discussion that such an act was treasonous. In retrospect, it is surprising how quickly the concept of obligatory service to the state emerged in the fifteenth and early sixteenth centuries.

This idea of service contained significant social implications and was eventually applied to other groups in the population, especially the peasants. The assumption arose that peasants, too, owed an obligation to the state, which could best be met by service to their landlords, be they princes, monasteries, boyars, or servitors. Moreover, as a money economy grew with the expansion of the state, peasants became more indebted to landlords, and the terms of loans and of sharecropping arrangements became increasingly burdensome. As a result, although serfdom (the binding of the peasant to the land) did not develop fully until some decades later, by the early 1500s the peasant's right to move to other land or to the service of a different lord had been restricted to a two-week period in the fall, after the harvest was in.

Commerce remained a significant part of economic life in Muscovy. One of the first European travelers to report his observations of the city, Ambrogio Contarini, an Italian diplomat traveling home to Venice from Persia, passed through Moscow in 1476. He described the Moscow market as follows:

> By the end of October the river which passes through the city is frozen over, and shops and bazaars for the sale of all sorts of things are erected on it, scarcely anything being sold in the town. They do this, as the river, from being surrounded on all sides by the city, and so protected from the wind, is less cold than anywhere else. On this frozen river may be seen daily numbers of cows and pigs, great quantities of corn, wood, hay, and every other necessary, nor does the supply fail during the whole winter. . . . [Cows and pigs] are frozen whole, and it is curious to see so many skinned cows standing upright on their feet. . . . A great many merchants frequent this city from Germany and Poland during the winter for the sole purpose of buying pelts such as the furs of young goats, foxes, ermines, squirrels, wolves, and other animals.[2]

The tsar engaged actively in trade, and as in other areas of Muscovite society, he did his best to control the commercial life of the city.

Concomitantly with the increase in the power of the grand prince and tsar, the authority, wealth, and importance of the Russian Orthodox Church grew. After 1453, when the Turks seized Constantinople, the Russian churchmen concluded that the tasks of defending Orthodox Christianity and ensuring the purity of the faith had fallen to them. This gave rise to the theory of the Third Rome, which, put most simply, declared that the first Rome had fallen because of heresy within the church, that the second (Constantinople) had succumbed to the Turks, and that Moscow was the third, the new center of true Christian belief; a fourth Rome there would not be. Primarily a religious explanation of secular events, this concept did not produce, as some Russophobes have contended, a Muscovite plan for expansion and for conversion of the non-Orthodox world. But the outlook reflected in the Third Rome concept certainly did make the Russian Orthodox Church (and therefore much of imperial Russian society) overly defensive and quite intolerant of ideas and influences from outside, including those from the Catholic (and later Protestant) West. To some extent, the strong streak of xenophobia that kept surfacing in the Russian Empire in subsequent centuries can be traced back to the self-righteous commitment to protect the one true faith inherent in the theory of the Third Rome.

An important issue for the Russian Orthodox Church, one common to organized religions that have expanded and become rich, was the proper role and function of the church in society. In the latter part of the 1400s and the first half of the 1500s, the Trans-Volga Elders, a group of reformers led by the monk Nil Sorskii, challenged the church leadership, urging the renunciation of worldly goods and pursuit of a simple monastic life. They wanted the church to give up its landholdings and other wealth and to emphasize instead contemplation and the striving for moral perfection. In the long run, the reformers were defeated. As a result, the Russian Church became even more focused on ritual and tradition and less concerned with intellectual innovation and the welfare of the people.

The challenge of the Trans-Volga Elders to established church policy posed a dilemma for Tsars Ivan III and Vasilii III. Past relations between the church and state had seldom been contentious. The metropolitans of Moscow had worked hand in hand with the Muscovite princes to advance their shared interests—the expansion of state and church. On a few occasions, the metropolitans had virtually ruled the principality when a prince was very young or there was a succession struggle. By the end of the fifteenth century, however, the tsars began to look greedily upon the church's vast landholdings: they could use more land, both to support their courts and to parcel out as pomestie to their growing body of servitors.

Consequently, when the reformers first called for the church to give up its estates, Ivan III was sympathetic to their position, apparently hoping that the state would acquire these holdings. On the other hand, the Trans-Volga Elders also insisted on the complete separation of church and state, demanding that the tsar and his government stay completely out of religious affairs. This plank of their platform was clearly less attractive since victory for the reformers would have ended the close, mutually beneficial cooperation between the secular power and the religious authority that had been so instrumental to Moscow's rise.

The church leaders, in opposing Nil Sorskii and his followers, argued that the interests of the Orthodox Church and the Muscovite state were closely linked and that the church should support and obey the tsar. This fitted well with the emerging concept of state service, and finally, after some wavering, both Ivan III and Vasilii III backed the church hierarchy in condemning the reformers.

CONCLUSION

The Muscovite state arose out of a need for security and unity in the forested wilderness. The core of the state-building experience was the constant struggle against first the Mongols and other princes, then the Lithuanians, the

Novgorodians, and the Mongols' descendants, the Tatars. Because the Moscow princes were talented and long-lived, they were better able to provide protection and ensure cohesion in their own domains. But in return, they demanded service to themselves and to the emerging state. Assertion of the rights of boyars, merchants, or peasants could lead to disunity and insecurity. Pluralism was not encouraged, and traditional privileges were slowly eroded and, finally, largely abolished.

A second tenet on which unification of the region rested was a belief in the worth of the community, of the people as a whole. It was not only that group or individual rights posed a threat but also that society highly valued community preservation and cohesion. This view, dating back to the Kievan Rus' concept of *sobornost'* ("spirit of the congregation") in the Orthodox Church and in the collectivity of spontaneously formed peasant communes, was now reaffirmed in a new form: the common purpose and significance of the society as a whole as represented by the Muscovite state.

A third important view that predominated in Moscow was a sense of inferiority and the need to overcome inherent liabilities. To survive and to expand, limited resources had to be husbanded and used efficiently. Surrounded on all sides by powerful enemies, Moscow's rulers were driven to mobilize the people and the society in order to prevail. Everything had to be subordinated to the effort to equalize the balance of forces.

At the same time, the people also benefited from the "gathering of the Russian lands." Christianity and other important elements of Kievan Rus' civilization were preserved and transmitted. A reasonable degree of internal peace was achieved, and economic recovery from the Mongol period began. The region reestablished extensive relations with the West in the 1400s, and divergent views and patterns still existed in Muscovite society. Yet, over the next hundred fifty years, the state steadily strengthened its position and imposed increasingly heavy burdens on the bulk of the Muscovite population.

FURTHER READING

Fedotov, G. *The Russian Religious Mind*. 2 vols. Cambridge, MA: Harvard University Press, 1966.

Fennell, John L. *The Crisis of Medieval Russia, 1200–1304*. London: Longman, 1983.

———. *The Emergence of Moscow, 1305–59*. Berkeley: University of California Press, 1968.

Hellie, Richard. *Enserfment and Military Change in Muscovy*. Chicago: University of Chicago Press, 1971.

Kaiser, Daniel H. *The Growth of Law in Medieval Russia.* Princeton, NJ: Princeton University Press, 1980.

Khodarkovsky, Michael. *Russia's Steppe Frontier: The Making of a Colonial Empire, 1500–1800.* Bloomington: Indiana University Press, 2002.

Kollmann, Nancy Shields. *Kinship and Politics: The Making of the Muscovite Political System, 1345–1547.* Stanford, CA: Stanford University Press, 1987.

Martin, Janet. *Medieval Russia, 980–1584.* Cambridge, UK: Cambridge University Press, 1995.

Thompson, M. W. *Novgorod the Great: Excavations at the Medieval City Directed by A. V. Artsikhovsy and B. A. Kolchin.* New York: Praeger, 1967.

Thyrêt, Isolde. *Between God and Tsar: Religious Symbolism and the Royal Women of Muscovite Russia.* DeKalb: Northern Illinois University Press, 2001.

Voyce, Arthur. *The Art and Architecture of Medieval Russia.* Norman: University of Oklahoma Press, 1964.

CHAPTER 4

IVAN THE TERRIBLE AND THE TIME OF TROUBLES, 1533–1618

The unification of Russia and neighboring territories under Moscow had laid the foundations of state and society, but the events of the next hundred fifty years built up and completed the structure of what became the Russian Empire. Political changes in the eighty years between the death of Vasilii III in 1533 and the election of Michael Romanov as tsar in 1613 marked a major turning point in the region's history, equal in importance to the reign of Peter the Great in the eighteenth century or to the Bolshevik and Stalinist revolutions in the two decades after 1917 (see Table 4.1 on p. 59).

Ivan IV (1533–1584) was known as *groznyi* in Russian, a word poorly rendered in English as "terrible." It is more correctly translated as "awesome" or "inspiring reverential dread." Nevertheless, because it is so well known, we will use the customary designation Ivan the Terrible, hoping that the reader will bear in mind that people of his time and later viewed Ivan with both admiration and fear.

Ivan the Terrible sought, however irrationally at times, to expand considerably the borders of Muscovy and to unify and control the lands he ruled. The social conflict and oppression this generated, combined with an economic crisis and the huge cost of major foreign wars, brought state and society to near collapse and temporary anarchy. The newly enlarged state narrowly missed dissolution again into petty principalities and was nearly conquered by Sweden and Poland. Yet, by an extraordinary effort, foreign enemies were repulsed, civil war ended, and state and society rebuilt. And making these turbulent times even more dramatic, love, hate, madness, deception, and heroism all figured significantly in the events of this era.

THE PERSONALITY AND CHARACTER OF IVAN THE TERRIBLE

Everyone agrees that Ivan the Terrible was violent and cruel and acted at times in a paranoiac fashion. Some historians go further, believing he had a severe personality disorder bordering on madness. Others argue that although he certainly behaved irrationally on occasion, Ivan was driven by the conviction that, divinely inspired, he was carrying out God's will and that the eradication of sin and purification of society necessitated the torture and the slaughter of "enemies." One interesting analysis, based on study of Ivan's exhumed skeleton, concludes that he may have suffered from an extremely painful spinal cord disease and that contemporary medication for this (mercury and laudanum) may have caused his unpredictable and violent fits of rage.

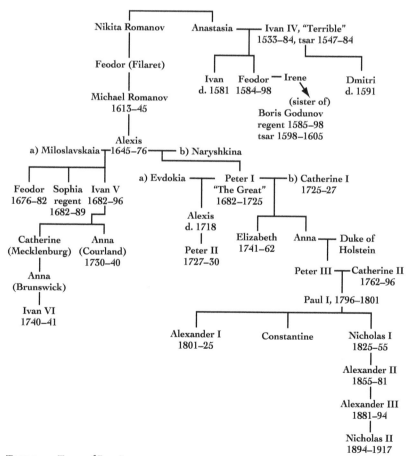

TABLE 4.1. Tsars of Russia, 1547–1917

FIGURE 4.1. Ivan IV (the Terrible). (V.M. Vasnetsov, *Tsar Ivan Vasilievich the Terrible,* 1018. Courtesy of the State Tretyakov Gallery)

His general levels of ability and intelligence remain in dispute as well. Traditionally, Ivan had been viewed as well educated for his time, widely read, and possessing some skill as a writer and thinker. More recently, it has been alleged that letters attributed to him were forgeries and that, in fact, he was a quite unlettered and altogether crude and uncultured person. In our view, he was certainly literate, and whether or not he actually wrote the pieces bearing his name, he was a clever and unusually able leader, though obviously emotionally unstable.

Without undertaking a complex Freudian analysis, we can see that Ivan the Terrible's childhood and upbringing clearly distorted his personality, values, and outlook on the world. His father, Vasilii III, died in 1533, when Ivan was only three. For another five years, his life remained reasonably normal; Ivan was a child ruler with his mother serving as regent in concert with her advisors. Unfortunately, the most powerful boyars resented her position, and when she died (perhaps by poisoning) in 1538, a bloody, no-holds-barred struggle for power between two prominent boyar families, the Shuiskiis and the Belskiis, erupted. Ivan, caught in the middle and alternately ignored or abused, witnessed beatings, torture, and murder. The intrigues and violence surrounding him undoubtedly made Ivan, apparently a sensitive boy, suspicious and resentful. The film *Ivan the Terrible*, made in the 1940s by the great Soviet movie director Sergei Eisenstein, melodramatically portrays this atmosphere.

Ivan also developed at this time a streak of cruelty and suppressed rage as well as a deep-seated determination to revenge himself on those responsible for his mistreatment and humiliation. Though perhaps exaggerating, Ivan later in life wrote:

> But when I had entered upon my eighth year of life and when thus our subjects had achieved their desire, namely to have the kingdom without a ruler, then they did not deem us, their sovereigns, worthy of any loving care, but themselves ran after wealth and glory. . . . How many boyars and well-wishers of our father . . . did they massacre! And the courts and the villages and the possessions of our uncles did they seize.

Yet not only the usurpation of power and wealth irked Ivan; petty harassments aroused his indignation as well:

> They began to feed us as though we were foreigners or the most wretched servants. What sufferings did I [not] endure through [lack of] clothing and through hunger! For in all things my will was not my own.[1]

As he entered his teens, Ivan began to assert his rights, and in 1547, when he was sixteen, he had himself crowned tsar and married Anastasia, one of the Romanovs, a well-liked boyar family. Though a political marriage, it turned out well, and Ivan lived happily with Anastasia until her death thirteen years later. Many historians believe she was a beneficent influence on the tsar, and it is certainly true that his more unorthodox and violent behavior began after Anastasia died.

THE REFORMS OF IVAN IV

In 1547, the year of Ivan's coronation, extensive rioting occurred in Moscow, and social disorder broke out in other parts of the country. These events were symptomatic of major problems that came to a head about the time Ivan ascended the throne. The most general problem was that the Muscovite state, comprising at this point about nine or ten million people and having expanded too rapidly, possessed an insufficient resource base to support itself and too small and antiquated an administration and social system to manage itself well. Ivan attempted both to build up the strength of Russia and to rationalize and improve its governance. The first task led him into conflict with aggressive foreign foes—Tatars, Swedes, and Poles—and the second into a remorseless and violent struggle with the most powerful single group in the land: the aristocracy of princely families and boyars.

At first, Ivan the Terrible's reforming efforts went well. He surrounded himself with a group of able advisors, including Macarius, metropolitan of the Orthodox Church; Sylvester, a well-educated priest; and Adashev, a talented servitor. These men and Ivan's other close collaborators came to be known as the Chosen Council, although it is unclear whether the council ever existed as a formal body. Ivan did not directly challenge the boyar *duma*, the ancient consultative body to the Russian princes, trying instead to work around it. In 1549, he convened a much broader advisory group, known eventually as the *zemskii sobor* (assembly of the land), representing not only the boyar elite but the gentry (servitors), church officials, townspeople, and, on one occasion, a few state peasants (from estates owned by the tsar or the government). Information on the composition and actions of this zemskii sobor is lacking, but Ivan probably discussed with it the reform measures he was about to undertake. Several times in later years, he called together and consulted with zemskii sobors.

Ivan placed high priority on improving the army's fighting capacity. Top commands were held by the highest-ranking boyars, regardless of ability, and this system often created serious leadership deficiencies. Although Ivan could not abolish the boyar-defended system of command by elite birth or rank, he managed to institute rules that permitted exceptions under special circumstances. In this way, he was able, for certain campaigns and battles, to advance the best officers to top posts. Ivan also regularized the terms of military service—how long a boyar or member of the gentry had to serve and what his responsibilities were. Finally, he accelerated and strengthened earlier efforts to form specialized military units of musketeers (called *streltsy*), artillerymen, and contract cavalry, all of whom were especially useful in manning the growing number of forts and outposts along Muscovy's continuously expanding frontier.

Ivan also supervised the collection and codification of the laws and local government reform. The latter was greatly needed, since governors and other local officials were often corrupt and systematically exploited the local population. The new system did not end all abuses, but it was a step forward at least.

Additionally, Ivan convened a major council of the Orthodox Church, which came to be known as the Council of the Hundred Chapters (from the number of charges given to it). It clarified a number of issues in internal church administration, strongly endorsed the close tie between the tsar and the church, and limited the church's right to acquire more land.

Finally, Ivan the Terrible made a strong effort to strengthen Muscovy's ties with Europe. He invited European specialists to Moscow to help improve the army, to erect buildings and churches, to introduce new technology, and to practice medicine. Only a few came, but they were instrumental in introducing stimulating ideas and techniques to Muscovite society. In the 1570s, Ivan established a special suburb of Moscow for foreign residents, many of whom, by the 1600s, were performing important services for Ivan's successors. Ivan also ordered the construction of Saint Basil's, the wonderfully ornate and colorful cathedral in Red Square with many octagons and shimmering, bulbous domes.

Through good luck, Ivan also established friendly and profitable relations with England. In 1553, Richard Chancellor, an English explorer searching for a northern route to the Orient, happened into the White Sea in northern Russia. He went on to Moscow, where Ivan cordially welcomed him, and an important trade relationship grew out of this chance encounter. Some English specialists also came to Muscovy in the latter part of the 1500s.

IVAN VERSUS THE ARISTOCRACY

In none of his early successes did Ivan confront head-on the basic question of Muscovite politics: Could the tsar exercise unlimited authority, or did the customary privileges of princely families and boyars restrict his growing power? In this contest, the aristocracy had several advantages. The first was tradition. From the very founding of Kievan Rus', the aristocracy had been the state's senior warriors and administrators and the closest advisors to the princes of Kiev and later of Moscow. It was unthinkable that the tsar could act and the state function without their close cooperation and full support. Second, they wielded considerable power: they owned the largest estates, could provide the greatest numbers of armed men for the tsar's army, and had almost total control over the population on their lands. Third, the boyars institutionalized access to power through the boyar duma and held most of the top positions in the army and the government.

At the same time, the boyars, particularly when compared to the landed nobility of Europe, were quite weak. They were few in number, including probably less than two hundred families in the 1500s. They had no corporate identity and, indeed, could not rely on any extensive body of custom or law that gave them privileges and rights as a class (instead of as individuals). Moreover, they were deeply fragmented, quarreling endlessly over precedence and rank and resorting to intrigue and brutality in their internecine struggles instead of uniting against the tsar. Finally, the rise over the preceding century and a half of the gentry, or men of service, had gradually undercut their position. The gentry, originally considered a clearly inferior class, at first held their estates only as long as they served the grand prince, and they were clearly dependent on the tsar; the boyars, however, had hereditary title to their land and, in theory, could leave the tsar's service at any time. Gradually, but steadily, in the 1500s, the distinctions between boyars and gentry disappeared: both held their land on a hereditary basis, and both owed obligatory service, although some boyars fled to Lithuania to escape this burden.

The tsar also had certain advantages in an open struggle with the boyars. He had the backing of the church as an institution, no matter what individual prelates and priests might feel. In addition, the theory and aura of autocracy, or unlimited rule, inherited from the Byzantine Empire and nurtured under Ivan III and his successors, although not fully accepted by the Muscovite society of the mid-1500s, served to strengthen Ivan the Terrible's claim to absolute authority. Finally, he could count on the support of the gentry, who, of course, stood to gain much from the diminution of the boyars' position. Ivan, however, unlike his contemporary absolute monarchs in the West, such as Henry VIII of England, did not have a strong merchant class or autonomous towns on which to draw for financial and political backing.

In retrospect, we may view the fierce struggle between Ivan the Terrible and the boyars that broke out in the 1560s as an unnecessary and even tragic contest, with neither side taking into account how much the struggle endangered the state. In the end, although the boyars' power was not totally broken, the principle of state service and the growing authority of the tsar were confirmed and enhanced. At the time, however, it was far from clear what the outcome would be, and the resulting bloodshed and disruption very nearly brought down the Muscovite regime altogether. Had Ivan not won, the nature of Russian society and the subsequent course of the area's history would certainly have been quite different.

Although the evidence is contradictory, two developments seem to have triggered the bloody showdown between Ivan the Terrible and the boyars. One was an unlucky event: the serious illness of the tsar in 1553. At that time, he asked his privileged subjects, including top government officials and boyars, to swear allegiance to his son Dmitrii as heir to the throne. Some did, but many at first refused, apparently because Dmitrii was still a child and because they feared another period of minority rule marked by internal strife and weakness, as had occurred in Ivan's boyhood. The incident infuriated and frightened Ivan, who, when he recovered from his illness, apparently marked down for future retribution those boyars whom he believed had wanted to usurp his family's right to the throne.

Although the Muscovite state had formally thrown off the Mongol yoke in 1480, the Mongols' descendants continued to harass the region from the south and east in the 1500s. Deciding that bold measures were needed, Ivan in 1551 launched a campaign against Moscow's nearest enemy, the Tatar Khanate of Kazan. In 1552, after a long siege, Kazan, a city on the Volga River east of Moscow, was itself captured, and by 1557, Ivan's state had annexed the whole khanate. In 1556, Ivan also succeeded in capturing the Khanate of Astrakhan at the mouth of the Volga and adding it to his domain (see Map 5.1 on page 89). These conquests brought mainly non-Slavs into the expanding state and added to the considerable diversity of Muscovite society. However, the Tatars of the Crimean Khanate remained independent and, backed by the Ottoman Turks, launched major attacks against Ivan on several occasions throughout his reign. The subsequent Russian Empire did not finally subdue them for more than two hundred years.

In addition to security against the Muslim Tatars, Ivan had an important foreign policy goal in the other direction, toward Europe. Ever since Ivan III's absorption of Novgorod, the Muscovite state had had a toehold on the shore of the Baltic Sea. Ivan the Terrible wanted to increase his state's territory on the Baltic coast and to expand trade with northern and central Europe. Blocking his way were the Livonian order of Germanic knights, who held what is today Estonia and Latvia, and the Polish-Lithuanian state in the south (see Map 3.1). In 1558, Ivan launched what came to be known as the Livonian War and at first met with great success. By the early 1560s, the Livonian order had been destroyed and some territory captured from Lithuania. It was, however, a bloody and expensive war, one in which Ivan's state was fighting on two fronts simultaneously, requiring higher taxes and more army recruits. Not only was there popular grumbling, but some of Ivan's advisors, including members of the Chosen Council, warned against getting too deeply involved in a costly military struggle in the west.

In 1560, as the policy dispute over the Livonian War was heating up, Ivan's first wife, Anastasia, died suddenly. Whether removal of her loving and calming influence was a factor in Ivan's subsequent irrational behavior is unclear, but in any case, Ivan launched an extraordinary vendetta against his friends and the leading boyar families shortly after her death. Accusing his trusted colleagues Sylvester and Adashev of conspiring to poison his wife, Ivan sent

Sylvester into remote exile and threw Adashev into prison, where he died. Ivan then turned against their circle of friends and began, mercilessly and without trial, to have them tortured and executed. There seemed to be no rhyme or reason to his actions, and during this reign of terror, a number of prominent officials and boyars fled to Lithuania. Ivan the Terrible immediately branded these flights as treason and increased the fury of his persecution against those who remained.

One bizarre episode followed another until, suddenly and without explanation, the tsar left Moscow in late 1564 with the treasury, withdrawing to a monastery some distance from the city. This action created bafflement and uncertainty, and since no one knew what to do, emissaries from Moscow begged the tsar to return. Finally, several months later, he reappeared, looking haggard and distraught. He agreed to resume his position as tsar only if his authority to punish traitors and evildoers as he saw fit were confirmed and he were allowed to set up a separate and autonomous area within the Muscovite state entirely under his control, conditions that the leading officials accepted.

Thus originated the strange institution called the *oprichnina* (pronounced "uh-preechneena"), literally, "the area set apart." This area under Ivan's personal rule consisted of scattered territories and estates, many of which were seized from princely families and boyars. The oprichnina included some of the best land as well as districts of several cities. The rest of the country was left under regular administration. In 1572, Ivan, apparently convinced that he had broken the back of the opposition, ended the oprichnina and reunited it with the Muscovite territories.

The precise purpose and significance of the oprichnina remains unclear. Ivan the Terrible probably saw it, first and foremost, as a weapon in his struggle with the boyars and princely families. To administer the oprichnina, he appointed ambitious and obedient servitors who did not hesitate to take harsh actions against his enemies and whom he rewarded with land grants and wealth. Ivan ignored or degraded the regular officials and boyars, confiscating the estates of many as a means of both punishing them and undermining their economic and social position. At times, the tsar was subject to fits of paranoia and rage against his imagined persecutors. He personally participated, and according to some accounts delighted, in the torture and murder of individuals and groups. On one occasion, he killed his favorite son during a furious outburst. At other times, he repented of his deeds and sought solace and atonement in contemplation and prayer.

The oprichnina as an institution, combined with Ivan's unbridled anger and violent oppression, succeeded in weakening and demoralizing the boyars, and for the last twenty years of his reign, Ivan encountered little opposition to his half-mad rule. But the cost was enormous. The division of the state into two parts wrecked the administration and seriously damaged the economy. The aura of terror and suspicion made normal social or political life impossible, and educated Muscovite society became paralyzed and cowed. Ivan the Terrible, with no one to gainsay him, plunged ahead with the draining Livonian War, exhausting the country and sapping its resources. Moreover, the fortunes of war turned against him: when peace was finally made in 1583, after twenty-five years of wasting struggle, he had lost almost everything originally gained, and the state was back where it had started. Or perhaps the country was worse off, because in the course of the war, the Swedes had entered the fray and were now allied with the Poles as deadly enemies of Moscow.

What did it all mean? Clearly Ivan the Terrible was mentally and emotionally disturbed, at the very least, and we need only look to our own recent history, to the case of Adolf Hitler, to appreciate how terrible the consequences can be when an intelligent person with a pathological personality wields absolute power. Yet it would be a mistake to write Ivan off as simply deranged. His struggle with the aristocracy was also a contest for control of the state, and although his opponents were perhaps less serious a threat than he imagined, the outcome confirmed the supreme power of the tsar. The shape of the full absolutism that was to take final form in the Russian Empire of the 1600s and 1700s was clearly presaged by the rule of Ivan the Terrible.

At the same time, the cost was exorbitant. The people were oppressed and squeezed, the economy ravaged, and the society nearly torn apart by civil persecution and unrelenting terror. Although Ivan succeeded in securing his eastern frontier, his grand design for the Baltic collapsed, and he was unable to subdue the Crimean Tatars in the south. Most significantly, the fears and tensions of his rule as well as the near ruination of the country set the stage for one of the most sensational and dramatic periods in the region's history, aptly named the Time of Troubles.

THE TIME OF TROUBLES, 1598–1613

Three main issues characterized the tumultuous era of the Time of Troubles: a struggle for political power, a widespread social revolution, and a national movement to prevent foreign domination of the lands controlled by the state created in large part by Ivan the Terrible. These themes were closely intertwined and often played out simultaneously. Nevertheless, to make comprehensible the confused events of the Time of Troubles, we will consider each of them in turn.

The Struggle for Political Power

The main thread of Muscovite history into the 1500s was the extension of the personal power and authority of the grand prince from his own estate to the larger principality and, finally, to the unified lands that would later be known as the Russian Empire. Facilitated by the continuity of a dynasty descended from Kiev, this process had culminated in the expansionist and absolutist rule of Ivan the Terrible. Tradition and the God-given status of the tsar glued the diverse Muscovite holdings together and shored up state power. But the 1598 death of Ivan's successor, the weak and sickly Feodor, without an heir not only provoked a major crisis but very nearly led to the complete dissolution of the state that had been slowly built up during the preceding two hundred fifty years.

The bitterness and resentment still felt by the upper classes as a result of their forcible subjugation by Ivan the Terrible exacerbated the turmoil that followed the end of the dynasty. The great boyar families were determined to recoup their fortunes and recapture their dominant political status in Muscovite society. The gentry, who had benefited from Ivan's oprichnina but were suffering economically, were no less determined to advance their interests by seizing as much political power as possible. The merchants, who had not fared particularly well under Ivan and were considered second-class citizens by the others, believed a golden opportunity to improve their position was at hand. The stage was set for political strife and intermittent civil war.

The prologue was provided by a twenty-one-year period, from 1584 to 1605, during which the talented Boris Godunov dominated political life. A minor boyar who participated in the administration of Ivan the Terrible's oprichnina, he was a brother-in-law of Tsar Feodor. Through his sister, Godunov acquired a commanding position in affairs of state early in Feodor's reign. Beginning in 1587, he served as regent and was in fact the ruler, while Feodor, who was extremely devout, concentrated on religious affairs. Godunov was talented and just, attempting to settle the country down domestically and to patch up the quarrels with Sweden and Poland. He skillfully helped engineer the establishment in Moscow of a patriarchate, the highest administrative unit in the Orthodox Church, and had his friend Metropolitan Job named the first patriarch. This arrangement permitted enlargement of the church hierarchy and enhanced Moscow's international prestige because the other patriarchs in the Orthodox Church were located in areas under Turkish rule.

Nonetheless, Godunov had two strikes against him. Although he promoted trade and ties with the West, he could do little to overcome Moscow's fundamental economic problems: declining agriculture and huge losses caused by Ivan's wars. He also had no legitimate claim to the throne. As a consequence, his enemies spread rumors that he had been involved in a 1591 conspiracy that resulted in the death of Ivan the Terrible's youngest son, Dmitrii (a story dramatically told in Modest Mussorgsky's great opera, *Boris Godunov*). In any case, in 1598, when Feodor died childless, Godunov clearly aspired to succeed him.

In this unprecedented situation, a zemskii sobor of some five hundred representatives of the boyars, gentry, clergy, and townspeople was convened. For the first time in the history of Moscow, no natural heir to the throne existed. Moreover, there was no law of succession. Because of the powerful position he had developed over the preceding decade and because he was undoubtedly the most suitable candidate available, the zemskii sobor elected Godunov tsar in 1598.

His reign began auspiciously, but before long, events over which he had little control undermined his position. First, between 1601 and 1603, the region suffered a terrible drought and famine. Despite extraordinary efforts by the government to relieve the misery, people were reduced to eating fodder and bark and even, on occasion, to cannibalism, as this contemporary account makes clear:

> But I swear by God that in Moscow I saw, with my own eyes, people who rolled in the streets and, like animals, ate grass during the summer and hay during the winter. . . . Human flesh, finely ground, baked in pies (a kind of pastry), was sold and consumed like beef. . . . Daily, on the Tsar's orders they collected hundreds of corpses and carried them outside the city in wagons—an undertaking which was awesome to observe. Specially appointed people washed the dead, wrapped them in a white cloth, put red shoes on them, and wheeled them to the church to be buried.[2]

Second, beginning in 1603, rumors began to spread that Ivan's last son, Dmitrii, had not died in 1591; it was whispered that he not only still lived but was preparing to assert his rightful claim to the throne. Despite his best efforts, Tsar Boris was unable to squelch these allegations. Moreover, stories also began to circulate that Godunov was a murderer and usurper and that the land was being punished by God for Godunov's sins. How much Boris's boyar opponents were behind these stories is unclear, but there is no doubt that the boyars fanned the flames of slander, some because they were jealous of Godunov's position, others because they had been slighted or oppressed by his policies.

The upshot was that, in the fall of 1604, a major rebellion against Tsar Boris erupted, headed by a pretender to the throne known retrospectively as the first False Dmitrii. Allegedly a former monk, he believed that he was indeed the lawful heir to the throne. His supporters included a group of Polish nobles, who were patently using him to further their own ends, and a motley collection of other discontented individuals, some who were convinced he was in fact Dmitrii and others who did not care about his claims as long as they could channel their grievances against the government through him.

The challenge of this first pretender opened eight years of chaotic and complex maneuvering for political supremacy among the boyars, gentry, and merchants, who backed first one candidate to the throne and then another. At the nadir of this unseemly contest, there was no tsar at all, and it seemed the vaunted Muscovite autocracy would disappear altogether. Greatly complicating the political struggle was the eruption of a major social revolution shortly after the appearance of the first False Dmitrii.

Social Revolution

Although a number of fringe and semicriminal elements participated, the main groups involved in the widespread 1605–1606 social revolution were peasants, Cossacks, slaves, and runaway serfs. By the early 1600s, serfdom—the binding of peasants to the land—had developed quite a bit, though the process was not yet complete. In the last part of the sixteenth century, an agricultural depression and the exactions accompanying Ivan the Terrible's oprichnina and his wars had made the situation of the rural population grave, and the drought and famine of 1601 and 1602 made it desperate. As a result, particularly in what is today central and southern Russia, almost all groups in the countryside, whether made up of free peasants, those loosely bound to their landlords by debts, the fully enserfed, or fugitives from their obligations and their lords, could unite against the upper classes and the government. And since symbolism and superstition were important in their lives, so much the better if they could believe their rebellious fury was being expended in support of the "true" tsar and the righting of a dynastic wrong.

The Cossacks need a special word of explanation. The name "Cossack," originally derived from a warlike, nomadic group of horsemen in central Asia, began at this time to be applied to bands of independent frontiersmen who lived on the southern and eastern borderlands of the Muscovite state. Some Cossacks were mainly freebooters and brigands; others were farmers and herders. Cossack bands frequently included escapees from authority, such as tax evaders, runaway serfs, and fugitives from justice. Proud of their skills as horsemen and fighters, determined to remain free, and fickle in their political loyalties during the Time of Troubles, the Cossacks were an effective but volatile force in both the struggle for power and the social revolution. On a number of occasions, they switched sides unexpectedly, tipping the balance in favor of

FIGURE 4.2. False Dmitrii I. (INTERFOTO / Alamy Stock Photo)

one faction or another. The Cossacks would continue to play a significant role in subsequent Russian history.

When the first False Dmitrii invaded Russia in October 1604 with his Polish supporters, the first to rally to his cause were the Cossacks. But other dissatisfied rural elements soon swelled his ranks, and in the spring of 1605, after the unexpected natural death of Boris Godunov, Dmitrii's forces captured Moscow, and he was installed as tsar. Ugly and ungainly in appearance, he tried to placate the boyars and the general populace, but word of his idiosyncratic habits and the haughty conduct of his Polish entourage began to spread. After he had been on the throne for less than a year, the first False Dmitrii was killed in a coup led by the boyar prince Vasilii Shuisky, who then arranged to have himself proclaimed tsar. Dmitrii's ashes were supposedly loaded into a cannon and fired back toward Poland.

With Shuisky on the throne, the boyars had seemingly won the political contest. The new tsar was compelled to provide the boyars guarantees against arbitrary treatment and punishment, and his policies reflected their interests. Though his "election" as tsar had been enthusiastically endorsed by the Moscow mobs, who were particularly incensed against the Polish clique that had dominated the city during the brief reign of the first False Dmitrii, Shuisky could offer them little once enthroned. As a result, they soon turned against him and joined a countrywide revolt to overthrow the boyar tsar.

With the central authority tarnished and weakened by dynastic struggle and successive coups, the country began to dissolve into anarchy. Local governors rebelled, as did non-Russian ethnic groups who opposed Muscovite repression. Most importantly, the lower classes in southern Russia rose in a massive conflagration that raged throughout 1606 and 1607. The rebels' leader, Ivan Bolotnikov, a colorful and extremely able demagogue of obscure origins, roused and organized the masses to fight for their own interests and needs and to destroy the boyars and landlords.

During this period, various new pretenders emerged, including one who claimed to be the son of Tsar Feodor, even though the record was clear that Feodor had had no sons. Finally, in August 1607, a second False Dmitrii appeared and quickly gathered a considerable following. Although neither he nor his close advisors took his claim to the throne seriously, many were happy to follow his banner in the hope of seeing order restored and obtaining what they wanted. In two bizarre episodes, the mother of the real Dmitrii, now a nun, declared the second False Dmitrii to be her child, and the Polish wife of the first False Dmitrii recognized him as her husband and bore him a son. As the social revolution burned itself out during 1608, and with the boyar tsar, Vasilii Shuisky, and the second False Dmitrii unable to defeat each other, a stalemate developed.

The Movement for National Defense

At this juncture, a new theme emerged: a struggle against foreigners meddling in local affairs. This had been presaged by the resentment against the Polish followers of the first False Dmitrii, but it became a major element in the Time of Troubles in early 1609, when Tsar Vasilii, with his back to the wall, turned to Sweden for help. In return for territorial concessions along the Baltic and a promise that the Russian state would ally with Sweden against Poland, the Swedes provided troops, who helped Vasilii Shuisky's army to chase away the second False Dmitrii.

To counter this outside assistance for Shuisky, some of the second False Dmitrii's supporters appealed to the king of Poland, Sigismund III, for help. Anxious to extend his influence in Muscovy and to thwart a Russian-Swedish alliance, Sigismund invaded Russia and agreed to have his son placed on the throne. But, most historians agree, Sigismund really wanted to rule Muscovy himself, and he apparently saw to it that negotiations over the conditions under which his son would become tsar broke down. Polish forces occupied

Moscow, the Swedes attacked in the north because the Russians had allied with the Poles, and the second False Dmitrii reappeared in the southeast to make another try for the throne. In the midst of these disasters, Tsar Vasilii was deposed and sent to a monastery.

This was certainly the low point in the fortunes of the Muscovite state: with no tsar, the capital occupied by Poles, the northwest controlled by Swedes, and a pretender stirring up trouble in the countryside, its chances for survival seemed slim. Yet the very gravity of the situation sparked an upsurge of anti-foreign feeling and a determination to restore Muscovy's independence as well as some semblance of order. The upper classes appear to have played the dominant role, and for good reason. They had the most to lose from Polish domination and continuing civil disorder and the most to gain from the resurrection of the Muscovite state of the 1500s, albeit without the arbitrary persecutions of Ivan the Terrible. Moreover, the effort at national regeneration began in the towns of northern Russia, which had been least affected by the social revolution and could still command enough economic resources to support the drive to expel the foreigners.

This national revival also contained a strong religious element. The Catholic Poles, the main enemy, were considered heretical, and the head of the Russian Orthodox Church, Patriarch Hermogen, played an important role in initiating the national resistance movement. In all likelihood, many illiterate but devout Russians, bewildered by the kaleidoscopic events of the preceding few years, were delighted to be told at last who the true enemy was: the heretical Poles.

In 1612, two remarkable individuals, a butcher named Kuzma Minin, and an experienced general, Prince Dmitrii Pozharsky, combined their organizational, fighting, and inspirational talents to form a national army that had liberated Moscow from the Poles by the end of the year. Large contributions made by citizens of many towns supported the army, and this national movement clearly represented a determined effort by the local population to take their destiny into their own hands.

Significantly, once the Poles were driven out, the leaders of the national resistance moved at once to restore tsarist rule. A zemskii sobor convened in early 1613 chose Michael Romanov as tsar after considerable deliberation, putting in power the family that would rule the Russian Empire until 1917. Only sixteen, Michael had not been compromised in the earlier civil wars of the Time of Troubles. He was a grandnephew of Anastasia, Ivan the Terrible's "good" wife, and thus indirectly related to the old dynasty. Perhaps most importantly, Patriarch Hermogen had backed him, and Michael's father, Metropolitan Filaret, was a popular and influential churchman and former boyar.

CONCLUSION

The new government of Tsar Michael was weak, and disorder and civil strife continued until at least 1618, the year marking the beginning of firm rule and the end of the Time of Troubles. The most important direct results of this period include the expulsion of the foreigners and Catholics, the preservation of the Muscovite state and the purity of the Orthodox Church, and the restoration of tsarist authority. Under the surface, however, the upper classes salvaged their position (even though the boyars' effort to seize power was defeated), while the lower classes succeeded only in postponing the day of their final enserfment, and the development of autocratic rule resumed.

The most interesting question is why absolutist authority first expanded greatly under Ivan the Terrible, then survived, despite the wrenching crisis of the Time of Troubles, to become the dominant political institution of modern Russian history. Although any answer must be speculative, four main factors explain this phenomenon, in our view.

First, given Muscovy's weak economy, strong central government was needed to mobilize the resources and people for the tasks of unification, growth, and defense. Because centralizing monarchs, fulfilling analogous goals, existed at about the same time in Western Europe, the Muscovite experience was hardly unique. But the power of the tsar to command obedience, sanctified by the Orthodox Church, Byzantine theory, and Mongol practice, was crucial to the further development and expansion of the Muscovite state.

Second, the tsar became a symbol of unity and security in a fragmented and hostile world. This role, enhanced by memories of Kievan Rus', had first taken shape when the prince was simply proprietor of an enlarged private estate turned into a principality; it had been expanded in the struggle to throw off the Mongol yoke and to "gather the Russian lands." Significantly, during the Time of Troubles, one common thread was the search for the "true" tsar, and again and again, the people, from both the upper and the lower classes, rallied around a pretender, no matter how flimsy his claims. Moreover, their first action to reunite the divided society was to elect a new tsar.

Third, the autocracy emerged, flourished, and survived because, from the earliest days, first during the Kievan Rus' period and then in the 1300s in Moscow, it was linked with the Orthodox Church. People of this period may have understood little of Christian theology or of the ideas and politics of the patriarchs, metropolitans, and archbishops, but they devoutly believed in the rituals and physical presence of the Orthodox Church. Thus, when state and church supported each other and the tsar acted as defender of the true faith as well as ruler of the Muscovite state, this association greatly reinforced his authority and his influence over the population.

Finally, it is important to remember that the tsars prevailed in part because no other group or institution seemed capable of organizing Muscovite society and building the state. The boyars fought each other as well as suppressed the lower classes. Although classes and institutions competitive with the king were growing stronger in Europe, they were declining in Muscovy. In fact, once Ivan the Terrible undercut the boyars' power, no group existed in Muscovy to seriously challenge the tsar's growing absolutism. The people could resist, as they did during Ivan the Terrible's depredations and during the Time of Troubles, but such resistance was either isolated defiance or disorganized rebellion. Even to make revolt coherent, it was necessary to raise the standard of a false or boyar tsar. Group fought group, the masses struck out blindly at the government and their economic oppressors, landlords, and merchants, but no alternative basis for organizing society was propounded. As a result, the region entered the seventeenth century with a battle-scarred, but well-entrenched, system of tsarist autocracy.

FURTHER READING

Barbour, Philip L. *Dimitry Called the Pretender, Tsar and Great Prince of All Russia, 1605–06.* Boston: Houghton Mifflin, 1966.

de Madariaga, Isabel. *Ivan the Terrible: First Tsar of Russia.* New Haven, CT: Yale University Press, 2005.

Dunning, Chester S. L. *Russia's First Civil War: The Time of Troubles and the Founding of the Romanov Dynasty.* University Park: Pennsylvania State University Press, 2001.

Hellie, Richard. *Slavery in Russia, 1450–1725.* Chicago: University of Chicago Press, 1982.

Longworth, Philip. *The Cossacks.* New York: Holt, Rinehart and Winston, 1970.

Perrie, Maureen. *Pretenders and Popular Monarchism in Early Modern Russia: The False Tsars of the Time of Troubles.* Cambridge: Cambridge University Press, 2002.

Platonov, S. *The Time of Troubles: A Historical Study of the Internal Crises and Social Struggle in Sixteenth- and Seventeenth-Century Muscovy.* Translated by John T. Alexander. Lawrence: University Press of Kansas, 1970.

Plokhy, Serhii. *The Cossacks and Religion in Early Modern Ukraine.* New York: Oxford University Press, 2001.

Skrynnikov, Ruslan G. *Ivan the Terrible.* Edited and translated by Hugh F. Graham. Gulf Breeze, FL: Academic International, 1981.

———. *The Time of Troubles: Russia in Crisis, 1604–1618.* Edited and translated by Hugh F. Graham. Gulf Breeze, FL: Academic International, 1988.

CHAPTER 5

THE MOLDING OF IMPERIAL RUSSIAN SOCIETY, 1613–1689

Forenoon prayers had not quite ended when Tsar Alexis heard a great hubbub outside the church. It was a hot summer morning, July 25, 1662, and the tsar, perturbed by this unexpected interruption of his daily devotions, called loudly to attendants in the courtyard beside the church, demanding to know what the commotion was all about. He soon learned that a mob was clamoring to see him, insisting that they be allowed to present their grievances to the tsar in person.

Alexis acted decisively and courageously. Ordering his wife and children as well as some of the officials against whom the mob was railing to take refuge in his nearby summer palace, the tsar walked out of the church to deal with the protesters. He was unaware that earlier that morning in Moscow, some ten miles from his summer retreat, riots had broken out over high taxes and allegations of corruption and that the crowds had accused several of his closest advisors of treasonous support for the king of Poland, with whom Russia was at war. A few hotheads had persuaded the mob to march out of the city to find Tsar Alexis himself.

A direct approach to the tsar was unprecedented. He was ordinarily a remote and haughty figure, with whom only a few high officials, clergy, and court attendants were permitted to communicate. Nonetheless, in this crisis Alexis listened to the rancorous and sometimes profane complaints of the mob's leaders. They demanded a lowering of taxes and the surrender to them of the officials and merchants they had accused. According to historian Joseph T. Fuhrmann, the tsar handled the situation masterfully:

> Alexis spoke to the rioters in a quiet way, hoping to calm them and persuade them to leave. He promised after Mass to return to Moscow, to conduct a personal investigation, to right all wrongs. Several of the crowd

grabbed Alexis by the buttons of his coat, shouting, "Whom do you believe—the traitors or us?" Alexis swore before God that his faith was in his subjects, and one member of the crowd stepped forward to seal this covenant by shaking the tsar's hand.[1]

Later that same day, the tsar behaved quite differently. When a second mob approached him just as he was setting out for Moscow in accord with the promise he had made earlier, Alexis ordered loyal troops who had rallied round him in the interim to disperse the crowd by force. Over one hundred rioters were driven into a nearby river and drowned. Thousands were captured and flogged on the spot. In the next few days, several hundred ringleaders were hanged publicly, and several thousand rioters were exiled to southeastern Russia and to Siberia. At the same time, the tsar richly rewarded the officers and troops who supported him. Somewhat later, he undertook a few of the reforms the Moscow mobs had demanded.

This major disturbance in Moscow in 1662 was preceded by citywide riots in the capital in 1648 and by uprisings in other cities and in scattered rural areas. Subsequently, between 1667 and 1671, a major rebellion broke out in southeastern Russia that mustered an armed force of over twenty thousand men and threatened to topple the government. It was led by Stenka Razin, a colorful and energetic Don Cossack (a freebooter from the Don River region), who roused the poorer Cossacks and the lower classes in the south against all officials and authority with a vague but appealing cry for freedom and an

FIGURE 5.1. Stenka Razin. (Heritage Image Partnership Ltd / Alamy Stock Photo)

end to taxes. Much to the relief of Tsar Alexis, who had personally trained the troops to be sent against the rebels, some rich Cossacks betrayed Stenka Razin in the spring of 1671 and turned him over to the government. He was tortured and executed in Moscow in June of that year. But Stenka Razin remained a hero to the oppressed masses and passed into folk legend and song as a romantic Robin Hood capable of extraordinary feats in defending the poor from the depredations of the rich.

As melodramatic as some of these instances of popular unrest in the 1600s were, they served merely to underscore the overall helplessness of the people under the dominant institutions of Russian society that took shape in that century. During the reigns of three tsars and a regent—Michael (1613–1645), Alexis (1645–1676), Feodor (1676–1682), and the notable female leader Sophia (1682–1689)—a major effort to secure and expand the Russian state and to build a viable military and governmental system was made. It largely succeeded, but because Russia's physical and economic resources were limited, the average subject had to bear most of the burden. By 1690, some fifteen million people of many ethnicities, languages, and religions were struggling to support a huge state that stretched from the Pacific Ocean into Eastern Europe.

In this chapter, we will examine three chief pillars of tsarist society: the system of serfdom that lasted to 1861, the institution of the autocracy that was reestablished and refined in the 1600s and persisted until 1906 (and with minor modification, until 1917), and the nature and function of the Orthodox Church, which has changed little up to the present day. In the last two parts of the chapter, we will look at the Russian Empire's territorial expansion in its continuing search for security as well as at the development of closer relations with the West, which had a portentous initial impact on the empire's thought and society.

SERFDOM

Human bondage is an ancient phenomenon, dating back at least to early recorded history and still persisting in some parts of the world even today. Yet it emerged in Russia and adjacent lands late, soon took an unusually widespread and oppressive form, and lasted for over two hundred years, down to 1861.

Most people who farmed in Kievan Rus' times were free. Many were organized in communes, or *obshchinas*, and possessed their own land. Nevertheless, even then some peasants had begun to incur obligations to others, usually large landholders. In return for assistance—seed, tools, money, the use of more land—a peasant would agree to do a certain amount of work for the lord or to pay back a given sum in cash or in kind. When these debts were paid, the peasant was free once more. Until then, the peasant could not leave the land and the obligations he had accepted.

In this way, some peasants were moving toward enserfment. During the decline of Kiev, the civil strife that followed, and the invasion by the Mongols, many peasants found making ends meet difficult. Crops were seized, fields and tools destroyed, and villages burned. Moreover, storms, drought, and pests could wipe out any year's harvest. Finally, taxes imposed by the Moscow grand princes and tsars made it even more difficult to subsist without falling into debt. For example, scattered evidence indicates that during the last half of the 1500s there was a serious agricultural crisis, probably caused by a combination of bad weather and the exactions resulting from Ivan the Terrible's *oprichnina* and his foreign wars. By 1601, a terrible famine had gripped the region. Clearly, many peasants were being driven by economic necessity to take on obligations they had little hope of ever repaying. Thus, their bondage became permanent and serfdom spread.

But it might never have become so extensive had not state policy at this very time acted to bolster and intensify the natural economic trend toward serfdom. To unify and defend the state, the tsars had to finance their armies and reward their servitors. Although they earned some profits from trade in furs and other commodities, the most valuable resource available to the Ivans and Vasiliis of the fifteenth and sixteenth centuries was land, land whose products they could requisition or tax or that they could give to fighting men in return for service. Yet neither sort of land was valuable without peasants to work it. If peasants could run away to the frontier or escape to the Cossacks, the land became worthless and the tsars and their state bankrupt.

As a consequence, the tsarist government followed several policies that helped establish serfdom in the countryside. First, they gave many grants of land (*pomestie*) to servitors; most of these grants included peasants who owed service to the tsar's servitor in return for their continued right to use the land.

Second, the tsars began to interfere in the customary rules that had governed obligations between lord and peasant. Traditionally, peasants who paid their debts (sometimes their debts were paid by another lord, who wanted their labor) were free to leave the land and the lord's service at the end of the harvest season, during the two weeks before and after Saint George's Day (usually falling in November). But beginning in the latter part of the 1500s, the state now and then decreed a "forbidden" year, that is, abolished in a given year the right to move during the period around Saint George's Day. Before long, every year was "forbidden," and the peasants were prohibited from leaving at any time. De facto, they were bound to the land and, after a while, personally to the lord.

Third, the government, at the urging of major landowners, made it more and more difficult for peasants to run away, to escape their obligations by flight. By long custom, if the lord could not recapture a fugitive serf within a certain period (in Western Europe, it was "a year and a day"), the serf had won his freedom. In the Russian Empire, the tsars kept extending the length of time in which a lord could recover a fugitive serf, first to three years, then to five, and finally indefinitely. Thus, an individual, even if he escaped, was always subject to reenserfment. As an additional support for the landowner, the government decreed increasingly harsh penalties for those who aided or harbored runaway serfs.

In these ways, state policy and economic necessity reinforced each other in transforming most peasants into serfs. The process was a gradual one, covering approximately two centuries, but it culminated distinctly in the Ulozhenie, or the Law Code, of 1649. Its provisions forbade serfs to leave at any time and gave landowners unlimited time and rights to reclaim runaway serfs. From that time on, the position of the serf deteriorated. Landlords not only required labor or payments in cash or produce in return for serfs' right to use their land but also began to exercise judicial and administrative control over them. By the end of the 1600s, the serf had become the personal chattel of the landlord and was approaching the status of a slave.

What happened to the peasant commune in this process? Interestingly, it was preserved as the peasant passed from free person to serf to near slave. The sense of community was maintained, and decisions in the obshchina continued to be made fairly democratically, that is, by a consensus of the heads of all the households participating. The lord used the obshchina as an administrative device, making the commune responsible for the peasants' obligations to him, and later the government also exacted taxes and recruits for the army through the instrumentality of the commune.

Not all peasants became serfs of private landowners, though 60 to 70 percent of the population held this status by the end of the seventeenth century. The remainder were predominantly state or church peasants. They lived on landholdings of the tsar, the state, or the Orthodox Church, and they owed obligations, usually in kind or in cash, less often in labor, to their respective institutional overseers. Their conditions of work and service were generally less onerous than those of serfs belonging to private landowners. Finally, a small number of peasants remained entirely free, especially those on the eastern and southern frontiers of the vast country.

Why did serfdom come to the Russian Empire so late, and why did it become such an extensive and long-lasting institution? One answer is summed up in the aphorism "Serfdom is the price paid for the sake of survival." In other words, the tsars, ruling a poor country but determined to build the imperial state and to defeat its enemies on several fronts, could only mobilize the required resources by demanding service from the whole population. The gentry provided military and administrative services and were paid with land. The peasants, in return for order and protection, served at first by paying taxes and providing recruits for the army. Later, however, they served by supporting the gentry so the latter could in turn serve the tsar and the state. They made the gentry's land valuable either by working on it for a certain number of days per week or by paying the lord (usually in produce) to use the land.

Yet the question remains, why did serfdom emerge in the Russian Empire at the very moment it was disappearing in Western Europe? European kings were also trying to unify their territories and set up centralized systems of government, but they did not have to resort to enforced service. The simplest answer is that, in attempting similar tasks, the Russian tsars and the European kings commanded quite different resources. The latter could draw on the accumulated wealth of towns and merchants who had been engaged in profitable local, regional, and international trade for some time as well as on an increasing agricultural surplus generated by new farming techniques and technology developed during the High Middle Ages. In imperial Russia, by contrast, agriculture remained at a low subsistence level, and there was little commercial surplus concentrated in towns and in the hands of rich merchants. As we saw earlier, the Mongols had appropriated the few resources of the country during their rule, and under the Muscovite tsars, trade and towns had grown only slowly. No capital had been amassed on which Russian imperial rulers could draw in their long struggle to consolidate and strengthen the state. Service (and serfdom) had to substitute for capital.

Perhaps if Kievan Rus' had not been cut off from European technology in the 1200s and 1300s; perhaps if Muscovy had participated with the Europeans in the overseas discoveries of new lands and the rich trade with the Americas, Africa, and Asia of the 1400s and 1500s; and perhaps if the early grand princes and tsars had tried more actively to improve agriculture and promote commerce; perhaps if Muscovy had not been strained by long wars with its neighbors, like Ivan the Terrible's Livonian War, the economy would have flourished without serfdom. But history is not made up of "ifs." None of those things happened, and we will never know whether the area might have escaped serfdom under different circumstances. Instead, we know that serfdom became the dominant social institution in the 1600s and persisted for over two hundred years.

This system influenced the region's future development in several important ways. First, it meant that the economy remained predominantly agricultural, that the level of productivity remained low, and that trade, towns, and

the merchant class all grew rather slowly. Second, it created a deep and virtually unbridgeable split in Russian imperial society between the great mass of
the population (the lower classes, the people, or, in Russian, the *narod*), comprising serfs and second-class citizens of the state with many obligations and
few rights, and a tiny upper elite who were privileged and mostly conservative.
Finally, almost from the beginning, serfdom created a great moral dilemma.
How could one justify subjugating millions of one's subjects? That both serfs
and their lords were Christians simply made the serfs' degradation more stark,
the situation more indefensible. These economic, social, and moral dimensions
of serfdom became persistent issues throughout the eighteenth and into the
nineteenth century.

THE AUTOCRACY

The autocracy—the unlimited rule of the tsar—nearly disappeared in the turmoil
and upheavals of the Time of Troubles. Yet the tsar's importance as the symbol
of the state and the focus of imperial unity was shown by the repeated attempts
during those stormy years to put forward a pretender to the throne and by the
decision of the 1613 *zemskii sobor* to elect a new tsar, young Michael Romanov.

For the first part of his reign, Michael ruled in concert with boyar advisors
and, from 1619, with his father, Patriarch Filaret. Following the latter's death in
1633, Michael ruled alone until he died in 1645, after a reign of thirty-two years.
His successor, Alexis, also had a long reign, lasting thirty-one years until 1676.
The very length of the rules of these first two Romanov tsars contributed significantly to restoring stability and authority to the tsarist system. Moreover,
both Michael and Alexis were moderately capable, if not particularly brilliant
or farsighted.

More important in resurrecting the autocracy, however, was the failure of
any alternative system or center of power to develop. Certainly in 1613, at the
accession of Michael, it seemed probable that the zemskii sobor, or assembly of
the land, which had played such a key role in the national resurgence against
the Swedes and Poles and had been ruling the country for some months, would
emerge either as an executive body coequal to the tsar or at least as an institutionalized advisory council representing the interests and views of the upper
classes in Russian imperial society. And indeed, in the first years of Michael's
rule, the zemskii sobor was in almost continuous session. It was also convened
on occasions of major foreign policy or domestic crises in the 1630s through
the 1650s. Yet it met infrequently after midcentury and died out by the end of
the 1600s.

No definitive explanation for the demise of the zemskii sobor can be affirmed, but we can speculate about two possible reasons. The first is a paradox: its very success in sharing power with the tsar led to its curtailment. It helped Michael and Alexis to rebuild the tsarist state and overcome foreign and domestic challenges by rallying support from the upper classes of society. But once the autocratic system, with assistance from the zemskii sobor, had recovered from the ravages of the Time of Troubles and the state had begun to grow and expand again, Tsar Alexis hastened to discard any restraints on his authority and gladly let this institution fall into disuse.

The second reason is that, unlike the parliaments of Western Europe developing around the same time, the zemskii sobor had no legal, theoretical, or ideological basis on which to build an ongoing role as a political institution. In an emergency, the tsar had convened it to rally support behind him and to give him advice. It was an ad hoc device and never developed an independent position in the Muscovite structure. Consequently, when the tsar no longer needed it and stopped convening it, the zemskii sobor disappeared from the landscape of imperial Russia.

In a larger sense, the dying out of the zemskii sobor reflected the weak political position of the upper classes, whose representatives made up the assembly. If the boyars, the high clergy, the gentry, and the rich townsmen had had independent power positions as separate classes, they might have acted to limit the growing absolutism of the tsar. But the boyars, who during the Time of Troubles had made a remarkable recovery from the setbacks they had suffered at the hands of Ivan the Terrible, were still unable in the 1600s to act together as a class or to assert political rights against the tsar. They continued to squabble over rank and position, they were often venal and narrow-minded, and Tsars Michael and Alexis were able to keep them under control. Moreover, their ranks were swelled greatly in the 1600s by marriage and by the appointment of servitors essentially loyal to the tsar. They became an elite of privilege and wealth but posed no threat to the autocracy.

During the Time of Troubles, high church officials had worked closely with other national leaders to save the country, and in the 1620s Patriarch Filaret had been virtual co-tsar with his son Michael. But the overriding tradition of the Orthodox Church was to support the autocracy and to work closely with it rather than to challenge it. As we shall see shortly, one seventeenth-century churchman did defy the tsar's authority, but his bid to share power was quickly quelled. By the end of the century, the Russian Orthodox Church, weakened by internal dissension, was politically helpless and wholly dependent on the tsar, a position quite different from that of many Protestant and Catholic churches in Western Europe.

The gentry and the townspeople had even less chance to limit the burgeoning autocratic power. The gentry were essentially the tsar's men. Even though, by the end of the 1600s, they had achieved considerable status and hereditary rights to their lands, the gentry, like the boyars, did not consider themselves or act as a class with group interests to defend or rights to assert. Although the gentry did show some political muscle in the 1700s, they were then in a stronger position than they had been in the seventeenth century.

The townspeople of the Russian Empire had almost no political influence, partly because they lacked clear status as a class but most importantly because towns were mainly administrative centers, extensions of the authority of the tsar, whereas in Western Europe, they were commercial and financial centers with autonomous charters and independent wealth. The tsar himself was the richest merchant, and although some individuals became wealthy in commerce and production, no autonomous merchant or financial class existed. There were no guilds, banks, or companies for the accumulation of capital, the protection of economic privilege, and the eventual assertion of political influence.

It is therefore hardly surprising that the autocracy grew and flourished during the seventeenth century to become the overriding political institution of tsarist Russia for almost three hundred more years. To be sure, the tsar's power was limited, but not by individuals, classes, or institutions. First, it was limited in spiritual terms: the autocrat was to rule according to God's will, and it would have been impossible for the tsar to act in a way that directly contravened the Orthodox faith and belief of his people. In fact, Tsar Alexis had to face just such a crisis, during which many hundreds of thousands of his subjects rejected his authority over a religious issue.

Second, the sheer size of his realm and the magnitude of the task of governing it tempered the tsar's absolutism. No tsar could do everything. Each tsar had to depend to a considerable extent on his military and civilian advisors and officials. Thus, beginning earlier but accelerating in the 1600s, the tsar's army and civil service grew rapidly. The tsar set general policies and even made final decisions on relatively small matters, but the day-to-day business of administration, such as keeping order, making judgments, and collecting taxes, was left to an increasing number of clerks and bureaucrats. The local self-government established under Ivan the Terrible had disappeared during the Time of Troubles, so the first Romanovs relied heavily on military governors to manage local and regional affairs. Corruption and harassment of the people were widespread, and some historians believe that the urban riots in Moscow and other cities in the 1600s, and even the great rebellion of Stenka

Razin, were sparked largely by resentment against the venality and petty op-
pressions of local officials rather than by any broad rejection of the tsarist
system.

THE ORTHODOX CHURCH

In the 1600s, as the restored imperial autocracy increased its centralized power,
the might and authority of the Russian Orthodox Church also expanded. But
two events, occurring about the same time in the third quarter of the century,
greatly weakened the church and prepared the way for its complete subjugation
to the state by Peter the Great in the early 1700s. Both events were associated
with one imposing, talented, and strong-willed individual, Patriarch Nikon,
head of the church from 1652 to 1667.

Unlike most high clergy, Nikon came not from the upper classes but was
of peasant descent. Extremely bright and well educated, Nikon had come to
the attention of young Tsar Alexis early in the latter's reign. Nikon's powerful
personality and erudition soon exerted considerable influence over the tsar.
Nikon, apparently partly through ambition and partly through his interpretation of the role of the church in the Byzantine system, asserted in the late
1650s that the church was independent of, or even in some respects superior
to, the state. He demanded to share authority with the tsar. This action flew
in the face of long-standing Russian Orthodox tradition and soon provoked a
political storm. The tsar finally broke with Nikon, and in 1666 and 1667, a high
church council, including prelates from other parts of the Orthodox world,
rejected Nikon's claims, unseated him as patriarch, and exiled him to a remote
monastery. That was the last time in Russian history that the spiritual power
attempted to challenge the secular authority of the tsar.

Of even more long-lasting consequence, however, was Nikon's other major
action: a thoroughgoing reform of Russian Orthodox texts and rituals. What
seemed a perfectly reasonable proposition—the correction of errors that had
crept into liturgical materials and church services over the centuries—soon
turned into a major struggle that divided the Russian Orthodox Church irrevocably and sparked social conflict, leading to thousands of deaths.

To us, the issues may appear obscure or even ridiculous: they included, for
example, whether the sign of the cross should be made with three fingers or
two, the correct spelling of Jesus's name, and the direction the procession that
makes up part of the Orthodox Mass should take around the church. But to
both sides in the mounting controversy, such questions were connected with

the fundamental question of what was the true Christian faith. Moreover, each side was led by a powerful, determined, and eloquent individual: the reformers by Patriarch Nikon and the defenders of the old forms by Archpriest Avvakum, whose autobiographical account of his sufferings is a major work of Russian-language literature.

The whole affair, known as the Schism (*Raskol* in Russian) because it split the church, began innocently enough as a by-product of the expansion and increasing sophistication of the Russian church. Early in Nikon's tenure as patriarch, well-educated and scholarly clergy, some of whom came from Ukraine, which had recently been added to the church's jurisdiction, as well as Russia, called to Nikon's attention certain parts of the Russian-language liturgical texts and rituals that did not correspond with Greek versions. The latter were considered more "correct" since they were closer to the original sources, and it was alleged that errors in translating materials into Russian had occurred at various times during the long period since the conversion of Kievan Rus' to Orthodoxy. Nikon, who was anxious to upgrade and improve the Russian Orthodox Church in various ways, soon accepted this point of view and began an intense campaign to eliminate the errors and to reform the ecclesiastical books and the Mass accordingly.

To his surprise and then anger, a number of high prelates disagreed with him and refused to accept the proposed changes. Before long, hundreds of thousands of parishioners had joined the opposition. After some indecision, Tsar Alexis and the government as a whole backed the reforms and soon began to use force against those who opposed them. Nikon was determined to impose the reforms on the whole church, but his opponents were equally adamant in rejecting them. As a consequence, the Russian Orthodox Church was torn apart, and those who opposed the reforms went their own way, becoming known thenceforth as Old Believers. Paradoxically, the same high church council that deposed Nikon in 1666 for his political ambitions nonetheless fully endorsed his reforms in 1667.

Both the church and the government exerted great moral pressure and even physical coercion in an effort to bring the Old Believers back into the fold. But few returned. And some, perhaps as many as twenty thousand, convinced that the changes presaged the end of the world, burned themselves to death. Others defied the government, and Old Believers at the Solovetskii Monastery in northern Russia held out against repeated military assaults for eight years, from 1668 to 1676.

Archpriest Avvakum was imprisoned and then burned at the stake in 1682 as part of a general persecution of opposition leaders. Nevertheless, the Old Believers survived to become a significant religious and social force in the eighteenth- and nineteenth-century Russian Empire, numbering some ten or twelve million adherents in 1900. Some Old Believers live today in the Russian Federation and Ukraine, and a few schismatic sects persist among Russian and Ukrainian emigrants in Canada and the United States.

What led the Old Believers to resist so fiercely what were, after all, superficial changes, emendations that did not touch basic doctrine and tenets of faith? In part it was a commendable devoutness, a profound emotional and intellectual passion to preserve what they believed was the purity and sanctity of true Christianity, as this appeal of Archpriest Avvakum makes clear:

> Come, Orthodox people, call upon the name of Christ. . . . Do not falter. I, together with ye, am ready to die for Christ. Although I have not much understanding—I am not a learned man—yet I know that the church, which we have received from our Holy Fathers, is pure and sacred. As it came to me so shall I uphold my faith until the end. It was established long before our time, and thus may it remain for evermore.[2]

An innate conservatism, bordering on superstition, also factored into the position taken by the Old Believers. Illiterate and insecure for the most part, they feared change and became convinced that altering the Mass or correcting the texts could only be the work of the devil, designed to bring God's wrath down on them. For some schismatics, xenophobia may also have played a role: the changes came from Greek-trained or Greek-oriented scholars and threatened what they perceived as true practices. The purity of the faith could only be preserved by rejecting these influences from the outside.

Finally, there may have been an element of sociopolitical protest in the Old Believer movement. Some of the schismatics were extremely poor and may have used the religious issue as a way of expressing their opposition to the government and the existing order. In any case, once the tsar and his administration sided with the church hierarchy, many Old Believers moved willingly to open rebellion against all authority, religious and civil, and waged guerrilla warfare against both the established church and the state. This marked a major crisis in the reign of Tsar Alexis, one that he barely overcame before his death in 1676.

The Schism seriously weakened the Russian Orthodox Church. The church lost some of its ablest leaders and some of its most devout and vital congregations. Moreover, the triumph of the reformers meant that form won out over content, ritual over feeling and ideas. As a result, Orthodoxy became increasingly formalistic and stultified, with less and less intellectual, social, and political influence in society.

As a corollary effect, life became more secularized. After the Schism, the role of religion and the church at the court and among the upper classes was reduced, a change that helped pave the way for Peter the Great's Westernization program forty years later.

THE EXPANSION OF THE RUSSIAN IMPERIAL STATE

The seeker of patterns in the region's historical development could reasonably argue that before the 1600s, the growth of the principality of Moscow and the expansion of the tsarist state were essentially defensive in nature, necessary to the consolidation of power and territory and to securing the Russian Empire's borders against a host of enemies on three sides. But after 1600, it is harder to maintain that the additions to these lands were primarily for self-protection. The tsars now appeared more interested in aggrandizement, power for the sake of power, and territories that would benefit the empire economically. Moreover, prior to the seventeenth century, the state annexed lands predominantly inhabited by ethnic Russians, except for Finno-Ugric groups in the north and Tatars and indigenous non-Slavs in the conquered khanates of Kazan and Astrakhan. Yet in the 1600s and after, most of the peoples who fell under Russian imperial rule were either fellow Eastern Slavs, such as the Ukrainians, or not Slavic at all, such as Balts, Caucasians, and Central Asians. The Russian Empire became a multinational state, but generally ethnic Russians and other Slavs continued to rule and dominate it.

In the 1600s, the two main directions of Russian imperial expansion were eastward and southwestward (see Map 5.1). The former, a push all across the Eurasian continent to the Pacific Ocean, added an enormous sweep of territory to the empire but had little political or strategic significance at the time. The latter, which brought part of today's Ukraine, including Kiev, into the tsars' realm, involved only a small amount of land but was very important politically and strategically.

Expansion across the Ural Mountains and into Siberia had begun in the latter part of the previous century but advanced eastward in the 1600s another three thousand miles. By the 1640s, explorers had reached the Pacific Ocean, and one expedition even sailed through the Bering Strait. The Russian imperial advance was checked only when it ran up against the outposts of the Qing Dynasty in China. With the signing of the Treaty of Nerchinsk in 1689, the Russian Empire's eastern border with China was established just short of the Amur River.

For a long time, the acquisition of furs remained Siberia's major advantage for the Russian imperial state. After the 1600s, migration to and colonization of

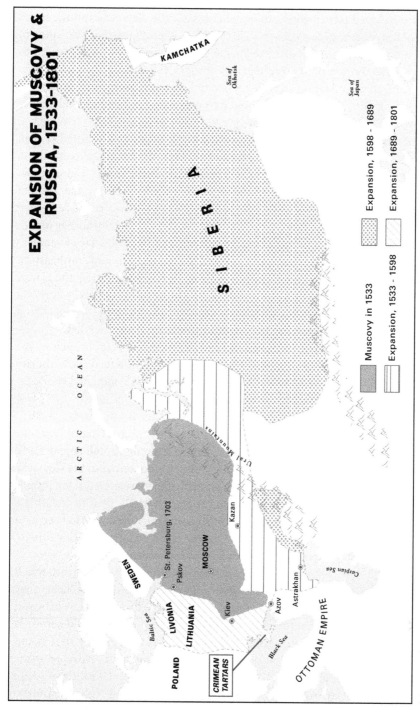

MAP 5.1. The expansion of Muscovy and the Russian Empire, 1533–1801.

Siberia developed rather slowly, mainly because of the distances and the harsh climate, but Siberia did offer a chance to escape the oppressive conditions of life in central Russia, and it attracted some peasants and serfs soon after it was opened up. Moreover, on its southeastern borders, the Russian Empire consistently spurred colonization in order to extend its frontiers against Asian nomads and Muslims. Fortified towns and outposts were built farther and farther toward central Asia, and settlers were given attractive incentives to live there.

The Russian Empire's acquisition of the eastern half of Ukraine between the 1640s and the 1660s was closely connected with the tsars' continuing struggle against Poland, which, in the seventeenth century, was a more powerful country. After the Polish effort to conquer Muscovy during the Time of Troubles had been rebuffed, relations between the two Slavic states remained strained, though a peace treaty was finally signed in 1634 after another inconclusive war. The situation was complicated because the Poles faced increasing difficulty controlling the population on Poland's eastern and southeastern lands, territory that had been part of the Kievan Rus' confederation and is now located in Ukraine. Most of the people were Orthodox peasants, whereas a majority of the landowners were Polish Catholics. The Ukrainians considered themselves oppressed socially and religiously by their Polish overlords. In the late sixteenth century, the Poles had helped establish a special branch of the Catholic Church called the Uniate Church, which acknowledged the authority of the pope in Rome but followed Orthodox liturgy and conducted the Mass in a Slavic language. Although some Orthodox Ukrainians accepted the new church, the majority did not, exacerbating the religious division in Ukraine.

The Poles were also having trouble with a special group living in Ukraine, the Dnieper Cossacks. The Polish government gave them limited support and permitted some continuation of traditional Cossack autonomy, but the Cossacks could not be won entirely to the Polish cause since they were Orthodox in religion and had close ties with the Ukrainian people as a whole. By dint of ruthless repression and at considerable cost, the Polish government was able to keep a lid on the situation until 1648, when the Ukrainians, led by a great national hero, Bogdan Khmelnitsky, started a large-scale rebellion against Polish rule.

Although the Ukrainians achieved considerable success against much larger Polish forces, in the long run they would clearly need outside help. They turned naturally to their coreligionists in Moscow. At first, Tsar Alexis and his advisors were reluctant to aid the Ukrainian rebels, which would certainly mean war with Poland, an expensive and risky proposition. Finally, in 1653 and 1654, with the approval of a zemskii sobor, Alexis responded favorably to the Ukrainians' request for assistance, in return for which the Ukrainians swore allegiance to the tsar. As a result of the ensuing war with Poland, territorial settlements were finally reached in 1667 and 1686, by which all the lands on the left, or eastern, bank of the Dnieper River, plus the cities of Smolensk and Kiev, became part of the Russian Empire.

Ukrainian historians and nationalists have strongly criticized the imperial Russian absorption of Ukraine, but it is hard to see how an independent Ukraine could have survived, sandwiched as it would have been between Turkey, Poland, and the Russian Empire. On the other hand, Russian imperial authorities, though also Slavic and Orthodox, proved stern masters. They failed to respect Ukraine's autonomy as stipulated in the arrangements of 1654 and 1667, and before long, they imposed serfdom in much of its territory. Later, they tried to suppress the development of Ukrainian literature and culture, which produced tensions that continue to strain the relationship between Russia and Ukraine today.

RELATIONS WITH THE WEST

Although Moscow had some contact with central and Western Europe in the 1300s and 1400s through Novgorod and Poland-Lithuania, the emerging Russian imperial state was largely isolated from the West during the period of its unification and rapid expansion. Increasingly in the 1500s and 1600s, relations were reestablished. Not only did trade expand, but ambassadors were exchanged, a few imperial subjects visited the West, and several thousand Westerners traveled to or lived in the empire. These contacts stimulated intellectual exchanges, first in religious matters and technology but later in secular knowledge and general culture.

The tsarist state benefited from closer ties with the West in several important ways. First, trade, though not extensive, was an important source of revenue and brought to the Russian Empire a variety of goods and finished products that otherwise would have been unavailable. Second, the Romanov tsars drew on Western military ideas and technology as they built up their armies. Finally, Western artisans and entrepreneurs played a significant role in developing early imperial mining and manufacturing enterprises, for example, in glassmaking and ironworking.

In the long run, the West's deepest impact on the Russian Empire was in the realm of ideas. Part of this intellectual stimulation was a by-product of religious competition between the Orthodox Church and the Catholic and Uniate churches. Orthodox leaders recognized that if they were to prevent the influx of Catholicism in Ukraine and the empire's other western borderlands, they needed better-educated clergy. Spurred by the model of Metropolitan

Peter Mogila's educational institution in Kiev, the authorities encouraged the establishment of schools in Moscow staffed largely by learned monks from Ukraine. These efforts culminated in the opening in 1687 of the Slavonic-Greek-Latin Academy, the region's first establishment of higher education, which taught not only those languages, but also rhetoric, philosophy, grammar, and theology.

At the same time, some secular literature modeled on Western forms began to appear, and the first theater was established under the patronage of Tsar Alexis. Not only the tsar himself but also elite imperial society displayed a growing interest in things Western. European dress, food, tobacco, furniture, and baroque architecture were all in vogue among upper-class imperial Russians, and smoking spread rapidly through all levels of the population.

In short, by the third quarter of the seventeenth century, there was a growing receptiveness to Western thought, manners, and institutions, an attitude that certainly prepared the ground for Peter the Great and his all-out effort to Westernize the Russian Empire in the early eighteenth century.

The psychological side effects of this openness to European civilization must not be overlooked. Because the Europeans were richer, thanks to the agricultural and commercial revolutions they were experiencing and to their profitable overseas trade, and because they were more advanced technologically, some imperial subjects felt inferior to the West and were anxious to catch up. Yet it is important to remember that, in some respects, the Russian Empire possessed a more advanced society than its Western neighbors; for example, they had a centralized, cohesive state, whereas the Italians and Germans still lived in a motley collection of city-states, tiny principalities, and feudal fiefdoms. They enjoyed a common religion and relative peace at a time when Europe was rent with religious strife and recurring warfare. The Russian Empire of this period was certainly different from Europe in many respects, but whether it was better or worse off is a highly debatable point.

CONCLUSION

In many ways, the seventeenth century was a transitional period in the development of Russian imperial society. The state, after a long period of growth and after nearly breaking apart in the Time of Troubles, was consolidated and centralized. Nevertheless, despite some reforms and an expansion of the bureaucracy, it had an archaic outlook and administration. The role of the tsar remained highly personalized, and government was not very efficient. At the same time, the economy developed only slowly, while Western European countries were accumulating wealth and laying the basis for the Industrial Revolution of the next century. The Russian Empire's expansion into Ukraine added important territory as well as several million fellow Slavs and coreligionists. On the other hand, its expansion eastward brought Asians under tsarist rule and had economic and strategic significance only much later.

In the 1600s, class divisions in imperial Russia hardened, and, in particular, a large proportion of the peasants became permanently enserfed and sank toward the level of slaves. The institution of serfdom widened the gap between a small elite and the bulk of the population, creating a major social and moral issue for the next two centuries. The Schism weakened the Orthodox Church, with a large minority of dedicated outcasts breaking away from the established religion. In the largest sense, the seventeenth century bridged Kievan Rus', Mongol Russia, and Muscovy to the Russian Empire, which was soon thrust precipitously into modern times.

FURTHER READING

Avvakum, S. *The Life of the Archpriest Avvakum by Himself.* Translated by Jane Harrison and Hope Mirrlees. London: Weidenfeld and Nicolson, 1968.

Blum, Jerome. *Lord and Peasant in Russia from the Ninth to the Nineteenth Century.* Princeton, NJ: Princeton University Press, 1961.

Bushkovitch, Paul. *Religion and Society in Russia: The Sixteenth and Seventeenth Centuries.* New York: Oxford University Press, 1992.

Crummey, Robert O. *Aristocrats and Servitors: The Boyar Elite in Russia, 1613–1689.* Princeton, NJ: Princeton University Press, 1983.

———. *The Old Believers and the World of Antichrist: The Vyg Community and the Russian State, 1694–1855.* Madison: University of Wisconsin Press, 1970.

Fuhrmann, Joseph T. *Tsar Alexis: His Reign and His Russia.* Gulf Breeze, FL: Academic International, 1981.

Fuller, William C., Jr. *Strategy and Power in Russia, 1600–1914.* New York: Free Press, 1992.

Hellie, Richard. *The Economy and Material Culture of Russia, 1600–1725.* Chicago: University of Chicago Press, 1999.

Hughes, Lindsey. *The Romanovs: Ruling Russia, 1613–1917.* New York: Hambledon Continuum, 2008.

Kappeler, Andreas. *The Russian Empire: A Multi-Ethnic History.* Harlow, Essex, UK: Longman, 2001.

Khodarkovsky, Michael. *Russia's Steppe Frontier: The Making of a Colonial Empire, 1500–1800.* Bloomington: Indiana University Press, 2002.

Kivelson, Valerie A. *Autocracy in the Provinces: The Muscovite Gentry and Political Culture in the Seventeenth Century*. Stanford, CA: Stanford University Press, 1996.

Michels, Georg Bernhard. *At War with the Church: Religious Dissent in Seventeenth-Century Russia*. Stanford, CA: Stanford University Press, 1999.

CHAPTER 6

PETER THE GREAT AND THE CONUNDRUM OF WESTERNIZATION, 1689–1725

The thud of axes slicing into wood resounded through the walls of the small log house on the riverbank. Peter, tsar of the Russian Empire, stirred in his sleep, then sat up quickly. Seeing daylight under the door, he cursed himself and jumped out of bed, throwing on his clothes as he hastened outside. He liked to be first on the job, but already carpenters perched on top of and around the frames of several large ships nearby. After momentarily warming his hands over a fire alongside several just-arisen workmen, Peter picked up his own hammer and axe. Energetically, he clambered up the scaffolding surrounding a galley under construction and threw himself into the work. Peter looked supremely happy. As he wrote in a letter at that time, "We are eating our bread in the sweat of our face."

No one seemed surprised to see his tsarist majesty, the "most pious father of his people," laboring as hard as any peasant in the shipyard. Most of his coworkers were already accustomed to the unorthodox ways of the young tsar, and they respected him for his skill as a shipwright and his willingness to tackle the toughest jobs. On this occasion, in March 1696, both Peter's talents and his leadership were being tested to the fullest. Reigning tsar for only two years, he had suffered a serious defeat at the hands of the Turkish Ottoman Empire the previous summer, and there was already considerable grumbling against him in Moscow. In 1695, Peter had tried to capture the fortified town of Azov, which commanded the entrance to the Sea of Azov at the mouth of the Don River (see Map 5.1). Peter's army besieged Azov, but because Peter had no support ships on the river, the Turks were able to relieve the garrison with reinforcements and supplies brought in by sea. Peter finally had to retreat.

Undaunted, Peter, as soon as he returned to Moscow in December, decided to resume the attack the following summer, but with a newly created imperial fleet to control the river. That meant he had only five months to build from scratch the armada he needed, twenty-five seagoing galleys and over a thousand barges for troops and supplies, an almost impossible task even under the best of conditions! Yet Peter had little to work with. It was winter, with numbing cold, ice, and shortened days; there was no shipyard anywhere in the southern area of the empire; no one in that region knew how to build large ships; and there was no prepared timber or other supplies for ship construction. As a biographer of Peter observed:

> Peter's plan, then, was to build the shipyards, assemble the workmen, teach them to mark, cut and hew the timber, lay the keels, build the hulls, step the masts, shape the oars, weave the ropes, sew the sails, train the crews, and sail the whole massive fleet down the Don River to Azov. All within five winter months![1]

Despite bad weather, delays in the arrival of skilled craftsmen, and the desertion of many conscripted laborers, Peter drove the project through to completion. In early May, he sailed down the Don at the head of his small navy, whose ships compared favorably with Turkish and Western ships of the time, and by the end of July had captured Azov. In the triumphal procession several miles long that entered Moscow the following October to celebrate this important victory, Tsar Peter walked on foot, among the other captains of the galleys, wearing a plain black uniform with only a white feather in his hat indicating he had any special status.

As this episode illustrates, Peter the Great was determined to use modern techniques and weapons to strengthen his country and unstintingly applied his considerable energy to this task. The Russian Empire had already begun to change under the impact of new ideas and increasing contact with Europe, and doubtless, even without Peter, it would have eventually been transformed into a more modern society. What Peter did was to accelerate this transition greatly. At the same time, because he forced the pace of change, he widened the gulf between the Westernized and unreformed sectors of imperial society. In their hearts, many subjects refused to accept the reforms Peter insisted on.

Moreover, in some respects, Peter the Great failed. On the surface, to be sure, imperial society, or at least the upper classes, appeared to adopt European ideas, technology, and attitudes; in retrospect, however, the result can be seen as a rough and uneven patchwork of the new and the traditional, with many anomalies and incongruities. Like many societies that have come in contact

FIGURE 6.1. Peter the Great. (Everett – Art / Shutterstock.com)

with Western science, technology, and power, the Russian Empire during Peter the Great's reign in all likelihood had no choice but to modernize. To ignore or reject Europe's influence meant isolation, backwardness, and eventual subjugation. Peter saw this clearly and did everything possible to propel his state into the modern era. He competed successfully with his powerful, nearest Western neighbors, Sweden and Poland, and he greatly increased the empire's security and prestige. He also set in motion far-reaching changes in almost every sector of life. However, he did not tamper with the institution of serfdom, which meant that society-wide modernization could not develop in the empire until after the liberation of the serfs in 1861.

Peter's impact was muted for two related reasons. First, unlike the Western European nations, the Russian Empire lacked the resources to move quickly to a basic overhaul of its institutions and way of life. It had a relatively small population of about fifteen million, and at the end of the 1600s it was still a poor country with low agricultural productivity, few cities, limited trade, and no substantial surplus. For Peter, even to make headway in establishing the empire's place in the European state system and in raising the level of culture in the country required a ruthless mobilization of the state's every available means and heavy exactions on the population.

Second, again unlike the West, the Russian Empire lacked many of the institutions and attitudes that could help carry out modernization. In the West, a reforming church, an entrepreneurial class, a developed higher educational system, and well-established guilds and other associations all stood ready to assist any king or group of leaders who proposed modernizing techniques and changes. On the other hand, Peter and his advisors had to act almost alone: the established church was apathetic and the Old Believers hostile; the merchants were weak, and the nobles as a group were divided, indifferent, and recalcitrant; education was almost nonexistent; corporate bodies were absent; and the bulk of the population formed a conservative opposition. It is no wonder that many believed Peter to be the Antichrist and that he could make progress only by compulsion and through his astounding energy and will.

PETER'S COMING OF AGE

Peter, like Ivan the Terrible, did not have a happy childhood, punctuated as it was by fights among noble families vying for power and by periods when the boy tsar was isolated and ignored. Peter was born in 1672, the first son of the second wife of Tsar Alexis I. His mother, Natalia Naryshkina, a member of a prominent family, was politically ambitious but traditional and conservative. As a young man, Peter quickly rejected her position and point of view.

On his death, Tsar Alexis I was succeeded by Feodor III, his eldest surviving son by his first wife, Maria Miloslavskaya. After a reign of six years, Feodor died in 1682 without an heir. A hundred years earlier, a similar succession crisis had opened the door to the Time of Troubles, but this time the Naryshkins quickly had Peter, a boy of ten, proclaimed tsar. Their claim was almost immediately contested, however, by the Miloslavsky faction, backed by special army regiments known as *streltsy*, or musketeers. During the subsequent fighting, Peter saw some of his mother's supporters murdered. It was finally agreed that Ivan V, Peter's elder half brother, would be senior tsar and Peter junior tsar. An older daughter of Alexis, Peter's half-sister Sophia, ruled as regent, with some effectiveness, until 1689, when a disastrous military campaign in the south against the Crimean Tatars led to her political downfall. Sophia was packed off to a convent, and Peter, who seemed uninterested in exercising power, permitted his mother and her family and supporters to manage affairs of state. After five years, his mother died, and in 1694, at the age of twenty-two, Peter began to direct policy. In 1696, the sickly co-tsar, Ivan V, died, and Peter assumed full authority.

In the 1680s, while Sophia was in charge, Peter had been shunted off to a village outside Moscow, where he was largely left to his own devices. As a result, he had little formal schooling but did a great deal to educate himself, particularly in practical matters about which he was intensely curious. Moreover, he was able to choose his own companions and develop his own interests. He surrounded himself with a motley crew of local people and a few foreigners, selected not because of birth or position but because Peter liked them or because they had talents he wanted to tap. As recreation, Peter was allowed to form his own "play" army, with which he first displayed his love of organization and his genius at military tactics. These young playmate-soldiers later formed the core of the first guards regiment in the Russian Empire. These military units lasted until the upheavals of 1917.

PETER'S PERSONALITY AND CHARACTER

Gargantuan is an adjective frequently used to describe Peter the Great, and it is indeed apt. Physically, he was huge and very strong. Doubting that Peter was "nearly seven feet tall," this book's coauthor John Thompson visited a Moscow museum that displayed a dummy of Peter in battle dress, and he put his six-foot, five-inch frame alongside Peter's mannequin. To Thompson's surprise, Peter towered comfortably above him, certainly not seven feet in height but probably a commanding six feet, eight inches tall. Living in an era when most people were only a little over five feet tall, how Peter must have dominated any meeting or gathering!

Peter's energy, his appetite for food, drink, and work, and his enthusiasm and intellectual curiosity were all virtually boundless. He wanted to do everything, know everything, observe everything. He drove his officials, soldiers, and people hard, but he drove himself harder. Determined to make the Russian Empire stronger and better, Peter the Great worked as single-mindedly for education and science as he strove fiercely for victory in battle. Peter cajoled and goaded his countrymen, and when all else failed, he coerced them down the path of modernization.

Darker sides to his personality and character should not be overlooked. Peter was often rude and inconsiderate. He was frequently ruthless and cruel. The tsar personally participated in the torture and execution of some members of the streltsy who had rebelled against his rule.

Like so many extremely talented and determined people, Peter tried to do too much. He took on more than he could manage; as a result, some of his actions were haphazard and some of his reforms uncoordinated and incomplete. Nonetheless, Peter accomplished more than a dozen others could have.

Characteristic of his outlook and behavior was the extended trip to Western Europe Peter undertook early in his reign. As a youth, he absorbed information and techniques in a wide range of civil and military trades from specialists residing in the foreigners' quarter of Moscow. Peter was particularly fascinated with shipbuilding and navigation. Although he had helped establish shipyards and construct vessels from 1694 to 1696, Peter wanted to learn still more and looked naturally to the West. In addition, he hoped that in the course of visiting European nations, he might enlist their support in his continuing struggle against the Turkish Ottoman Empire.

Consequently, he set out in the spring of 1697 as part of a delegation of over two hundred representatives from the empire. Peter attempted to travel incognito as simply a member of the group, but his size made him easily identifiable. Moreover, as the first tsar to travel in Europe, he was the center of attention not only among European governments but among the general public as well. He spent almost a year and a half abroad, visiting Holland (today part of the Netherlands), England, and the Austrian Hapsburg Empire; he was about to continue on to Italy when political turmoil in the Russian Empire compelled him to return home.

The tsar's "Grand Embassy" was largely successful. Peter spent the most time in Holland, acquiring a great deal of information about seafaring and boatbuilding, and hiring a number of Dutch specialists to work for him back home. He learned a great deal there and in other countries about European attitudes, customs, and education, although his own rowdy behavior at times shocked the Europeans. Peter did not succeed in forging an alliance against the Turks, but he did establish personal ties with European officials that were useful in his later diplomatic pursuits. Most of all, he returned to Moscow with his head full of ideas about ways to modernize his tradition-bound homeland.

PETER IN WAR AND DIPLOMACY

Peter greatly changed imperial Russian society, but not the empire's foreign policy. He consistently pursued objectives abroad that were similar to those of his predecessors dating back to the fifteenth century. Peter's highest priority was securing his empire's vulnerable borders, particularly in the south and the west. Next came the task of expanding the state's contacts and territory, especially in ways that would liberate the empire from its long isolation as a landlocked country. Finally, Peter, like Ivan the Terrible and the first Romanov tsars, encouraged exploration and expansion in Asia in search of new opportunities and trading partners.

The main threat to the Russian Empire in the south came from the Crimean Tatars, who were descendants of the Mongols who periodically attacked the state from their well-defended khanate on the Crimean Peninsula in the Black Sea. Since the late 1400s, the Tatars had been under the protection of the Turks, and the Ottoman Empire was therefore the target of Peter's first campaign. In 1695, shortly after assuming full authority as tsar, Peter attacked Azov, finally subduing it in 1696 with the help of his newly constructed southern fleet.

Later on, after a second war against the Turks in which Peter narrowly escaped a major defeat, he had to give back Azov and dismantle his Black Sea fleet. Nevertheless, he set a precedent for imperial expansion to the Black Sea, and by the end of the eighteenth century, the Russian Empire had established a firm foothold along the northern shore of that important inland waterway.

Ivan the Terrible had made a major effort to reach the Baltic Sea but was ultimately defeated. In the Great Northern War, which lasted the greater part of Peter's reign, from 1700 to 1721, the modernizing tsar renewed this struggle. His two main objectives were to break the power of Sweden, at that time the dominant country in northern central Europe, and to open trade and contact directly with Europe via the Baltic Sea, his "window to the West." Although partners in the anti-Swedish coalition shifted with the fortunes of war, Poland and Russia were Sweden's main opponents during most of the Great Northern War.

When the war began, Sweden seemed at a disadvantage: not only had most of the states of the region allied against it, but Sweden's new king, Charles XII, was not yet twenty years old. Charles, however, proved to be a formidable adversary, an energetic and talented leader, and a military genius. Before his death on the battlefield at the age of thirty-seven, he conducted brilliant campaigns and won a number of major victories.

One of Charles's first triumphs was the defeat of Peter and his much larger army at Narva (located in modern-day Estonia) in late 1700. Dismayed but not discouraged, Peter began at once to rebuild and reorganize his whole military establishment, including training methods, artillery, and supply. In addition, Peter worked to mobilize the civil government behind the war effort.

Luckily for Peter, though Charles could have forced the Russian Empire's withdrawal from the war had he pursued an offensive toward Moscow, he instead turned his attention southward against Poland, which he considered the main enemy. Peter the Great took maximum advantage of this respite, expanding and reshaping his army and developing a fleet for use in the Baltic Sea. Beginning in 1701, imperial forces captured most of Estonia and Livonia (in present-day Latvia) along the Baltic shore, and in 1703, Peter founded a city strategically located in the northeastern corner of the Baltic Sea at the mouth of the Neva River (see Map 5.1). Soon named St. Petersburg (after Saint Peter, not Peter the Great), it served as the capital of the Russian Empire from 1713 to 1728 and again from 1732 to 1918.

Charles XII finally defeated the Poles and thus could focus fully on Peter and his forces. In 1708, he and his army crossed into the empire from Poland, but instead of heading directly for Moscow, the Swedes turned south into Ukraine, hoping to win over the Cossacks and to establish a firm base there. Several thousand Cossacks did join forces with Charles, but the majority of Ukrainians remained loyal to Peter and the Russian Empire. After a preliminary battle in which Peter captured some reinforcements and relief supplies intended for Charles, the main struggle was joined in July 1709 at Poltava. Outnumbered almost two to one, the Swedes fought heroically but finally suffered a crushing defeat:

> At 9 o'clock . . . the Swedish army turned and moved south to get into a position parallel to that of the Russians. Opposite . . . [were] two packed lines of Russian infantry . . . supported by seventy field guns. . . . The Russian first line of twenty-four battalions was 10,000 strong, the second [of eighteen battalions] 8,000. . . . The enemy superiority in numbers was terrifying. So was their superiority in firepower.
>
> Within half an hour the battle was over. The Swedes were either casualties of the battle or . . . fled to the safety of the baggage and reserve regiments at Pushkarivka.
>
> Charles XII on his stretcher [from an earlier wound] had been at the head of the right infantry wing. When the panic spread to that sector of the thin line, his cry of "Swedes, Swedes" went unheeded. His stretcher was hit by musket bullets and destroyed. It looked as if the king would become a prisoner of the Russians. . . . Lewenhaupt's call that the king was in danger brought, however, a front of soldiers willing to delay the enemy by laying down their lives for his. Charles forced himself onto a horse, the bandages on his foot came undone, and blood dripped from [his] wound that opened with the unwonted activity. The horse was shot under him and was replaced.
>
> The Russians did not pursue the Swedes. The fight had been one between infantry in the main, and the foot soldiers of Tsar Peter were nearly as shaken as those of Charles. . . . The Swedes had left some 10,000 on the battlefield, 6,901 dead and 2,760 prisoners of the Tsar. Russian losses were relatively light: 1,345 killed and 3,290 wounded.[2]

Charles managed to escape southwest into Turkish territory. But the reconstructed imperial army had acquitted itself well under Peter's personal leadership, and he had every reason to be proud of the progress his European-izing program had achieved. Peter quickly followed up the victory at Poltava, capturing the Baltic coast from Riga to southern Finland in 1710, which se-cured his new city of St. Petersburg.

Shortly thereafter, however, he became embroiled with the Ottoman Em-pire again, and the war with Sweden, though essentially settled at Poltava, dragged on for over another decade. Peter made further gains along the Bal-tic shore, and in the Peace of Nystad in 1721 brought the long Great Northern War to an end. The Nystad treaty confirmed the Russian Empire's possession of territory between St. Petersburg and Finland as well as of what are today the countries of Estonia and Latvia. The empire at last had secure access to the Baltic Sea and, through it, to Western Europe. Even more importantly, the Russian Empire replaced Sweden as the dominant power in northern central Europe and was able to concentrate its energies during the rest of the century on a contest with Poland for supremacy in Eastern Europe. As British historian B. H. Sumner succinctly summed up the outcome, "Peter made Russia a power in Europe and all three knew it."

In recognition of his success, Peter received the honorific "the Great." Moreover, by adding the Balts and Finns to his group of subjects, Peter ex-tended the multinational character of the empire, a feature that persisted to 1991. Finally, while the Russian Empire reached its geographic limits in the west, its eastern and southern expansion continued steadily into the 1860s.

Although Peter's main concerns in foreign affairs were his wars with Tur-key and Sweden, he had a continuing interest in Asia. He maintained relations with China, encouraged explorations and contacts in the Pacific and with Mongolia and central Asia, and occupied Persian territory (contemporary Iran) along the Caspian Sea, although those lands were returned shortly after his death. Peter even planned an expedition to establish ties with India. As a leader of vision, the tsar clearly understood that because of the empire's location in Eurasia, it was bound to have increasing intercourse with the Asian peoples and cultures lying to the southeast. Furthermore, Peter wanted to know more about these other societies, so he encouraged his subjects to study them.

PETER'S REFORMS

In undertaking major changes in imperial Russian society and government, did Peter have a grand design, or was he driven helter-skelter from one reform to another by the need to keep his war machine going? Proponents of the latter view point out that the Russian Empire was at peace for only a little over two years during the whole period of Peter's reign and that for a society with a poorly developed economy, the major wars Peter waged demanded an all-out effort and overshadowed any other purpose or activity. On the other hand, those who believe Peter had a plan can point to his own justifications for the changes he made and to reforms he undertook that were quite unrelated to the military mobilization of the empire.

As in so many historiographic controversies, the answer seems to lie somewhere between the two positions. Peter certainly had a definite purpose: he intended to introduce into his state the modern ideas, technologies, methods, and institutions he had learned about or observed on his mission to Europe. These, he was convinced, would both make the empire stronger and improve the welfare of its people. On the other hand, Peter certainly did not have a carefully worked out and consciously timed scheme for Europeanizing the country. He often did things impulsively and in an uncoordinated fashion. And certain measures were clearly related directly to the war effort and to the support of his new army and navy.

Though not a philosopher or theoretician, Peter the Great had a practical sense of the sort of state and society he was trying to shape. His models were the European nations of his time, monarchies with effective bureaucracies and commercial economies. Peter accepted completely the concept of autocracy, the idea of centralized absolutism. The governmental reforms he carried through were designed not to limit the tsar's rule but to make it more effective. He did try to change the ideology of autocracy by secularizing and depersonalizing the tsar's role. The tsar was to remain an absolute ruler, but not for his own sake or even for God's. Instead, the tsar-emperor was to serve the state, as everyone else did. Peter wanted the people to obey not the tsar as a person or a patriarch but as a symbol of sovereignty, as the first servant of the state. The bulk of the population, however, continued to see the tsar as both a "father" and a ruler anointed by God.

Consonant with his view of power was Peter's belief that all should serve the state. Neither religion nor wealth nor birth should exempt one from fulfilling a primary obligation to that entity. Civil and military service were the highest callings, and everything should be done to ensure that the army and the bureaucracy were efficient, honest, and just.

So should economic life also benefit the state? Peter accepted the tenets of mercantilism, then the dominant economic theory in Europe, holding that production should be stimulated and trade managed in such a way as to accrue maximum advantage to the state. At the same time, the state should encourage and support science, technology, and education, which were needed for effective governance and for expanding the economy.

As we already noted, Peter carried out a complete overhaul of the imperial army and founded the imperial navy in order to better wage war against the Ottoman Empire and Sweden. In his military reforms, Peter changed almost everything, including the design, production, and procurement of weapons and ships; the recruitment, training, and supply of enlisted men and officers; as well as transport, deployment, and battlefield tactics.

To ensure the manning and command of his armed forces and his civil service, Peter required that everyone serve. To be sure, the Muscovite tsars had established this principle earlier, but Peter made the obligation universal and lifelong and saw that it was enforced. Nobles served with their units as long as they were fit, and peasant recruits were drafted for life, although the term was reduced to twenty-five years later in the 1700s. Peter also decreed that appointment and advancement in civil and military service would be awarded according to ability and merit, not privilege, birth, or influence. To this end, he set up the Table of Ranks, which contained fourteen parallel grades in the civil and military service. Peter provided his own best example, working his way up in both the army and the navy until he became a general and later an admiral. Peter encouraged upward social mobility. A person who attained the eighth rank of the civil service, for example, automatically became a noble.

Moreover, Peter chose his own closest advisors not primarily from the old boyar and gentry families but from all classes in society, selecting individuals he thought had special skills or unusual ability. Alexander Menshikov, Peter's most trusted confidant, whom he later made a prince, was of humble origins and reputedly worked as a street vendor in Moscow before becoming the tsar's orderly and rising to prominence. Other high officials in Peter's reign included several Swiss, Scots, and Germans as well as a former serf, a shepherd, and a clerk. At the same time, one of his ablest generals was a member of an old noble family.

However, it is important to note that Peter did not alter serfdom. He seemed unaware that it was probably an inefficient system of agricultural production, apart from the moral issues it raised. Yet in other areas of economic life, Peter did his best to stimulate activity and output. He established hundreds of small manufacturing enterprises—most, to be sure, primarily to supply the armed forces—and he introduced a number of new products and trades into the empire. He provided subsidies to promote exports and assisted local artisans. Because of the heavy costs of his wars, however, the imperial economy hardly flourished in the Petrine era, and some estimates suggest that the state was worse off at the end of Peter's reign than at the beginning.

There is certainly no doubt that the average citizen carried a heavy fiscal burden under Peter's rule, as the state budget more than doubled between 1700 and 1725. Peter and his advisors were ingenious at devising new taxes, including some intended to discourage traditional practices, such as those on beards and Old Believers. A reform of lasting significance was Peter's decree changing the basis of taxation on the peasantry from the household to the individual. It was suspected, probably correctly, that peasants were crowding together in ever larger households in order to spread the burden of the steadily increasing exactions levied by the central government. In order to prevent this and to make sure everyone paid, Peter's government carried out a crude census and then decreed a "soul tax" that assessed each adult male. There is some speculation that this led to the setting up of new households and eventually to a marked rise in fertility and population later in the century. In any case, since both serfs and household slaves were counted and taxed without distinction, Peter's fiscal policies further erased any lingering distinction between them: all became the movable property of their owners.

In a related fashion, a reform Peter designed with another purpose in mind helped eliminate the difference between estates held for service and those that were hereditary without any legal service obligation. In a decree of 1714 (which was reversed after his death), Peter attempted to end the traditional practice of dividing an estate among all the male heirs, since it resulted in ever smaller and less efficient landholdings. The new single-inheritance (or primogeniture) law required designation of one son as sole heir, with the eldest male child receiving title if no one else was named. At the same time, the decree made no distinction among estates, assuming that all were hereditary and that all estate owners owed service.

Peter's desire to make the tsarist system work better led to much tinkering with government institutions and procedures. The result was a patchwork of the old, the adapted, and the European. Because he was frequently away campaigning, Peter originally established the Senate, a senior council of about a dozen officials, to rule in his absence. After a while, the Senate came to have considerable administrative and judicial power and turned into a permanent institution of the empire. Peter ceased appointing boyars, and the boyar duma and *zemskii sobor* both disappeared. Peter thoroughly reorganized the central bureaucracy, setting up a series of colleges to handle such matters as foreign affairs, the army, the navy, justice, finance, mining, and commerce. Modeled on Swedish institutions, the colleges were to be run by a council or collegial group. In theory, this system would prevent abuse of power by one individual and provide a wider range of experience and judgment in making important decisions. In practice, the colleges were quite unwieldy but nevertheless lasted for almost a century.

In provincial and municipal government, Peter took some bold initiatives, but his reforms were largely unsuccessful. As the Russian Empire grew, it became harder and harder to manage and govern, a problem that not only Peter but his successors failed to overcome.

Though Orthodox, Peter engaged at times in drunken and blasphemous parodies of church rituals and celebrations while relaxing with his friends. As in other fields, he called freely on the talents of several educated and able clerics, but he saw little role for the traditional church in the modernized state he was trying to mold. Since the general thrust of his policies was to secularize society, he tried to minimize the church's role in the empire. To make sure the church would be subservient to the state, Peter left the patriarchate vacant when Patriarch Adrian died in 1700. Later, he abolished the post, replacing it with the Holy Synod, a body of high clerics supervised by a lay official, the over-procurator of the Holy Synod. This arrangement lasted until 1917 and permitted the government to keep a tight rein on church activities and policies. Not yet recovered from the turmoil of the Schism, the church could do little to resist its subjugation by Peter.

Peter was an enthusiastic supporter of education. Training schools for the armed services naturally received high priority, but Peter also encouraged lay schools. He was particularly eager to advance the sciences and technology and laid plans for a national academy of sciences, which came into being shortly after his death. He established the first general hospital and surgical school at Moscow in 1706. Later, he reorganized medical affairs under the Medical Chancery headed by a foreign-educated imperial physician.

To make education more accessible to the average citizen, he oversaw a simplification of the Old Church Slavonic alphabet. To disseminate culture, he sponsored the first newspaper and greatly expanded book printing in the empire. The number of titles issued during his reign rose annually from six or seven to forty-five, and the content of these books broadened to include scientific and secular as well as religious topics. Peter's efforts in education, though extensive, were in fact only a tiny beginning. As one of the young subjects he sent abroad to study observed, "How can I learn geography without knowing the alphabet?" The Russian Empire needed to establish a much broader base of elementary and secondary schools and a better organized system, tasks that Catherine the Great undertook later in the 1700s.

To a considerable extent, Peter's most lasting reforms were cultural and psychological. His symbolic gestures, such as cutting off boyars' beards or forcing them to wear European dress, seem almost silly, but behind them was his relentless determination that the imperial elite change their outlook and attitudes, giving up the parochial, religious, old-fashioned ways and ideas of Muscovy for the worldly, secular, progressive lifestyle and thought of Europe. Many resisted or ignored him, but in the long run, Peter did succeed in orienting society in a different direction, in forcing it to look to the future instead of the past. This wrenching change of direction had two fateful consequences, however. It alienated the educated elite from the mass of the people, and before long, it led to a fundamental questioning of imperial society as a whole and to ideas of revolution.

RESISTANCE TO PETER

In attempting to transform the state, Peter was determined and ruthless. As early as 1696, he established permanent political police to persecute his opponents. Nevertheless, many people openly criticized his reforms, and millions more passively resisted, clinging stubbornly to the old ways. For the majority of peasants, Peter's reign meant not only new burdens but the introduction of strange and unorthodox customs, both of which they deeply resented. Many believed Peter was the Antichrist and feared the end of the world was near.

The most important rebellion against Peter broke out in southeastern Russia, centered in the city of Astrakhan, in 1705. Peter was then heavily engaged in the Great Northern War and could ill spare troops to send against the rebels. Moreover, since the leaders of the uprising espoused a broad range of popular grievances against both central and local government, the insurrection could easily have spread to other parts of southern Russia, the traditional seedbed of rebellion. Peter's opponents in Astrakhan included runaway serfs, Old Believers, and Cossacks but also many conservative subjects outraged by the combination of new taxes and iconoclastic policies that Peter had imposed on them. In appealing to the Don Cossacks for help, the rebels declared:

> We wish to inform you of what has happened in Astrakhan on account of our Christian faith, because of beard-shaving. . . . How we, our wives, and our children were not admitted into churches in our old Russian dress. . . . Moreover, in the last year, 1704, they imposed on us, and collected a [new] tax. . . .They also took away all our firearms . . . and our bread allowance [for those serving as frontier guards].[3]

The rebels' anger soon turned to violence, with the killing of the military governor and several hundred officials and nobles. A regular army under one of Peter's leading generals was required to suppress the uprising. Some of its leaders were publicly executed in Red Square as an example to the population.

Nevertheless, in 1707 and 1708, a new insurrection erupted, this time in the south, led by a disgruntled Don Cossack named Kondratii Bulavin, who exhorted his followers to reject serfdom and the government. With a motley army of over fifty thousand, Bulavin occupied several key towns and tried to persuade the Dnieper Cossacks to join him, but he was finally defeated by government troops.

At the same time that he was suppressing these revolts, Peter had to contend with sporadic uprisings among the Bashkirs, a Turkic people on the empire's eastern frontier who resented imperial domination and the taxes of Peter's government.

Those in government circles and among the old boyars and conservative churchmen who opposed Peter's policies hoped to use the heir to the throne, Peter's son Alexis, as the spearhead of their discontent. Intelligent but weak-willed and dissolute, Alexis, under pressure from Peter, renounced his right to the throne. Soon afterward, he went into self-imposed exile abroad. He was finally persuaded to return to the empire, but before long, his name was linked to plotting against Peter. Relations between father and son had never been good, and now Peter acted willfully against Alexis. In 1718, a broadly composed, extraordinary tribunal sentenced Alexis to death, but shortly thereafter, he died or was murdered in prison. Five years later, Peter promulgated a new succession law, declaring that the tsar had the right to name the heir to the throne, but he died in 1725 without doing so.

CONCLUSION

Within fifty years of Peter's death, some writers were arguing that his reign had greatly benefited the Russian Empire, while others claimed that it had ruined the country. This controversy became a major issue during the 1840s, when a debate arose between the Westernizers, who approved of Peter's policies, and the Slavophiles, who denounced them. In the 1860s, the conservative journalist Michael Katkov concluded that Peter's rule was "a catastrophe that . . . disrupted the organism of national life and . . . deprived [us] of the instinct and feeling of personal life . . . remaking us into senseless imitators doing everything on order of the government."

Peter's reign can best be summed up as a series of paradoxes that help explain why it is so controversial:

- Peter coerced the Russian Empire into modernization, but it was coming anyway.
- Peter had a vision of a more efficient, modernized empire, but his reforms were often haphazard, forced on him by military necessity and the pressure of events.

- Peter wanted to drive barbarism out of the state but relied on barbaric methods to achieve that goal.
- Peter wanted to change and improve society but left it with serfdom, an entrenched, privileged nobility, and a cumbersome and often corrupt bureaucracy.
- Peter cared about the welfare of his people, but his wars and fiscal demands left them burdened, exhausted, and resentful.
- Peter sought good government and encouraged individual merit, but his reign heightened the arbitrary power of the state.
- Peter set a fast pace and employed coercion to make progress, but this practice alienated most people and undercut the changes he was trying to make.
- Peter made the Russian Empire a great power in Europe, but he achieved this through aggression against its neighbors and at great cost to the empire itself.

In evaluating Peter the Great, we can make three major conclusions concerning his reign. First, he was clearly one of the most influential personalities in modern history. While the Russian Empire undoubtedly would have entered modernity, Peter greatly accelerated the process and, in so doing, changed imperial society fundamentally. Second, Peter propelled the empire onto the European stage and made it a great power. Finally, Peter forced the population to face some fundamental questions: How could imperial society react to new ideas and technology and still be true to its own traditions and unique culture? Should the West be imitated, or could Western attitudes and methods be modified and adapted to serve local needs and interests? Was it possible to fuse local beliefs and Western thought? And finally and most fundamentally, what was the true essence of Russian, Ukrainian, and the other Slavic and non-Slavic civilizations that existed during Peter's time and continue to exist today?

FURTHER READING

Anisimov, Evgenii V. *The Reforms of Peter the Great: Progress Through Coercion in Russia.* Translated by John T. Alexander. Armonk, NY: M. E. Sharpe, 1993.

Bushkovitch, Paul. *Peter the Great.* 2nd ed. Lanham, MD: Rowman & Littlefield, 2016.

Cracraft, James. *The Petrine Revolution in Russian Culture.* Cambridge, MA: Belknap Press of Harvard University Press, 2004.

————. *The Revolution of Peter the Great*. Cambridge, MA: Harvard University Press, 2003.

Engel, Barbara Alpern. *Women in Russia, 1700-2000*. Cambridge, UK: Cambridge University Press, 2004.

Hughes, Lindsey. *Peter the Great: A Biography*. New Haven, CT: Yale University Press, 2002.

————. *Sophia: Regent of Russia, 1657-1704*. New Haven, CT: Yale University Press, 1990.

LeDonne, John P. *Absolutism and Ruling Class: The Formation of the Russian Political Order, 1700–1825*. New York: Oxford University Press, 1991.

————. *The Russian Empire and the World, 1700–1917: The Geopolitics of Expansion and Containment*. New York: Oxford University Press, 1997.

Marrese, Michelle. *A Woman's Kingdom: Noblewomen and the Control of Property in Russia, 1700–1861*. Ithaca, NY: Cornell University Press, 2002.

Marsden, Christopher. *Palmyra of the North: The First Days of St. Petersburg*. London: Faber and Faber, 1942.

Meehan-Waters, Brenda. *Autocracy and Aristocracy: The Russian Service Elite of 1730*. New Brunswick, NJ: Rutgers University Press, 1982.

Sunderland, Willard. *Taming the Wild Field: Colonization and Empire on the Russian Steppe*. Ithaca, NY: Cornell University Press, 2004.

Wirtschafter, Elise Kimerling. *Social Identity in Imperial Russia*. DeKalb: Northern Illinois University Press, 1997.

Zitser, Ernest A. *The Transfigured Kingdom: Sacred Parody and Charismatic Authority at the Court of Peter the Great*. Ithaca, NY: Cornell University Press, 2004.

CHAPTER 7

CHANGE AND CONTINUITY, 1725–1801

A large party, in carriages and on horseback, approached Peterhof, the summer estate of the tsars. Since it was early summer, the gardens were at their most colorful, and the elaborate system of fountains was playing beautifully. Tsar Peter III, at the head of the group, looked forward with pleasure to the expected festivities that evening in honor of his name day, July 9, 1762. His wife, Catherine, who was staying at Peterhof while he was at another palace, was a renowned hostess, and he could anticipate a fine time, even though he and Catherine were not on good terms. Recently at a state dinner, he had publicly called her a fool, angering her partisans. Lately, there had even been rumors that she was plotting against him, taking advantage of his unpopularity with many prominent officers, nobles, and clerics who resented his often boorish behavior, his open hostility to the Russian Orthodox Church, and his decision to ally with Frederick the Great of Prussia, the Russian Empire's archenemy for the last seven years. As Peter and his companions rode into the courtyard of Peterhof, they were surprised to find no one about to greet and assist them. But when they entered the palace, they were dumbfounded and dismayed. Neither Catherine nor a single person from her retinue was there. Peter found only her ball gown ready for the party.

What Peter did not know and only learned several hours later was that early that morning, Alexei Orlov, one of five brothers—all guards officers who were Catherine's closest supporters—had roused the tsarina and hustled her into a waiting carriage for an emergency trip to St. Petersburg, the capital. The conspirators against Peter's rule had planned to wait several more weeks to depose him, but the arrest of one of their number had forced their hand. They were determined to win over key elements in the army before Peter even learned what was afoot. Later on the morning of July 9, a travelling carriage drew up outside the barracks of the Izmailov Guards Regiment on the outskirts of St. Petersburg. A Guards regimental officer descended and disappeared hastily inside. A few moments later, as a drummer alerted the soldiers, a woman of about thirty, dressed in dusty black, with her hair unpowdered, was handed down from the carriage and almost engulfed by a crowd of shouting and cheering soldiers. Shortly afterwards the crowd parted, and an elderly Orthodox priest advanced bearing aloft the cross. In loud tones officers and men . . . swore allegiance to the newly proclaimed Empress Catherine, Autocrat of all the Russias.[1]

The new empress then proceeded to the barracks of the other Guards regiments, all of whose members enthusiastically declared their support for her. By noon, she was at the Kazan Cathedral, where the highest church prelates confirmed her title, and later that day, the archbishop of Novgorod administered the oath of allegiance to troops drawn up in front of the Winter Palace. All but a few officers, who protested and were promptly arrested, ignored the point that, only six months previously, they had sworn loyalty to Peter.

The deposed Tsar Peter III, after learning of the coup d'état, awaited his fate. Catherine herself rode out to arrest him, and a few days later, while in custody, he was strangled by Alexei Orlov and others, allegedly in a fight. Catherine, determined to keep the throne, overlooked the murder, declaring Peter had died of "a hemorrhoidal colic," and rewarded her conspirators lavishly.

Catherine the Great knew where she was headed: to sit on the imperial Russian throne and to make her mark in modern European history. But where was the empire headed? Catherine herself, in our view, was not quite sure. If the empire was moving in the direction of becoming an "enlightened" society, then something would have to be done about serfdom, a reform that might unravel the whole social system and would certainly arouse the bitter opposition of the serf-owning nobility, the state's chief supporters. If the Russian Empire were to evolve toward a society based on law and institutions or even on classes, then the arbitrary authority of the autocracy would have to be curbed and alternate centers of power created almost from scratch. Although Catherine nodded a few times in this direction, she had no intention of surrendering her autocratic prerogative. If the empire was to proceed down the path toward industrialization, as England was just starting to do, the role of the state in economic life would have to be greatly reduced, private entrepreneurs encouraged, markets found, and techniques learned. This course was beyond the resources available to Catherine. In all cases, she had to work with what Peter the Great and his successors had left her.

In two important ways, Peter's efforts survived him and shaped the future course of his country: the Russian Empire remained a major European power, and Europeanization continued to develop and take root. Nevertheless, in other significant ways, the eighteenth century saw fundamental divergences from Peter's program of service to the state and modernization. First, during the 1700s, obligatory service for the nobility was abolished, though many nobles continued to serve. But because the nobles did not succeed in establishing an institutional basis for themselves as a class, they were unable to turn their freedom into a regularized device for limiting the autocracy. Moreover, since the nobles no longer owed service to the state, the political and moral justification for their role as serf owners was weakened. Others' criticism and self-criticism of their position mounted.

Second, the 1700s saw little progress toward Peter's goal of establishing a regulated state that rested on efficient institutions and fixed laws. Instead, the political system remained, despite a burgeoning bureaucracy, largely dependent on the personal authority and quasi-religious image of the tsar and on the privileged status and role of the topmost nobility who filled the chief military and administrative positions in the imperial government. No competing sources of power emerged to challenge the autocracy and to push it toward modernity. By the end of the eighteenth century, while a few intellectuals and conscience-stricken nobles had begun to question the morality of serfdom and the political validity of the tsarist system, both persisted largely unchanged.

Third, the Russian Empire continued to develop economically, largely under state encouragement, intervention, and control, but it did not possess the requisites to participate in the Industrial Revolution that occurred at the end of the century in Europe. Thus, by 1800, the empire's rate of economic growth had begun to fall markedly behind that of the Western European nations, and its agricultural productivity remained low.

Fourth, the empire's continuing expansion brought new, non-ethnic Russian peoples under tsarist rule. Their mistreatment by the government sowed the seeds of later conflicts between a Slavic majority and non-Russian minorities.

Fifth, by the end of the 1700s, the Russian Empire had begun to develop a national consciousness and literature, which laid the foundation for the remarkable flowering of culture in the nineteenth century.

In this chapter, we will begin with a concise sketch of political developments from the death of Peter the Great in 1725 through the end of Catherine's reign in 1796.

PETER'S SUCCESSORS, 1725–1762

For one hundred years, beginning with Peter the Great's death and ending with the Decembrist Revolt of 1825, the question of who was to sit on the tsarist throne created political turmoil in the Russian Empire. This seems puzzling, when one considers the dominant position that Peter occupied, but several factors help explain the uncertainties that followed his reign. Peter himself muddied the succession issue by treating the state as private property. In 1722, he declared that he alone would name his successor, but he then failed to do so. Moreover, the nobles, who wanted to exert more political influence, could achieve their goals only through control of the tsar, whom Peter had made the embodiment of the supremacy of the state in society. The locus of power was in the tsar. There were no well-defined estates, no autonomous church, no municipalities, no middle class, and not even an independent bureaucracy. Control of the throne itself was the key to political success.

Yet in the thirty-seven years after Peter's death, his immediate successors were neither capable individuals nor strong rulers. Notably, three women, Catherine I, Anna, and Elizabeth, reigned in this period. Each possessed a strong personality and had her own ideas, but lovers, courtiers, and advisors largely set and executed policy. The sequence of rulers in the eighteenth century was as follows:

Catherine I	1725–1727
Peter II	1727–1730
Anna	1730–1740
Ivan VI	1740–1741
Elizabeth	1741–1762
Peter III	1762
Catherine II (the Great)	1762–1796
Paul I	1796–1801

Catherine I, the second wife of Peter the Great, was of humble Latvian origins, but possessed the backing of Peter's colleagues and friends, although Peter's grandson, Peter II, was the logical heir. Pressure from the guards regiments, set up originally by Peter the Great and manned in all ranks mainly by nobles, finally settled the issue in Catherine's favor. On four more occasions in the 1700s, the guards, who directly represented noble interests, intervened to determine who should be tsar. In this way, the nobility played a significant political role but never found a way to institutionalize this influence.

Moreover, the nobles were not a unified and coherent group, and the one attempt they made to formalize their participation in the government foundered on divisions among them. On Catherine's death, Peter II succeeded her, but he died of smallpox in 1730, which left no male Romanov in line for succession. A small clique of upper-crust nobility, including members of the Supreme Privy Council, a type of executive body on which Catherine had relied, decided to offer the throne to Anna, a daughter of Peter the Great's stepbrother, Ivan V. In so doing, they asked Anna to accept a number of conditions that sharply limited her autocratic power. In effect, she was to rule jointly with the council. Anna, eager to ascend the throne, agreed. However, less privileged members of the nobility, jealous of the ploy effected by the council, demanded their share of the political pie, and when Anna arrived to be crowned, the guards demonstrated in her favor. Taking advantage of this turmoil, Anna tore up the conditions and dissolved the Supreme Privy Council.

Anna ruled for the next ten years as empress, but she relied heavily on a group of advisors who were predominantly Germans from the Baltic region. One of them, her favorite, Count Biron, was particularly corrupt and cruel, and his persecutions of Old Believers and others aroused bitter enmity among imperial subjects of all classes.

Before dying in 1740, Anna appointed her grandnephew, Ivan VI, as tsar, but he was only an infant when he ascended the throne, and the so-called German Party continued to rule the empire. Again in 1741, the guards staged a coup d'état, putting Peter the Great's daughter, Elizabeth, in power. Though quite capable and well meaning, Empress Elizabeth was also vain, lazy, and extravagant. She, too, ruled through favorites, though now they were ethnic Ukrainians and Russians rather than Germans. During her reign, the influence of French culture spread in the empire, but Elizabeth did little to tackle the country's basic social, economic, and administrative challenges.

In 1762, when Elizabeth died, Peter III, Peter the Great's grandson by his oldest daughter and a German princeling, succeeded to the throne. Brought up in a German household, Peter moved to the Russian Empire when he was a teenager, but he never lost his suspicion of his new surroundings and his admiration for things German, including the leading German sovereign, Frederick the Great of Prussia. In several areas, Peter III's policies were quite forward looking, but his attacks on the Orthodox Church, his attempt to Prussianize the imperial army, and his radical switching of sides in the Seven Years' War, in which he made peace with the empire's traditional enemy Prussia on the verge of Prussia's defeat, alienated broad circles in imperial society. Moreover, Peter III's crude, adolescent, and unpredictable behavior gave the people little hope for improvement in his rule. The result was yet another palace revolution, carried out by elements of the Guards regiments, with his wife Catherine's connivance. The unfortunate Peter III was soon dead, perhaps by accident, perhaps by assassination—the exact circumstances of his death will likely never be known.

CATHERINE THE GREAT, 1762–1796

Although Catherine the Great did not have so abrupt and marked an impact on Russian and European history as Peter the Great, she was a powerful and effective ruler for over three decades. She was both extremely able and a charmer, as the British ambassador to Russia made clear in a 1762 dispatch to London:

> Her Imperial Majesty is neither short nor tall. . . . Her features were far from being so delicately and exactly formed as to compose what might pretend to regular beauty, but a fine complexion, an animated and intelligent eye, a mouth agreeably turned, and a profusion of glossy chestnut hair produce that sort of countenance which, a very few years ago, a man must have been either prejudiced or insensible to have beheld with indifference. . . . Her eyes are blue, their vivacity tempered by a languor in which there is much sensibility and no insipidity. . . . She expresses herself with elegance in French, and I am assured that she speaks Russian with as much precision as German, which is her native language. . . . She speaks and reasons with fluency and precision.[2]

Outgoing, intelligent, hardworking, ambitious, and self-confident, Catherine the Great poured all of her considerable energy and skill into the task first of ascending the throne and then of advancing the cause of the Russian Empire, her adopted land, and of herself as its "enlightened" ruler.

In almost every respect, Catherine was a self-made woman. Born Sophie of Anhalt-Zerbst, a small German principality, she lived as a child in modest circumstances and without great expectations. It was assumed that, at best, she might be married to some minor German princeling or nobleman, and it was only a stroke of great good fortune that, through complicated family connections, at age fifteen Sophie was selected by Empress Elizabeth as the fiancée of the heir to the Russian imperial throne, the future Peter III. She and her mother were commanded to go to St. Petersburg to live at Elizabeth's court. Before long, her mother was evicted as an agent of the Prussian king, and Sophie realized that her betrothed Peter III was coarse, poorly educated, and emotionally underdeveloped.

With skill and determination, she nevertheless set about preparing herself for her future role as a tsar's wife. She converted to the Orthodox faith, was re-baptized as Catherine, learned Russian, and plunged assiduously into finding out all she could about her new country and the larger world. She read widely, particularly in the works of the French writers of the Enlightenment, and stud-ied politics and human nature close up, first observing the maneuvering and intrigues at Elizabeth's court and then taking part in them. Caught out on one occasion, Catherine shrewdly threw herself on the mercy of Empress Eliza-beth, protesting her devotion to the state and the monarch. Elizabeth forgave her, and by the time Peter III ascended the throne, Catherine, in sharp contrast to her husband, had thoroughly Russianized herself and developed a wide cir-cle of powerful friends among the elite of imperial society.

Through self-education and by character and inclination, Catherine the Great was indeed an "enlightened despot" comparable to other European monarchs accorded that designation in the eighteenth century. She believed in natural law, the rule of reason, religious toleration, and the orderly function-ing of government for the good of society (see Figure 7.1). Although happy to use her acquaintance and correspondence with Voltaire and other leaders of the European Enlightenment to boost her own ego, to build support for her regime, and to spread her fame abroad, she was also genuinely stimulated and inspired by their ideas and advice.

Regarding the empire, her intentions were good, but her dilemma was that, having usurped the throne, she never felt entirely secure on it and thus hesitated to undertake basic social reforms, such as the abolition or ameliora-tion of serfdom. She feared destabilizing the system and alienating her chief political supporters, the nobility. Moreover, she was dealing with a vast coun-try with huge problems, and on some practical matters, she simply felt she could make little headway. She remained dedicated to the ideals of the Enlight-enment and to improving Russian society, but as she wrote Denis Diderot, the French philosopher, "You only write on paper, but I have to write on human skin, which is incomparably more irritable and ticklish."

Though adhering to principles of the Enlightenment, Catherine strength-ened rather than curtailed the autocracy and opposed the French Revolution. This was not hypocritical. In both the concept of enlightened despotism and the empire's political tradition, beneficial change was to be directed from above, and the monarch was not to relinquish authority but to use it wisely. Moreover, Catherine never espoused radical eighteenth-century ideas such as representative government and liberty. She wanted a more efficient, more hu-mane autocracy, but nevertheless an autocracy.

FIGURE 7.1. A portrait of Empress Catherine the Great that suggests her forceful personality. (Heritage Image Partnership Ltd / Alamy Stock Photo)

Catherine was particularly sensitive about her authority because, despite her repeated proclamations after her husband's deposition that she was acting in the interests of all the people and for the good of the whole country, she was in fact an outsider, a German upstart, who had seized the throne by force and had no legal claim to it. To make her even more nervous, two legitimate heirs to the throne existed, and several pretenders arose. Ivan VI, although deposed in 1741, was still alive but also still imprisoned. In 1764, however, he was killed by his guards during a failed attempt to rescue him and use him against Catherine. A second threat was Catherine's son Paul, born in 1754. Although recognized as Peter III's son and therefore heir to the throne, Paul was almost certainly sired by a lover of Catherine, Sergei Saltykov. As Paul grew to adulthood, he posed the continuing danger that he might become a rallying point for opposition to Catherine.

Among the pretenders, the most important was Yemelyan Pugachev, a Don Cossack, who in 1773 and 1774 led the last major peasant revolt in a series that dated back at least to Ivan Bolotnikov's rebellion in 1607. Although this widespread uprising was directed more against the system than Catherine personally, it was a frightening affair since it dramatically revealed to her the deep-seated weaknesses in the empire's central and provincial administration as well as the extent of the country's social inequities. The spectrum of those who joined Pugachev reflected the diversity of groups with major grievances against the regime: Cossacks whose privileges and autonomy were being undercut, Bashkirs and Tatars whose culture and ethnic rights were being trampled on, Old Believers persecuted by the Orthodox Church and the government, factory serfs condemned to work in the mines and manufacturing enterprises of the Ural region in inhuman conditions, agricultural serfs ground down by increased taxes and recurring army conscription, and fugitives of every kind, from army deserters to runaway serfs and criminals.

Claiming to be Peter III, Pugachev declared an end to serfdom, taxes, and the draft as well as a war on landlords and the government. Molding his motley supporters into a surprisingly effective force, Pugachev ranged along the Ural and Volga Rivers and briefly captured a number of important towns. Because the Russian Empire was then engaged in a major war with Turkey, the government nearly panicked, fearing at one time that Pugachev might march on Moscow. Repeatedly defeated by regular troops, he was finally captured and, as one account put it, "drawn and quartered, but not tortured"! The Pugachev revolt strengthened Catherine's political alliance with the nobility, virtually the only group that supported the government in the disaffected regions. It also bolstered her resolve to undertake fundamental reforms of the imperial administration.

Aware when she came to power in 1762 that governance in the empire was chaotic, Catherine, with her usual determination and acumen, set about putting state affairs into better order. She reformed the Senate to make it more efficient as an administrative overseer, improved tax collection, and revamped the budget and fiscal policy. At the same time, interested in a broader and deeper-rooted approach to the state's problems, she decided to convene a representative body of leading officials and citizens to initiate a codification of the laws (the last had been in 1649) and to study what basic reforms should be undertaken. Known as the Legislative Commission, it included delegates from the nobles, townspeople, the government, state peasants, and non-Russian ethnic groups, but no serfs and only one cleric. Opening its sessions in 1767, Catherine presented the commission with a long set of "instructions" that she had labored over for many preceding months. Drawing heavily on Enlightenment thinkers, Catherine had personally written many sections of her charge to the commission, which was quickly translated into all the main European languages.

After almost two years of deliberations, the commission adjourned. It had served quite effectively as a broadly constituted consultative body. It did not reach definite conclusions partly because of its unwieldy size (it included almost six hundred members) and because few delegates had the education, experience, and judgment to turn Catherine's theoretical considerations into practical law or policy. But it also gave no specific policy direction because it mirrored differences within society, particularly between nobles and merchants, as well as the general reluctance of any group to attack the root institution of serfdom. The Legislative Commission, however, did have several positive results: it educated Catherine concerning the basic problems of the society she presided over and the limits of what she could alter; it provided concrete information and opinions that she later incorporated in her administrative reforms; and its subcommittees, which met for several more years, drew up a number of useful proposals.

Partly spurred by the Pugachev revolt, Catherine in 1775 instituted a major reorganization of the imperial administration, which included changes that lasted, in some cases, until the 1860s and, in others, until 1917. The most important reform was to divide the nation into provinces (*guberniia*) equal in population—there were fifty by the end of Catherine's reign—subdivided into equal districts. The provincial governors were responsible for coordinating government policy and for overseeing the operations of functionally separate judicial, legislative, and administrative departments in each province. Although not ideal, this was a marked improvement over previous patterns of governance.

In 1785, Catherine undertook two other major reforms, granting a charter of rights and obligations to both the nobility and the towns. The former was more important because it confirmed the liberation of the nobility from compulsory service, first decreed under Peter III in 1762, and because it established noble organizations in the provinces and districts of the reorganized empire. A few historians have argued that the Charter of the Nobility was the first step toward the formation of independent interest groups in imperial history and that it might have opened the door to eventual representative government. But this interpretation is off the mark. Indeed, Catherine wanted to establish the nobility as a separate and privileged order in society, but mainly so that it could serve the government more effectively. She certainly did not intend for them to develop into an alternate center of power. The nobles themselves did not attempt to turn their charter into a weapon against the autocracy. The complicated and limited system of governance set up for the towns in 1785 did not entirely work, and municipal administration remained a problem for Catherine's successors.

Catherine was, of course, active in many other areas, including social policy, education and culture, economic development, minority affairs, and foreign policy, and her role in these matters will be discussed in the following sections as part of our review of long-term trends in Russia during the whole period from Peter's death to the end of the eighteenth century.

RUSSIAN IMPERIAL EXPANSION AND COLONIZATION

Throughout the 1700s, but particularly during Catherine's reign, the Russian Empire continued to expand its frontiers in all directions and to settle new areas. In many respects, this trend marked a continuation of earlier policies and movement, but in the eighteenth century, much of the new territory acquired had never been under Kievan Rus' or earlier Russian imperial rule, and most of the peoples absorbed were not ethnic Russians or even Slavs. By 1800, the state was an enormous, multinational empire, prominent in both Europe and Asia.

After Peter the Great's death, the Russian Empire maintained its influential position in European politics, and the government also continued Peter's interest in exploring and colonizing in Asia. The empire's foreign policy in Europe was directed in large part toward weakening its two major western neighbors, Poland and the Ottoman Empire. Since Austria was also concerned about the same countries, the Russian and Austrian empires were allied for much of the century. The empire also tried to stay on good terms with Britain, its largest trading partner.

It is hard to evaluate Russian imperial foreign policies from the sixteenth to the twentieth centuries. Were the empire's leaders motivated primarily by considerations of defense and national security? Were they trying to protect its borders and forestall possible attacks by enemies? Or were they mainly interested in extending the empire's rule and influence over other countries? Were they imperialistic, seeking widened power and profit in Europe and Asia (and perhaps the world)? Unfortunately, the historical records of the 1700s provide no clear answers to these questions.

On the one hand, it can be argued that the Ottoman Turks and particularly their protégés, the Crimean Tatars, posed a constant threat to the southwestern flank of European Russia. Similarly, the Poles, historically inhabiting a larger and more developed kingdom, could be viewed as a danger. But in fact, the Tatars were more of a nuisance than a threat, and the Ottoman Empire was already in the period of decline that led to its collapse in World War I. Moreover, Poland, economically weak and wracked by internal problems, was in no position to menace the Russian Empire. And in Asia, no power posed any possible danger to the state. On balance, then, imperial foreign policy in the 1700s appears more aggressive than defensive, although the state's expansion to the Black Sea under Catherine fulfilled a long-cherished goal dating back to Kievan Rus' times and extended the empire's southern border to its natural geographic limit.

The chief loser in the game of eighteenth-century European politics was Poland, which was swallowed up by its neighbors before the end of the century (see Map 5.1). While the details of the diplomatic maneuvering that resulted in three partitions and the eventual disappearance of the Polish state are beyond our scope, the general circumstances of Poland's annexation are important, not least because they shed light on the strong antipathy most Poles have today for ethnic Russians. To be sure, the Poles were, to some extent, their own worst enemies, but essentially, Poland was victimized by stronger neighbors coveting its land.

Although Poland recovered from its defeat by Charles XII of Sweden during the Great Northern War, it was weakened throughout the 1700s, partly because it could command fewer resources than most of its neighbors, and partly because it was being torn apart by social, religious, and political conflict. Polish peasants struggled against their landlords, Catholics persecuted those of other faiths, and the Polish nobility steadily undermined the power of the king. Finally, in the 1760s, civil war erupted in Poland, an irresistible temptation for the major surrounding countries to interfere in its affairs. This led in 1772 to the first partition, under which Russia, Austria, and Prussia each took Polish territory adjoining their states, the whole totaling about one-third of the territory of Poland. Although Russians, Belarusians, and Ukrainians inhabited most of the land Catherine annexed, the predominance of these nationalities hardly justified the action. The humiliation of the first partition led to a national revival in Poland that greatly strengthened the country but also alarmed its neighbors.

After some maneuvering, the powers joined in two more partitions in 1793 and 1795 that eliminated Poland from the map of Europe. In these, the Russian, Prussian, and Austrian states annexed lands inhabited primarily by ethnic Poles, who became an important and hostile minority within each empire. Although prestige, economic benefit, and security were advanced as reasons for this barefaced dismemberment of an independent state, greed, opportunism, and a determination to share in the spoils seem to have been the basic motivations. As one contemporary noted about Maria Theresa, the empress of Austria, "She wept, but she kept on taking." The Poles, of course, were bitterly resentful, rebelling against their imperial Russian masters three times in the 1800s before resurrecting their country in 1918 in the aftermath of World War I.

The Russian Empire's other major territorial gains were in the southwest as the result of several wars against the Ottoman Empire, the most important of which occurred under Catherine the Great between 1768 and 1774. By the end of the century, the empire had acquired all the territory north of the Black Sea from the Dniester River eastward, including the mouths of the Don and Dnieper Rivers; had annexed the Crimea, the home of the Crimean Tatars; had obtained commercial rights in the Black Sea and through the Straits at Constantinople; and was vaguely authorized to act as protector of Orthodox Christians under Turkish rule. Strategically, economically, and politically, the Russian Empire gained a great deal, securing its southern border, opening up profitable trade through the Black Sea, obtaining rich agricultural lands, and weakening one of its main enemies. Nevertheless, the Turkish problem remained a major issue in imperial foreign policy throughout the next century.

Imperial colonization of Siberia and the fringes of central Asia had begun in the 1600s but was stepped up in the 1700s. In addition to encouraging ethnic Russians, Ukrainians, and other Slavs to move out to the frontier regions, the government invited a large group of Catholic and, later, Mennonite Germans to settle along the Volga River. And after acquisition of territory north of the Black Sea, Russians and Ukrainians were settled there in large numbers. Although in earlier times Jews had been prohibited from living in the Muscovite state, Catherine encouraged the immigration of Jews, both into western Russia and into the new lands in the south. Incorporation of the Polish territories also added a number of Jews to the empire's population. At first, they were granted equal rights as citizens, but in the 1790s, for reasons that are unclear, an imperial decree assessed double taxation on Jews of all classes.

As the empire expanded by conquest and colonization, administration of this vast state became more and more difficult. In foreign policy, Catherine essentially followed the lead of her predecessors; that is, she treated the new territories and peoples as integral parts of the Russian Empire. This meant that, with a few exceptions, centralized rule was established, local rights were ignored, and efforts were made to Russify the non-Russian ethnic populations, including other Slavs such as Belarusians and Ukrainians. Ukrainians in particular lost the last vestiges of their autonomy and were fully absorbed into the empire. Serfdom was also permitted in western Ukraine and selectively in the new lands north of the Black Sea, although not in Siberia and the Asian borderlands.

ECONOMIC AND SOCIAL DEVELOPMENT

The Russian Empire, like much of Europe, experienced a remarkable population boom in the eighteenth century. The reasons for this growth are not clear, but improved public order and public health, a feeling of greater security and stability, and an increase in the acreage farmed may all have contributed. In any case, the population more than doubled in about four generations, from roughly thirteen million in 1722 to twenty-nine million in 1796. To the latter figure were added another ten million people living in the recently acquired Polish and southwestern lands. The result was a much larger workforce and potential market, but the boom also produced more mouths to feed, while agricultural productivity had increased little. The overwhelming majority of the population remained serfs and state peasants living at a bare subsistence level.

Although towns grew with the increasing population, the urban-rural ratio changed slowly: in the early 1700s, about 97 percent of the people lived in the countryside and 3 percent in towns, and by 1800, the figures were 92 to 94 percent and 6 to 8 percent, respectively. The upper nobility remained a tiny fraction of the population, numbering in the tens of thousands, and the whole noble class reached only into the hundreds of thousands, comprising barely 1 percent of the population at most. Over 90 percent of the population were peasants, and the proportion of those who were privately owned serfs grew slowly in the 1700s, reaching an estimated 55 percent by the end of the century, when serfdom was at its height. This meant that, by 1800, between fifteen and twenty million imperial subjects were virtual slaves. Another ten to fifteen million were state peasants of various categories who owed heavy obligations in money or kind but were slightly better off than the private serfs.

During the 1700s, while the percentage and total number of serfs increased, their situation deteriorated. Not only did the eighteenth-century tsars give to favorites, military heroes, high nobles, and other worthies land containing hundreds of thousands of peasants (often from non-Russian but ethnic Slavic areas in Ukraine and eastern Poland), thereby making the inhabitants serfs, but they also gave all serf owners greatly increased power over their serfs. For example, owners could now interfere in serf marriages, send recalcitrant serfs into the army, and administer judicial and physical punishment to serfs, including banishment to Siberia.

Advertisements offering serfs for purchase resembled those for the sale of slaves in the American South: "For Sale: two plump coachmen, two barbers, one knows how to play musical instruments." Unlike slavery in the United States, however, serfdom in the Russian Empire was not limited to one region of the country, but existed almost everywhere, except in the far north, Siberia, and parts of the Asian reaches of the state. Finally, the data are insufficient to determine how much state taxes on the peasants increased in the eighteenth century, but it would be reasonable to estimate that they doubled. In short, the 1700s marked the apogee of the institution of serfdom in every respect: numbers, extent, conditions, and oppressiveness. Catherine, though concerned in principle, apparently believed, particularly after the Pugachev revolt, that tampering with serfdom would threaten the whole social system. Consequently, she attempted only minor reforms, encouraging voluntary emancipation of serfs and limiting the use of serf labor in industry.

The inefficiencies and lack of incentives to produce associated with serfdom help explain why the economy in the eighteenth century advanced only slowly. Serfdom held back the development of a national market, slowed capital accumulation, and hindered technological innovation and entrepreneurship. But the economic policies of the state were also at fault. Catherine, for example, offered inducements for nobles to found industries and enter trade, but this policy also discouraged merchants and townspeople. Serf artisans and producers, though they made a substantial contribution to the economy, were not encouraged. As a result, although nonagricultural output grew in the course of the century, the ground was not prepared for a major takeoff into industrialization, like that occurring in Western Europe. At the end of the century, the empire was a leading producer of iron and copper, with its output of pig iron in 1790 equaling that of England, but in the first decades of the nineteenth century, the state fell far behind in economic terms.

THE CHANGING ROLE OF THE NOBILITY

The nobility began the eighteenth century tightly harnessed to state service by Peter the Great. Noble sons were expected to be ready for education or duty in their teens and were to serve for life. By the end of the century, nobles owed no service in peacetime, though they could be summoned in time of need. The nobles had become a dominant and privileged elite in imperial society, far and away the state's best-educated and wealthiest element. The steps along their path to liberation were many, and we need note only a few major ones here. In 1736, the term of service for nobles was reduced to twenty-five years. In the 1740s, one son in each noble family was exempted from service so that he could stay home to manage the family's land and affairs. Another decree stipulated that only nobles had the right to own serfs. Finally, in 1762, under Peter III, nobles were exempted from state service in peacetime altogether, a privilege confirmed in Catherine the Great's 1785 Charter of the Nobility.

Although service was no longer obligatory, the imperial crown still strongly encouraged it, and in fact, most nobles continued to serve in some military or bureaucratic capacity. It was expected that those who did not would run their estates in the countryside and be active in local affairs, including the provincial and district assemblies of nobles established in the 1785 charter. But few had any altruistic interest in improving production on their lands, and there was little incentive to do so as long as they did not go too far into debt. Out of boredom or a sense of responsibility, some did participate in local administration, but many frittered away their time or simply vegetated.

In any case, the nobility was not a homogeneous group, as evidenced when it split over the conditions the Supreme Privy Council tried to impose on Anna. In addition to differences along lines of rank, wealth, and political influence, the nobility was divided by location and education. At the top of the social pyramid stood the nobles of the two capitals, St. Petersburg and Moscow. These individuals either held important state posts or were wealthy enough to keep a town house in one of the two major cities. They would spend part of the year on their rural estates and part engaging in urban social life. Beneath this elite were the provincial nobility, that is, nobles who either resided or kept town houses in the other major cities of the Russian Empire. At the bottom of the scale were the rural nobility, probably half of all nobles, who lived on small estates, owned few or no serfs, and seldom if ever went to the towns. They were generally poor, some little better off than their peasants, and usually poorly educated. There were also "personal" nobles who owned neither land nor serfs.

Education became in the eighteenth century a major dividing line among the nobility and in imperial society generally. Before 1700, only high clergy and a few of the elite were educated at all—even parish priests were generally illiterate or had only the most rudimentary education. During the eighteenth century, the nobility, as part of their dominance, became much better educated, either through schools or through private tutors. Nobles who lacked the money or the opportunity for education soon found that the top jobs in the tsarist administration were out of their reach and that they were slipping into an inferior social status.

At the same time, education affected the outlook of the elite nobles in two ways. Since their education was primarily Western in orientation, they found themselves increasingly isolated from their fellow citizens, whether they were poorer, uneducated nobles or humble serfs. The sophisticated elite increasingly adopted European manners, customs, dress, and even language, thereby opening a huge and unbridgeable chasm between them and their fellow subjects. The noted writer of the nineteenth century, Alexander Herzen, characterized the alienation that resulted as follows: "Foreigners at home and foreigners abroad, idle onlookers—spoiled for Russia by their Western prejudices and spoiled for the West by their Russian habits—they constituted a strange kind of intelligent superfluity, and lost themselves in their artificial life, in sensual pleasures and in an intolerable egoism."

A small minority who found themselves adrift between two cultures but were determined to do something about it became radical critics of the situation in the Russian Empire. They concluded that imperial society as a whole, and particularly the institution of serfdom, needed fundamental change if it were to measure up to the standards that Enlightenment thinkers had postulated as the natural and inalienable rights of all peoples. These critics became the forerunners of the state's revolutionary intelligentsia of the nineteenth century.

Whatever the differences in education, rank, and wealth among the nobility, the question remains, why did they not become an independent political force in society once they had been liberated from obligatory state service? Two related factors were decisive, in our view. First, by the 1700s, the tsar largely determined entry into and placement within the noble group. Peter the Great's Table of Ranks institutionalized the nobility's dependence on state service, appointment to which the tsar and his close advisors controlled. To be sure, there were hereditary nobles, and old families persisted in positions of influence and wealth. But status and power mostly depended on service, and the tsar decided who would serve and therefore who would be important. This was true whether service was obligatory or voluntary.

Second, and a natural corollary, the nobility had no separate or autonomous institutional base outside the government. They were not organized as a class; they had no corporate rights—except petitioning the tsar—but only rights as individual nobles; and they had no mechanism, since the end of the boyar duma and the *zemskii sobor*, for representation as a group before the tsar. Although Catherine the Great's provincial and district assemblies of nobles could be viewed as the embryo of an independent organization, they were in fact creations of the state, serving mainly state administrative purposes. Only on a few rare occasions in the nineteenth century were they turned to the purpose of representing the independent interests and views of the nobility.

EDUCATION AND CULTURE

As an enlightened despot, Catherine worked hard to broaden and improve education in the empire. Theoretically, a well-run state required an educated populace; practically, Catherine desperately needed trained individuals to staff her administration and help her govern an immense country. More sensibly than Peter the Great, who tried to build an educational system from the top down, Catherine the Great strove to develop an integrated system at all levels.

Some of the state schools Peter had founded failed for lack of funds, teachers, or students, but a few survived, and during the middle of the eighteenth century, these were complemented by the opening of a number of private schools. Moscow University was founded in 1755, although it enrolled barely one hundred students in its first few decades. Catherine began with an idealistic plan for a network of state boarding schools that would produce an enlightened elite. This plan proved impractical, although it did encourage the founding of the first school for women, the Smolny Institute in St. Petersburg, which during the Revolution of 1917 became the headquarters of Lenin's Bolshevik Party. Finally, in the 1780s, a system of general public and free education was instituted; schools were opened in provincial cities and district towns but not in the countryside. At the same time, the first teachers' training institute was founded. By 1796, over twenty thousand pupils were enrolled in the recently created elementary and secondary schools, a paltry number in a country of the empire's size, but a start and an authentic triumph for Catherine, who had to overcome lack of interest and funds to create the system.

For most imperial subjects of Slavic origin, despite the growing Westernization of elite society, cultural life continued to revolve around Orthodox religion and folk beliefs and tales. The village church remained the center of worship and edification, and communal celebrations focused on religious festivals and holidays. Faith in God and the saints as well as the rites of baptism, marriage, and death ordered and undergirded existence even for those backsliders who infrequently attended Mass. Sickness and nature's vagaries were coped with through folk wisdom and traditional remedies dispensed by influential women healers in the village. Most of imperial culture remained Orthodox, Slavic, and fatalistic.

In sharp contrast, Catherine the Great vigorously promoted Western-oriented cultural activities, beginning with her own court, where plays, readings, and musical soirées intermingled with games, balls, and other light entertainment. The number of books published in the empire more than tripled during Catherine's reign as compared with the total output up to that time. The empress also encouraged periodicals and newspapers, and as education spread among the nobility and townspeople, an informed and interested, if tiny, reading public developed. Catherine also encouraged the arts, and the theater flourished, producing mainly European plays but also plays by local authors.

As with much of the cultural development of the 1700s, painting, architecture, and music largely imitated Western models. But to a considerable extent, this schooling in European styles and values was the indispensable preparation for the astounding outburst of independent artistic creativity in the nineteenth century that so enriched world culture. The literature of the eighteenth century foreshadowed the cultural efflorescence to come, with the development of the first modern poets, playwrights, and authors in the empire, including Antiokh Kantemir, Michael Lomonosov, Denis Fonvizin, and Nicholas Karamzin. Lomonosov was also a gifted scientist and a leader of the Russian Academy of Sciences, which was founded after Peter the Great's death. By the end of the century, Russian, Ukrainian, and other writers had developed a distinct style and an independent identity, which can be characterized as the beginnings of a definite national consciousness.

Intellectual debate and social criticism, both important aspects of the European Enlightenment, developed in the Russian Empire as well. In Catherine's time, the boldest commentator on imperial society, Alexander Radishchev (1749–1802), was an outstanding example of a type of intellectual that became both prominent and troublesome to the government in the next century. Radishchev, of noble birth and well educated in Germany and at home, entered state service and performed creditably as a middle-level administrator in Catherine's regime. At the same time, under the influence of Enlightenment thought, particularly the writings of Jean-Jacques Rousseau, Radishchev became increasingly disturbed by what he observed around him in society and found the moral and social implications of the serf system particularly appalling. Employing a typical eighteenth-century literary device, the travelogue, he poured out a devastating criticism of serfdom in his book *Journey from Petersburg to Moscow*, which was published in 1790, but privately because of its controversial nature. Catherine, already alarmed at what she considered the excesses of the French Revolution, banned Radishchev's book and had him arrested and imprisoned in Siberia. Thus, at the end of Catherine's reign, the state, which had fostered the spread of culture and of "enlightened" ideas, turned to censorship and repression against theories and individuals considered harmful to state interests—a policy followed, with rare respites, by subsequent imperial administrations.

THE REIGN OF PAUL I, 1796–1801

The brief rule of Catherine's son Paul supplied a disturbing coda to eighteenth-century imperial history. Harsh manifestations of Russian civilization that had been suppressed or minimized under Catherine bubbled to the surface during Paul's reign. While his mother emphasized civil administration and civic

FIGURE 7.2. Paul I. (V.L. Borovikovsky, *Portrait of Pavel I.,* 4957. Courtesy of the State Tretyakov Gallery)

development, Paul was a militarist above all. While Catherine emphasized reason and thoughtfulness, her son was often irrational and quixotic. While his mother tried to encourage and lead her people, or at least her officials and the educated public, into accomplishing what had to be done in their and the state's interest, Paul gave orders with little or no explanation.

In Paul's defense, however, his background may partly account for his instability and failure as a ruler. Although he was undoubtedly an illegitimate son, Paul was accepted by all as the legitimate heir. Catherine, a strong-willed mother, found it difficult to mold Paul as she would have liked. In addition, she continually feared him since he had a stronger claim to the throne than she and could always serve as a rallying point for opposition, should it develop. Consequently, fairly early in her reign, when Paul was still a young man, she shunted him aside. He was kept out of state affairs and encouraged to busy himself with military training, which he loved, on his own estates near St. Petersburg.

Moreover, because Catherine lived well into her sixties and reigned for over thirty years, Paul had to wait a long time for the throne and had plenty of opportunity to build up resentment against his mother, her advisors, and their policies. Finally, near the end of her reign, Catherine indicated fairly clearly that she would probably name her grandson Alexander (who became Tsar Alexander I) as her successor; he was a handsome and intelligent young man, who, with his brother Constantine, had been taken away from Paul and his wife at an early age and reared by grandmother Catherine with tenderness and in accord with "enlightened" principles. In short, Paul had a good deal to be disgruntled about when his mother died unexpectedly in late 1796. Since she had not yet named a successor, Paul ascended the throne at the age of forty-two.

Not unlike his father, Peter III, Paul instituted some progressive measures in his short reign, encouraging religious toleration and education and attempting to have the obligations of serfs defined and limited. He also finally settled the succession issue that had created such political turmoil throughout the century, decreeing that the throne was to pass to the eldest male heir. But both his policies and his style upset the nobility and the bureaucracy, on whom the administration and welfare of the state mainly depended. He was high-handed, which was bad enough, but also inconsistent and unpredictable. As one critic put it, his reign could be characterized as "Order, Counterorder, Disorder." Paul tried to enforce Prussian-style discipline on the army and conducted endless parades and drills, all of which antagonized both officers and enlisted men. Moreover, he seemed completely insensitive to the feelings of either individuals or the citizenry as a whole, perhaps because he was wholly self-centered and made a bit giddy by the assumption of despotic power after waiting so long. He reportedly told a senior official on one occasion, "The only person in Russia who is important is the person I am speaking to, and only as long as I am speaking to him."

Paul was thoroughly conservative and probably little understood and cared little for the ideas of the Enlightenment or the aspirations of his mother. He tightened censorship, relied on political repression, and joined the European coalition against revolutionary France. But as in other matters, his foreign policy was contradictory and unpredictable. In 1800, disgusted with his allies, Paul switched sides, joined Napoleon, and ordered some Don Cossacks to set off in a foolish attempt to oust the British from India. His alliance with France may have been the final straw in the developing resistance to Paul's rule, and in early 1801, he was deposed and killed in yet another coup d'état.

CONCLUSION

By the end of the eighteenth century, the Russian Empire was largely what Peter and Catherine had made of it. In many respects, Catherine completed what Peter had begun, adding, however, a more reasoned and humane touch to the changes affecting society. The result was a country of extreme contradictions: it was Europeanized in elite culture and thought, military affairs, and even technology, but deeply traditional in popular culture, religion, social system, and agriculture; it was a leading power of Europe politically, but had an arbitrary and repressive autocracy and a relatively backward economy; it had a modern educational system as well as an ordered and even "enlightened" administration that supervised a degrading and inefficient social system and relied heavily on censorship and coercion.

The Russian Empire's historical experience differed from that of Western Europe, and even the most passionate Westernizer in the realm knew this. Nonetheless, the empire could not turn its back on Europe with its new ideas and inventive technologies—the empire had to exist in and adjust to a European-dominated world. Neither Peter nor Catherine had found a magic formula to blend the best of Europe with the best of their state, but none probably existed, and none of their successors fared any better.

To Catherine's great credit, she demilitarized the society, tried to improve governance, promoted education, helped found a national culture, and confirmed the nobility in their rights while trying to inspire them to higher ideals of rationality and service. On the other side of the ledger, however, she was unable to cope with the problem of serfdom, she enhanced autocratic power without removing its inherent arbitrariness, and she expanded imperial rule over Poles, Ukrainians, and non-Slavs with little moral or other justification. On balance, one has to conclude about the fascinating Catherine that she did what she could, which may not have been enough for the Russian Empire's needs, but was far more than her immediate predecessors and most of her successors accomplished.

FURTHER READING

Alexander, John T. *Catherine the Great: Life and Legend.* New York: Oxford University Press, 1989.

Catherine II. *The Memoirs of Catherine the Great.* Translated by Lowell Blair. New York: Bantam Books, 1957.

Garrard, J. G., ed. *The Eighteenth Century in Russia.* Oxford: Clarendon, 1973.

Kamenskii, Aleksandr. *The Russian Empire in the Eighteenth Century: Searching for a Place in the World.* Translated and Edited by David Griffiths. Armonk, NY: M. E. Sharpe, 1997.

Kelly, Catriona. *A History of Russian Women's Writing, 1820–1992.* Oxford: Clarendon, 1994.

Leonard, Carol S. *Reform and Regicide: The Reign of Peter III of Russia.* Bloomington: Indiana University Press, 1992.

Madariaga, Isabel de. *Russia in the Age of Catherine the Great*. New Haven, CT: Yale University Press, 1982.

Marrese, Michelle. *A Woman's Kingdom: Noblewomen and the Control of Property in Russia, 1700–1861*. Ithaca, NY: Cornell University Press, 2002.

McGrew, Roderick E. *Paul I of Russia, 1754–1801*. Oxford: Clarendon; New York: Oxford University Press, 1988.

Raeff, Marc. *Origins of the Russian Intelligentsia: The Eighteenth-Century Nobility*. New York: Harcourt, Brace & World, 1966.

———. *Understanding Imperial Russia: State and Society in the Old Regime*. Translated by Arthur Goldhammer. New York: Columbia University Press, 1984.

Ragsdale, Hugh, ed. *Paul I: A Reassessment of His Life and Reign*. Pittsburgh, PA: University Center for International Studies, University of Pittsburgh, 1979.

Ransel, David L. *The Politics of Catherinian Russia: The Panin Party*. New Haven, CT: Yale University Press, 1975.

———. *A Russian Merchant's Tale: The Life and Adventures of Ivan Alekseevich Tolchënov, Based on His Diary*. Bloomington: Indiana University Press, 2009.

Rogger, Hans. *National Consciousness in Eighteenth-Century Russia*. Cambridge, MA: Harvard University Press, 1960.

Whittaker, Cynthia Hyla. *Russian Monarchy: Eighteenth-Century Rulers and Writers in Political Dialogue*. DeKalb: Northern Illinois University Press, 2003.

Wirtschafter, Elise Kimerling. *Social Identity in Imperial Russia*. DeKalb: Northern Illinois University Press, 1992.

CHAPTER 8

AUTOCRACY, DISSENT, AND FERMENT, 1801–1855

An icy gust of wind from the Neva River swept across St. Petersburg's Senate Square, causing the soldiers drawn up in ragged ranks to hunch down into their tunics. Eyes watering from the cold, they looked about vainly for a sign from their officers. Some units had been there since early that wintry morning, December 26, 1825. For two weeks, confusion reigned over who would succeed the deceased tsar, Alexander I. His oldest brother, Constantine, had renounced the throne in favor of a younger brother, Nicholas, in accord with a secret memorandum approved by Alexander several years earlier. But when Alexander died, Nicholas, reluctant to appear a usurper, had hesitated, providing an opportunity for a group of revolutionary army officers to attempt to seize power. They called out elements of four regiments, some three thousand troops in all, to demand that Constantine be made tsar. The Decembrists, as the dissident officers came to be called, wanted a number of liberal reforms in the Russian Empire, but the soldiers understood little of this, as is illustrated by the apocryphal story that they clamored for "Constantine and Constitution," believing the latter (a feminine noun in Russian) to be the name of Constantine's wife.

Earlier that morning, the soldiers shot and fatally wounded their commanding general when he had appeared to persuade them to surrender. A high church official, Metropolitan Seraphim, had fared better when he appeared in full vestments and bearing a cross to appeal to them to give up: the soldiers had merely shouted at him to retire to the cathedral and pray for their souls. The future tsar, Nicholas I, had himself barely escaped when he met a company of disheveled and disgruntled soldiers in the nearby Palace Square in midmorning. Intending to put the men in formation, Nicholas, without identifying himself, called, "Halt!" to which the troops replied, "We're for Constantine." To avoid a confrontation, Nicholas simply told the unit it should go to the Senate Square to join their comrades who were already there.

By afternoon, the impasse between the rebels ranged in front of the Senate Building and some twelve thousand loyal troops confronting them across the square remained unbroken. The two top leaders of the Decembrists were nowhere to be found at this crucial moment, and junior conspirators were uncertain what to do.

Because of St. Petersburg's northern latitude, in mid-December, dusk comes to the city as early as three in the afternoon. Fearing that the rebellion might spread under cover of darkness, Nicholas finally ordered his artillery to fire grapeshot at the mutineers. Some sixty or seventy were killed, more were wounded, and the rest fled. One hundred and twenty-one leaders of the Decembrist movement were arrested, of whom five were put to death after an official investigation and trial. Decisive action might have carried the day for the revolutionaries, but since their goals and motives were vague and unpublicized, it seems unlikely they could have succeeded in the long run.[1]

What sort of society were the Decembrists rebelling against? By the early 1800s, the Russian Empire was a huge but economically underdeveloped country, profoundly conservative yet with the first stirrings of revolutionary ferment, powerful militarily but inherently weaker than its Western rivals, and socially repressive despite spreading education and bursting cultural creativity. In this chapter, we will explore these paradoxes, focusing in turn on the empire's serf economy, political stagnation punctuated by reform efforts under Tsars Alexander I (1801–1825) and Nicholas I (1825–1855), the flowering of literature and the arts, the development of revolutionary ideas, and the empire's dominant role in Europe and Asia. We will sketch the picture of what was in many respects a faltering giant: a great empire with endemic structural weaknesses, a socially divided citizenry, and uncertain and conflicting values.

By the early 1800s, the Russian Empire included 41 million people, as compared with 26 million in France, 18 million in Great Britain, and 8 million in the United States. Geographically, it stretched from central Europe to the Pacific Ocean and from the Arctic to the Black Sea. Although Russians were the majority ethnic group, other Slavs such as Belarusians and Ukrainians, along with Germans, Finns, Jews, Tatars, Baltic peoples, and Asians of various nationalities also lived in the empire. Most Slavs were overwhelmingly Orthodox in religion, but there were also significant numbers of Catholics, Lutherans, Jews, and Muslims. Official policy increasingly advanced Russification, a policy that imposed the Russian language, culture, and imperial administration on all subjects. The government also encouraged Russian Orthodoxy as the preferred faith. Fewer than 2 million people lived permanently in towns and cities. The imperial capital St. Petersburg had the largest population, 308,000 inhabitants, with Moscow next at 270,000.

An authoritarian government headed by the autocratic tsar and run by an extensive bureaucracy managed this huge and diverse empire. Administration was cumbersome, inefficient, and often venal. Civil liberties were limited, and censorship, arbitrary actions, and repression were common. Some four hundred fifty thousand people were nobles, but the largest landholders and serf owners totaled less than thirty thousand individuals. Two million people served in the military, and another two million were clergy, merchants, artisans, and urban laborers. All the rest, almost thirty-seven million subjects, were privately owned serfs and state peasants. State and society were richer than they had been in the eighteenth century but were rapidly falling behind the wealth and progress of Western Europe.

Most imperial subjects were formalistically religious, little educated, vaguely loyal to the tsar, and increasingly resentful of the harsh life they endured and of the privileged elite who appeared to reap the benefits of their sacrifices. Within imperial Russian culture as a whole, and particularly among the educated elite, a deep-seated and divisive clash of values was developing. On the one side were secular, rational, worldly ideas and attitudes associated with the European Enlightenment. Opposed to them were religious, emotional, traditional views and feelings derived from the old Kievan Rus' and Muscovite cultures. Eloquent spokesmen for both positions and philosophies arose, and a lively debate ensued throughout the 1800s.

THE SERF ECONOMY

Since much of imperial society and the economy were built on the peasantry and the system of serfdom, we need to take a closer look at rural life and its institutions. The primary social unit was the extended peasant family, which customarily included grandparents, parents, and children, with a son's wife moving into his family's household. The dominant authority in the family was normally the senior male, but if such an individual were absent or incapacitated, a grandmother or mother could fill the role. The family unit shared work and property and held joint responsibility for taxes and other obligations.

Marriage, usually arranged, took place early in life. Women bore children almost annually since the household needed workers, and 45 percent of children died before their fifth birthday. Peasant huts were small, crowded, dirty, smelly, and, in cold weather, smoky, as the one stove was poorly ventilated. Except in times of famine, peasants had enough to eat, probably faring as well or even better than European farmers of the same era. Disease and the chance that young males might be taken for twenty-five years' service in the tsarist army were constant threats. Many peasants looked to God, spirits of nature, or a "good tsar" to protect them in adversity.

Imperial Russian villages were clusters of dwellings, usually laid out side by side along one or two muddy streets, averaging forty to fifty houses and several hundred to a thousand people. Each small dwelling had space within it for animals, such as a few cows, pigs, geese, or chickens, as well as a tiny orchard and vegetable garden in back. In most villages, the surrounding lands were divided into grazing, timber cutting, and tillable fields (the same held for the lord's acreage). Each household had the right to farm strips of land in the crop fields.

A collective village institution, the *obshchina*, or commune, whose forerunner arose in Kievan Rus' times, allocated these farming strips among households, usually every ten years, on the basis of the size and needs of the household. Composed of heads of all the households in the village, the obshchina made general agricultural decisions, such as what and when to plant, but each household worked its strips individually. The obshchina was also responsible as a whole for a village's general obligations: work or payments to the lord, taxes, and conscripts for the tsarist government.

In central and southwestern Russia, serfs worked the lord's land as well as their own; in other parts of the country, serfs and state peasants owed payments in produce or money in lieu of labor on the lord's fields. Depending on the size of his landholdings, his financial situation, and his inclinations, a noble landowner might closely supervise farming on his estate or show little or no interest in it, leaving agricultural decisions almost entirely to overseers and managers. During the nineteenth century, the financial position of most noble landholders declined markedly, and by midcentury, well over half of them were in debt.

Even this cursory description of the agricultural system demonstrates its inefficiency and low productivity. Serfs and state peasants had little incentive to produce since a good part of the fruits of their labor went to the lord or to the state in the form of taxes. Moreover, even an ambitious peasant was restrained by having to tailor his farming to the pattern set by common obshchina decisions on sowing, tilling, and harvesting. Nobles had little incentive to invest in agriculture or to introduce new farming techniques. As long as their estates produced enough for them to live comfortably, they were content to follow traditional practices. As a result, the land as a whole produced only a modest surplus, enough to feed the cities and to export a bit to Western Europe, but not enough to accumulate rapidly the capital needed for large-scale industrialization.

Nevertheless, even had there been general recognition that the serf economy was not very efficient or productive, changing it would have been difficult.

As an institution, serfdom remained a useful administrative and social mechanism. It permitted the nobles and the government to control the bulk of the population, maintaining the peasants at a subsistence level. The nexus of lord, commune, and household facilitated keeping order, collecting taxes, and manning the army. Moreover, because the system was so widespread and because so much of privileged imperial society appeared to depend on serfdom, most officials feared the social disruption its abolition would cause. In particular, they were afraid that the nobility would turn against the government. Only a major military defeat and rapidly changing attitudes finally permitted, in 1861, the dismantling of this antiquated socioeconomic system.

The rest of the imperial economy in the first half of the nineteenth century suffered from the same drawbacks that it had in the 1700s, particularly a limited internal market, insufficient capital for investment, state restrictions and interference, and a small and timid entrepreneurial class. At the same time, it did begin to grow, laying the foundations for its remarkable development in the latter part of the century. The number of manufacturing enterprises doubled, while the number of workers increased fourfold. Particularly significant was the increasing use of free hired labor, which led some to conclude that the empire would be better off without serfdom. New branches of production were established, and a major cotton textile industry was developed. Transport and communications were greatly expanded, with the building of canals and railroads and the use of steamships on rivers and seas. Trade and a money economy grew, and the Russian Empire became an exporter of grain and other raw materials to Western Europe. The number and size of towns increased, and the urban population had almost doubled by midcentury.

Despite nascent industrialization and slowly improving productivity, the empire remained essentially underdeveloped with an economy linked too heavily to an inefficient agricultural system. In terms of both economic growth and economic strength, the Russian Empire began to fall markedly behind Western and even central Europe. This trend had two significant results: the empire became increasingly dependent economically on Europe, and though it still played the role of a great power, it remained relatively weak politically and militarily.

THE DILEMMA OF REFORM

At the time, few people were aware of this erosion of the empire's position. Reforms were discussed in the reigns of both Alexander I and Nicholas I, but no fundamental changes in the political and social system resulted, despite

an abundance of new ideas and the first emergence of a revolutionary movement. In part, this stagnation can be explained by the fact that the Russian
Empire continued to enjoy great success as a participant, often even an arbi-
ter, in European affairs. Defeat was needed to force change. But in part, the
"frozenness" of imperial life in this era stemmed from the fact that, under the
autocracy, only the tsar could initiate peaceful change, and neither Alexander I
nor Nicholas I was prepared to undertake radical reform, instead preferring to
tinker with the system.

In particular, Tsar Alexander I disappointed those who looked for new
directions for society. A favorite grandson of Catherine, he enjoyed a privileged childhood and an exemplary education supervised by a private tutor
committed to the ideals of the Enlightenment. He was born and trained to
rule brilliantly. Moreover, he was a striking and charming individual. Tall,
blond, gracious, and with a lively imagination, Alexander I commanded admiration and respect from friends and enemies alike. But he also had an enig-
matic personality and character: restless, vague, inconsistent, and, in the end,
quite mystical. He had difficulty putting his ideas into practice, vacillated on
important issues of state policy, and finally came down much more clearly on
the side of absolutism as opposed to enlightened change.

Some historians have suggested that the uncertainties and vagaries in Alexander I's behavior resulted from his rather tortured upbringing, torn as he
was between his father, Paul, and his grandmother, Catherine the Great, while
trying to please both, as well as from guilt over his father's murder during the
coup d'état that brought Alexander to the throne. Although these are plausible
suppositions, it is important to note that flights of mysticism and erratic action
occurred more often in Alexander's later years and that as a young tsar—he
was twenty-three years old at the time of his accession in 1801—he was quite
decisive and seemingly well balanced.

In fact, Alexander's reign had a promising start. He annulled some of Paul's
most unpopular measures and amnestied a number of people whom Paul had
disgraced, exiled, or imprisoned. Alexander then began regular meetings with
a small group of young and liberal-minded advisors to plan improvements in
society. This coterie, which came to be known as the Unofficial Committee,
discussed frankly what changes should be made in the autocratic system and
whether serfdom should be abolished. All the participants, including Alexander, soon confronted the great complexity and delicacy necessarily involved in
reforming the two major institutions of imperial society. No comprehensive
plan was propounded, but the discussions of the Unofficial Committee did
yield useful administrative changes, including the strengthening of the Senate
instituted in the time of Peter the Great and the establishment of ministries to

FIGURE 8.1. Alexander I. (Heritage Image Partnership Ltd / Alamy Stock Photo)

run various departments of government. Regulations for the personal manumission of serfs were decreed, and serfs in the Baltic provinces were emancipated, though without land. A number of new universities and schools were founded, and the educational system was both extended and improved.

Though the Russian Empire's joining in a European war against Napoleonic France in 1805 interrupted Alexander's concern with domestic issues, he returned to a consideration of reform between 1807 and 1812. The most radical proposal came from Michael Speransky (1772–1839), a remarkably able and far-sighted official, who on the basis of his talent, education, and effectiveness rose from humble origins to become a close advisor of both Alexander and Nicholas. In 1809, Speransky drew up an elaborate system of governance for the empire, which in fact amounted to a constitution. It provided for separation of the administrative and judicial functions of the state as well as for legislative bodies at four levels and the specification and protection of certain rights for citizens. It was a bold plan, and had it been adopted, it would have moved the Russian Empire much closer to the patterns of political development then unfolding in Western Europe. But Alexander put into effect only a small part of Speransky's project, and later, in 1820, he also failed to implement a constitutional proposal submitted by another advisor. At the same time, Alexander strongly supported constitutions for France after Napoleon's defeat and for the kingdom of Poland set up under imperial control after the Napoleonic wars. This anomaly in Alexander's political policies is one of the enigmas of his character that have never been fully explained. In our view, Alexander retained the basic attributes of the autocratic system in the empire outside of Poland in part because he enjoyed the power and authority he wielded and in part because his exploration of radical reform in the deliberations of the Unofficial Committee had convinced him that giving the average Russian a say in government might undermine the whole system and lead to revolution.

In the latter part of his reign, Alexander continued to approve some minor reforms, but also adopted strongly conservative policies in education and social affairs, including a scheme proposed by the reactionary General Alexis Arakcheyev known as military settlements. These were estates and villages inhabited by enlisted soldiers who, between military assignments, farmed the land under strict discipline and harsh conditions. Moreover, Alexander pursued antiliberal policies abroad and spearheaded efforts to suppress revolutionary movements in Europe. Alexander I also maintained a large army and navy, with over 40 percent of the state budget in 1825 allotted to military expenditures.

Alexander's unwillingness to introduce basic reforms to the empire's social system and political order evoked disillusionment, frustration, and despair among those of the educated elite who opposed serfdom and autocracy and favored the institution of civil rights and some form of representative government. Particularly disaffected were numbers of younger military officers, most of whom had served in the campaigns in Europe against Napoleon and been exposed to the liberal ideas of the Enlightenment during their service in France as well as in their education and reading. Largely of noble background, these young men, after their return home, formed secret societies to discuss their hopes and ideas for reform and to plot a course of action. Proud of their country's victory over Napoleon and its role in European affairs, they found themselves ashamed of and distressed by the empire's economic backwardness, social oppression, and political obscurantism; as men of action, they determined to do something about the situation. By the early 1820s, these idealists formed two main groups: the Northern Society, whose moderate leaders espoused a limited constitutional monarchy, and the Southern Society, whose more radical thinkers urged the tsar's overthrow, the establishment of a republic, and possibly the abolition of serfdom.

Reports of these dissident activities reached Tsar Alexander, but he seemed little concerned, probably because he was aware that they involved only a small group with no following among the people as a whole. When confusion over the succession followed Alexander's unexpected death (he was only forty-eight years old), the conspirators seized this opportunity to move against the government. Their plans were not well laid, they were muddled and timid in executing them, and the Decembrist rebellion was a fiasco.

Although many of the Decembrists were noble officers in guards regiments, like their forebears who had participated in seizures of power in the eighteenth century, the Decembrist revolt was not a palace revolution of the traditional type. The Decembrists did not want simply to change tsars but rather to change government and society. In that sense, even though they acted in isolation from the masses, the Decembrists were the first modern revolutionaries in the Russian Empire. Perhaps their goals were idealistic and their methods hopelessly impractical, but the Decembrists had a vision of a better state and a determination to realize that dream. Consequently, they were soon idolized as revolutionary pioneers, and their tradition inspired the empire's revolutionary movements throughout the nineteenth century.

Alexander's youngest brother, Nicholas I, came to the throne at age twenty-nine in late 1825, during the tumult of the Decembrist uprising, and reigned for almost thirty years. Nicholas was militaristic in outlook and deportment. Half Prussian through his mother and tutored by a general, he had felt most comfortable as a youth in military drill and routine. He wanted the Russian Empire to be well ordered, efficient, and strong, and he applied his considerable determination and capacity for hard work to that end. Meticulous about detail, he personally supervised the investigation and trial of the Decembrists, clearly convinced that such dangerous and harebrained activities should never be allowed in a properly run autocracy.

Although reserved, suspicious, and characterized by an almost fanatical sense of duty, Nicholas was by no means stupid, and he was well aware that the empire faced serious problems. In 1842, Nicholas stated candidly:

> There is no question that serfdom in its present state in our country is an evil palpable and obvious to everyone. However, to attack it now would be, of course, an even more disastrous evil.[2]

Nevertheless, he took several steps to mitigate the harshness of serfdom, and decreed that serf families could not be broken up and that serfs could not be sold apart from the land. He also supported directives regularizing and ameliorating the obligations of state peasants. At the same time, he carried out a number of administrative and bureaucratic reforms designed to make the existing system work better. Among the most significant were a massive codification of the law in 1838 overseen by Speransky and a series of financial improvements supervised by his minister of finance, Egor Kankrin.

The government's slogan of "Autocracy, Orthodoxy, and Nationality" summed up the ideology of Nicholas's conservative regime. He reinforced the tradition of the authoritarian state and is reputed to have said, "I regard the whole of human life as service." Defending the prerogatives of the autocracy, Nicholas did not hesitate to resort to arbitrary action, censorship, police surveillance, and harassment to hector the government's critics and suppress dissent. Although the notorious Third Section of His Majesty's Own Chancery, established by Nicholas, was a forerunner of the political police set up by twentieth-century dictatorships, it was quite inefficient and unwieldy and achieved rather minuscule results, despite enormous efforts.

Nicholas strongly supported the Orthodox faith and espoused Russian nationality as a supreme good. He applied Russification measures to the western provinces of the empire, and after the Poles revolted against imperial rule in 1830, Nicholas suppressed the rebellion bloodily and abolished the Polish constitution, replacing it with new regulations that greatly restricted Polish autonomy and repressed Polish culture.

Overall, he maintained and extended the ideal of service to the state, together with the authority of the government. The autocracy and serfdom remained basically unchanged, while the bureaucratic civil service grew to oversee almost every aspect of life. Society was still divided into classes, or estates, with the upper nobility retaining extensive privileges of status, wealth, and influence. Although merchants, artisans, and other free townspeople existed, almost no middle class or bourgeoisie comparable to that in Western Europe developed. This was because the empire had a predominantly agrarian economy and the government dominated all activity: its bureaucrats outnumbered all other nonlaboring and nonagricultural workers, it controlled education and the professions, and it played a leading role in finance, production, and trade. Even the towns were, or had until recently been, predominantly administrative centers. In such a centralized, hierarchical structure, there was no place for independent interest groups or pluralistic inputs to policy and operations. Finally, except among those who espoused the ideals of the Enlightenment, the rights and aspirations of the individual were largely ignored in imperial society. State, church, army, and village commune all stressed the good of the whole community over that of the individual person.

CREATIVITY AND DISSENT

What causes sudden surges of human creativity, such as the Renaissance or the Enlightenment? How can one explain a flurry of brilliant artistic activity, as occurred in the mid-nineteenth-century Russian Empire? In the space of not more than thirty or forty years, a dozen individuals produced some of the greatest works in world literature and Western music. It was an astounding and largely inexplicable performance. Paradoxically, these creative heights were reached at the very moment when imperial society, under Nicholas I, was culturally repressed. The government attempted to block new ideas with censorship and persecution, and the atmosphere was one of stagnation and disillusionment. Moreover, the official and widely held values were mystical and religious, related to the traditional tenets of Orthodox Christianity and the conservative principles of autocracy and privilege. Under such circumstances, how could magnificent secular works of literature and music be written and composed?

It is tempting to answer that the coincident movement of dissent and criticism stimulated this creative flowering, but it is almost impossible to support such a causal connection. Most of the literature was about life, not revolution, and the writers represented a broad spectrum of political and social views. One can only say that artists and revolutionaries existed side by side and that, to some extent, both combined what the empire had learned from Western culture with local traditions and ideals to create brilliant new art and thought. It is also true that both writers and critics of the system moved in the same circles, forming a special group in imperial society known as "the intelligentsia."

This subclass comprised individuals well educated in both local and Western culture whose main focus was intellectual life and discussion and who were deeply concerned about the nature of their own society and the empire's future. The intelligentsia, although its members came predominately from the upper classes, included the sons and daughters of the poorer clergy, of lower-ranked civil servants, and of service and professional townspeople. They worked at all sorts of jobs, from tutoring and teaching to serving in the tsarist army and bureaucracy. Most felt alienated from the government and "official" society; at the same time, though its members did not always acknowledge it, the intelligentsia was almost completely cut off from the peasantry and the small but growing number of workers. They made varying criticisms of the existing situation and system while propounding a wide range of solutions, from conservative to revolutionary. While it is common to make the mistake of equating the intelligentsia with revolutionaries, in fact a majority of the intelligentsia preferred peaceful change in imperial society.

The remarkable outpouring of outstanding literature from writers among the intelligentsia began in the 1820s and 1830s with the poetry and prose of Alexander Pushkin, perhaps the most versatile and lyrical of all writers during the period. His long poem *Eugene Onegin* describes "the superfluous man," the individual who restlessly but in vain seeks a place and purpose in life and society, a story that became the basis of a magnificent opera by Pyotr Tchaikovsky. Unfortunately, Pushkin's brilliant career was cut short when, at the age of thirty-eight, he was killed in a duel. His place as the premier poet of the era was taken by Michael Lermontov, who composed moving romantic poems and also wrote a superb realistic novel, *A Hero of Our Times*. He, too, died in a duel when only twenty-six years old.

Nicholas Gogol, often considered the founder of romantic realism, wrote about everyday life. His rollicking comedy *The Inspector General* and highly enjoyable novel *Dead Souls* satirize rural society and its petty landlords and officials. In such short stories as "The Overcoat" and "The Nose," Gogol, with macabre humor but considerable empathy for his protagonists, depicts the dreary life and outlook of the common person, the downtrodden bureaucrat or citizen struggling to exist in a society filled with pomposity and privilege. Although Gogol was politically conservative, his work was hailed by the radical critics among the intelligentsia who urged that literature be used as a weapon against the evils of government and society.

From the 1850s to the 1870s, three giants dominated literature. Ivan Turgenev's most influential book, *Fathers and Sons*, incisively portrays the conflict between a more moderate, older generation and a new breed of radicals personified by Bazarov, a nihilist who rejects all old values and mores in the name of materialistic science. Fyodor Dostoyevsky, perhaps the greatest of the psychological novelists, depicts daily life realistically in such works as *Crime and Punishment* and *The Brothers Karamazov*. Yet the essence of his books is the conflict between emotions and ideas. He was thoroughly critical of Western materialism and values, while seeing true salvation in a refinement of selfless love attained only through suffering.

Dostoyevsky's contemporary, Leo Tolstoy, remains a favorite epic novelist, best known for the broad sweep and riveting detail exemplified in his lengthy depiction of the Russian Empire's struggle against Napoleon, *War and Peace*. Tolstoy had the knack of making scenes and characters seem more vital and absorbing than reality itself. In the late 1870s, Tolstoy underwent a religious rebirth and became an influential advocate of nonviolence and a devastating critic of the artificiality and immorality of modern life.

Artists of the mid-nineteenth century excelled in music as well as literature. The first great composer in the empire was Michael Glinka, who lived from 1804 to 1857. His operas as well as those of other composers later in the century effectively join classical musical forms from Europe with Russian folk melodies, songs, and stories. This tradition was followed in the 1860s through the 1880s in the works of a group of outstanding composers known as the Mighty Bunch or the Five: Modest Mussorgsky, Nikolai Rimsky-Korsakov, Milii Balakirev, Cesar Cui, and Aleksandr Borodin. Working separately at about the same time was Tchaikovsky. Together, these six composers produced romantic ballets, operas, symphonies, and other pieces that have enchanted lovers of classical music ever since.

While writers and musicians were producing impressive masterpieces, essayists and social critics such as Vissarion Belinsky were engaged in a lively debate over philosophical and political issues. Much of the discussion focused on the nature of society and the direction it ought to follow. Although almost all the debaters were schooled in a common body of European philosophy, especially German idealism, they reached diverse and often conflicting conclusions. Most were optimistic about the empire's future, rejecting Peter Chaadayev's gloomy assessment in 1836 that because "we are not Western or Eastern and have the traditions of neither," the Russian Empire had contributed nothing to world culture.

The two main schools of thought that developed were the Westernizers and the Slavophiles, small informal groups of noblemen intellectuals located mostly in Moscow. The former, as the name indicates, believed that the empire should adapt essential values and institutions developed in the West to the needs of local society. The Westernizers stressed secular and rational thought and were voluntarists; that is, they believed that individuals and groups could act to change and improve society. Looking with favor on Peter the Great, they urged the expansion of education and the reform of imperial institutions. Although some later became revolutionaries, most Westernizers urged the introduction of civil freedom and constitutional government through peaceful, evolutionary change. Two prominent Westernizers, Alexander Herzen and Michael Bakunin, became increasingly critical of the government and went into exile in Europe in the mid-1840s. Herzen became a prominent journalist and mild revolutionary, while Bakunin moved in a sharply radical direction to become a leading anarchist.

The Slavophiles were romantic nationalists who idealized the Kievan Rus' and Muscovite past, rejected Western civilization as a model for imperial Russian development, and espoused a future good society based on the spiritual values of Russian Orthodoxy and the social values of the people, especially as expressed in the peasant commune. At the same time, they were critical of the government and the tsar, arguing that the bureaucracy's interference and the changes introduced by Peter had broken the mystical bond that existed in Kievan Rus' and Muscovite times between ruler and people. It was therefore necessary to restore a simpler, purer form of rule that would both protect the rights of all subjects and give the tsar freedom to act benevolently. The Slavophiles also criticized the Russian Orthodox Church, urging its purification and the widespread propagation of basic ideals. With these changes, the Slavophiles concluded, the Russian Empire could build a unique civilization far superior to Western societies that would contribute constructively to world culture. This visionary future would be based on brotherly love, peace, and harmony. These contrasting attitudes toward the West and differing views of the empire's mission and future remained important issues of intellectual discourse during the nineteenth and early twentieth centuries.

THE RUSSIAN EMPIRE: ARBITER OF EUROPE, COLONIZER OF ASIA AND AMERICA

In the first half of the nineteenth century, many considered the Russian Empire to be the most powerful country in Europe, and the empire played a prominent, if not the dominant, role in European affairs. This position stemmed from its major contribution to the defeat of Napoleon and to the subsequent peace settlement. At the same time, the empire was busy extending its borders, primarily in Asia, where Tsars Alexander I and Nicholas I annexed most of the Caucasus, and expanding its colonies in North America. Finally, throughout this period, the imperial government was deeply involved with the Ottoman Empire (centered in modern-day Turkey), an imbroglio that culminated in the 1853–1856 Crimean War.

Tsar Alexander I came to the throne determined to keep his country at peace, but in the first ten years of his rule, the Russian Empire waged war with Persia (modern-day Iran), the Ottoman Empire, Sweden, and France. The struggle with Persia grew out of a request for protection from the small Christian state of Georgia in the Caucasus. The Russian Empire assisted the Georgians against both Persian and Ottoman incursions and pressures, and by 1810, it had incorporated Georgia and several small neighboring areas (see Map 9.1). Conflict with the Ottoman Empire from 1806 to 1812 and with Sweden in 1808 and 1809 resulted in the empire's acquiring two strategically important territories on its western border, Bessarabia (located in modern-day Moldova and Ukraine) and Finland.

But the main foe during Alexander I's reign was revolutionary France, led by Napoleon. Alexander opposed France because of the empire's political ties to Austria, Prussia, and Great Britain, its close economic relations with Great Britain, and Napoleon's plans for transforming and dominating Europe. Alexander considered Napoleon a parvenu and usurper. Armed conflict raged from 1805 to 1807, but Napoleon soundly defeated the Russian Empire and its allies at the battles of Austerlitz, Eylau, and Friedland. In July 1807, Napoleon and Alexander signed a peace accord at Tilsit, and for the next four years, the two major continental European powers were uneasy allies.

The Tilsit agreement eventually broke down over several issues. First, Napoleon wanted the Russian Empire to adhere strictly to his "Continental System," which was essentially a Europe-wide economic blockade against Great Britain, France's major remaining foe. Not only did many Russian subjects ignore the restrictions and continue to trade with Britain, but to the extent the blockade was observed, it harmed the Russian Empire's export economy, since the English had been the empire's major trading partner over the preceding decades. Moreover, the Russian Empire resented its defeat at the hands of the French and the growing French domination of Europe. The French, in turn, considered the Russian Empire to be an unreliable ally and the only important obstacle to complete French hegemony on the continent. Finally, in addition to other minor irritants in the relationship, the two governments differed over policy in the Middle East, the Balkans, Poland, and Northern Europe.

In June 1812, without declaring war, Napoleon invaded the Russian Empire with the largest military force ever assembled in Europe, known as the Grand Army, which at its height included over six hundred thousand troops. While many of the soldiers in this force were French, Napoleon's reluctant allies in Austria, Italy, Poland, the German states, and elsewhere supplied the remainder of this massive force. Outnumbered more than two to one, the Russian imperial army was forced to fall back steadily before Napoleon's advance. Eventually, in September 1812, imperial Russian troops, under a newly appointed and popular commander, Prince Michael Kutuzov, made a stand at Borodino, a village near Moscow. In one of the bloodiest battles in history, the imperial Russian army lost over one-third of its force, some forty thousand men, while Napoleon's army suffered proportionate losses, over fifty thousand casualties, in just one day. Though the Russian imperial army was forced to retreat, few prisoners were taken, and Napoleon could not destroy the army's remnants. Napoleon entered Moscow unopposed a few days later, believing the capture of the empire's former capital, important economic center, and spiritual home would compel Alexander to surrender. However, Alexander I rejected Napoleon's indirect overtures for peace.

Imperial subjects of all classes rallied patriotically around Alexander and the army, and Napoleon soon found himself in an untenable position. Harassed by Kutuzov's forces, confronting greatly extended communications and supply lines, Napoleon was unable to draw much support from Moscow itself, which had been first evacuated and then partially destroyed by intentionally set fires. Facing the approach of the harsh Russian winter, Napoleon withdrew his forces in mid-October. In one of the great disasters of military history, the Grand Army, weakened by disease, dwindling supplies, the raids of guerrilla bands, and the bitter cold, staggered out of the Russian Empire. Only fifty thousand men out of the original six hundred thousand escaped death or capture. In the succeeding months, the victorious imperial army carried the war to Europe and played a major role in Napoleon's ultimate defeat. The campaign concluded with Alexander's marching into Paris at the head of his victorious troops.

Paradoxically, the triumph of 1812 and 1813 was seen at the time and subsequently as both a source of national pride and a reminder of the Russian Empire's vulnerability to attack from the West. Victory over Napoleon greatly increased the empire's prestige in Europe and ensured it major influence in European affairs for several decades to come. At the same time, it may have led the empire's leaders to consider their country more powerful than it in fact was and, thus, reduced the pressure for basic reforms.

Alexander was a leader at the Congress of Vienna, which worked out a peace settlement for post-Napoleonic Europe in 1815. Under pressure from the other powers, the Russian Empire had to settle for a smaller kingdom of Poland under its rule than Alexander had sought, but the tsar did obtain approval for his formulation of the Holy Alliance, an agreement between the leading monarchs that they would band together to promote peace and Christian brotherhood in the world. Its practical manifestation was the Quadruple Alliance, which consisted of the Russian and Austrian empires along with Prussia, Great Britain, and France, which joined in 1818. The Quadruple Alliance was a powerful political coalition that acted to regulate the affairs of Europe for over a decade. In particular, the alliance, under prodding from Vienna and St. Petersburg, moved firmly to suppress revolutionary movements in various parts of the continent. Although an internationalist in outlook, Alexander I saw collective action primarily as a means of safeguarding the restored order in Europe and forestalling revolution.

Tsar Nicholas I pursued the same goals but did so with such added vigor that he earned the unfortunate sobriquet of "the gendarme of Europe." In 1830, when revolutions broke out in France and Belgium, the Poles also rose in revolt against their imperial masters, and the imperial army had to be employed to restore order there. When revolution again swept across Europe in 1848, Nicholas I sent imperial troops to help quell the uprising in Hungary.

Nicholas also extended the gains his predecessors had made in the Caucasus, acquiring part of Armenia in 1818 and waging a long war against Caucasian mountaineers led by the brilliant and tenacious warrior Shamil. In the Pacific region, Nicholas encouraged the development of Russian America, which included Alaska. In 1867, Nicholas's successor, Tsar Alexander II, sold Alaska to the United States in large part because of the territory's remoteness, competition from Great Britain and the United States, and the perception in St. Petersburg that Alaska had become unprofitable.

Although the Russian Empire had been in conflict with the Ottoman Empire since the sixteenth century, only in the first half of the nineteenth century did the empire's increasingly tense relationship with the Ottomans, known as the Eastern Question, become a major issue in imperial foreign policy. The Russian and Ottoman empires fought four major wars during the nineteenth century for several reasons. As an Orthodox state, the Russian Empire asserted its right to protect Christian minorities living in the Ottoman Empire (particularly in the Balkans), some of whom were fellow Slavs. Officials in St. Petersburg also claimed they should be allowed to manage and safeguard Christian holy places in Jerusalem and elsewhere in the Middle East, preserving them from not only Muslim but also Catholic interference.

A second set of issues centered on economic and strategic control of the Black Sea and the Bosphorus straits, the passage between the Black Sea and the Mediterranean. In the 1800s, the imperial Russian government struggled to obtain the right of free passage through the straits, first for merchant vessels and later for warships.

Finally, relations between the Russian and Ottoman Empires were strained because Ottoman authority in Constantinople (the Ottoman capital), was rapidly weakening. In fact, the Ottoman state became known to its allies and enemies alike as "the sick man of Europe." As Ottoman power declined, the Russian Empire expanded into the Caucasus on the eastern border of the Ottoman state. Even more important was the fate of territories under Ottoman rule in the Balkans on the Ottoman's southwestern border. Balkan peoples rebelled against Ottoman authority in a series of nationalist uprisings, and the great powers, particularly the Austrian Empire, strove to exert influence in the Balkans. Consequently, while the Russian Empire tried to reduce or eliminate Ottoman control over the Balkans, it had to contend with the intrusion of Austrian and later German power there. At the same time, France and Great Britain were eager to prevent an Ottoman collapse, from which St. Petersburg would reap enormous gains, and as Ottoman power eroded, both Paris and London strove to block any excessive gain of influence by the Russian Empire.

In the 1820s, the Greeks rebelled successfully against their Ottoman over-lords, and Greece achieved its independence in 1832 after a long struggle. Recurring anti-Ottoman nationalist struggles also broke out elsewhere in the Middle East and the Balkans during this period. On almost every occasion, the Russian Empire and most other European great powers were drawn into these conflagrations; yet for three decades, a major war among them was somehow averted. In the late 1840s and early 1850s, however, Tsar Nicholas I, who had until then managed imperial policy quite skillfully, made two major miscalculations. He mistakenly counted on British backing and, misled by his emissary in Constantinople, underestimated Ottoman resistance to his state's pressure and demands.

Although the details of the negotiations and the particular issues at hand need not concern us, they resulted in the Ottoman sultan's appeal for support to the European powers, and when the Crimean War broke out between the Russian and Ottoman empires in 1853, France and Great Britain soon sided with the Ottomans. Austria, although not participating, maintained a threatening presence on the Russian flank, and Nicholas found himself isolated and outnumbered. In September 1854, an Anglo-French expeditionary force landed on the Crimean Peninsula. After a grueling campaign, marred by the gross incompetence of the generals on both sides and heavy sacrifices and casualties all around, the imperial Russian forces were defeated. In 1856, the empire had no choice but to sign the humiliating Treaty of Paris.

The Crimean War burst the bubble of the Russian Empire's superpower status in Europe, revealing to the West its military weakness and social and political backwardness. Although the empire continued to play a significant role in European affairs for the next sixty years, its position was now that of a second-rate power. Even more importantly, the war displayed in glaring fashion to the new tsar, Alexander II (Nicholas I died in 1855), and to the imperial elite the country's serious internal problems and the urgent need to reform both its archaic socioeconomic system and its cumbersome, inefficient government.

CONCLUSION

In several respects, the history of the Russian Empire in the first half of the nineteenth century represented a golden opportunity missed. With a burgeoning population and a slowly rising level of education, the imperial government, drawing on the experience of neighboring Europe, could have accelerated the state's economic growth and initiated processes of industrialization and modernization. Instead, the Russian Empire, although developing slowly, fell markedly behind the booming economies of western and central Europe. This inferior position left the Russian state considerably weaker than its great power rivals for the remainder of the nineteenth century and into the twentieth.

In order to move ahead economically, the imperial government would have had to abolish serfdom and greatly reduce its overbearing and stultifying intervention in all aspects of social, economic, and political life. To contemporaries, it seemed that Alexander I, the favorite of Catherine, a child of the Enlightenment, and a man of imagination and ability, could have been the perfect leader to undertake these necessary changes. Yet Alexander's complex personality and enjoyment of power prevented him from grasping the prickly handle of reform, even after his glorious triumph over Napoleon. Constitutional projects languished, and serfdom continued. Out of frustration with the lack of progress came the 1825 Decembrist Uprising and, in the 1840s, the beginning of a revolutionary movement among the intelligentsia.

Under Nicholas I, hopes for reform dimmed, given his character and outlook, with the result that the Russian Empire marked time, its social problems festering and its political climate frozen. Nicholas could wield the empire's great power status in Europe, and the empire's international prestige was high, but its humiliating defeat in the Crimean War burst even this bubble.

By 1856, imperial Russian society was in a fairly desperate situation. Much of its educated elite, although participating creatively in European culture and bringing renown to their country in such fields as literature and music, were alienated from the government and out of touch with 90 percent of the population, which remained uneducated, burdened, and a potential revolutionary force. Underdeveloped economically, repressed politically, and divided socially, the Russian Empire nevertheless continued to absorb European values and modernizing influences and tried valiantly to compete with Western societies that were already stronger and moving rapidly in quite a different direction. It was urgent that the empire seek its own salvation, find its own path, and move into the modern world on its own terms. The task facing the new tsar, Alexander II, was monumental.

FURTHER READING

Blackwell, William L. *The Beginnings of Russian Industrialization, 1800–1860.* Princeton, NJ: Princeton University Press, 1968.

Friedman, Rebecca. *Masculinity, Autocracy, and the Russian University, 1804–1863.* Houndmills, UK: Palgrave Macmillan, 2005.

Hartley, Janet M. *Alexander I.* London: Longman, 1994.

Hoch, Steven L. *Serfdom and Social Control in Russia: Petrovskoe, a Village in Tambov.* Chicago: University of Chicago Press, 1986.

Lincoln, W. Bruce. *Nicholas I: Emperor and Autocrat of All the Russias.* Bloomington: Indiana University Press, 1978.

Lovell, Stephen. *Summerfolk: A History of the Dacha, 1710–2000.* Ithaca, NY: Cornell University Press, 2003.

Malia, Martin E. *Alexander Herzen and the Birth of Russian Socialism, 1812–1855.* Cambridge, MA: Harvard University Press, 1961.

Martin, Alexander M. *Romantics, Reformers, Reactionaries: Russian Conservative Thought and Politics in the Reign of Alexander I.* DeKalb: Northern Illinois University Press, 1997.

Monas, Sidney. *The Third Section: Police and Society in Russia Under Nicholas I.* Cambridge, MA: Harvard University Press, 1961.

Moon, David. *The Russian Peasantry, 1600–1930: The World the Peasants Made.* London: Routledge, 1999.

Polunov, Alexander. *Russia in the Nineteenth Century: Autocracy, Reform, and Social Change, 1814–1914.* Translated by Marshall S. Shatz. Edited by Thomas C. Owen and Larissa G. Zakharova. Armonk, NY: M. E. Sharpe, 2005.

Riasanovsky, Nicholas V. *Nicholas I and Official Nationality in Russia, 1825–1855.* Berkeley: University of California Press, 1959.

Roosevelt, Priscilla. *Life on the Russian Country Estate: A Social and Cultural History.* New Haven, CT: Yale University Press, 1995.

Wortman, Richard S. *Scenarios of Power: Myth and Ceremony in Russian Monarchy from Peter the Great to the Abdication of Nicholas II.* New abridged ed. Princeton, NJ: Princeton University Press, 2006.

Zhuk, Sergei I. *Russia's Lost Reformation: Peasants, Millennialism, and Radical Sects in Southern Russia and Ukraine, 1830–1917.* Washington, DC: Woodrow Wilson Center Press; Baltimore: Johns Hopkins University Press, 2004.

CHAPTER 9

REFORM, REACTION, AND MODERNIZATION, 1855–1904

During the nineteenth century, crowds in imperial Russia were proud of the country's armed might and loved to watch parades and other military ceremonies. The tsar, the first soldier of the Russian Empire, often presided at these occasions. In that respect, Sunday, March 13, 1881, seemed like many other holidays. Tsar Alexander II, known to many as the Tsar-Liberator for freeing the serfs in 1861, planned to review a parade around noon, then to visit a royal cousin on his way back to the Winter Palace in the heart of St. Petersburg. Unbeknownst to Alexander, however, twenty-seven determined revolutionary terrorists, members of a radical fringe group called the People's Will, had fixed that Sunday as his date of execution.

After four unsuccessful attempts to assassinate the tsar, the terrorists rented a small basement shop in one of St. Petersburg's main streets, from which they halfheartedly sold cheese to disguise their main activity: burrowing a tunnel under the street with the aim of blowing up the emperor's carriage should it pass that way. On March 13, just before Tsar Alexander left for the parade, his mistress had persuaded him not to return by his usual route, which would indeed have taken him along the street in front of the cheese shop. But the terrorists, aware that the tsar often took alternate ways home as a precaution, not only kept a large cache of dynamite in their tunnel under the street but posted five of their number along other streets and squares of the capital. Four of them were armed with a primitive, nearly suicidal bomb of nitroglycerin that had to be tossed at extremely close range; the fifth, Sophia Perovskaia, a young woman of twenty-six from a noble family, was the lookout and supervisor.

As soon as Sophia saw that Alexander intended to take a different route back to the palace, she signaled by hand for the bomb throwers to take up new positions. A short while later, when the imperial entourage started down

FIGURE 9.1. A painting showing a bomb exploding under Alexander II's carriage during his assassination by terrorists, March 1881.

a street called the Catherine Canal Embankment, Nicholas Rysakov stepped close to the carriage and hurled his weapon (see Figure 9.1). The explosion wrecked the wheels of Alexander's carriage and wounded several onlookers, but the tsar himself was unhurt. Overcome by curiosity and concern for the wounded, Alexander dismounted from the carriage and approached Rysakov, whom the police had instantly seized.

At that moment, a second assassin moved out of the crowd to within a few yards of Alexander and threw his bomb at the tsar's feet. Both Alexander and his assailant were mortally wounded, and both died several hours later. Twenty others were also wounded, and blood was spattered across the snow banked on both sides of the street. Later, the Church of the Savior's Blood was built in St. Petersburg on the spot on the street where Alexander was killed.

Five terrorists were executed, but one of their leaders declared triumphantly, "An overwhelming weight has fallen from our shoulders. Reaction must end in order to make way for the rebirth of Russia." That did not happen, making the terrible events of that gray, late winter afternoon in St. Petersburg only one episode in a continuing pattern of violence, reform, and reaction that marked the second half of the 1800s in the Russian Empire.[1]

In the two decades before his assassination, Alexander II presided over an impressive burst of reforms that considerably altered the old order. With these changes, and under the impact of the country's rapid economic development and social transformation, the Russian Empire moved belatedly down the path of modernization. At the same time, however, retrograde forces—from individual tsars and officials, through most of the landed nobility, down to ultranationalist elements in the cities—strongly opposed reform and tried to bind the empire in a traditional framework. They insisted on long-established values and fought bitterly to preserve privilege and autocratic rule. This reactionary attitude and its reflection in state policy, together with the dislocation and discontent caused by the massive socioeconomic changes taking place as well as a disastrous military defeat at the hands of the Japanese Empire, led to conflict and finally to the Revolution of 1905.

THE ERA OF THE GREAT REFORMS, 1855–1881

In three important respects, the Russian Empire at the time of the accession of Alexander II in 1855 differed markedly from the state his uncle, Alexander I, had inherited half a century earlier. First, the empire was a good deal bigger, both in territory and in population. Finland, Bessarabia, and the Caucasus were added, but even within its old boundaries, the number of inhabitants of the state had increased dramatically, from about forty-one to fifty-nine million people. This meant that the agricultural economy, with little or no increase in productivity, had more people to support and less land per person. The result was widespread peasant unrest. Second, though the economy as a whole was changing, it was falling farther behind that of Western Europe. The first signs of nascent industrialization appeared, the number of free workers grew, and trade and a money economy expanded, while the position of the nobility deteriorated. In these circumstances, continuing the system of serfdom made less and less sense to a number of contemporary observers. Finally, after its defeat in the Crimean War, the Russian Empire was considerably weaker vis-à-vis its rivals in Europe than it had been in 1801.

Alexander II, the eldest son of Nicholas I, ascended the throne in 1855 at the age of thirty-seven, having been prepared for his responsibilities both through tutorial education and occasional participation in state affairs. Conservative in outlook and upbringing, he seemed an unlikely candidate for the role of tsar-liberator. Yet several factors worked to turn Alexander II into an effective reformer. Since he was realistic and hardheaded, Alexander concluded early in his reign that serfdom would have to be eliminated and other changes made if more serious difficulties were to be avoided. He was also patriotic, deciding that if the Russian Empire were to be powerful again, its government

FIGURE 9.2. Alexander II. (Courtesy of the Library of Congress, LC-USZ62–128131)

and social system would have to be brought up to date. Moreover, Alexander, respecting the ability of the senior civil servants charged with implementing change, steadfastly supported them, even in the face of strong noble opposition. Like his predecessors, Alexander had no intention of destroying the autocracy, but unlike them, he became convinced of the need for basic reform if it were to be saved.

This last point is well illustrated by Alexander's famous remark to the Moscow nobility in 1856: "It is better to begin to abolish serfdom from above than to wait until it begins to abolish itself from below. I ask you, gentlemen, to think over how all this can be carried out." Thus, starting with the elimination of serfdom, Alexander launched his series of Great Reforms, which transformed society, but by no means solved all its problems. Affecting some fifty-two million people, over 85 percent of the entire population, ending serfdom in the Russian Empire was at the time the most extensive and influential government-directed social change undertaken in human history. Extremely difficult and complex, the reform was carried out remarkably smoothly and quite effectively.

Opposition certainly existed, particularly among the nobility and some bureaucrats. But the majority of educated society strongly favored emancipation, in our view, for three main reasons. First, the serf system was increasingly indefensible on moral grounds; hardly anyone could support the practice of one person owning another. As education spread in the 1800s, the imperial elite, including many nobles, found serfdom increasingly repugnant. Second, defeat in the Crimean War convinced the empire's military and bureaucratic leadership that a thorough overhaul of the country's antiquated economic and social system was needed. Armaments were outdated, transport and supply had failed during the war, and the state's serf army had no trained reserves. Finally, many people were beginning to realize that, to move ahead, their country needed free labor and expanding industry.

Although oversimplified, the main issue in the reform was who would get how much land. More conservative nobles suggested freeing the serfs without land and compensating the nobles for the loss of serf labor or their rent payments. The most radical position was to provide the peasants with all the land, not only the fields they worked for themselves, but also the landlord's tillable acres, with compensation to the landlord for the land, but not for lost services. The peasants apparently expected to get most of the land, as their proverb suggests: "O lord, we are yours but the land is ours."

For four years beginning in 1857, the terms of the emancipation were discussed in provincial committees of the nobility and in the Main Committee, the government's supervising body for the reform. Details were worked out in editing commissions, and on March 15, 1861, the emancipation manifesto was proclaimed, shortly before the United States freed its slaves. The compromise reached was quite reasonable under the circumstances. It favored the nobility, but not so greatly as one might have expected, given their long role as a privileged elite and the tremendous pressure they exerted on the tsar and the government during discussion of the reform. The peasants did not get as much land as they wanted, but their situation might have been tolerable had they not undergone a population explosion that doubled their numbers over the next fifty years and created a desperate need for land. The provisions of the reform let the landlord keep most of his land and, in principle, gave the liberated peasants what they had traditionally farmed. In practice, and particularly in central Russia, where land was most valuable, the peasants received some 10 to 25 percent less land than they had previously tilled. Moreover, the government compensated the landlord for the lost services of his serfs and collected this amount from the peasants in so-called redemption dues spread over forty-nine years. This became a heavy burden, which the peasants could not pay in the long run.

Because it was a useful social and administrative device, the reformers retained the *obshchina* (peasant commune), with two unfortunate effects. It meant the peasant was still bound to the village and its collective assembly, which determined when and how they would farm as well as their share of taxes to the government. As some cynics observed, the peasant, far from being emancipated, exchanged one master (the landlord) for another (the obshchina). However, as the peasant had always been part of the commune, this undoubtedly rankled less than their failure to obtain all the land. But keeping the obshchina also meant the peasant remained a second-class citizen, with special status and institutions and without the same standing as other subjects of the tsar. In fact, the government, concurrent with the emancipation, introduced new peasant courts and local organs of government (the *volost* system).

However much the terms of the emancipation favored the interests of the nobles, this arrangement did the nobility little good since few nobles were able to manage their estates profitably, and noble indebtedness steadily climbed in succeeding decades. The peasants' situation also deteriorated because of a population explosion combined with scarcity of land. In addition, having to stay in the commune dampened individual initiative, and the productivity of peasant farmers, even as free laborers, remained low.

Nevertheless, the emancipation had two important positive results: it removed a moral and economic millstone from around society's neck, and it provided a supply of free labor for development of agriculture and industry. Available for hire were household serfs who were freed without land and serfs who took "beggars' allotments," quarter-shares of land in exchange for no redemption dues, which proved too small to support them. In addition, some landed peasants left the village temporarily for off-season work in factories.

Most of the other Great Reforms followed the pattern of changes that had occurred earlier in Western society, but they stopped short of providing imperial subjects with full civil liberties or a national representative government. Instead, the reforms made governance of the country more orderly, efficient, and just, but within the framework of autocracy. The judicial reform of 1864 was a good case in point: it provided for trained and independent judges, open and sensible judicial procedures, and equality before the law. It gave the Russian Empire one of the most advanced and fair judicial systems in Europe. At the same time, because no political or constitutional reform accompanied it, the tsarist government was later able to carry out a number of extralegal actions through imperial decrees, administrative regulations, and so-called extraordinary measures, which amounted to a form of martial law.

Other important reforms established partial self-government at two local levels. A series of municipal institutions was created in 1870, and new district and provincial organs called *zemstvos* were set up in 1864. The latter were assemblies whose members were elected separately by all classes: nobles, townsmen, and peasants. Although the nobles predominated and the zemstvos had limited budgets and were restricted to managing only such local issues as education, public works, health, and welfare, they provided excellent training in politics and governance for future liberal opponents of the autocracy and served local needs quite well. While the central ministries in St. Petersburg and provincial governors continued to control most fiscal matters, the police, and economic activity, the zemstvos nonetheless succeeded in many areas.

Other reforms included an extensive reorganization of military affairs, the introduction of universal conscription with a six-year limit on terms of military service, and the creation of a reserve military force. Also, education was expanded and improved, journalism and book printing were encouraged, censorship was eased, and Russian Orthodox parishes and church administration were reorganized.

Taken together, the Great Reforms produced a significant transformation of imperial Russian society, though the core of the political system, the autocracy, remained largely untouched. The reforms served also as a safety valve, releasing long pent-up resentments and promising a better future. At the same time, the reform era aroused false hopes, leading some to believe that more had changed than was the case and encouraging others to dream of a constitutional system and the establishment of full civil freedoms.

For the long run, the reforms' most influential impacts were their stimulation of rapid social and economic change and fostering of accelerated industrialization and modernization. Although an important step in restoring the empire's strength, the reforms may have been too little, too late, as the country's rivals to the west and Japan to the east accelerated the pace of their social and economic development at about the same time, making it even harder for the empire to catch up to them.

TERROR AND REACTION

Although in 1880 and 1881 Alexander did not turn his back on reform, and was at the time considering a semiconstitutional project prepared by a liberal advisor, he disappointed many in the intelligentsia who believed his reforms had not gone far enough and were appalled at his occasional appointment of avowedly conservative ministers. Moreover, events in the 1860s strengthened the hand of those urging the tsar to hold back: outbreaks of student rioting, a revolution in Poland in 1863 that aroused nationalist and conservative feeling in the majority Russian and Ukrainian areas of the empire, and a failed attempt to assassinate the tsar in 1866. Moreover, in some areas, such as religion and education, the state gave conservatives virtually free rein. Religions other than Russian Orthodoxy were repressed, and measures were taken to squelch national movements in Poland and Ukraine. Romantic supporters of the government developed an idealized kind of Slavic nationalism known as Pan-Slavism. Vague and abstract, it argued that all Slavs in Russia and Eastern Europe, as true brothers, should be united in common purpose under the benevolent leadership of the Russian Empire, the largest Slavic country in the world.

A combination of dismay at apparent slips into reactionary policy under Alexander and disillusionment with the limited nature of his reforms produced in the 1860s a new, more radical opposition among the intelligentsia. This "generation of the sixties" voiced more fundamental criticisms of imperial society and espoused more revolutionary solutions than their forerunners of the 1840s. Many were nihilists who rejected old values, institutions, and policies on principle and, according to their detractors, stood for nothing, hence their name. In fact, they did believe in science and rationality, and some, like Nicholas Chernyshevsky, went on to advocate utopian societies of socialist harmony and plenty. In rejecting traditional authority and conventions, they sought a freer, simpler life for all as well as personal liberation. Also among their ranks were a number of able and courageous women who brought to the revolutionary movement a special emotional intensity and moral fervor.

Most revolutionaries of the 1860s favored radical change but urged peaceful means and popular education to bring it about. Their views, broadly categorized as populism, motivated several thousand of them to "go to the people" in the early 1870s. Young radicals went to the countryside to work among the peasantry, whom they idealized as a fount of moral purity and untainted simplicity. The peasants, bewildered and suspicious, did not know what to make of these well-meaning city folk who wanted to help them. A few cooperated, most ignored the populists, and in some case local peasants reported the new arrivals to the police for suspicious activity.

When it was clear that this and other efforts to promote radical change by education, example, and propaganda were having no effect, a small group of revolutionaries, the People's Will, broke off from the mainstream of populism and turned to terrorism. Although numbering probably no more than a hundred, these zealous revolutionaries succeeded in killing more than a dozen prominent officials and frightening much of society. Andrei Zhelyabov, speaking in his own defense at his trial for complicity in the 1881 assassination of Alexander II, explained the revolutionaries' rationale:

This temporary movement to the people showed our ideas to be impracticable and doctrinaire.... From dreamers we became workers. We took to deeds, not words. Action meant some use of force.[2]

The program of the People's Will, adopted a year earlier, also defended violence:

The purpose of terroristic activities . . . is to break the spell of governmental power, to give constant proof of the possibility of fighting against the government, to strengthen in this way the revolutionary spirit of the people and its faith in the success of its cause, and, finally, to create cadres suited and accustomed to combat.[3]

In practice, however, terrorism and assassination repelled much of educated society, puzzled the peasants, and strengthened conservatives' position and determination. Thus, the era of the Great Reforms ended not only in the murder of the Tsar-Liberator but in a period of reaction and counterreform that immobilized political life in the empire for twenty-five years.

Since Alexander III (1881–1894), who became tsar at age thirty-six, greatly admired his grandfather, Tsar Nicholas I, the striking parallels between their reigns were perhaps no accident. Both rulers came to the throne after periods of change and reform that had ended in tragedy: a revolt and an assassination. Both were determined to restore law and order, both wanted a well-regulated and efficient state, both believed in the sanctity and power of the autocracy, and both were ardent ethnic Russian nationalists. To some extent, both also reacted against their predecessors' policies. Alexander III had never been close to his father, and in the last years of Alexander II's reign, the son had deeply resented the father's open flaunting of a mistress.

Whatever personal and psychological reasons might have influenced Alexander III to reject his father's reform policy, it is also clear that he did not believe further change would be good for the empire. From the late 1860s, long before he came to power, he had increasingly adopted a traditional and religious outlook consonant with the philosophy of his former tutor, Konstantin Pobedonostsev, a conservative intellectual who served after 1880 as head of the Holy Synod, the council that managed the affairs of the Orthodox Church. Pobedonostsev was highly critical of the Great Reforms and believed wholeheartedly in defending and buttressing the tsar's autocratic power. He stressed moral values while sharply criticizing science, materialism, and the empire's growing industrialization.

Austere, not especially bright, and somewhat self-righteous, Alexander III did his best to turn back the country's clock, a singularly inappropriate effort as the empire's society and economy were at that very moment changing rapidly and fundamentally. Consequently, political retrenchment made subsequent readjustment efforts more difficult. The only areas in which Alexander III's administration took account of the new realities were fiscal policy and labor legislation designed to ameliorate slightly the dreadful conditions under which the empire's new working classes toiled.

Otherwise, stern repression and systematic reaction ruled. For example, in the countryside, although unable to reverse the emancipation of the serfs, Alexander III and his conservative advisors created a new instrument of control that bypassed both the existing administrative framework and the earlier institutions of volosts and zemstvos: the post of land captain, an official charged with supervising all rural affairs and granted both judicial and administrative authority in direct violation of the separation of functions sought by the reformers of the 1860s. Alexander III and his counterreformers also limited the jurisdiction and effectiveness of the self-governing zemstvos and the municipal institutions that were set up under Alexander II.

At the level of the central government, little was done to modify autocracy, but the complexity of governing a slowly modernizing society meant in fact that Alexander III had to rely, more than any of his predecessors, on the state bureaucracy, which on occasion blocked some of his reactionary measures. Most policies were approved, however, including tight restrictions on the press and universities, and Alexander III did not hesitate to resort to extralegal steps, such as sending opponents into exile in Siberia and decreeing areas of the empire subject to stringent "temporary regulations," which amounted to extralegal punishment.

A dedicated nationalist, favoring, as one observer put it, "Russian principles, Russian strength, Russian people," Alexander III disliked Germans and detested Poles and Jews. During his reign, anti-Semitism flourished. Admission quotas for Jews in secondary schools and universities were established, and restrictions limiting Jewish habitation to the so-called Pale of Settlement, an arc of territory in modern-day Belarus, Latvia, Lithuania, Moldova, Poland, Ukraine, and western Russia where Jews had traditionally lived, were enforced. The first pogroms, or riots, directed against Jewish property and Jewish individuals occurred, if not with government encouragement, at least with government indifference. In the non-Russian territories of the empire, Russification policies begun earlier in the nineteenth century were greatly intensified, provoking nationalistic resistance among many ethnic and religious groups.

In 1894, Alexander III died unexpectedly of a stroke, and his son Nicholas II ascended the throne at the age of twenty-six. More intelligent than his father but not broadly educated, Nicholas was weak-willed and irresolute, perhaps because his father had tyrannized him. Although a devoted family man and quite charming when he wished to be, Nicholas was also suspicious and narrow-minded. He had few qualities necessary to lead a complex society in turbulent times. He did not really understand the swift changes taking place in the empire and remained committed to preserving the autocracy and traditional values. Early in his reign, he labeled the aspirations of a group of liberal aristocrats for limited representative government as "senseless dreams," and during the first decade of his rule, he continued his father's reactionary policies. He also supported Russification, extending it even to Finland, which had enjoyed some autonomy since it came under imperial rule in 1809.

Nicholas, however, could be influenced by powerful personalities, and he supported for a time the program of economic modernization advanced by his minister of finance, Sergei Witte. An individual from nonnoble origins who worked his way up in government service by talent, hard work, and imagination, Witte typified the new bureaucrats emerging in the latter half of the nineteenth century. He believed fervently that if the Russian Empire were to remain competitive with European nations, the state would have to modernize, particularly by exploiting its natural resources and building up its economy. He supervised what has been called "the Witte system," which included subsidies and tariffs to promote heavy industry and exports; extensive borrowing from abroad to accelerate industrialization; stabilization of the fiscal system, including adoption of the gold standard; the building of railroads; and the accumulation of capital by selling grain in European markets. Witte was astonishingly successful, but the cost to the peasantry was heavy, contributing to widespread agricultural disorders that began in 1902 and lasted off and on through 1907.

ECONOMIC AND SOCIAL MODERNIZATION, 1861–1905

Witte's efforts were part of a larger process of economic and social development that swept over the Russian Empire in the forty-odd years from the emancipation of the serfs in 1861 to the Revolution of 1905. The newly freed peasants were perhaps least affected by these sweeping changes in society, but even they felt the impact of rapid modernization. In the first place, new factories and workshops drew heavily on peasant labor. At first, peasants worked in industry primarily on a seasonal basis, returning to their villages for key agricultural tasks such as sowing and harvesting. But later, they resided permanently in the cities, perhaps leaving their families in the countryside until they could earn enough to support them in town. Under either arrangement, part of their wages went to paying their share of village and communal taxes. In the second place, improved transportation and communication meant that new ideas, including appeals for revolution, spread across much of the empire. If not fully aware politically, peasants at least began to think about joint action against the landowners and the government.

Historians differ about the peasants' economic situation after emancipation. Some argue that their standard of living declined, particularly for those in the densely populated "black-earth" provinces in what is today southern Russia. Others believe that the peasants lived reasonably well and developed a more balanced diet in the late 1800s. This increased prosperity may have led peasants to want more (such as more land, better tools, and new crops), and resulted in a revolution of rising expectations that threatened social and political stability. All agree that the peasant population more than doubled in this period, increasing on an average by eight hundred thousand persons a year and reaching almost one hundred million by 1905. Although some peasants emigrated to Siberia and to the far reaches of the empire in Asia, their numbers were far fewer than the natural increase of people. This population boom resulted in part from improved conditions of health and public order in the villages. Peasants also ate better, and some areas widely adopted a new and reliable crop, potatoes, to add variety and carbohydrates to the customary rural diet of coarse rye bread and cabbage. Peasants may also have had a more positive attitude about the future as a result of emancipation and so risked having ever-larger families.

This population explosion soon produced a shortage of land. From 1861 to 1905, the average size of a peasant's share of communal land decreased by 46 percent, and his livestock holdings dropped by one-third. The price of land doubled. By 1900, the peasants' redemption dues were 119 percent in arrears. A serious famine occurred in 1891, and extensive peasant disorders broke out in 1902 and 1903. Yield per acre increased in the late 1800s, but the obshchina system of collective ownership and farming provided little incentive to improve farming methods or work harder.

To the peasants' difficulties of growing numbers and insufficient land must be added the government's heavy exactions. Quite deliberately, successive imperial administrations from the 1870s onward squeezed the peasantry to support the state budget and help finance industrialization. Three methods were used: direct taxes levied through the commune; indirect taxes on such

FIGURE 9.3. A meeting of village elders, 1910. (© Victoria and Albert Museum, London)

widely used items as vodka, salt, and kerosene; and the purchase of grain at relatively low cost and then its export abroad at higher prices. At times in the 1800s, vodka revenues alone made up one-third of all state income, making the government a chief contributor to public drunkenness and burgeoning alcoholism among much of the male population.

The nobility, as both an economic force and a social class, declined in the postemancipation era. Noble landholding fell by almost 30 percent, and much of the land the nobles retained was mortgaged. Only a small minority ran their farms well or developed large, capitalist-style agricultural enterprises. Another small group went into industry, banking, or professional work, but the majority remained civil servants or barely subsisted on their estates. Still influential at court and in the bureaucracy, nobles nevertheless faced increasing challenges from upstarts from the lower social echelons, such as Witte.

While agriculture lagged and the aristocracy struggled, industry was growing by leaps and bounds. Several factors promoted an industrial boom. First, the Russian Empire, like the United States and Japan, benefited from earlier European experience with industrialization by installing the latest technology and machinery and drawing heavily on European capital for investment. Second, the Great Reforms not only furnished a pool of peasant labor for the new factories but created an atmosphere of legality and stability that encouraged both local entrepreneurs and foreign investors. Finally, the tsarist government actively supported industrialization through subsidies, tariffs, large government orders, and outright ownership of key sectors, such as railroads.

Between 1861 and the 1880s, industry grew at a moderate pace, with the number of factories increasing from about ten to twenty thousand and the value of their output from about two hundred million to one billion rubles. By 1905, the number of factories passed forty thousand, and total output soared to over four billion rubles. Railroad track distance grew from about one thousand to over twenty-five thousand miles between 1860 and 1905. The Russian Empire became a major producer of coal, iron, and petroleum and began to export manufactured goods to Asia and parts of Europe. The empire's rate of industrial growth in the two decades before the Revolution of 1905 was 8 percent a year, equaling that of the United States at a comparable period in its development.

This first surge of industrialization had certain distinguishing characteristics. Production was highly concentrated, both in a few major cities and regions, such as Moscow, St. Petersburg, the Ural Mountains, and Ukraine, and in large factories, such as the Putilov factory, which gathered thousands of workers in one place. This concentration resulted in some economies of scale, but also produced large clusters of workers, giving them greater solidarity and later facilitating the spread of revolutionary ideas among them.

Another special feature of the growth of industry was the dominant role played by the state, both directly through state investment, management, and purchases and indirectly through favorable economic and fiscal policies. The other major bloc of capital for industrialization came from abroad, from European and American investors. Foreign investment in the Russian Empire grew from one hundred to nine hundred million rubles between 1880 and 1900, and by 1914, one-third of all the empire's industry was foreign owned.

The dominance of state and foreign capital in the economy had several important effects. It meant revolutionaries could charge that foreigners and a privileged few around the tsar were exploiting the country, especially its working class. In addition, loans from France helped bind the two countries diplomatically and militarily. Moreover, the prominent role played by the government and foreign investors stunted the development of a capitalist class. Local businessmen never had the economic strength and political clout their counterparts enjoyed in Europe and the United States. They were never powerful enough to force needed political changes, and even when they worked together with the empire's professional classes, as during World War I, they succeeded only in harassing the autocracy rather than reforming it.

The social impact of industrialization on the Russian Empire was much like its effects in Western Europe a half century earlier. Cities expanded in size and number, and the urban population of the state doubled. The number of workers shot up, reaching over 2.25 million by 1905. Most of the proletariat worked and lived under deplorable conditions, as the following excerpts from reports of government factory inspectors in the 1880s show:

> Sanitary conditions in the workers' settlement of Yuzovka [the city of Donetsk in modern-day Ukraine] are highly conducive to the contraction and spread of disease. The market place and streets are full of filth. The air is rotten with the stench from factory smoke, coal and lime dust, and the filth in gutters and organic wastes on streets and squares. . . . The majority of workers live in so-called "cabins" built in the outskirts of the settlement. . . . These cabins are simply low, ugly mud huts. The walls are covered with wood planks or overlaid with stones which easily let in the dampness. The floors are made of earth. These huts are entered by going deep down into the ground along earthen stairs. The interiors are dark and close, and the air is damp, still, and foul-smelling. . . . The furnishings are completely unhygienic, although frequently the workers live here with their families and infant children.
>
> The very worst, most unhealthy conditions I saw were in tobacco factories. . . . The shops where tobacco is chopped and dried are so filled with caustic dust and nicotine fumes that each time I entered one of these rooms I had spasms in my throat and my eyes watered. Yet, even women sometimes work in this atmosphere. . . . Children work in these tobacco factories as wrappers, baggers and packers. There were even children under twelve working there.[4]

In addition, wages were low, hours were long, and the workers were at the mercy of arbitrary regulations and fines imposed by management. Forming unions and striking were prohibited, although as early as the 1870s, the first strikes occurred.

Almost as important as their physical situation in creating a revolutionary frame of mind was most workers' difficulty adjusting to factory discipline and city life. Away from the traditional routine and values of family, village, and church, they sought some new purpose and anchor for their lives. Some fell into drunkenness and petty crime; others readily joined social or discussion groups. Open to new ideas, such workers' circles debated Marxism and other revolutionary creeds under leaders who were usually members of the intelligentsia, not the working classes.

COMPETING IDEOLOGIES

As the pace of economic and social change quickened in the last quarter of the nineteenth century, intellectual ferment accelerated as well. Most educated subjects sought solutions to the empire's problems in two schools of political philosophy that had developed earlier in Europe: socialism and liberalism. Among the intelligentsia, two main categories of socialism emerged in the 1880s and 1890s: Marxism and peasant socialism. After the start of the twentieth century, an organized liberal movement developed. Since all three ideologies played important roles in the revolutionary events of the 1900s, we need to examine each of them briefly.

Writing in Germany, Karl Marx developed his theories in the midst of the Industrial Revolution in western and central Europe. Outraged by the misery and exploitation he saw all about him, he concluded that the promise of freedom and equality trumpeted by the leaders of the French Revolution remained unfulfilled. Marx explained the injustice of contemporary life by arguing that the material world—in society, this meant the economic factor—was the basic reality; under industrialization, therefore, the productive forces (the factories) and the relations of production (factory ownership) determined social, political, and intellectual life. Applying this materialist, or economic, interpretation to history, Marx argued that, powered by conflict between positive and negative forces (the dialectic method), human development would pass, according to immutable laws, through six stages: primitive communism (what we might term today a hunter-gatherer society), slaveholding, feudalism, capitalism, and socialism. When society reached the final phase of history, known as communism, the dialectic contradictions within it would cease and a utopian society for all humanity would begin.

From this set of ideas, known as dialectical and historical materialism, Marx drew certain conclusions about the society around him. Europe, he believed, had passed from feudalism to capitalism in the upheaval of the French Revolution, and another great revolution would be needed to complete the passage from capitalism to socialism. This revolution, Marx was convinced, was inevitable and, in fact, was being prepared by the capitalists themselves. Driven by economic necessity, they were exploiting the workers so unmercifully that the capitalist system, forced into a crisis of diminishing profits and overproduction, would eventually collapse. Confronted with their imminent demise, the capitalists would resist, only to be overthrown by an organized and class-conscious proletariat. By this time, workers would comprise the overwhelming majority of the population, and they would establish a dictatorship of the majority as a transition to a single-class society in which the state as a coercive mechanism would wither away. In the new socialist society, all citizens would own the productive forces, thereby liberating them from the artificial constraints on production imposed by the capitalists. This would produce a superabundance of goods, and each individual could then receive under socialism enough to meet basic needs. At the same time, each socialist citizen, eager to help the whole society, would work and contribute to the full extent of their talents. According to Marx, the socialist or proletarian revolution needed to bring all this about had not yet occurred anywhere in Europe, but the crisis of capitalism was deepening all the time.

At this point, one might wonder how these theories of Marx, so closely tied to the Western European experience and the advanced industrialization of that region, could have any relevance for the underdeveloped, predominantly agricultural Russian Empire. Marx himself never satisfactorily answered this question, although on several occasions he talked optimistically about the possibility that the empire might be able to develop a unique brand of socialism, building on the collective tradition of the peasant commune. In the 1880s, a few revolutionaries, eyeing the rapid industrialization of the empire, began to speculate that Marxism might be a useful political program if it could be adapted to local conditions. Before long, wretchedness and desperation made imperial workers quite willing to listen to any theory that promised to improve their lot and put them in charge, no matter whether its fine points really applied to their society or not.

A few populists, many of whom were in exile in western or central Europe, converted to Marxism, and by the 1890s, several dozen Marxist revolutionaries were active within the empire itself and led workers' discussion circles. An early Marxist was Vladimir Ulyanov, who later adopted the revolutionary pseudonym Lenin. Lenin grew up in moderate circumstances and excelled at school. Not unhappy or deprived, he turned to revolution mainly from idealism, but partly also because his older brother Alexander Ulyanov was executed in 1887 for complicity in a plot to assassinate Tsar Alexander III. Expelled from university for participation in student agitation, Lenin read widely in European political philosophy and the history of revolutionary movements. Lenin later joined the Marxist Russian Social Democratic Labor Party, and in 1897 the state sentenced him to exile in Siberia for propagandizing and organizing labor efforts among the workers of St. Petersburg. Lenin used this time to study and write, and after his exile ended in 1900, Lenin became a leader of the Marxist Russian Social Democratic Labor Party (RSDLP). In 1903, this organization, commonly known as the Russian Social Democratic (SD) Party, split into the Menshevik and Bolshevik (led by Lenin) parties, which we will examine later.

During this period, Lenin and his colleagues engaged in extensive po-
lemics against two competing sets of ideas, which they were convinced would
undercut the development of a strong Marxist revolutionary movement. One
was economism, a view held by some workers and intellectuals that their main
goal should be to improve the proletariat's economic and social conditions.
They sought shorter hours, higher wages, improved factory safety, and decent
housing. The SD Party argued that such a program only deceived the workers. As long as capitalists owned the factories and used their economic power
to control the government (although in the Russian Empire they in fact did
not), concessions wrung from them would be only temporary and inadequate.
The only correct course of action was political: organizing the workers for the
eventual socialist revolution. The SD Party made some headway in its arguments, though in practice it often had to lump the workers' economic demands
in with its Marxist political platform.

The other ideology against which the Marxists struggled was peasant
socialism, which grew directly out of the earlier populist movement. Its proponents argued, however, that instead of education or "going to the people,"
organization and revolutionary activity were the correct weapons for effecting
radical change. The leaders of peasant socialism believed that society could
avoid some of the worst evils of capitalism as it had developed in Europe by
moving directly from its present agricultural, semifeudal system to socialism, drawing heavily on the peasantry and their socialist experience with the
peasant commune. In the 1890s and the first decade of the 1900s, the peasant
socialist movement spread rapidly, and its followers were soon organized as
the Socialist Revolutionary (SR) Party, becoming a main rival of the SD Party
from then on. The SR Party, though counting heavily on the peasants, also
courted workers, establishing cells at factories and workers' settlements and
enjoying considerable success.

Although both SD and SR parties favored revolution to bring about the
changes they desired, large numbers of people in the professions, among the
nobility, and in the civil service opposed using violence and espoused peaceful,
evolutionary reform. They were just as strongly hostile to the tsarist government, but their vision of the future was not socialism but liberalism. This was
a rather loose set of social and political principles that had evolved in Europe
in the nineteenth century, building on the ideas of the Enlightenment and the
experiences of the French and American revolutions of the eighteenth century.
Unlike socialists, liberals had no strict doctrine, but they generally believed in
full civil freedoms; equality for all citizens (including the peasantry); benevolent social and economic reforms with no infringement of private property,
free trade, and laissez-faire economic policies; and some form of representative

government through a constitution or some other mechanism. A few believed in abolishing the autocracy and establishing a republic, but most would have been content to see the empire reformed under a constitutional monarchy over which the tsar could still preside. The liberals also began to organize in the early years of the twentieth century, forming the Constitutional Democratic Party in 1905 (known as the Kadets from its Russian initials, KD).

At about the same time that the socialist and liberal movements were established, nationalism increasingly affected some of the non-Russian ethnic and religious groups within the empire. Polish demands for the reestablishment of an independent Poland, or at the very least for greater Polish autonomy, revived throughout the nineteenth century, culminating in the rebellions of 1830 and 1863 and reviving again in the 1890s. The Finns, particularly after the repression practiced under Nicholas II at the turn of the century, clamored for a separate or autonomous Finland. To a lesser degree, they were joined by the Baltic peoples (Estonians, Latvians, and Lithuanians) and by Armenians and Georgians in the Caucasus. Even more threatening to the centralized structure and policies of the Russian Empire was the emergence of a nationalist movement among Ukrainians. Growing out of a literary renaissance and an interest in Ukrainian history, Ukrainian nationalism was beginning by 1900 to press social and political demands against ethnic Russian dominance.

These threads of disaffection within the imperial state—socialism, liberalism, and nationalism—began to come together in the early 1900s to threaten the tsarist autocracy. Their impact was greatly intensified when imperial society suffered, in short order, an economic and then a foreign policy crisis. The economic emergency was created by a severe depression just after 1900 and by sporadic peasant disorders across a number of provinces in 1902 and 1903. How serious these economic disruptions would have become is unclear because in 1904 they were overshadowed by the empire's involvement in a calamitous war with Japan that helped spark the Revolution of 1905.

FOREIGN POLICY

Before looking at that dramatic revolution, we need to review the way in which developments in foreign policy ended in the empire's going to war. The Crimean War reduced the state's influence in Europe and checked its expansion into the Balkans. But this was only a temporary setback. Before long, the Russian Empire joined its fellow empires Germany and Austria-Hungary in an informal alliance system known the Three Emperors' League that lasted from 1873 to 1887. Involvement in this organization meant the Russian Empire was once again an active participant in European politics and in the European balance of power.

Moreover, the Russian Empire was soon embroiled with the Ottoman Empire again. New crises arose when Ottoman subject peoples in the Balkans tried to fulfill their nationalist aspirations by rebelling and when the European powers, who had lent the Ottoman sultan large amounts of money, were dissatisfied with his fiscal policies and plans for repayment. The Russian Empire would probably have been dragged in anyway, but the sudden upsurge among the educated classes of vociferous Pan-Slavic feeling put great pressure on the government to assist the empire's Slavic and Orthodox brethren in the Balkans.

Between 1875 and 1877, a string of events occurred, any one of which might have been resolved peaceably, but their cumulative effect was to bring the Russian and Ottoman Turkish states to the brink of war. The Ottoman Empire, rejected by Western public opinion after its bloody suppression of a Bulgarian revolt, was prepared to make substantial concessions, but Tsar Alexander II, pushed by inflamed nationalist feeling at home, took the Russian Empire into war against it. After an early defeat, the imperial army's superior numbers brought it a considerable victory, reflected in a preliminary Russo-Turkish peace treaty signed in March 1878 that gave the Russian Empire substantial gains in the Balkans. However, at the Congress of Berlin, a subsequent conclave of all the European powers, the Russian state's spoils were somewhat reduced. After 1885, when the Bulgarians repudiated imperial Russian tutelage, the empire's influence in the Balkans was minimal for the next twenty years. Nonetheless, when new crises erupted in the area after 1908, great power entanglements eventually led the Russian Empire into the conflagration of World War I.

After the Congress of Berlin, European statesmen encouraged the Russian state to look in other directions. Otto von Bismarck, the architect of Germany's unification, who had claimed for himself the role of "honest broker" at the Congress of Berlin, declared, "Russia has nothing to do in the West. She only contracts nihilism and other diseases. Her mission is in Asia. There she . . . stands for civilization." In fact, the empire did expand notably in that direction from the 1840s on (see Map 9.1). At first, the push was into Central Asia, an area of steppe, desert, and high plateaus inhabited by various groups of mostly Persian and Turkic descent. To forestall some of these people's constant raids, the imperial state established control over much of the region in the 1860s and 1870s. The British were alarmed and feared an imperial Russian threat to Afghanistan and perhaps even to British India itself. By the end of the nineteenth century, however, the main focus of imperial Russian interest had shifted to East Asia.

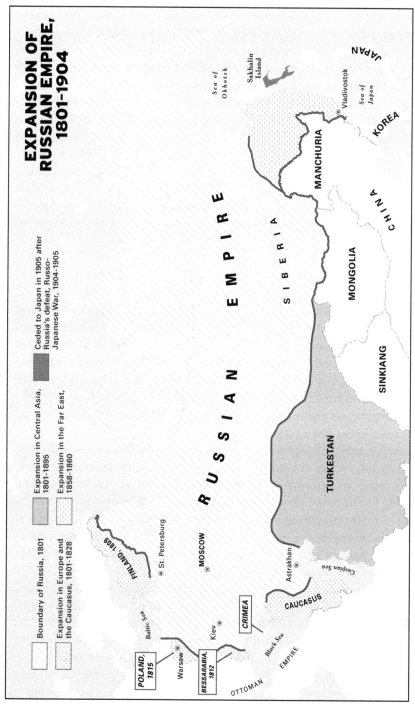

MAP 9.1. The expansion of the Russian Empire, 1801–1904.

At the urging of administrators in St. Petersburg and the empire's eastern reaches, the Russian Empire acquired the northern shore of the Amur River in the 1850s, occupied the southern half of Sakhalin Island north of Japan, and founded the important Pacific port of Vladivostok, meaning "ruler of the East," in 1860. In the early 1890s, the empire began construction on the Trans-Siberian Railroad, which eventually linked Moscow and Vladivostok. By the early twentieth century, the empire was also extending its influence into Chinese-controlled Manchuria and Korea, which Japan coveted for itself. The Russian Empire confronted not only the ineffective resistance of the declining Qing Empire but also the vigorous expansionism of a newly modernized and ascendant Japan, which had recently experienced the transformative Meiji Restoration. This clash of interests led to war with Japan in 1904–1905 and to a major crisis in imperial Russian society.

CONCLUSION

Not since the days of Peter the Great had imperial society been in such ferment as it was in the second half of the nineteenth century. The decision to emancipate the serfs transformed a socioeconomic system that had predominated for nearly two hundred fifty years. Together with the other Great Reforms and growing economic ties with Europe, the abolition of serfdom helped launch an accelerating modernization of the empire's society and economy. By 1900, the Russian Empire was partly industrialized and, with its rich natural resources, had the basis to become a powerful, modern nation.

However, substantial problems remained unsolved. Backward and inefficient agriculture acted as a brake on the economy. Overpopulation and government taxation created a desperate and impoverished peasantry ripe for revolution. In the cities, an uprooted and exploited proletariat listened attentively to calls for action from a spectrum of revolutionary agitators. In the borderlands of the empire, non-Russian minorities, resentful of the government's Russification policies and stoked by nationalist enthusiasm, struggled for autonomy or independence.

These issues, however, might have been ameliorated if only the empire had changed as much politically as it had socially and economically. But sporadically under Alexander II and blatantly under Alexander III and Nicholas II, the imperial government acted to preserve the autocratic system virtually unaltered. The tsar remained an absolute sovereign, and no national policies could be carried out without his sanction. Nor were the people as a whole, not even interest groups among them, to have any say in national governance, whatever small measure of self-government existed at the local level. The tsar needed the bureaucracy to rule, to be sure, but the bureaucracy could do nothing without the tsar's approval.

As a result, the ruling elite became increasingly isolated from the rest of imperial society, and both sides girded for a decisive struggle over what the empire's future should be. As the country changed and the political crisis matured, the empire continued to play a major role in European and world policies. But if it could not resolve its domestic schism, it was hardly strong enough to survive a major showdown on the international stage.

FURTHER READING

Black, Cyril E., ed. *The Transformation of Russian Society: Aspects of Social Change Since 1861*. Cambridge, MA: Harvard University Press, 1960.

Blackwell, William L. *The Industrialization of Russia: An Historical Perspective*. 2nd ed. Arlington Heights, IL: H. Davidson, 1982.

Breyfogle, Nicholas B. *Heretics and Colonizers: Forging Russia's Empire in the South Caucasus*. Ithaca, NY: Cornell University Press, 2005.

Brooks, Jeffrey. *When Russia Learned to Read: Literacy and Popular Literature, 1861–1912*. Evanston, IL: Northwestern University Press, 2003.

Brower, Daniel R. *The Russian City Between Tradition and Modernity, 1850–1900*. Berkeley: University of California Press, 1990.

Emmons, Terence, ed. *The Emancipation of the Russian Serfs*. New York: Holt, Rinehart and Winston, 1970.

Engelstein, Laura. *Slavophile Empire: Imperial Russia's Illiberal Path*. Ithaca, NY: Cornell University Press, 2009.

Fischer, George. *Russian Liberalism: From Gentry to Intelligentsia*. Cambridge, MA: Harvard University Press, 1958.

Gregory, Paul R. *Before Command: An Economic History of Russia from Emancipation to the First Five-Year Plan*. Princeton, NJ: Princeton University Press, 1994.

Heretz, Leonid. *Russia on the Eve of Modernity: Popular Religion and Traditional Culture Under the Last Tsars*. Cambridge, UK: Cambridge University Press, 2008.

Hunt, R. N. Carew. *The Theory and Practice of Communism: An Introduction*. 5th rev. ed. New York: Macmillan, 1957.

Keep, John. *The Rise of Social Democracy in Russia*. Oxford: Clarendon, 1963.

Kolchin, Peter. *Unfree Labor: American Slavery and Russian Serfdom*. Cambridge, MA: Harvard University Press, 1987.

Leonard, Carol. *Agrarian Reform in Russia: The Road from Serfdom*. Cambridge, UK: Cambridge University Press, 2011.

Lincoln, W. Bruce. *The Great Reforms: Autocracy, Bureaucracy, and the Politics of Change in Imperial Russia*. DeKalb: Northern Illinois University Press, 1990.

Maynard, Sir John. *The Russian Peasant and Other Studies*. London: V. Gollancz, 1942.

Menning, Bruce W. *Bayonets Before Bullets: The Imperial Russian Army, 1861–1914*. Bloomington: Indiana University Press, 1992.

Miller, Forrest A. *Dmitrii Miliutin and the Reform Era in Russia*. Nashville, TN: Vanderbilt University Press, 1968.

Mosse, W. E. *Alexander II and the Modernization of Russia*. New rev. ed. New York: Collier Books, 1962.

Pierce, Richard. *Russian Central Asia, 1867–1917: A Study in Colonial Rule*. Berkeley: University of California Press, 1960.

Robinson, Geroid T. *Rural Russia Under the Old Regime: A History of the Landlord-Peasant World and a Prologue to the Peasant Revolution of 1917*. New York: Macmillan, 1949.

Rogger, Hans J. *Russia in the Age of Modernization and Revolution, 1881–1917*. New York: Longman, 1983.

Staliunas, Darius. *Making Russians: Meaning and Practice of Russification in Lithuania and Belarus After 1863*. Amsterdam: Rodopi, 2007.

Stites, Richard. *The Women's Liberation Movement in Russia: Feminism, Nihilism, and Bolshevism, 1860–1930*. Princeton, NJ: Princeton University Press, 1978.

Treadgold, Donald W. *The Great Siberian Migration: Government and Peasant in Resettlement from Emancipation to the First World War*. Princeton, NJ: Princeton University Press, 1957.

Von Laue, T. *Sergei Witte and the Industrialization of Russia*. New York: Columbia University Press, 1963.

Worobec, Christine D. *Peasant Russia: Family and Community in the Post-Emancipation Period*. Princeton, NJ: Princeton University Press, 1991.

CHAPTER 10

REVOLUTION, REFORM, AND WAR, 1904–1917

In the fall of 1905, three men sat inside the cabin of a small steamer that rolled from side to side, but they were oblivious to this motion as they bent their heads over several sheets of paper on the table in front of them. They engaged in animated discussion, and from time to time, one of them corrected the document's Russian script. In less than an hour, they arrived at their destination, disembarking at Peterhof, the country palace of the emperor, Nicholas II. While two of the men waited in an anteroom, the third, Sergei Witte, met with Nicholas and his advisors, including the tsar's uncle, Grand Duke Nikolai. A sense of urgency marked the meeting, for a general strike was paralyzing St. Petersburg, the capital, and riots and disorders were spreading throughout the Russian Empire. It was clear to everyone that decisive action had to be taken promptly.

Witte, who had returned only a few weeks previously to public acclaim for his successful negotiation of a peace treaty with Japan at Portsmouth, New Hampshire, submitted a report to Nicholas II the day before urging reform as the best means of choking off the growing revolution. He now summarized that report and concluded by explaining his view that the tsar had only two alternatives. Either Nicholas could move along a path of reform, or he must choose a dictator to suppress the civil unrest by force. The meeting adjourned without a decision, but was reconvened after lunch, when Witte presented a draft imperial manifesto promising reform, the document that he and his colleagues had been working on during the boat trip to Peterhof. No one raised objections during the meeting, but the next day, the tsar asked other senior officials to make recommendations. Witte, learning this, sent word to Nicholas that he would be willing to head a government committed to restoring order and initiating reform, but only on the basis of the report they had just discussed, without modifications.

The following morning, October 30, 1905, Baron Vladimir B. Fredericks, secretary of the imperial court, explained to Grand Duke Nikolai that since

Witte would be available only on his own terms, the tsar would have to establish a dictatorship after all, and that the grand duke was the logical appointee. Hearing this, the grand duke pulled a revolver from his pocket and exclaimed, "Do you see this revolver? I am now going to the tsar and will ask him to sign Count Witte's program and manifesto. Either he will do this or I shall shoot myself in the head!" Whether the grand duke repeated his dramatic threat to the tsar is unknown, but returning a short while later, after seeing Nicholas, he reported that the tsar would accept Witte's program and manifesto.

After meeting with Witte again that afternoon, Nicholas II signed the document, which was immediately promulgated and became known as the October Manifesto. It only partially succeeded in quelling the revolutionary movement, but it did establish civil freedoms and a limited form of constitutional government, a system that lasted, with some modifications, until the collapse of the autocracy in the Revolution of 1917. That Nicholas was not entirely happy with his decision is shown by what he confided to his diary that night: "After such a day my head began to hurt and my thoughts were confused. God help us and comfort Russia."[1]

Nicholas's "headache" over granting extensive reforms within the empire's autocratic system is understandable. He had come to the throne determined to preserve the autocratic legacy of his predecessors. Yet imperial Russian society was changing rapidly, and when the tide of unrest and revolution threatened to sweep away the traditional system, Nicholas decided his only course was to give only a little ground. The tsar remained committed to the absolutist principle and resented the concessions he was being forced to make. As a result, the period between the Revolution of 1905 and the outbreak of war in July 1914 saw a changing society, but one whose top leadership still clung to an outmoded past. As economic development and social transformation altered imperial Russian life irrevocably, the tsar and his conservative supporters were able to block the evolution of the political system, preserving many old ways of governance. The Russian Empire on the eve of World War I was markedly asymmetrical: an antiquated state structure ruled a modernizing society. Whether the former would eventually have changed enough to synchronize with the latter remains a fascinating but unanswerable question, since the cataclysm of the First World War changed the equation forever.

THE REVOLUTION OF 1905

The early-twentieth-century popular uprising against the tsarist government is known as the Revolution of 1905 because the peak of revolutionary activity occurred in that year. In fact, however, its first manifestations date to 1904, and the revolutionary movement in the countryside and army continued until 1907. During these years, the imperial regime faced a major challenge to its authority, with the breadth and intensity of the opposition reflecting in part the enormous socioeconomic changes that had taken place in recent decades. Comparing the Revolution of 1905 to the Decembrist Revolt only eighty years earlier, one is struck by how isolated from and unrepresentative of the whole society the Decembrists were and how, by contrast, almost every social group participated in the 1905 Revolution.

Some participants came from totally new classes: industrial workers and people from the professions and business. Others, such as the national minorities, were newly aroused, whereas the peasants had a long tradition of rebellion but had never acted countrywide and en masse before. Finally, mutinies in the army and navy marked the first time that military rank and file had risen against authority in Russia. The revolutionary forces' very breadth in 1905 also presented an element of weakness. Each group had somewhat different aims and favored different methods of struggle. Yet the wide range of revolutionary actors—women, middle-class liberals, workers, peasants, non-Russian minorities, soldiers, and sailors—and the spontaneous nature of much of their antigovernment activity clearly foreshadowed the Revolution of 1917, and for these and other reasons, Vladimir Lenin called 1905 a "dress rehearsal" for the more decisive uprising twelve years later.

Russia's 1904–1905 war with Japan triggered but was not the primary cause of the Revolution of 1905, which grew instead out of long-standing grievances, social injustices, and political frustrations in imperial society. The strain and sacrifice of war, coupled with humiliating losses and the empire's final defeat by Japan, provided the immediate pretext to attack the government.

During the empire's expansion into East Asia and well into the war with Japan itself, members of the tsarist administration consistently underestimated the strength and skill of the Japanese government. The minister of the interior even went so far as to observe that "a short victorious war" might not be a bad thing since it would dampen the growing popular unrest. Yet the imperial army suffered a series of defeats on land as well as a naval disaster at the Straits of Tsushima between Korea and Japan, where Japanese warships almost totally destroyed a major Russian fleet that had sailed halfway around the world from the Baltic Sea. It was only because the Japanese state was feeling the war's financial burden, and because Witte exercised keen diplomatic skill that the empire was able to salvage a reasonable peace, the Treaty of Portsmouth, signed in August 1905 at Portsmouth, New Hampshire, under the auspices of President Theodore Roosevelt. The Russo-Japanese War was significant in two major respects: it marked the first defeat in modern times of a European power by an Asian nation, and it added fuel to the burgeoning revolutionary movement in the Russian Empire.

In the first years of the twentieth century, grain prices in the empire dropped, and agricultural wages declined, worsening the peasantry's plight and seeming to confirm the peasant adage, "The shortage will be divided among the peasants." As the following description shows, most peasants lived at the margin of existence:

> [In] a village eighty miles from Moscow . . . the people lived in wooden huts . . . thatched with straw. . . . The stoves were great erections of clay, upon which some of the family slept. Many had no chimney. There was a little opening over the door near the roof, which let out the smoke after it had warmed and blackened both walls and people. . . . Clay was the material for cooking vessels, and clay or wood for plates and dishes. China was a rarity for holidays. Splinters of wood supplied the function of forks. The general sleeping place was the floor, on straw, which was brought in each night and taken out in the morning. All clothes were home spun. . . . The usual footgear was birchbark sandals; leather boots only on holidays and to church, and a pair lasted more than ten years. . . . For a long time there was only one cloth coat in the village: it was borrowed by friends for festive occasions. . . . Meat was a rarity. The rye-bread was supplemented by cabbage soup and barley porridge.[2]

Under such conditions it is hardly surprising that, beginning in 1902, peasants began to protest, particularly in the areas of greatest hardship in southern and central Russia. A wave of peasant disorders started in 1904 and expanded considerably in 1905.

At about the same time, strikes were spreading through a number of industrial centers, and by 1905, hundreds of thousands of workers were on strike. A number of these strikes included demands for political reform as well as insistence on higher wages and shorter hours. Terrorist activity, dormant for a number of years, resurfaced, and several imperial officials were assassinated.

But it was the liberals who took the political initiative in challenging the tsarist government. In November 1904, a meeting of representatives of *zemstvo* organizations called for equal status for the peasantry, civil freedoms, and a representative legislative assembly. In March 1905, the Union of Unions was formed to bring together over twenty professional associations of lawyers, doctors, engineers, and other occupations, and it sought similar reforms.

The first dramatic clash between the government and the people took place in an incident on January 22, 1905, a day subsequently known as Bloody Sunday. In hopes of diverting radical workers from direct antigovernment activity, the Ministry of Internal Affairs had begun in 1904 to support associations of workers organized and supervised by the police. In St. Petersburg, an ambitious, idealistic, and slightly muddled priest, Father George Gapon, headed such a group. On Bloody Sunday, he led a crowd of peaceful working-class petitioners—men, women, and children carrying icons and pictures of the tsar— to the imperial palace. Unaware that Nicholas II was away, they intended to present him with an address couched in the high-flown rhetoric customarily used in such petitions to the throne. The address proved ominously prophetic. It said in part:

> Lord, we workers, our children, our wives and our old helpless parents have come to seek justice and protection from you. We are impoverished and oppressed, unbearable work is imposed on us, we are despised and not recognized as human beings. . . . We are pressed ever deeper into the abyss of poverty, ignorance and lack of rights. . . . We have no strength left, O Lord. . . . If thou wilt not respond to our plea, we shall die here on the square before thy palace.[3]

And die they did. In a tragic display of incompetence, security officials in St. Petersburg, without the knowledge of the tsar or higher authorities, chose to disperse the unarmed crowd by force and fired into several columns of protesters, killing over a hundred people and wounding many more. Public opinion reacted strongly against the government, and Bloody Sunday marked an important turning point in the development of the revolutionary movement by destroying the myth of a mystical bond between the people and a gentle and caring father-tsar.

From January 1905 on, the government found itself increasingly powerless, as a series of parallel protest activities by liberals, workers, peasants, national minorities, and soldiers and sailors engulfed the state. It was an impressively broad national movement for change, manifesting itself in speeches, meetings, proclamations, mutinies, strikes, riots, assassinations, land seizures, and demonstrations. A popular rejection of the tsarist administration, the revolution was largely leaderless and spontaneous.

The government could do little. In August, the unpopular and ruinous war with Japan finally ended. That month, the tsar issued a decree establishing a consultative legislative assembly to be elected by a restricted franchise. But this was clearly too little, too late. By October, the strike movement had culminated in a general strike that shut down almost all activity in St. Petersburg and produced the urgent conference between Nicholas II and Witte described earlier.

The October Manifesto that Witte proposed and the tsar signed, albeit reluctantly, promised the people a broadly representative legislative assembly, to be called the Duma, as well as full civil liberties—that is, freedom of press, assembly, and speech. A short time later, the tsar made further concessions, legalizing trade unions, canceling the remaining redemption dues owed by the peasants, and relaxing restrictions against minority nationalities. Although disorder continued, these reforms divided the opposition and thus marked the first step in the government's regaining control of the situation. To be sure, the far-left-wing parties, the Marxist Social Democrats (SDs) and the peasant Socialist Revolutionaries (SRs), together with most workers, rejected Nicholas's package of concessions as totally inadequate and continued to clamor for a constituent assembly and radical economic changes. The peasants, who wanted land, were hardly mollified. But much of the educated public, especially the middle and professional classes, was satisfied. The Kadets (members of the leading liberal Constitutional Democratic Party) decided that, though the reforms did not go far enough, they would press for further change within the system granted, and they condemned continuing violence. The Octobrists, a newly established party of businessmen and moderately conservative landowners, concluded, as their name indicates, that the October concessions were sufficient and no further reforms were needed. By December 1905, although imperial society was still seething below the surface, articulate elements at the top had opted for peaceful evolution and begun to rally around the government in its efforts to restore order.

Two developments in the fall of 1905 had particularly frightened educated and propertied circles in imperial society: the peasants' continuing violence and illegal land seizures, and the political radicalization of the workers, especially in St. Petersburg and Moscow. During the October strikes, workers of the capital had spontaneously formed a coordinating committee of elected representatives from many of the main factories to supervise and direct the strike movement. Modeled on similar committees formed that summer in several small industrial towns, which in turn may have been adaptations to the city and the workers' situation of the traditional communal assembly in the village, the St. Petersburg committee took the name Soviet (meaning "council") of Workers' Deputies. This body soon began to exercise a number of welfare, administrative, economic, and political functions and was the forerunner of the soviets that, after their reestablishment during the Revolution of 1917, became the basic institutions of the postrevolutionary state.

Although the St. Petersburg soviet and the soviets that soon sprang up in a number of other cities throughout the empire were formed by and for the workers and most remained worker dominated, the radical parties did their best to use the soviets as platforms for revolutionary agitation and as political weapons against the factory owners and the government. They had some success with these efforts; in particular, Leon Trotsky, a talented speaker and writer for the Social Democrats and a leader of the Bolsheviks in 1917, gained considerable renown as chairman of the St. Petersburg soviet and a forthright champion of the rights of the masses. But the continuous upheavals and constant strikes began to take their toll among the tired and poverty-stricken workers, and in mid-December 1905, when the soviet tried to organize a massive strike to win the eight-hour day for workers, the movement collapsed, and the government arrested the soviet's leaders. In protest, the Moscow soviet took to the barricades, and for eleven days, workers in Moscow battled government troops and artillery in a heroic but ultimately futile struggle.

Emboldened by its success against the soviets, the government, backed by much of public opinion, enlarged its efforts to restore order. It attacked the peasant revolution directly by sending punitive military expeditions into the most disaffected provinces to put down peasant unrest by force. It dispatched similar repressive units to the Baltic provinces to quell nationalist disorders there.

Several factors, in addition to the shift of public attitudes against further violence and the exhaustion of the workers, worked in the government's favor. With the war over in East Asia, the government was able to bring back to European areas of the empire reliable units to be used in suppressing civil disorder, though mutinies and unrest in the armed forces continued sporadically through 1906. In addition, the government's financial position, badly weakened by the war with Japan and the revolutionary disruption of the economy, was salvaged when Witte managed to secure a major loan from France. Finally, conservative forces began to organize and soon were actively supporting the government's repressive policies. A far-right-wing organization, the Union of the Russian People, was formed, with a reactionary political, religious, and ethnic Russian nationalist platform. Furthermore, the police tolerated conservative gangs called the Black Hundreds. Spurred by primitive anti-Semitism, they were involved in pogroms against the Jews that broke out frequently in 1905 and 1906. On a few occasions, honest government officials or military officers intervened to protect the Jews and Jewish property, but more often, the authorities stood by and let the mobs wreak havoc on the Jewish community. In the late 1800s and early 1900s, an estimated 2.5 million Jews fled the Russian Empire, with many settling in the United States.

By the spring of 1906, when the First Duma convened, the government had clearly mastered the revolution, although peasant and military disorders continued throughout the year and into 1907. The Revolution of 1905 had succeeded in forcing the tsarist regime to make significant changes, but it had failed in its larger purpose of toppling the old structure entirely.

THE DUMA PERIOD, 1906–1914

Between the Revolution of 1905 and the outbreak of World War I in 1914, the Russian Empire experienced a brief interlude of somewhat normal development, marked by limited constitutionalism, renewed economic growth, rapid social evolution, basic changes in agriculture, and a remarkable spurt of cultural creativity. Some historians see this period as the beginning of the peaceful emergence of a modernized, democratic society, quite similar to Western societies. Others, however, see these few years as a desperate, last-ditch effort by reactionary forces to paper over some of the state's most fundamental flaws, a ploy doomed to failure whether the war came or not. In their view, the changes of the Duma era succeeded only in temporarily staving off an inevitable and sweeping social revolution, the first portents of which appeared in 1913 and early 1914.

In December 1905, when the government still felt threatened, the tsar approved a broad franchise for elections to the Duma, the legislative body promised in the October Manifesto. Virtually all adult male subjects could vote, although voters did not elect representatives directly, but through assemblies of electors. By April 1906, when Nicholas II issued the Fundamental Laws, a constitution that set forth the specifics of the new system, the government felt strong enough to water down the Duma's power in several ways. A reorganized State Council (an advisory body set up by Alexander I) was designated an equal legislative chamber, alongside the Duma, with its members chosen to ensure that it would be highly conservative: half were appointed by the tsar, and half were chosen by several elite groups and institutions. In addition, the Fundamental Laws contained a provision that allowed the tsar to issue legislation when the Duma was not in session, although that body was to approve or reject such laws when it reconvened. Finally, the first section of Article I of the Fundamental Laws reaffirmed the basis of imperial autocracy in the following terms: "The All-Russian Emperor possesses Supreme and Autocratic Power. To obey His authority not only from fear but also from conscience is ordered by God Himself."[4] Other sections reserved to the tsar and his ministers authority over foreign and military affairs and over certain parts of the state budget.

The elections to the First Duma evoked some lively campaigning. Although most members of the radical parties boycotted the election, opponents of the government still won a comfortable majority of the seats. This was no small shock to the government, which had expected the peasants to be a conservative political force.

The scene when Tsar Nicholas II convened the Duma in April 1906 reflected some of the basic divisions of imperial society, with the Orthodox clergy on his right hand, the higher nobility on his left, and the rest of the Duma deputies in front of him. In the Duma sessions, the opposition, emboldened by its electoral success, pressed vigorously for additional concessions. They wanted to exert greater control over the state budget and to make the tsar's ministers responsible to the Duma, and they particularly urged sweeping land reform. When the government resisted staunchly on these issues, an impasse resulted. Only three months after the Duma was convened, the tsar dissolved it. Some two hundred Duma deputies challenged the government by calling on subjects not to pay taxes or serve in the army until the government made further concessions, but the public did not respond, and the deputies were arrested. At the same time, the government continued its policy of forcibly restoring order, not hesitating to use such extralegal measures as military courts-martial, which condemned several thousand people to death in 1906 and 1907, as well as administrative banishment, which sent over twenty thousand individuals into exile in Siberia.

Individuals from the extreme left, such as the SDs and the SRs, decided to participate in the voting for the 1907 Second Duma, and peasant electors, angered by the government's recalcitrance on the land issue, supported radical candidates, with the result that the Kadets lost ground to the leftists, while government and conservative parties gained seats but remained in a minority. Therefore, the Second Duma proved even less tractable than the first, from the government's point of view, and after three months of wrangling, it too was dissolved.

The government, now led by a resolute prime minister, Peter Stolypin, acted illegally to change the electoral law, issuing in July 1907 new regulations that greatly reduced the representation of peasants and national minorities and provided that the gentry would choose one half of the electors. Put another way, under the revised franchise, each elector represented 250 landowners, 1,000 large urban property holders, 15,000 small property holders, 60,000 peasants, and 125,000 workers. This weighting of the elections had the desired result, as the Third Duma consisted of 270 conservative deputies, 114 Kadets, 30 leftists (mostly SDs and SRs), and 17 nonparty deputies, giving the government a comfortable working majority.

Third Duma deputies served their full terms from 1907 to 1912, and the Fourth Duma, elected in 1912, lasted almost to its prescribed end, before the revolution interrupted its work in the fall of 1917. Although the tsarist government controlled both the Third and Fourth Dumas, the evolutionary impact of these two bodies is important in two ways. First, the Dumas provided useful political experience, not just for the deputies and party members themselves but for the articulate public as a whole, which followed Duma debates closely and expressed opinions in newspapers and journals on a wide range of issues that the Dumas considered. In other words, the educated populace not only had a little taste of political democracy but obviously savored it. Second, the Dumas did accomplish a good deal in noncontroversial areas. For example, they pushed the government to begin improving and modernizing the empire's armed forces. Duma committees helped work out important legislation related to public education, labor safety, and social insurance. The Dumas also encouraged more effective economic and fiscal policies.

Finally, the Dumas played some role in the most significant legislation of the prewar period: the Stolypin reforms in agriculture. The general features of these changes in rural life had been developed during Witte's premiership in 1905 and 1906. A major goal was to make agriculture more productive so that it would act as less of a brake on the economy as a whole. Another objective was to give peasants a sense of proprietorship, thereby encouraging them not to seize land illegally as they had in 1905 and not to follow the enticements of revolutionary parties that promised to expropriate land on their behalf. Witte believed that to accomplish these aims, it would be necessary to break up the village commune, making each peasant an individual owner, and to eliminate the old strip system of farming, instead giving each peasant a consolidated plot of land. Since the individual peasant would then control his own land, crops, and profits (after government taxes), he would have an incentive to work harder and to use newer farming techniques, thereby notably raising yield per acre throughout the country.

Stolypin took over this program, and between 1906 and 1911, it was initiated in a series of laws and administrative regulations. Since the war cut short its implementation, it is difficult to assess how successful the Stolypin land reform might have been, but one has to respect Lenin's judgment that, if completed, it would have significantly reduced the potential for revolution among the peasantry. Like the emancipation of the serfs, it was a major social revolution, and it would have turned some hundred million peasants into small landowners. An estimate is that by 1915, only a little over a million peasant families, having withdrawn from the commune, had both acquired ownership of their land and consolidated their strips into a single plot. On the other hand, almost a quarter of all peasant families had left the commune and owned their own land, though it was still scattered among the various communal fields. The remaining peasants were only in the preliminary stages of the reform process.

How did the peasants feel about the Stolypin program? No one is entirely sure because most of our evidence is filtered through the government agencies responsible for administering the reform at the grassroots level. It is significant, however, that although the commune continued to exist until the collective farm system replaced it in 1928–1929, many peasants during the Revolution of 1917 seized land and used it as if they owned it individually. On the other hand, since the Stolypin policies provided only limited opportunities for the peasants to acquire more land and since the peasant population continued to multiply, one wonders whether even the most successful promotion of private ownership and land consolidation could have blunted the peasants' desperate hunger for additional land or solved the problem of the growing numbers of landless and nearly destitute peasants.

During the Duma years, the imperial economy resumed the rapid industrial growth that had characterized it in the 1890s. Between 1906 and 1914, industry increased at about 6 percent a year, and enough miles of railroads were added to make the Russian Empire second only to the United States in total track distance. New manufacturing sectors developed, banking and service enterprises expanded, and mining and other extractive industries grew rapidly as the richness of the land's natural resources began to be tapped. The pre-1900 pattern of heavy concentration in large factories and a few urban locations, including but not limited to Moscow and St. Petersburg, continued. Foreign capital retained its major role in many sectors of the economy. The labor force increased to about 3.5 million workers. Just before the outbreak of World War I, labor unrest revived notably, and in the spring and summer of 1914, on the eve of the war, the strike movement reached its highest peak since 1906. Clearly, this restiveness reflected basic divisions and unresolved tensions in imperial society. Moreover, despite its impressive economic growth, the empire remained substantially less developed and modernized than the nations, particularly Austria-Hungary and Germany, with which it was competing in foreign affairs.

Were imperial subjects better off in 1914 than before the Revolution of 1905? Unfortunately, there is no clear answer to that question. It is likely that the average real income of both peasants and workers was slightly higher in 1914, although some of the poorest individuals were in desperate straits. Yet even if the standard of living was rising in the prewar empire, so were the people's expectations. Many certainly wanted far more than they were getting. The masses' resentment of privileged elites was manifested in a hostility that had simmered just below the surface for centuries with only occasional eruptions, like the Pugachev Revolt, and was perhaps nearing the boiling point. After the Revolution of 1905, the people felt less powerless, and for the first time, they began consciously to heed the appeals of the revolutionary intelligentsia. Convinced they were being deprived of basic equity and increasingly desperate over the conditions in which they lived, the bulk of the empire's workers and peasants were attuned to revolution.

Another factor helping to create a revolutionary situation on the eve of the war was the rigid and unyielding nature of the imperial regime. The tsar, his closest advisors, and the conservative elite were determined to resist change, and the bureaucracy was so structured that major reform of the political system could come only from the top. Since no established mechanism for innovation existed, only occasional powerful personalities, like Witte and Stolypin, could develop new approaches. And though both of those men were politically conservative, their fates were hardly encouraging to potential reformers: Nicholas II, pressed by reactionary circles, dismissed Witte as premier in April 1906, and Stolypin was assassinated in 1911. After that, no strong, reform-minded individual appeared inside the government. There was no further opportunity for the system to modify itself before it was blown away by the revolutionary storm of 1917.

Does all this mean that the state was moving steadily and inexorably toward revolution? Not necessarily, argue many historians, who point to several signs of peaceful progress during the Duma era. Not only were peasants being encouraged to become stable individual proprietors, but the economy was booming, and the benefits of that boom were just beginning to reach the workers. Higher education spread, and the government and the Duma, working together, initiated a broad educational program designed to put all children into elementary school within fifteen to twenty years. Other positive trends included a dramatic increase in cooperatives, continuing improvement in communications and transportation, slow but steady progress in public health, the beginnings of an intellectual and social renaissance among a few Orthodox religious thinkers, and rapidly advancing science and technology. But these evolutionary trends needed time to make their impact felt, and that time was simply not available. In any case, the changes of the Duma years may have taken place too late, after centuries of social oppression, political absolutism, religious obscurantism, and personal exploitation. We can conclude that too many grievances and too much resentment had accumulated in society to avert the violent explosion that the country's disastrous involvement in World War I made almost certain.

THE SILVER AGE: RUSSIAN IMPERIAL CULTURE, 1890–1917

In the years immediately preceding the war, the Russian Empire experienced not only economic and social change but also a surge of artistic and intellectual creativity. Perhaps not as dazzling as the cultural outpouring in literature and music that marked the mid-1800s, this new outburst nevertheless made major contributions to world culture in such areas as poetry, theater, ballet, music, design, and painting. Artists participated significantly in the twentieth-century modernist movement, and today we still enjoy and benefit from the pioneering works of those who were active in the period from the 1890s to the Revolution of 1917.

Culture in this era could draw on its own rich past as well as receive stimulation from the ferment and excitement of such European artistic movements as realism and impressionism. Moreover, after 1905, the intellectual climate in the empire was freer, with little censorship and an increasingly appreciative public. On the other hand, the achievements of the outstanding artists of this Silver Age are all the more remarkable when set against the relatively low cultural level of the country as a whole. Although the number of school and university graduates was shooting up, on the eve of the war, 50 percent of the empire's population was illiterate, and the overwhelming majority of the people was acquainted only with folk culture and the emotional religious experience of the village church.

Theater developed remarkably in the last part of the nineteenth century and the first years of the twentieth. Particularly prominent were a famous director, Konstantin Stanislavsky, whose method has influenced actors ever since; an outstanding theater company, the Moscow Art Theater; and a subtly powerful playwright, Anton Chekhov. Chekhov also wrote wonderful short stories, but beginning in 1895 until his death in 1904, he produced a string of successful plays that deal with such timeless themes as loneliness, boredom, alienation, and frustrated dreams. Among the classics Chekhov bequeathed to playgoers, the best known are *Three Sisters* and *The Cherry Orchard*.

Emerging early in the 1900s, the empire's first major revolutionary author, Maxim Gorky, drew on his experiences drifting about the land as a youth for such realistic works as the play *The Lower Depths* and the novel *Mother*. Bitterly critical of imperial society, Gorky eloquently argued the need for radical change. Embracing the Revolution of 1917, he remained the dean of Soviet writers, despite disagreements with Lenin and Stalin, until his death in the 1930s.

In sharp contrast to the psychological probing of Chekhov or the revolutionary realism of Gorky was the symbolism of writers, primarily poets, who emerged after 1905. They espoused aestheticism, beauty, "art for art's sake," and individual lyricism, exploring and expanding language in new and dramatic ways. The most talented was Alexander Blok, famed for his mystical poem about the revolution, "The Twelve," but the most active politically was Vladimir Mayakovsky. He threw himself into propaganda work after 1917 and in the 1920s helped develop an avant-garde revolutionary theater; however,

disillusioned and depressed, he committed suicide in 1930. A few lines from his
poem "A Cloud in Trousers" suggest his imagination and brashness:

> *But it seems,*
> *before they can launch a song,*
> *poets must tramp for days with callused feet,*
> *and the sluggish fish of the imagination*
> *flounders softly in the slush of the heart.*
> *And while, with twittering rhymes, they boil a broth*
> *of loves and nightingales,*
> *the tongueless street merely writhes*
> *for lack of something to shout or say.*[5]

In the early 1900s, artists excelled at bringing together various art forms in
a single presentation that was markedly more than the sum of its parts, what
today we might call a "multimedia" work. This approach was pioneered by a
group of young artists who published a daring journal, the *World of Art*, that
combined prose, poetry, and criticism with beautiful typography, layout, and
illustration. The *World of Art* movement soon spread to the ballet and theater, where the artist Alexandre Benois and the impresario Sergei Diaghilev
brought the best dancers, such as Anna Pavlova and Vaslav Nijinsky, together
with the music of the most daring new composers, such as Igor Stravinsky, and
mounted the performance against sets, costumes, and lighting designed by
outstanding modern artists. The resulting integrated and stunning presentations were the sensation first of the empire and then, when Diaghilev took his
Ballets Russes company abroad, of all Europe.

At about the same time, a brilliant group of avant-garde artists influenced by Post-Impressionism in Europe was developing in the Russian Empire
and contributed importantly to modern art in the West after World War I.
For example, Vladimir Tatlin was an important leader in the constructivist
movement, Natalia Goncharova and Mikhail Larionov developed Rayonism,
Kazimir Malevich initiated Suprematism and was a forerunner of minimal
art, and Marc Chagall and Wassily Kandinsky, both of whom emigrated to the
West after the Revolution of 1917, were important abstract artists.

Finally, intellectuals contributed significantly to modern science and
scholarship in this period. Scientists built on earlier achievements in such fields
as mathematics, chemistry, and engineering. At the same time, they made new
contributions in physics, biology, physiology, psychology, and history. Both
scholars and scientists were supported by an expanding system of higher education, including new universities and research institutes.

Put briefly, the quality and output of intellectual and cultural life on the eve of the war were remarkably high, especially in relation to the general level of education and culture in the country. Whatever its deficiencies in social and political terms, imperial society could be proud of its artistic and creative contributions, an area in which the nation was not backward but instead a leader of world culture.

THE RUSSIAN EMPIRE IN WORLD WAR I, 1914–1917

The Russian Empire's path to World War I began in the 1880s and early 1890s, when St. Petersburg replaced traditionally close links to Germany and Austria-Hungary with a newfound friendship with France. The French alliance seemed to defy common sense. Not only was France far away, anti-autocratic in ideology, and a potential rival in the Middle East, but it was also isolated, vengeful, and therefore a potential troublemaker on the European scene. But the Russian Empire wanted support against its chief rival in the Balkans, Austria-Hungary, and it also feared the increasingly aggressive and militaristic German Empire. The Russian Empire, like France, seemed alone and vulnerable in the lions' den of European power struggles once treaties with Germany and the Austrian Empire had been dissolved in the 1880s. Finally, France was the empire's chief creditor, which suggested that a political-military alliance could only strengthen the economic connection between Paris and St. Petersburg.

With the establishment of the Franco-Russian Alliance in the early 1890s, the French cleverly drew the Russian state into their military embrace, ensuring that the vast numbers of the empire's peasant army would be thrown against the Germans should the French ever have the chance they had sought for so long to avenge their defeat at the hands of the Germans in 1871 and to recover the lost territories of Alsace and Lorraine. Following the defeat by Japan, the French alliance seemed even more important to imperial leaders. Supplemented in 1907 by an understanding with Great Britain, the empire felt secure in a powerful system, which was soon known as the Triple Entente. The difficulty, however, was that the opposing system, the Triple Alliance of Germany, Austria-Hungary, and Italy, emboldened the Russian Empire's archenemy in the Balkans, the Austrians, to be more aggressive in that region.

Beyond our scope are details of the militarism, diplomatic maneuvering, and imperialistic rivalry that marked international relations in Europe in the decade before 1914. In 1908, however, during a crisis over Bosnia, and to a lesser extent in 1912 and 1913 during the Balkan Wars, the imperial government in

St. Petersburg believed it had been forced to back down diplomatically under pressure from the Austrians, supported by Germany. Therefore, when in 1914, as restitution for a Serbian nationalist's assassination of the heir to the Austrian throne, the Austrian government tried to wrest humiliating concessions from Serbia, the Russian Empire's ally in the Balkans, imperial leaders were in no mood to compromise, believing their status as a great power to be at stake.

Intense nationalist feeling exacerbated the crisis in all countries, and the Russian Empire was no exception. Although some government officials knew that the empire was no match for German economic and military power, and one predicted that its defeat would result in "hopeless anarchy, the outcome of which cannot be foreseen," others feared that a retreat might lead to the country's eventual domination by its central European rivals, and publicists and orators beat the drums for ethnic Russian patriotism and Slavic unity among the Russian, Ukrainian, and Belarusian populations of the empire. Consequently, when the crisis turned into war between the Allies (which included the Russian Empire, France, and England) and the Central Powers (which included the Ottoman Empire, Germany, and Austria-Hungary), public opinion in the Russian state welcomed the conflict. All parties and groups, except Lenin and the Social Democrats, rallied around the throne and vowed enthusiastically to support the war effort.

In the beginning, the Russian state's war aims were simply to check the ambitions of Germany and Austria-Hungary, to fulfill its treaty obligations to France, and to defend its territory. With the Ottoman Empire's entry into the war, the empire added the goal of seizing the Bosphorus and the Ottoman capital of Constantinople. In a secret treaty signed in 1915, France and England agreed to support this acquisition of Ottoman territory after the war.

The imperial army fared poorly on the Eastern Front against Austria-Hungary and Germany. The Russian Army's opponents had a fivefold advantage in artillery and three times as many rifles and machine guns. Imperial troops fought bravely, but they were poorly led and supplied. Mismanagement and inefficiency plagued the government's conduct of the war. As the French had hoped, the large Russian Army managed to tie up many German divisions in 1914 and helped to save France from being overrun, but by 1915, the Central Powers had crossed Poland and advanced into the Russian Empire proper. Refugees from the occupied western regions poured into the central cities, adding to the already existing problems of food, housing, and fuel supply.

The imperial army remained intact, but its defeats and losses mounted. By the end of the fighting in late 1917, the empire had mobilized over fifteen million men and lost six to eight million who were killed, wounded, or taken prisoner, with perhaps another two million having deserted. Mobilization of such large numbers of men both weakened the domestic economy and changed the character of the army. Its largely untrained peasant recruits, uprooted from traditional routines and circumstances, became radicalized under conditions of defeat and harsh discipline into a potentially revolutionary force.

On the home front, the strain of the war had led to a gradual breakdown of the economy and a sharp decline in civilian morale by 1916. A number of the empire's educated elite had thrown themselves into the war effort, attempting in several public and voluntary organizations to make up deficiencies in medical and hospital services, war production, food distribution, and other areas. But the transport system could not meet the enormous demands placed on it, and supplies to the cities began to dwindle. Resulting shortages worsened the plight of urban workers who were already suffering as the cost of living rose faster than their wages. In the countryside, the peasants, short of labor because of the army mobilization and facing low prices for grain and high prices for the few manufactured products available, began to produce less, mainly feeding themselves, a course that naturally intensified the food supply problems in the cities.

FIGURE 10.1. Nicholas II and his family, with members of the court. Uniforms and military ceremonies played an important role in court life. (Courtesy of the Library of Congress, LC-USZ62–46347)

Even the economic hardships, coupled with the military defeats and sacrifices, might have been bearable if the empire's diverse peoples possessed some sense of what they were fighting for and if they had an inspired leader. Instead, the tsar and his advisors refused to promise reforms after the war while furnishing only incompetent and aimless direction of the war effort. The disintegration of the imperial government at its highest levels was symbolized by the notorious influence of Gregory Rasputin. A self-proclaimed holy man, Rasputin was able to affect government appointments and possibly even policies because Nicholas's wife Alexandra believed "Our Friend," as she called him, was able to stop the bleeding of Alexei, her hemophiliac son and the heir to the throne (see Figure 10.1). Realizing that Rasputin's presence in court circles discredited the monarchy, conspirators shot Rasputin after he appeared impervious to the cyanide-laced food and drink they had given him at a party.

The government refused to accept proposals for reform and cooperation made by a large majority of deputies to the Fourth Duma, and the tsar continued to endorse the appointment to ministerial posts of cronies and incompetents. Even the tsar's cousin commented, "The Government itself is the organ that is preparing the revolution." In 1916 and early 1917, as economic and living conditions worsened and the military situation deteriorated, rumors of a coup d'état circulated in the capital, now renamed Petrograd because St. Petersburg had too Germanic a sound in the Russian language. Many predicted revolution, yet when it actually occurred, it happened suddenly and with no immediate warning.

CONCLUSION

It is difficult to see how the Russian Empire, once involved in a massive, draining war, could have avoided some sort of violent upheaval. In four important ways, World War I brought on a revolutionary crisis. First, the war accelerated the disorientation of society that the processes of modernization, industrialization, and urbanization had launched in the preceding decades. Tens of millions of imperial subjects were physically displaced: some were mobilized into the army, others became refugees from the war zone, and many more moved voluntarily to undertake work in factories and various war industries. This great migration of individuals within the country disrupted old ties, habits, and attitudes and exposed people to new ideas and experiences. The result was a weakening of the fabric of the old society, leaving many people and groups searching for new roots and increasing the potential for radical social and political change.

Second, the war intensified the sense of injustice and resentment that had been building among the masses during the previous decades. After the first surge of patriotic support for the war, people became both exhausted and bitter as the fighting dragged on. Losses in people, territory, and destruction were enormous; many families suffered personally and directly, and almost everyone was affected indirectly. The harsh conditions under which workers and peasants labored and lived seemed increasingly intolerable, and the sacrifices of the soldiers at the front, pointless. As one historian of the Russian Army has concluded, "The soldiers felt they were being used and recklessly expended by the rich and powerful, of whom their officers were the most visible, immediate representatives."[6] War weariness, despair, and hatred of the old system dominated all levels of society. The people's only hope lay in victory, which seemed increasingly distant and illusory, or in radical change, some sudden liberation from their bonds and burdens.

Third, the war caused a partial collapse of the economy, resulting in deteriorating conditions in the major cities. As the real income of both workers and peasants declined, as the transportation and distribution systems ceased to function effectively for civilian needs, and as food and fuel shortages in the cities worsened, people's attitudes toward the government and the war hardened until, finally, they simply refused to tolerate the situation any longer.

Finally, the empire's participation in the Great War completely discredited Nicholas II and his already weak regime. People were therefore able to discard the tsar and his government entirely, with almost no one coming forward to defend them. For centuries the masses had retained faith in the divinely inspired tutelage of the benevolent father-tsar. But in the twentieth century, this faith dissipated as workers and peasants wondered why the tsar did nothing to ameliorate their lot. During the war, many held Nicholas responsible for the grief, suffering, and fear it had brought: If the tsar were a good tsar, they wondered, why could he not save the empire?

Nicholas's own actions did not help matters. He associated himself personally with the war effort, made himself commander in chief of the army, and moved to the general headquarters at the front to oversee operations. In this way, Nicholas became linked to the continuing defeat, loss of life, and sacrifice. He did nothing to correct the incompetence and moral corruption of the government. People despised the tsarist ministers and bitterly criticized their mismanagement of the war effort. It was bad enough to suffer and to lose, but to do so in part because the country was being run by a clique of misfits and sycophants, some of whom Rasputin himself had selected, was intolerable.

By 1917, imperial society was twice changed: first by the economic, social, and political developments of the late nineteenth and early twentieth centuries and then by the disruptions, sacrifices, and despair of World War I. The tsarist leaders aside, it was clear to nearly everyone in the crumbling empire that the old system could not go on, but what new order would replace it? The answer lay in the circumstances of the dramatic revolution to come.

FURTHER READING

Ascher, Abraham. *P. A. Stolypin: The Search for Stability in Late Imperial Russia*. Stanford, CA: Stanford University Press, 2001.

———. *The Revolution of 1905*. 2 vols. Stanford, CA: Stanford University Press, 1988–1992.

Chulos, Chris. *Converging Worlds: Religion and Community in Peasant Russia, 1861–1917*. DeKalb: Northern Illinois University Press, 2003.

Daly, Jonathan W. *The Watchful State: Security Police and Opposition in Russia, 1906–1917*. DeKalb: Northern Illinois University Press, 2004.

Gatrell, Peter. *Russia's First World War: A Social and Economic History*. Harlow, UK: Pearson/Longman, 2005.

Gorshkov, Boris B. *Russia's Factory Children: State, Society, and Law, 1800–1917*. Pittsburgh: University of Pittsburgh Press, 2009.

Gray, Camilla. *The Great Experiment: Russian Art, 1863–1922*. New York: H. N. Abrams, 1962.

Haimson, Leopold. "The Problem of Political and Social Stability in Urban Russia on the Eve of War and Revolution Revisited." *Slavic Review* 59, no. 4 (2000): 848–875.

———. "The Problem of Social Stability in Urban Russia, 1905–17." *Slavic Review* 23, no. 4 (1964): 620–642; 24, no. 1 (1965): 1–22.

Harcave, Sidney. *Count Sergei Witte and the Twilight of Imperial Russia: A Biography*. Armonk, NY: M. E. Sharpe, 2004.

Hosking, Geoffrey A. *The Russian Constitutional Experiment: Government and Duma, 1907–1914*. New York: Cambridge University Press, 1973.

Keep, John L. H. *Last of the Empires: A History of the Soviet Union, 1945–1991*. Oxford: Oxford University Press, 1995.

Kennan, George F. *The Fateful Alliance: France, Russia and the Coming of the First World War*. New York: Pantheon Books, 1984.

Lieven, Dominic. *Nicholas II: Twilight of the Empire*. New York: St. Martin's, 1996.

Lincoln, W. Bruce. *In War's Dark Shadow: The Russians Before the Great War*. New York: Dial, 1983.

Mehlinger, Howard D., and John M. Thompson. *Count Witte and the Tsarist Government in the 1905 Revolution*. Bloomington: Indiana University Press, 1972.

Nathans, Benjamin. *Beyond the Pale: The Jewish Encounter with Late Imperial Russia*. Berkeley: University of California Press, 2003.

Petrone, Karen. *The Great War in Russian Memory*. Bloomington: Indiana University Press, 2011.

Retish, Aaron B. *Russia's Peasants in Revolution and Civil War: Citizenship, Identity, and the Creation of the Soviet State, 1914–1922*. Cambridge: Cambridge University Press, 2008.

Ruthchild, Rochelle Goldberg. *Equality and Revolution: Women's Rights in the Russian Empire, 1905–1917*. Pittsburgh: University of Pittsburgh Press, 2010.

Smith, C. Jay. *The Russian Struggle for Power, 1914–1917: A Study of Russian Foreign Policy During the First World War*. New York: Philosophical Library, 1956.

Stavrou, Theofanis George, ed. *Russia Under the Last Tsar*. Minneapolis: University of Minnesota Press, 1969.

Wallace, Sir Donald Mackenzie. *Russia: On the Eve of War and Revolution*. New York: Vintage Books, 1962.

CHAPTER 11

REVOLUTION, CIVIL WAR, AND THE FOUNDING OF THE SOVIET STATE, 1917–1928

Everyone was glad it was warmer that spring. During street demonstrations of the past two days, people had shivered and nearly frozen, but despite the bitter cold, they had continued their protests against the shortage of bread and the war. Now, by midmorning on Saturday, March 10, 1917, the thermometer had climbed to 20 degrees Fahrenheit, and crowds of strikers, unemployed workers, students, and housewives were again on the streets, heading for the center of Petrograd,[1] the capital of the Russian Empire. The demonstrators' mood on the previous two days had been amiable, almost jolly, as if they were on holiday. On Saturday, however, more clashes with the police occurred as more and more workers left work to join the protest marches. By noon, three hundred thousand people, or about one-fifth of the city's total population, were milling about. Some, besides demanding bread, shouted, "Down with the tsar," and a few even called out a truly revolutionary slogan, "Down with Tsarism!" Nevertheless, Tsarina Alexandra, who despite her involvement in government affairs during the war understood almost nothing about popular attitudes, wrote to her husband Tsar Nicholas about the disorders, "If the weather were very cold, they would all probably stay at home."

In Znamenskaia Square, at the end of Nevsky Prospect, the city's main street, a revolutionary speaker was addressing a large crowd when mounted police arrived to break up the demonstration. The speaker urged the throng not to move on as ordered. The detachment commander then raised his pistol and took aim. Before he could fire, a Cossack, who was a member of the capital's security forces, rode forward and cut the commander down with his saber. Although Cossacks and army troops had previously behaved with tolerance toward the demonstrators, this was the first time that anybody from the government's side actively supported the protesters. The next day, soldiers from the Pavlovskii Guards Regiment attacked a police unit, and that night members of the Volynskii Regiment, who, under orders, had fired on unarmed demonstrators in the morning, vowed not to do so again. The next morning, when their commanding officer again ordered them out against the crowds, the soldiers mutinied and killed him.[2]

These incidents marked the turning point in the revolution that overthrew the imperial autocracy. Once Cossacks and troops stationed in Petrograd sided with the revolutionaries, the empire's government was helpless. The police were too few to restore order if military force could no longer be relied on. The subsequent arrest of the tsarist ministers and the abdication of Tsar Nicholas II were anticlimactic.

THE FEBRUARY REVOLUTION: THE COLLAPSE OF AUTOCRACY

The popular uprising that led to the disappearance of the imperial autocracy after three hundred years of rule by the Romanov dynasty, known in Russian and most Western historiography as the February Revolution, took place between February 24 and 28, 1917, according to the Old Style (Julian) calendar then in use in the Russian Empire. According to the New Style (Gregorian) calendar used in the West and adopted in Soviet Russia[3] in 1918, the tsar's downfall occurred between March 8 and 12, and as such is sometimes referred to as the March Revolution. Under either name, this revolution was the first of two that took place in 1917, and together they are usually designated the Russian Revolution. Since the second upheaval, which brought Vladimir Lenin and the Bolsheviks to power, happened between October 24 and 26 (Old Style) or November 6 and 8 (New Style), it is called the October Revolution.

The February and October revolutions were two separate events, but many historians argue that they were simply stages in one continuous, radical transformation of society in 1917, a people's rebellion sparked by the oppression and injustice of imperial rule that culminated in the founding of an entirely new social and political system, Soviet socialism. Others, minimizing the shifts in political power reflected by the two revolutions, stress the more fundamental and long-range modernization of society in its economic, social, and intellectual aspects, a process that began in modern times with the emancipation of the serfs in 1861 and was accelerated in the massive Soviet industrialization drive after 1928. In our account, we will try to include both perspectives on the Russian Revolution, its specific features and long-term impact on both the former Russian Empire and the rest of the world.

The protests over bread shortages, the strikes, and the street demonstrations in Petrograd that led to the collapse of the autocracy occurred spontaneously, without particular leaders or heroes, and involved many groups, particularly women. Although radical socialists egged the crowds on, the demonstrations constituted a genuinely popular revolution in which the bulk of imperial subjects expressed their refusal to tolerate the existing situation and government any longer. Casualties numbered about fifteen hundred individuals. Once the soldiers joined the crowds, the old regime simply disappeared, a deliquescence of authority repeated throughout the country. Nicholas II soon abdicated, without protest, and no one came forward to defend the autocratic system.

The nature of the February Revolution raises an important question about imperial Russian society: How could the old order be discarded so easily? The answer lies in part in the discrediting of the tsarist regime at the top and in the terrible burdens and discouragement of the war, for which people blamed the tsarist government. But the autocracy vanished in a moment because of more profound weaknesses as well. In the latter part of the nineteenth and the beginning of the twentieth centuries, the traditional belief system and norms that had bolstered the autocracy for so long began to erode rapidly. The tsar had counted on ingrained obedience and gratitude for his benign rule, on the rituals and divine support of the Orthodox Church, on a system of classes in which each group knew its place and acknowledged its obligation to serve the state, and on a mystical sense of the rightness and goodness of Slavic tradition. By the 1900s, these values had become diminished or outmoded, and no new conservative policies had emerged to replace them. The old order rested on custom and inertia; once these weakened, it was easily toppled.

In March, Tsar Nicholas abdicated in favor of his brother Grand Duke Michael Alexandrovich, who refused the throne. In any case, almost no one supported continuation of the monarchy, even if it were reformed. Nicholas and his family met a tragic fate. After spending some fairly pleasant months under mild "house arrest" in Siberia, the deposed tsar, his wife, and their five children were brutally murdered in July 1918 by local authorities to prevent their possible capture by anti-Bolshevik forces involved in the Russian Civil War that was then raging. The Bolshevik leaders in Moscow callously approved this execution.

Even before the tsar abdicated, a group of liberal leaders had formed a committee of Duma members, which soon appointed what came to be known as the Provisional Government. Its ministers included mainly members of the Octobrist and Kadet parties plus a few other moderates. From the start, the Provisional Government labored under several handicaps. Its own members as well as the populace at large considered it temporary and transitional, in power only until a constituent assembly democratically elected by all people could convene and decide on the Russian state's permanent future government. In addition, the Provisional Government represented a considerable range of political views, particularly after May 1917, when moderate socialists joined the cabinet. As a result, it could not agree on even temporary solutions for some of the country's most urgent problems. Finally, the Provisional Government tried to govern in an atmosphere of unrealistic popular expectations, revolutionary euphoria, and widespread feelings of liberation that impelled people to reject all authority.

In practical terms, moreover, the Provisional Government almost immediately found itself sharing power in the country with a grassroots organization, the soviet. On March 12, in the same Petrograd building in which Duma members were meeting to form the Provisional Government, a group of revolutionary activists assembled, including representatives of the workers, a few socialist and radical politicians, and some soldiers. They soon decided to reconstitute the soviet that had played such a dramatic role in the Revolution of 1905. In recognition of the contribution troops of the Petrograd garrison had made in the recent revolution, the resurrected organization was called the Petrograd Soviet of Workers' and Soldiers' Deputies. It chose an executive committee dominated by moderate socialist politicians.

The Petrograd Soviet soon exercised considerable authority because workers in such key sectors as transport, communications, and supply looked to it for guidance and because it had influence over troops stationed in Petrograd and other major cities. This was particularly true after March 14, when the Petrograd Soviet issued order number 1, a call for sweeping reforms in the army and the election of soldiers' committees in each unit. As it became established, the Petrograd Soviet acted as a check on, or watchdog over, the formal administration of the country, the Provisional Government, creating a situation of dual power that lasted until the October Revolution seven months later.

The February Revolution spread quickly throughout the crumbling Russian Empire. As in Petrograd, imperial authorities were replaced, usually without bloodshed, by public committees, and soviets soon formed, first in the cities and then more slowly in district towns and villages. Outside the empire, the Central Powers welcomed the revolution, thinking it might lead to an unraveling of society and a collapse of the Russian military's fighting capacity. The Allies and the United States were also delighted, first on ideological grounds since they could now fight side by side with another democracy instead of an autocracy and, second, because they hoped the new government would invigorate the Russian military's war effort and strengthen its contribution to the Western cause.

But what did the people think about the downfall of the tsar? Most of them were overjoyed, embracing the revolution as a panacea for all of the country's and their own problems. Exhilarated and optimistic, they exercised their new freedom to the fullest, attending meetings, founding parties, sending petitions and telegrams to Petrograd, and talking, always talking. At the same time, except for a common belief in the glory and value of "the Revolution," all had their own ideas about the future: workers expected higher wages, the eight-hour day, and better working conditions; peasants counted on more land and higher grain prices; the national minorities dreamed of autonomy, local rights, and, in a few cases, independence; soldiers and sailors wanted fairer treatment, civil and political rights, and their own committees. Moreover, most individuals believed their dreams would come true, if not right away, at least in the near future.

The reality, of course, was far different. The Provisional Government had to struggle with the same problems that the imperial regime had confronted, most prominently the war and its effects. In retrospect, we can see that the war was destroying orderly society and that, at heart, people were sick of it. But at the same time, inertia, the lingering effects of patriotism, fear of the Germans, and, among educated classes, a sense of duty to the nation's allies all combined to make it unthinkable that the country should pull out of the war. The Provisional Government announced it would continue to fight and support the Allied cause. The Petrograd Soviet also endorsed the war, although simultaneously calling for a redefinition of Allied war aims to eliminate annexations of others' territory and indemnities against the losers.

The Provisional Government promised independence to the Poles and full autonomy to the Finns but could not agree on policy toward the other national minorities such as the Ukrainians and Belarusians. Both the Provisional Government and the Petrograd Soviet backed expanded civil liberties, immediate elections to the Constituent Assembly, and the lifting of restrictions against religious minorities and Jews. But they were far apart on what social and economic policies should be followed. Nevertheless, the Petrograd Soviet decided to tolerate the Provisional Government as long as it kept its promise to uphold social freedoms and to oppose the remnants of the tsarist autocracy.

A month after the February Revolution, a new element was introduced into the situation when, on April 16, Lenin (see Figure 11.1), who had been in exile in Europe for ten years, arrived back in Petrograd. Although the German government helped Lenin return by letting him pass across German territory, and although the Bolsheviks later secretly accepted money from the Germans, neither Lenin nor members of his party were German agents, as some have charged. They took money from whatever source was available and used it for their own purposes. In this case, Lenin intended to stir up a radical revolution

FIGURE 11.1. Vladimir I. Lenin, 1870–1924. (Courtesy of the Library of Congress, LC-USZ62–101877)

at home, for which purpose the Germans assisted him, but he counted on that revolution spreading to Europe and to Germany itself.

Lenin was now leader of the Bolsheviks, an important faction of the Russian Social Democratic Party. Lenin and the Bolsheviks established a separate identity within the party beginning in 1903 at the party's Second Congress, where they had argued that the party should be a small, elite, highly disciplined band of professional revolutionaries. Their opponents, known as the Mensheviks, favored a larger, broadly based, more open party. After 1914, the two factions also disagreed over World War I. Lenin and the Bolsheviks interpreted the war as the result of struggles among the capitalists over colonial empires and trade and concluded that capitalism was in a final phase of decline, which Lenin dubbed "imperialism." While most Bolsheviks followed Lenin in denouncing all sides in the struggle and urging the workers to turn the imperialist war into a struggle against the capitalists, most Mensheviks approved defensive military action to protect the state while calling for a peace of justice and brotherhood.

The Mensheviks welcomed the February Revolution and accepted the Provisional Government in part because they clung to orthodox Marxist theory, which taught that all societies had to pass through a capitalist phase of development, however brief, before they could undergo a proletarian revolution and enter the final stage of history, socialism. For the Mensheviks, the February Revolution represented the overthrow of the old feudal order in Russia's equivalent of the French Revolution, and Russian society was now in its capitalist, or "bourgeois-democratic," phase. The Mensheviks considered it doctrinally correct to support the bourgeois-democratic Provisional Government and to use the freedoms it granted to proselytize to the workers about the forthcoming proletarian, or socialist, revolution. In a set of statements known as the April Theses, Lenin attacked this view. He called on the people to struggle against rather than support the Provisional Government, to begin at once to prepare the transfer of all power to the Petrograd Soviet, and to end the war immediately. This radical program shocked even his fellow Bolsheviks and was ignored by moderate socialist and liberal politicians as extremist nonsense.

Undaunted, Lenin continued to espouse his ideas, reflecting two of his most dominant traits as a revolutionary leader: his tenacious will that often wore down and overpowered doubting comrades' resistance and his devout conviction of both the necessity and the possibility of a socialist revolution. As the spring wore on, the tide of events began to move in a direction that favored Lenin's view of the situation. The war dragged on, and the Provisional Government was weakened by a crisis over its alleged retention of the imperialist war aim of acquiring Constantinople and the Turkish Straits from the Ottoman Empire. Social and economic conditions worsened instead of improving after the February Revolution. The Provisional Government made no progress on two key issues, land reform and rights for ethnic and religious minorities, partly because its liberal leaders stuck resolutely to democratic principles. They insisted that such fundamental questions as redistribution of land, which the peasants were vociferously demanding, and whether the future state should be a federal system, as the non-Russian nationalities insisted, could only be settled by the free vote of all citizens through their representatives in the soon-to-be elected Constituent Assembly. Yet the Provisional Government did not do enough to speed up preparations for the elections, and its members could not agree on how to meet the most immediate social and economic problems.

More important than the government's ineffectiveness, however, was the masses' growing disillusionment with the results of the February Revolution. Not only had it not solved everyone's problems, but most individuals were worse off. When it seemed they were no nearer to achieving their cherished goals, many people grew frustrated and bitter, blaming privileged elites, particularly the educated leaders of the Provisional Government, for the dashing of their hopes. War weariness was spreading rapidly, and even frontline troops became restive. The government nevertheless pushed forward with its plans to mount a major military offensive designed to relieve pressure on the Allies on the Western Front. Workers became embroiled in heated disputes with factory owners, and peasants began to seize private and state land illegally. As mass attitudes and actions became increasingly radical, authority and order began to dissipate in the country, and tensions mounted. Clearly a new crisis was imminent.

THE OCTOBER REVOLUTION: THE BOLSHEVIKS COME TO POWER

Two climactic events in the summer of 1917 paved the way for the Bolsheviks to take power with relative ease in the fall of that year. The first was the July Days, a spontaneous mass uprising in Petrograd on July 16 and 17. People poured into the streets of the capital with no specific purpose in mind except to show their dislike of the Provisional Government and their disgust with the existing situation. Some may have also vaguely wanted the Petrograd Soviet to replace the Provisional Government. Moderate socialists in the Petrograd Soviet did not believe they should assume power at a time not yet ripe for a socialist revolution. The riots in Petrograd died down, and the Provisional Government regained control of the situation for a time, but the July Days revealed the revolutionary nature of the masses and the instability of the Provisional Government.

The second event was a bungled attempt by General Lavr Kornilov to seize power and establish a military dictatorship in the country. After the major offensive planned by the Provisional Government had failed, in part because some military units proved unreliable, the prime minister, a socialist liberal named Alexander Kerensky, supported a movement within the top command to restore discipline in the army and to put down unrest on the home front. Kerensky thought he was using General Kornilov to strengthen the state, but Kornilov believed Kerensky was giving him a free hand. As a result of this tragicomic misunderstanding, Kornilov, encouraged by conservative elements in Petrograd, rashly ordered troops to move against the capital. Kerensky, fearing that Kornilov intended to take over the government, appealed to the Petrograd Soviet and the masses for support, thereby alienating himself from conservative circles and making him dependent on radical elements. Railway and communications workers prevented the movement of Kornilov's troops, while revolutionary agitators persuaded many of his soldiers to give up. As a result, the attempted coup was a fiasco, and the position of the radicals was strengthened. Even more importantly, most people were now frightened of the possibility that reactionary forces, however vaguely defined, might attempt a counterrevolution, threatening whatever gains the revolution had provided. Throughout the fall of 1917, the Bolsheviks effectively used the looming threat of counterrevolution in their bid for power.

By September 1917, the Bolsheviks' slogan "Peace, Land, and Bread" was winning over large numbers of workers, soldiers, and peasants. The Bolsheviks also promised non-Russian minorities, particularly Ukrainians and Belarusians, the right of self-determination. Their program fitted well with the goals of many citizens, and the Bolsheviks soon obtained a majority in the Petrograd and Moscow soviets. In the meantime, the war continued to go badly, and the Provisional Government under Kerensky seemed paralyzed, despite several attempts to rally democratic elements around it.

The vulnerability of the liberal-moderate socialist coalition that was trying to govern the state stemmed from several factors. It lacked strong leadership, Kerensky in particular being a vain, mercurial, and often impractical person who, between bouts of apathy and despair, rushed around giving speeches and exhorting his fellow countrymen without accomplishing much. Moreover, as noted earlier, moderate socialists were reluctant partners in the coalition cabinet since, according to Marxist theory, the government should have been a capitalist one. They were not willing to assume power themselves because it was the wrong historical moment for a socialist government, yet they were stalemated by the liberals from taking immediate steps to alleviate the nation's socioeconomic ills. Finally, the circumstances were such that even a united government with strong leadership could not have survived as long as it continued an unpopular war and refused to grant the people's most urgent demands. On the very eve of the Bolsheviks' assumption of power, several moderate socialists proposed a program of peace and land reform to Kerensky, but by then it was too late.

As the Mensheviks and the Socialist Revolutionaries, tainted by their association with the war and the Provisional Government, lost influence with the masses, the Bolsheviks gained strength. In an amazing turnabout, the Bolsheviks had grown from a tiny fringe group of around twenty thousand at the time of the February Revolution to a huge party of about two hundred sixty thousand with substantial influence in the army and among the urban masses. Within the party, a sharp debate erupted in September and October 1917 over whether to attempt an armed revolution. Lenin, with his brilliant political acumen, argued vigorously that now was the moment to strike, while the

Provisional Government was weak and while a majority of opinion favored the Bolsheviks. Others urged caution and a longer period of preparing the masses for action. Lenin finally forced through a decision to move toward revolution.

Two events occurring on the eve of the revolution facilitated the Bolsheviks' success in the October Revolution, during which they took power as it slipped from the hands of the Provisional Government. First, the Petrograd Soviet formed the Military Revolutionary Committee (MRC) in the third week of October. Although charged with preparing defensive measures in the event of a German attack on Petrograd and with coordinating the movement of troops in the capital, the MRC soon became a planning committee for the Bolshevik uprising under the forceful leadership of Leon Trotsky, a prominent Bolshevik. Several days before the revolution, the MRC posted its own commissars (political officers) with most military units in the capital and announced that no military orders were valid unless countersigned by the MRC. This meant that the Provisional Government had lost control of the troops in Petrograd, and although only a few of them joined in the Bolshevik uprising, the rest declined to defend the Provisional Government.

Second, Trotsky, who did an excellent job organizing and directing the revolution, cleverly managed affairs so that Kerensky was provoked to move against the Bolsheviks on November 5. This permitted them to appear not as illegal subverters of a democratic government but as righteous defenders of freedom and the revolution against the dark forces of reaction.

On November 6 and 7, the Bolsheviks took control of key locations in Petrograd—banks, post offices, railroad stations, and government buildings—most often without a struggle. On the night of November 7, they also captured the Winter Palace, former seat of the tsars, and arrested the ministers of the Provisional Government who had retreated there. Only a few military units tried halfheartedly to defend the palace, and Kerensky, after slipping out of the city, could not rally a sufficient military force from the regular army to recapture Petrograd from the Bolsheviks. Casualties during the October Revolution in the capital numbered only a few hundred, and most of the citizenry passively accepted the new order with a wait-and-see attitude.

On November 8, Lenin formed a Soviet government called the Council of People's Commissars and presented to the Second Congress of Soviets, made up of deputies from soviets throughout the country, decrees calling for immediate peace and for nationalization of all land and its transfer to the peasantry for their use. He also decided to proceed with elections to the Constituent Assembly late in November.

Outside Petrograd, the October Revolution proceeded unevenly. In some cities, power passed quickly to Bolshevik-dominated soviets, but in others, fighting erupted, and it was days or even weeks before the Bolsheviks established their authority. The peasants, happy with the decree on land, generally acquiesced in the Bolshevik takeover, and most of the army, except a number of officers, supported the new Soviet government after Lenin pushed through an armistice with the Germans, pending peace negotiations.

During his first weeks in power, Lenin had to deal with a serious political crisis. Most delegates to the Second Congress of Soviets, including many of the Bolsheviks, had been sent to the congress with instructions from local soviets to support the formation of a new government that included all the socialist parties, including the Mensheviks and Socialist Revolutionaries. But since the moderate socialists opposed the Bolshevik assumption of power and their delegates had walked out of the Second Congress on that issue, Lenin had formed an all-Bolshevik government. Not wishing to share power, Lenin would have preferred to continue that arrangement, but pressure not only from soviet representatives but from within the Bolshevik Party and from key trade unions forced him to enter negotiations with the Mensheviks and Socialist Revolutionaries for the creation of an all-socialist cabinet. By the end of November, the talks had collapsed, the pressure had dissipated, and Lenin had reorganized the Council of People's Commissars to include a few individuals from the Left Socialist Revolutionaries, a radical faction of that party. In this way, Lenin established a one-party government, which became a central feature of the Soviet system.

A couple of months later, Lenin made it clear that the Bolsheviks intended to dominate not only the government but also the general political life of the country. Lenin had permitted elections to the Constituent Assembly, as promised in the Bolshevik platform, but since the majority of voters were peasants and the Socialist Revolutionary Party was closest to them, the Socialist Revolutionaries won a majority of seats in the new assembly. When it convened in January 1918, and it became evident the Bolshevik minority could not control the assembly, Lenin forcibly dissolved it. Although the moderate socialist parties occasionally contested local soviet elections during the next few years, for all practical purposes, the Bolsheviks, by that act, had created a one-party dictatorship over the country, which was now known as Soviet Russia.

The October Revolution meant that in a few days, or weeks at most, power in the largest country in Europe had been transferred into the hands of a radical socialist minority bent on entirely restructuring society and carrying their proletarian revolution to the advanced countries of the West and, eventually, the whole world. Lenin justified the socialist revolution in the less-industrialized former Russian Empire by saying that special circumstances, such as the war and the revolutionary actions of the peasantry, had permitted it and that the October Revolution would fulfill the capitalist stage of history in Soviet Russia as it proceeded. It was a rather vague formulation, but Lenin counted on the socialist revolution's spreading to highly industrialized Western Europe; once the proletariat had come to power there, they could give Soviet Russia the assistance it needed to develop an advanced economy and support true socialism. As Lenin often put it, the Bolsheviks needed to hold onto power until their ally, the workers of the West, came to their aid.

We know that the October Revolution had fateful consequences for modern world history, but what sort of a revolution was it? It was certainly not an evil conspiracy designed to impose a new form of human bondage on the Russians, Ukrainians, Belarusians, and other peoples of the former Russian Empire, as some have argued. On the other hand, it was not a great libertarian revolution opening the way to freedom and plenty for all. Neither vilifying the Bolsheviks nor glorifying the masses is a convincing way to interpret the revolution. Rather, the Bolsheviks were able to build upon deep popular feelings— resentment of the injustice and oppression associated with privileged imperial elites, fear of counterrevolution, revulsion against the war and the sacrifices it entailed, and dreams of a better, securer, more just future—to come to power and win the chance to construct a new order. That many of the masses' aspirations remained unfulfilled and that the Bolsheviks built a revolutionary society quite unlike that which their early members had envisaged are key elements of the story that will unfold in the remaining pages of this book. But it is important to remember that the vision, the dream, the yearning for a future good society that animated so many people in 1917, not the reality of what actually happened afterward, had a powerful impact on the rest of the world.

CIVIL WAR AND FOREIGN INTERVENTION, 1917–1921

Almost immediately after coming to power, the Bolsheviks had to confront major internal and external challenges to their authority that led to a bitter, no-holds-barred conflict lasting almost three years. This raises intriguing questions: To what extent did this desperate struggle for survival determine the contours of Soviet society? How much of the harshness, intolerance, and authoritarianism of the Soviet system can be traced to its birth pangs in civil strife and economic stringency? Or, put another way, if the Bolsheviks had been allowed to put their ideas into effect without outside interference or the need to improvise to stay alive, what sort of socialist society might have emerged?

In considering these questions, we need to bear in mind several factors. First, the Russian Empire was not an advanced country in 1914, and regardless of the further devastation caused by the civil war, its three-year involvement in World War I had nearly wrecked the economy. So the Bolsheviks would not have had extensive resources to work with in any case.

Second, as we have seen, Lenin and his party made clear, well before major armed attacks against them began, that they would tolerate no interference with their rule and that they would share authority neither with other parties and interest groups nor with the people. This was partly because Lenin and the Bolsheviks believed the party should not only lead but act on behalf of the people and partly because Lenin was convinced that the Bolsheviks must hold power until the Russian Revolution could spark a revolution in Europe and the advanced proletariat of the West could come to the Bolsheviks' assistance. Consequently, Soviet Russia, even at peace, was not likely to be a democratic, participatory society. At the same time, it seems fair to conclude that the rigors and exigencies of the civil war and foreign invasion intensified authoritarian trends within Bolshevism and reinforced attitudes and policies that emphasized control, centralization, and the suppression of dissent.

The issue that touched off the civil war and intervention was not the dissolution of the Constituent Assembly or the Bolsheviks' radical economic measures, such as repudiation of the imperial state's foreign debt and nationalization of property, though these acts hardly pleased many people at home and abroad; rather, it was Lenin's policy toward the war. By making peace with the Central Powers, as he eventually did in the Treaty of Brest-Litovsk of March 1918, Lenin alienated millions of patriotic citizens, who concluded that the Bolsheviks had sold the country down the river, as well as the Allied powers, whose leaders believed the Russian state had betrayed their cause and were forcing the Western democracies to make even greater sacrifices to defeat Germany and Austria-Hungary. To be sure, neither the anti-Bolsheviks nor the Allied statesmen were delighted with the Bolsheviks' revolutionary policies and their appeals to workers throughout the world to revolt, but they took up arms against the new Soviet regime primarily because it had made peace with the German enemy.

Ironically, Lenin faced a no-win situation. He had promised the people peace; if he did not deliver, his government would not last long. Yet he knew that peace not only would entail humiliating concessions to the Germans but would probably also stir up widespread opposition to the Bolsheviks. Faced with this dilemma, Lenin risked the potential of attacks from foes within and without against the certainty of German occupation and popular rebellion if he tried to continue the war. Yet even within his own party, he had a major struggle before convincing a slim majority of Bolsheviks to accept the terms of Brest-Litovsk, under which Soviet Russia lost a quarter of its territory and population, a third of its industry, and three-quarters of its coal mines to Germany and Austria-Hungary. Lenin believed that the peace treaty was a temporary surrender, a scrap of paper to be torn up when the proletarian revolution broke out in Germany, as he was convinced it would. In fact, the treaty lapsed eight months after it was ratified in March 1918 not because of a revolution in Germany but because the Allies won the war.

In December 1917, at the time that armistice negotiations with the Germans began, the first anti-Bolshevik forces were formed in the south and primarily included high officers in the former imperial army and Cossack soldiers. Major hostilities did not begin, however, until May and June 1918, when a military front against the Bolsheviks was set up in Siberia supported by the Czechoslovak Legion, which had formed part of the imperial Russian army and was being evacuated to the Western Front when it clashed with the Bolsheviks. Other fronts were established in the north, supported by British and American troops, and before long in the northwest, also with British assistance. Later, anti-Bolshevik, or White, armies were also active in the southwest, supported by the French, and in the trans-Caspian area, supported by the British. The military history of the civil war is both extremely complex and beyond our scope, but as a glance at Map 11.1 shows, at one time, Soviet Russia was surrounded on all sides by anti-Bolshevik forces and compressed into a relatively small area.

The civil war was greatly complicated by the participation of non-Russian minorities, who often were at odds with the ethnic Russians who favored a centralized Russia and were generally unwilling to make concessions to the other nationalities. At various times in the period between 1918 and 1921, a majority of Finns, Baltic peoples, Poles, Armenians, Georgians, Ukrainians, and various Muslim peoples of Central Asia fought the Bolsheviks. To confuse the picture even further, some members of these national groups were Bolsheviks and supported Lenin and the Soviet government in their efforts to incorporate ethnic minority areas into Soviet Russia. When the struggle finally ended in the early 1920s, the Poles, Finns, and Baltic peoples had established their independence, and the others had been absorbed into the new Soviet Union.

The foreign powers that intervened in the civil war constitute another important element in this drawn-out and fierce struggle. In the summer of 1918, the Central Powers, worried that the Bolsheviks were not completing the economic payments required under the Treaty of Brest-Litovsk, occupied the western territory of Soviet Russia. At about the same time, Britain, France, the United States, and Japan decided to intervene, mainly in hopes of restoring a military front against the Germans but partly for anti-Bolshevik or imperialistic reasons. Although the American president, Woodrow Wilson, disapproved of this action, he went along with his allies as a gesture of wartime unity. Allied troops, mainly Japanese but including seven thousand Americans, landed in the Far East, and British and American troops landed in the north. In 1919, French troops were sent to Odessa in the south. The greatest Western

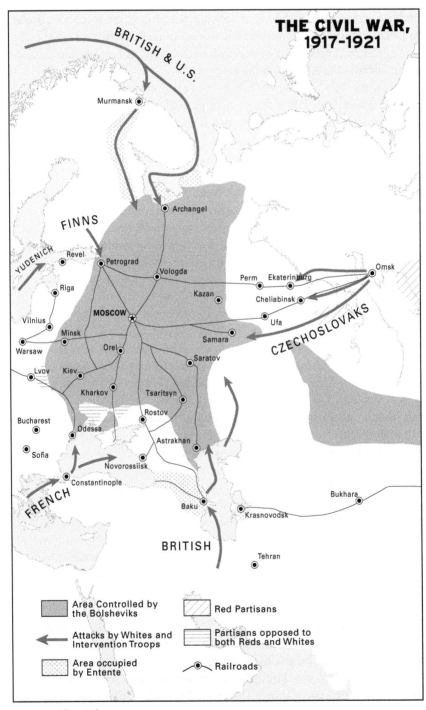

THE CIVIL WAR, 1917-1921

BRITISH & U.S.

Murmansk

FINNS

Archangel

YUDENICH

Revel

Petrograd

Vologda

Perm Ekaterinburg

Omsk

Riga

Kazan

Cheliabinsk

CZECHOSLOVAKS

Vilnius

MOSCOW

Ufa

Minsk

Samara

Warsaw

Orel

Saratov

Lvov Kiev

Kharkov

Tsaritsyn

Bucharest

Rostov

Odessa

Sofia

Astrakhan

Novorossiisk

Constantinople

Bukhara

FRENCH

Baku

Krasnovodsk

BRITISH

Tehran

Area Controlled by the Bolsheviks		Red Partisans
Attacks by Whites and Intervention Troops		Partisans opposed to both Reds and Whites
Area occupied by Entente		Railroads

MAP 11.1. The civil war, 1917–1921.

contribution to the anti-Bolshevik cause, however, was not direct military support, most of which was withdrawn in 1919 after the victory over Germany, but military equipment and financial assistance for the White forces. This aid unquestionably helped the anti-Bolshevik armies fight on considerably longer than they otherwise could have and was therefore a source of much Soviet resentment against the Western powers.

After the defeat of Germany, the Western intervention took on a decidedly anti-Bolshevik character, but public opinion in the democracies was unwilling to support a major effort to bring down the Bolshevik regime, and the whole enterprise had petered out by 1920 (although Japan did not remove its troops until 1922). The legacy of intervention was suspicion and mistrust between the Soviet government and the West, which hampered their relations over the next several decades.

At the same time that the Bolsheviks were desperately defending the Soviet state against White armies and foreign interventionists, they were also on the offensive, trying to stir up revolution in the West. For a time, Lenin convinced himself that the proletarian revolution predicted by Marxist theory was about to erupt in Europe, partly because of the Bolshevik example and partly because of disillusionment and economic hardship in Germany and Austria following their defeat. To distinguish his movement of revolutionary socialism from the moderate or evolutionary socialism in Russia and Europe, Lenin had his party renamed the Russian Communist Party (Bolshevik). He sent propaganda, agents, and a little money to spur the revolutionary cause in Europe, and short-lived Communist uprisings in Hungary and in southern Germany momentarily raised Lenin's hopes. In March 1919, Lenin founded the Communist International (Comintern), a league of revolutionary socialist parties dominated by the Bolsheviks and dedicated to promoting world revolution.

Although revolution did not spread to the West, neither were the Western powers able to snuff out the revolution in Soviet Russia. And although many in Europe and the United States were terrified of the "Red Menace" and the potential spread of communism, many others were swayed by Soviet appeals for peace and an end to intervention as well as Soviet calls for a new postwar order based on social justice and economic equality.

In the all-out struggle to survive, the Bolsheviks adopted stringent policies at home. As early as December 1917, they established the Cheka (from its Russian initials), the forerunner of the Soviet secret police, and by the summer of 1918, when a political opponent shot and wounded Lenin, the Bolsheviks resorted to extensive political coercion and terror by incarcerating "enemies of the revolution" in concentration camps. White forces also resorted to terror and arbitrary executions. Lenin and Trotsky tried to justify their repressive policies as necessary to the survival of the revolution and the Soviet state.

The social and economic policies the Bolsheviks adopted between 1918 and 1921 are sometimes called "war communism," and indeed, the demands of the war effort dictated many of these measures. But they might also be called "militant communism" because some policies were ideologically motivated and designed to introduce socialist concepts in Soviet Russia. Industry was nationalized and tightly controlled; private enterprise and trade were reduced to a minimum; the state provided all public and social services, including education and culture; and the Orthodox Church and other faiths were persecuted.

Soviet policy toward the peasants was contradictory. They were allowed to keep the land they had seized in 1917, and additional public land was given to them. At the same time, since the Soviet government needed grain to feed workers in the cities and the troops of the growing Red Army, it resorted to requisitioning peasant surpluses. This policy greatly angered the more prosperous peasants, and the civil war lasted as long as it did in part because peasants kept switching back and forth between the Reds and the Whites. At last, when they realized that the anti-Bolshevik forces were determined to take the land back and to restore many aspects of the old order, the majority of peasants passively sided with the Bolsheviks.

The Soviet government survived as much because of its opponents' deficiencies as its own strengths. To be sure, the Soviet forces had interior lines of communication, and the Red Army, built up to a force of several million men and effectively organized and led by Trotsky, often with assistance from former tsarist officers, fought bravely for the most part. Yet the disorganization, disunity, and reactionary attitudes and policies that characterized the Whites made them far less formidable opponents than they might have been. Moreover, they failed to reach an agreement with the national minorities, thereby losing valuable support. The Allied powers, in the face of a public weary of war and partially sympathetic to the Bolsheviks, could not provide decisive assistance.

The last episode of the civil war and intervention was an attack on Soviet Russia by Poland that led to a bloody summer of fighting in 1920. With the military situation stalemated in the fall, peace was agreed to on the basis of a compromise boundary line between the two countries.

THE NEW ECONOMIC POLICY AND COEXISTENCE, 1921–1928

By the winter of 1920 and 1921, when it was clear that Soviet Russia had survived, the major question for the Bolsheviks became "What next?" Lenin's hoped-for revolution in Europe had not materialized and did not seem imminent. Little help could be expected from that quarter, although Lenin hastened to restore diplomatic and commercial relations with the Western capitalist countries (except the United States, which, until 1933, refused to recognize the Soviet state), and he was quite happy to grant economic concessions to capitalists willing to invest in Soviet Russia. But few were interested, and it soon became apparent that Soviet Russia would basically have to go it alone.

At the same time, the Bolsheviks faced a disastrous situation at home. Civil war and intervention had completed the wrecking of the economy begun in 1914. By 1920, industrial production was at only 20 percent of its 1913 level, and even agricultural production was only two-thirds of what it had been. The country was virtually a wasteland, with some regions facing famine and spreading epidemics of typhus and smallpox. Some fifteen to twenty million people had been killed or had died of disease and starvation between 1914 and 1921. Moscow and Petrograd had shrunk to less than half their prerevolutionary sizes. Workers in the cities were dissatisfied, and several million Red Army veterans needed to be employed and resettled. The peasants violently resisted further requisitioning of their grain and demanded nonexistent manufactured goods before they would sell their produce. Peasant uprisings reminiscent of 1905 and 1917 broke out in a number of regions, and in March 1921, a major revolt erupted in Kronstadt, an industrial town and naval base not far from Petrograd. The Kronstadt rebellion was particularly alarming because, all through 1917 and much of the civil war, the Kronstadt rebels had been among the most loyal and spirited supporters of the Soviet government. Significantly, what they now demanded went to the heart of the political dilemma the Bolsheviks faced:

> Immediate re-election of the soviets by secret ballot and upon the basis of free political agitation, "in view of the fact that the existing soviets do not express the will of the workers and peasants," freedom of speech and press for "workers, peasants, and for the Anarchists and the left socialist parties"; freedom of meeting, and free trade unions and the formation of peasants' unions; liberation of all socialist political prisoners . . . abolition of all special political departments (in the army, navy, and transport) . . . equal rations for all, except those engaged in work detrimental to health . . . full rights for the peasants to "do as they please with all the land."[4]

Lenin had no intention of meeting the democratic political demands of the Kronstadt rebellion and ordered the uprising suppressed by force. But he fully recognized that economic concessions would have to be made to save the revolution and Bolshevik rule. At the Tenth Party Congress in March 1921, he set forth his reform program, the New Economic Policy (NEP). It was not a retreat to capitalism, as some anti-Bolsheviks believed, but rather an example of Lenin's tactical flexibility as expressed in his dictum, "One step backward, two steps forward." Lenin knew that changes were needed to restore the economy before a forward movement toward socialism could be contemplated.

The NEP had three main features, all designed to stimulate economic recovery. First, peasants were allowed to pay the government a fixed tax in money or in kind and could sell anything they produced beyond that in the open market; this was an effective incentive for them to grow and distribute more. Second, much of industry was denationalized, with the government retaining ownership of only "the commanding heights," that is, the largest factories, transportation, and the banks, with the rest reverting to private ownership. Finally, most retail trade and much of the labor market were freed from government control and allowed to operate privately and for profit.

The NEP worked exceedingly well, despite the famine of 1921 and 1922, which private relief assistance from the United States did much to alleviate. Industry surpassed its prewar output levels by 1926 and 1927, and agriculture nearly reached its 1913 production total in the following year. Moreover, with peace at hand, life settled into a normal routine, and many older Soviet citizens later viewed the NEP years as a happy and relatively prosperous time. Some outside observers have argued that the seminationalized, semiprivate structure of the Soviet economy under the NEP could have provided a continuing mechanism of economic and social development for Soviet Russia, even though it was not fully socialist. It is clear, though, that Lenin never envisaged the NEP as anything but a temporary measure. Before he was able to work out how Soviet Russia, still an under-industrialized country, could advance toward socialism in the absence of revolution in the West, he suffered a stroke in May 1922 and died twenty months later, in January 1924.

The March 1921 party congress was important not only because it launched the NEP but also because key decisions concerning the party and the state structure were taken. Throughout its history, the Bolshevik (Communist) Party had been regulated internally according to the rules of democratic centralism. Under those rules, ideas and policies could be freely debated at various levels of the party before a decision was made. Once the decision was taken, it was binding on all party members and units. In practice, however, party members had been free to continue discussion of controversial questions and had on occasion even formed groups within the party to oppose various policies. At the Tenth Party Congress, Lenin insisted on the adoption of a rule against "factionalism," which stated that, once a decision had been made, no organized group could continue to agitate against it. Although Lenin did not enforce this new provision rigidly, it gave Joseph Stalin, Lenin's successor, a powerful weapon against internal opposition and helped him establish a dictatorship within the party.

The March 1921 party conclave also encouraged the movement already developing to make Soviet Russia a federal state, giving the national minorities some cultural and structural autonomy as long as the Communist Party retained power in each region and ensured political subjugation to the national government. The result was the emergence between 1922 and 1924 of the Union of Soviet Socialist Republics (USSR), commonly known as the Soviet Union. Governments controlled by the Communist Party ran each of the union's republics, and although each of the eventual total of fifteen republics had the theoretical right to secede from the union, it was understood that such a step would never be taken since it would be inimical to the welfare of the larger state, the Soviet Union, the first socialist nation in the world.

During the NEP period, the Soviet government continued the contradictory foreign policy it had initiated in 1918 when it was struggling to survive. On the one hand, the government called for peace, normal relations between itself and all other nations regardless of their ideology, and active trade and commercial intercourse between Soviet Russia and the capitalist West; on the other, the Communist Party, which ran the Soviet government, agitated vigorously for immediate world revolution, the overthrow of capitalist governments in the West, and destruction of the traditional international order. Moreover, through the Comintern and its ties with Communist Parties abroad, the Russian Communists sought actively to promote these revolutionary objectives. No wonder Western politicians and diplomats were perplexed.

Nevertheless, with the exception of the United States, the Western nations, because they too wanted trade, peace, and normal relations, established ties with the Soviet state and even invited the Soviet leaders to such Europe-wide meetings as the Genoa Conference of 1922. This respectability nicely reflected Lenin's doctrine of peaceful coexistence, his view that socialist and capitalist states could live quietly, side by side, interacting on matters of mutual interest. At the time Lenin did not, however, stress another aspect of the theory of coexistence: socialist society should try to gain all possible advantage from such a relationship, and eventually, after an unspecified period, coexistence would disappear in a "frightful collision" between the socialist and capitalist systems, from which socialism would emerge triumphant on a global scale.

THE STRUGGLE FOR POWER

While Lenin lived, he dominated the Communist Party and Soviet state by virtue of his experience, intellect, and strong will. Although other comrades did not hesitate to disagree with him, he was widely admired and respected,

FIGURE 11.2. Joseph Stalin, 1878–1953. (Courtesy of
the Library of Congress, LC-USW33–019081-C)

and his views generally carried the day. In the early 1920s, however, even before
his first stroke in May 1922, Lenin began to lose his grip on the party and state.
In the first place, he was unsure, as we have seen, about how socialism could
best be built, and so he could not provide clear direction and ideological guidance. Moreover, since the party and state were larger and more complex than
they had been in the immediate aftermath of the October Revolution, it was
much harder for Lenin to be on top of everything. One of the younger party
members on whom Lenin came to rely for administrative and organizational
detail was Joseph Stalin, who became general secretary, or chief administrator,
of the party in 1922 (see Figure 11.2).

The name Stalin, meaning "steel," was a revolutionary pseudonym. His
real last name was Dzhugashvili, and he was born in the Georgian Caucasus
in 1878. The son of a poor shoemaker and rebellious as a youth, Stalin withdrew from the theological seminary to which his devoted mother had sent him
for a pious education and was soon involved in daring revolutionary activity,
including robberies to raise money for the cause. Stalin rose in the ranks of
the Bolshevik Party through determination, hard work, thoroughness, and,

perhaps, most importantly, self-effacement. How much the later abnormality of his personality can be traced to resentment over his humble origins, his abusive father, and the subsidiary role in which his better-educated and more brilliant comrades cast him is unclear; at the time, Stalin swallowed his pride and reliably and uncomplainingly carried out party assignments. Unscrupulous and extremely ambitious, he realized the importance of ingratiating himself with Lenin and, before World War I, had become the latter's assistant on issues affecting national minorities and the right of socialist self-determination.

Returning from exile in Siberia right after the February Revolution, Stalin was an industrious and loyal comrade in the years of the revolution and civil war. Although he had his first disagreement with Trotsky in 1919, Stalin was always willing to serve the party as needed. As early as 1921, when he helped arrange the forcible incorporation of his native Georgia into the new USSR, he showed he could be ruthless and decisive. Partly as a result of Stalin's methods and attitudes in that case, Lenin became increasingly critical of him in 1922 and 1923. After his first stroke, Lenin returned to work and planned to present to the Twelfth Party Congress in the spring of 1923 a major criticism of Stalin, recommending his demotion. Luckily for Stalin, just before the congress convened, Lenin had a further paralyzing stroke, which incapacitated him until his death in January 1924.

He had earlier written down, however, some of his growing doubts about Stalin, a document that came to be known as Lenin's Testament: "Comrade Stalin, having become *gensek* [general secretary of the party], has concentrated boundless power in his hands, and I am not sure that he will always manage to use this power with sufficient caution. . . . Stalin is too rude, and this fault . . . becomes intolerable in the office of general secretary. Therefore I propose to the comrades that they devise a way of shifting Stalin from this position."[5]

After Lenin's incapacitation, Stalin allied himself with two other party leaders, Lev Kamenev and Grigory Zinoviev, in an effort to isolate Trotsky and reduce his power. When Lenin died, Stalin delivered the funeral oration; for reasons that remain unclear, Trotsky failed to attend the funeral and did not publish Lenin's Testament (which also contained some milder criticisms of Trotsky), even though he was the best-known Bolshevik after Lenin and his logical successor. By early 1925, Trotsky had been replaced as commissar for war; in 1926, he was removed from the Politburo, the party's ruling executive committee, and then expelled from the party; in 1928, he was exiled; and finally, in 1940, an agent of Stalin's police murdered him while he was in exile in Mexico.

Beginning in 1925, Stalin turned against Zinoviev and what was known as the Left Opposition, allying himself with more moderate leaders in the party, such as Nikolai Bukharin. In 1928, however, following his triumph over Trotsky and the Left Opposition, Stalin reversed himself again, attacking his erstwhile supporters, dubbing them the Right Deviation, and reducing their role in the party to insignificance. As a result, Stalin emerged from the power struggle to succeed Lenin as undisputed leader of the party and dictator of the Soviet Union. He triumphed in part because his opponents consistently underrated him, in part through skill and ruthless ambition, in part because he cleverly controlled and manipulated the party from his position as general secretary, and in part because he espoused a persuasive ideological platform. Stalin's methods and his mastery of the party boded ill for the future of the Soviet people.

CONCLUSION

During the decade from 1917 to 1927, a centuries-old social and political system was jettisoned, a disastrous and brutal war was ended only to be followed by three more years of bitter fratricidal struggle, a new society struggling to find its identity and set fresh goals was born, and an unheralded yet powerful leader emerged to dominate the country and extend the revolution. It was little wonder that some Russians thought of this period as a new Time of Troubles.

In retrospect, we can see that those years had several distinguishing characteristics. First, the Russian Revolution saved Marxist socialism, which had been nearly destroyed as an influential movement by nationalist feelings aroused at the outbreak of World War I. Lenin and the Bolsheviks, even though they came to power in a backward country, rescued the socialist ideal and ensured that it would survive for most of the twentieth century as an alternative way of organizing modern society.

Second, the Russian Revolution fulfilled some aspirations of the people and dashed others. From it, the Bolshevik Party emerged as the strongest force in the new society, yet the events of 1917 intensified the Leninists' distrust of mass organizations and other parties. The course of the revolution reinforced their belief that they knew what was best for the people and that theirs was the correct way. The Bolshevik leaders had no intention of letting the masses decide important issues, and as a result, even though the people wanted an all-socialist government responsive to the popularly elected soviets, they were given a one-party dictatorship over the government and country, with the Bolsheviks dominating and using the soviets for the party's own purposes.

On the other hand, the Bolsheviks did meet popular demands in a number of areas: they gave the peasants land; they brought peace, at least temporarily; they tried to provide greater equity; and they gave many a sense of dignity and self-worth that they had never had before. In short, the people had gained, and they had lost, as so often happens at major turning points in human history.

Finally, the revolutionary years provided remarkable evidence that a single individual can affect the course of history. It is hard to conceive of the Russian Revolution without Lenin. He returned home to galvanize his party, insisted stubbornly on bidding for power at the only moment when the Bolsheviks could probably have succeeded, and forced through the peace with Germany, without which the revolution could not have survived.

FURTHER READING

Avrich, Paul. *Kronstadt 1921*. Princeton, NJ: Princeton University Press, 1991.

Bernstein, Frances Lee. *The Dictatorship of Sex: Lifestyle Advice for the Soviet Masses*. DeKalb: Northern Illinois University Press, 2011.

Figes, Orlando. *A People's Tragedy: The Russian Revolution, 1891–1924*. New York: Penguin Books, 1996.

Fitzpatrick, Sheila. *The Russian Revolution*. 3rd ed. New York: Oxford University Press, 2008.

Fitzpatrick, Sheila, Alexander Rabinowitch, and Richard Stites, eds. *Russia in the Era of NEP: Explorations in Soviet Society and Culture*. Bloomington: Indiana University Press, 1991.

Graham, Loren R. *Science in Russia and the Soviet Union: A Short History*. Cambridge, UK: Cambridge University Press, 1993.

Hirsch, Francine. *Empire of Nations: Ethnographic Knowledge and the Making of the Soviet Union*. Ithaca, NY: Cornell University Press, 2005.

Koenker, Diane P., William G. Rosenberg, and Ronald Grigor Suny, eds. *Party, State, and Society in the Russian Civil War: Explorations in Social History*. Bloomington: Indiana University Press, 1989.

Kotkin, Stephen. *Stalin*. Volume 1: *Paradoxes of Power, 1878–1928*. New York: Penguin, 2014.

Martin, Terry. *The Affirmative Action Empire: Nations and Nationalism in the Soviet Union, 1923–1939*. Ithaca, NY: Cornell University Press, 2001.

Mawdsley, Evan. *The Russian Civil War*. Boston: Allen & Unwin, 1987.

Osokina, Elena. *Our Daily Bread: Socialist Distribution and the Art of Survival in Stalin's Russia, 1927–1941*. Translated and edited by Kate Transchel and Greta Bucher. Armonk, NY: M. E. Sharpe, 2001.

Rabinowitch, Alexander. *The Bolsheviks in Power: The First Year of Soviet Rule in Petrograd*. Bloomington: Indiana University Press, 2007.

Raleigh, Donald J. *Experiencing Russia's Civil War: Politics, Society, and Revolutionary Culture in Saratov, 1917–1922*. Princeton, NJ: Princeton University Press, 2002.

———, ed. *Provincial Landscapes: Local Dimensions of Soviet Power, 1917–1953*. Pittsburgh: University of Pittsburgh Press, 2001.

Service, Robert. *Lenin: A Biography*. Cambridge, MA: Harvard University Press, 2000.

Smith, Scott B. *Captives of Revolution: The Socialist Revolutionaries and the Bolshevik Dictatorship, 1918–1923*. Pittsburgh: University of Pittsburgh Press, 2011.

Stites, Richard. *Russian Popular Culture: Entertainment and Society Since 1900*. New York: Cambridge University Press, 1992.

Swain, Geoffrey. *Trotsky*. Profiles in Power. Harlow, UK: Routledge, 2006.

Thompson, John M. *Revolutionary Russia, 1917*. 2nd ed. New York: Macmillan, 1989.

Tucker, Robert C. *Stalin as Revolutionary, 1879–1929: A Study in History and Personality*. New York: W. W. Norton, 1973.

Wade, Rex A. *The Russian Revolution, 1917*. 2nd ed. Cambridge, UK: Cambridge University Press, 2005.

Wildman, Allan K. *The End of the Russian Imperial Army*. 2 vols. Princeton, NJ: Princeton University Press, 1980–1987.

Wood, Elizabeth A. *The Baba and the Comrade: Gender and Politics in Revolutionary Russia*. Bloomington: Indiana University Press, 1997.

Yekelchyk, Serhy. *Ukraine: Birth of a Modern Nation*. Oxford: Oxford University Press, 2007.

CHAPTER 12

THE STALIN REVOLUTION AND WORLD WAR II, 1928–1946

Who broke the chains that bound our feet, now dancing,
Who opened lips that sing a joyous song,
Who made the mourners change their tears for laughter,
Brought back the dead to life's rejoicing throng.
Who is in heart, in every thought and action,
Most loving, true and wise of Lenin's sons—
Such is the great Stalin.[1]

This excerpt from "The Song of Stalin" illustrates the extent of the official adulation of Joseph Stalin at the height of his power. Yet this individual was responsible for launching a virtual civil war against the peasants in which millions died and for instituting purges and repression against the general population in which millions more perished. At the same time, he oversaw the industrialization of the Soviet Union, the survival and victory of the USSR in World War II, and the establishment of Soviet dominance in Eastern Europe after the war. Because he was a suspicious, secretive person presiding over a xenophobic, terror-ridden system, we know little about Stalin's motives and purposes, and he remains in many respects an enigma. Clearly, however, his tyrannical rule and the later reaction against it shaped Soviet society for much of the twentieth century and beyond.

STALINISM: INDUSTRIALIZATION AND COLLECTIVIZATION

In 1917, the Bolsheviks seized political power, but despite sporadic experiments under war communism, they did not radically transform Soviet Russia's socioeconomic system in their first decade of rule. Beginning in 1928 and 1929, however, Stalin and the Communist Party of the Soviet Union (CPSU) carried out a second major revolution, one that completely changed the configuration of Soviet society. Until the Chinese Communist revolution some twenty years later, it was the most sudden and thoroughgoing alteration in a people's way of life in history, even surpassing the French Revolution of 1789 in its sweep and the numbers of people affected.

Stalin and a few party leaders within the CPSU, not the people as a whole, decided on this revolution and then drove it through in the 1930s. The dislocation, suffering, and outright loss of life were enormous, but the achievements were also considerable. As a Soviet citizen once shouted at coauthor John Thompson when he questioned the costs of this second revolution, "Yes, yes, it was a frightful price to pay, but it was all worth it—it made us strong and respected!" Indeed, the goal of making the Soviet Union powerful enough to withstand any external threat strongly motivated Stalin and his comrades to force through rapid industrialization. In a 1931 speech, Stalin, in his usual blunt and didactic fashion, summed up this line of argument, dismissing complaints that the pace of industrialization was too fast:

> To slacken the tempo would mean falling behind. And those who fall behind will get beaten. But we do not want to be beaten. No, we refuse to be beaten! One feature of the history of old Russia was the continual beating she suffered because of her backwardness. She was beaten by the Mongol Khans. She was beaten by the Turkish beys. She was beaten by the Swedish feudal lords. She was beaten by the Polish and Lithuanian gentry. She was beaten by the British and French capitalists. She was beaten by the Japanese barons. All beat her—because of her backwardness, because of her military backwardness, cultural backwardness, industrial backwardness, agricultural backwardness. They beat her because to do so was profitable and could be done with impunity. . . . That is why we must no longer lag behind.
>
> We are fifty or a hundred years behind the advanced countries. We must make good this distance in ten years. Either we do it, or we shall go under.[2]

Just ten years and three months later, Adolf Hitler's Nazi armies invaded the Soviet Union.

Other reasons sparked the industrialization decision. Ideologically, Marxist theory ordained that a socialist society must be highly industrialized with an overwhelming preponderance of workers. Yet the Soviet Union under the New Economic Policy (NEP) was only partly industrialized, with fewer workers than peasants. Politically, Communist rule was to be on behalf of the proletariat. How long could the party continue to govern confronted by increasingly prosperous peasants, small businessmen, and private traders, whose class interest and actions were distinctly petty bourgeois? Economically, something had to be done. The post-1921 NEP recovery was faltering, and a different path to growth and prosperity had to be found.

All in the CPSU agreed on the necessity to industrialize, but the difficult question was how to do this in the absence of revolutions in the highly industrialized countries of the West. At the very end of his life, Vladimir Lenin talked vaguely about using cooperatives and the importance of stimulating revolutions in Asia, but he had no answer. How to industrialize, because it was such an urgent question for the CPSU, became an important issue in the debates that accompanied the struggle for power after Lenin died. The position of the Right Deviation, led by Nikolai Bukharin, was to industrialize through an intensified NEP, very much as the Western European countries had originally done. This would mean encouraging a productive agriculture, the surplus of which could be accumulated to invest in industry and trade abroad in exchange for advanced technology. In other words, the Soviet Union would benefit from the normal exchange between city and countryside, the former making larger numbers of manufactured goods to trade for the latter's increasing crop yields, with government taxation of this process providing capital with which to build new factories.

Opponents within the CPSU criticized the Right Deviation's plan on three main grounds. First, it was a slow process, as the Right leaders readily admitted, whereas the Soviet Union needed to build its strength and its socialist base quickly for both national security and ideological reasons. Second, it permitted politically unreliable peasants and traders to play a dangerously key role in the process. Finally and most damningly, the urban-rural economic nexus, instead of improving, began to break down in 1927 and 1928, when peasants reacted to higher government-set prices on the manufactured articles they desired by withholding grain from the market. Faced with unfavorable terms of trade, peasants ate more, stored grain, fed it to their livestock, and made it into illicit vodka. Supplies to the towns, to the army, and for export dwindled.

The Left Opposition, headed first by Leon Trotsky and later by Grigory Zinoviev, argued that only high-tempo industrialization could produce the rapid economic growth that the Soviet Union required. Consequently, the state must tax the peasantry and squeeze it in order to provide "primitive socialist accumulation" of capital, which could then be quickly infused into the rapidly expanding industrial sector. The Right denigrated this scheme as unrealistic, concluding, "You can't build today's factories with tomorrow's bricks."

But another aspect of Trotsky's views, part of his theory of permanent, or uninterrupted, revolution, was that the Bolsheviks must carry the proletarian revolution into Europe and Asia as quickly as possible because the building of socialism in the USSR depended on the triumph of the world revolution abroad. Also known as internationalism, the philosophy of Trotsky and his supporters argued that the Soviet Union could and should launch the process of rapid development, but that the USSR could complete the process only with the help of outside revolution, which the Communist Party should work vigorously to promote.

Between 1924 and 1928, Stalin occupied a middle position, not accepting high-tempo industrialization but criticizing the proposal of the Right as too slow and dangerous. Most importantly, Stalin vigorously attacked Trotsky's view that the Soviet Union had to depend on revolutions abroad, propounding instead a doctrine that came to be known as "socialism in one country." He based his case on a single quotation from Lenin, taken out of context. In a 1916 article, Lenin had speculated that, in exceptional circumstances, it might be possible for a country that experienced a proletarian revolution to build socialism alone, within its own borders, without help from the international socialist revolution that both Marx and Lenin had previously considered integral to the process. Lenin, however, made it clear that this could happen only in an advanced industrialized country. Stalin nevertheless applied the idea to the USSR, and naturally, it was immensely popular. In essence, Stalin exhorted his fellow citizens, "We Soviet comrades, by our own effort, sweat, and ingenuity, can build the glorious socialist future in our homeland without having to rely on help from outside." This appealing nationalistic vision helped him secure support from within the CPSU in his struggle against Trotsky and other rivals.

After he had defeated the Left opposition and as he was emerging in 1928 as the undisputed head of the party and leader of the country, Stalin adopted the Left's high-tempo plan as his own and determined to carry through a radical transformation of Soviet society. According to Robert C. Tucker, one of Stalin's best biographers, Stalin may have wanted to emulate his hero, Lenin: to make his own revolution to match the one Lenin had led in 1917 and, like him, to make his mark in Soviet and Communist history. The program Stalin espoused initially had three major components: complete nationalization and socialization of all nonfarming activity, from large industry to small service establishments; central state planning, under which economic decisions were made at the top and transmitted down to all enterprises; and extensive expansion of mechanization and new technology in every branch of economic activity. The State Planning Commission, known as Gosplan, drew up the First Five-Year Plan for the Soviet Union in August 1928, with the substantial but not unthinkable goal of increasing industrial output by 120 percent by 1934. In the following year, Stalin decided to up the pace of industrialization and doubled the goal. This required herculean efforts and seemed an unattainable objective.

Another aspect of Stalin's economic revolution was collectivization, the transfer of all peasant land, whether managed by the commune or individuals, into new agricultural units called collective farms. These were institutions which all peasants had to join and to which they were also required to contribute most of their livestock and tools. As you might expect, this pooling of assets delighted poor peasants with little to contribute and outraged better-off peasants with considerable assets to surrender. The party labeled the latter *kulaks* and, during collectivization, directed its main attacks against them.

Collective farms operated throughout the Soviet era. Members shared the work and the profits, according to the number of workday units an individual had contributed. But before it could take profits, the farm had to provide a certain share of its produce to the state. In 1929, this entailed a fixed amount to be delivered, then later, most commonly, a certain percentage of the output to be sold to state agencies. From the party's point of view, an obvious advantage of the collective farm system was that it gave party planners and state administrators greater control over agricultural production and, particularly, made the amount the state-run economy would obtain from agriculture more predictable. When peasants were individual proprietors and could trade on the open market, it was difficult for the government to know what would be produced and how much of it would enter the marketplace.

In our view, the desire for this degree of control was the main reason Stalin and his advisors finally opted for collectivization and pushed it so hard. The success of a forcible grain-collection campaign carried out in the Urals and Siberia in 1928 influenced Stalin to adopt compulsory collectivization. Nevertheless, according to some historians, Bolshevik planners never intended for collectivization to be the main method of organizing agriculture, but when peasants started to withhold grain from the market, thus threatening the industrialization drive, overzealous party officials at the national and local levels began to push collectivization as a way of intimidating the peasants, and the movement soon acquired a momentum of its own. In any case, at the end of 1929 and the beginning of 1930, collectivization was pursued so vigorously that Stalin had to make a speech, "Dizzy with Success," urging restraint on party cadres and offering peasants a chance to withdraw from the collective farms. Many did so, but in subsequent months, pressure to form such farms slowly but steadily increased until, by 1936, 90 percent of all farming in the Soviet Union was collectivized, with most of the rest organized in farms run directly by the state.

Many collective farms were organized by pressure and, if required, by force. Young Communist activists were recruited to go door to door in villages to persuade peasants to join. If the inhabitants were not won over, the army would be called in, the village surrounded, and the most recalcitrant peasants loaded on trucks to be taken to railheads for transportation to farms in Central Asia or to forced labor camps in Siberia. This campaign went hand in hand with an intensified Communist attack on organized religion. Many priests were arrested, and most Orthodox churches, synagogues, and mosques were closed. Schools and the media trumpeted atheism, and believers were harassed and persecuted.

Many peasants, rather than turn their livestock over to the collective farm, slaughtered them. As a result, Soviet livestock herds were reduced by as much as one-half and had not recovered their pre-1929 numbers when they were decimated again by World War II. In 1933, a major famine struck Ukraine and southwestern Russia, areas where resistance to collectivization had been strong. Stalin insisted that grain exports and government grain procurement be maintained, covered up the disaster, and made little effort to stop the famine. During this famine and the collectivization drive, some four to five million people perished.

Whatever the debates on the origins of collectivization, many analysts agree that the program was an economic disaster. Peasant disruption and resistance meant that under the First Five-Year Plan agricultural output increased by only 65 percent of its planned target, creating the necessity to ration food in the Soviet Union. Moreover, in the long run, collective farming did not prove to be efficient, and it remained a major problem for subsequent Soviet leaders.

Industrialization under the First Five-Year Plan enjoyed greater success. The plan was declared completed at the end of 1932, after four years and three months. Although there were many difficulties and its goals were not fully met, considerable progress had been made. The planners had counted on good weather, large crop yields, and substantial increases in agricultural productivity; in fact, there were two years of bad weather and crop failures, plus the disastrous collectivization already discussed. The planners had also assumed reduced defense costs and growing trade with the outside world. Instead, because of Japanese expansion in Manchuria, the Soviet Union spent more on defense, and the great world depression that began in 1929 meant that Soviet foreign trade fell off, with the Soviet Union therefore unable to buy as much Western technology as it needed.

The Second Five-Year Plan was completed between 1933 and 1937, and the Third Plan was two-thirds finished when Nazi Germany attacked the Soviet Union in June 1941. During the twelve years of intensive industrialization, from 1928 to 1940, Soviet industry grew fitfully, but at an average pace of 12 to 14 percent a year, an impressive performance. The urban population doubled, as did the number of workers. The plans emphasized heavy industry, which showed the greatest gains. For example, steel production increased fourfold, coal production fivefold, and generation of electric power ninefold. Plan goals were set in terms of quantity output, so quality was generally slighted. Improving the quality of goods in the Soviet economy persisted as a major objective of Soviet planners.

Outside heavy industry, the five-year plans achieved much less success. Production goals for light industry and consumer goods and services were consistently under-fulfilled, and agriculture lagged even further behind. As with raising quality, increasing agricultural output and production of consumer goods was a continuing concern of the Soviet regime.

No one can doubt that the massive effort to industrialize the Soviet Union in the 1930s produced a substantial economic base and paved the way for the nation to become the second-largest industrial power in the world (after the United States) after World War II. The more difficult questions are, How was it done, and what did it cost?

In an analysis of the Soviet performance, one feature stands out. Soviet industrialization required total mobilization of all of the country's resources, material and human. In turn, this demanded prescriptive centralized economic planning and maximum control over every institution and individual in society. High-tempo growth under Soviet conditions left little room for the operation of autonomous interest groups or the initiative and wishes of private individuals. The CPSU and the Soviet state set the goals, chose the methods, managed the effort, and ensured that each citizen made the contribution the plan required. In this way, industrialization greatly reinforced the authoritarian trends already present in Bolshevism with which Stalin was so enamored. As a result, the Stalinist system can best be summed up as a blend of Bolshevism (one-party rule) and industrialization (mobilization and total control) in addition to paranoia and the use of terror.

Stalin and the CPSU used three basic instruments to ensure the Soviet people's all-out participation in industrialization and the Stalinist system: persuasion, incentive, and coercion. All three played a continuing role in Soviet society. Western critics sometimes overlook the genuine enthusiasm with which many Soviet citizens supported the industrialization effort, despite the heavy sacrifices it required. Several appeals the party stressed were particularly enticing. First, the vision of the future encompassed good times and material comfort. The hard work, low pay, and wretched conditions of the present were simply a down payment on the better life for all that socialism promised.

"Perhaps you, but certainly your children, will enjoy prosperity and happiness in the decades ahead," exhorted party members and government propaganda.

Second, the party emphasized patriotism of both the ideological variety, calling for diligence and devotion in defending the socialist revolution and the first workers' state, and the nationalistic sort, urging ethnic Russians to sacrifice so that Mother Russia could become strong enough to repulse external enemies. Chauvinism became increasingly prominent as the threat from Nazi Germany grew.

Finally, there was the subtle call to commit oneself to this great crusade, to find personal satisfaction in working shoulder to shoulder with one's fellow comrades for the good of all. Some of these themes can be identified in the following passage from a Soviet novel about the heroic construction of a new factory:

> On the landing of the steel-trellised tower stood Gleb, Shidky, and Badin, the members of the Factory Committee. . . . Right and Left in long rows red flags blazoned like beacon-fires.
>
> The factory! What strength had been put into it, and what struggle! But here it was—a giant, a beauty! Not long ago it had been a corpse, a devil's mud-heap, a ruin, a warren. And now the Diesels roared. The cables vibrated with electricity, and the pulleys of the ropeway sang. Tomorrow the first giant cylinder of the rotary furnaces would begin to revolve, and from this huge smokestack grey clouds of steam and dust would roll.
>
> And he, Gleb, no longer existed; there was only an unbearable rapture in his heart which was almost bursting from the flooding blood. The working class, the Soviet, the great life they were constructing! God damn it, we understand how to suffer, but we also know the grandeur of our strength.[3]

As a second mode of mobilizing the citizenry for industrialization, Stalin and the party provided two kinds of incentives. The first was material, primarily higher pay for producing more or for working in dangerous conditions or in remote areas. Under war communism, some ideologues had wanted to move toward equal pay for all, but in the early 1930s, Stalin made it clear that in building socialism, the motto would be, "To each according to his work"; the slogan, "To each according to his needs," would come into effect only when socialism had triumphed completely on a global scale. Engineers, technicians, and skilled workers were paid more than laborers and unskilled workers, and almost everyone was paid on a piecework basis. Norms, or goals, of output were set for different categories of work, and those who over-fulfilled their norms were rewarded financially as well as lionized. In fact, the Soviet government encouraged a whole movement to stimulate record-breaking output, called

Stakhanovism after Aleksey Stakhanov, a Soviet coal miner who consistently produced amounts of coal way beyond his production quotas. Another, subtler incentive was the chance to move ahead in society, to quickly achieve higher status and more prestige. Those who were loyal to the party and worked hard could expect rapid promotion, and Stalin created a whole new generation of upwardly mobile administrators and technicians to staff the party and the government.

Finally, persuasion and incentives were backed by coercion. The state tightened labor discipline, and those who worked poorly faced not just peer pressure, ridicule, and ostracizing but loss of their jobs, cancellation of their work cards (needed for employment anywhere), and even sentencing to a correctional labor camp as a "wrecker" or "saboteur" of the industrial effort. Many of those sent to the camps were put to hard labor, undertaking especially dangerous or heavy construction tasks as well as timbering or mining in unbearable climatic conditions. Millions died in the forced labor camps. Moreover, coercion was used against peasants and religious believers, and anyone who resisted party policy, or just tried to stand aside, was subject to harassment, intimidation, and eventually arbitrary arrest, imprisonment, and dispatch to the camps.

These methods of ensuring total immersion of the whole population in the industrialization drive were applied in all areas of Soviet life. No area could escape being harnessed to the overall effort. The arts, science, education, sports, what was left of the Orthodox and other churches in the USSR, and even the writing and teaching of history—all were expected to orient their goals and activities to promote industrialization. It was a countrywide, across-the-board struggle.

What was the cost? Millions were dead, millions more struggled to survive in labor camps, and the CPSU and state intruded into every aspect of a person's life. Moreover, in the 1930s, Soviet wage earners suffered a decline in their standard of living from its 1920s level, and because of the influx of new workers into the cities, housing conditions deteriorated, and for several years food was rationed. Most peasants were clearly worse off, although many who moved to work in the new factories eventually improved their lots. Was industrialization worth the cost? Some Soviet citizens believed it was. Others did not, and the question can only be answered in the long run in terms of an individual's own values and principles. Nevertheless, in assessing the outcome of industrialization, it is important to consider whether another way, a different plan and set of methods, might have achieved comparable results at a lower cost.

STALINISM: SOCIETAL CHANGE AND REPRESSION

We noted earlier that the Stalinist system grew out of an agglomeration of three elements: the authoritarian traditions of Bolshevism, the total mobilization and control demanded by industrialization, and Stalin's suspiciousness and willingness to resort to terror. Before turning to this last point, we need to summarize the formal structure of Soviet society in the 1930s.

The country was a federation of Soviet socialist republics, as Stalin's new constitution of 1936 confirmed. The various republics and smaller national units operated under the slogan "National in Form, Socialist in Content." This policy meant that, although the party encouraged some autonomy in cultural matters and local government, it enforced Communist orthodoxy in ideology and exerted tight political control over minorities. On the one hand, the minorities fared better under this arrangement than they had under imperial-era Russification. They had a chance to develop their own languages, cultures, and traditions. They benefited from expanded educational opportunities, some economic development, and the exercise of local rights. On the other hand, the non-Russians felt oppressed and exploited, resenting Communist, predominantly ethnic Russian domination, the party's strict centralized control, and Moscow's siphoning of local natural resources and economic profits to fuel the Five-Year Plans. In addition, local environmental degradation, ethnic Russian migration into non-Russian republics, and limited openings at the apex of political power embittered the minorities.

Federal, republic, and local governments were all based on soviets, which were councils of deputies at various levels elected directly by all Soviet citizens. The population was exhorted, expected, and pressured to vote, and turnouts of 99 percent of the electorate were regularly achieved. Elections were not a political contest since only a single slate of candidates was presented to the voter (a few defiant voters crossed out the list or otherwise marred their ballots, but they were an exception). The CPSU arranged the nomination of candidates (not all were party members) and controlled the soviets' decisions. The highest representative body was the Supreme Soviet, which confirmed the official government, the USSR Council of Ministers.

Though only about 7 percent of the population joined the party, the party set and revised ideology and policy, managed and oversaw the government, and directed and controlled judicial, social, economic, and cultural life. It exerted its power through party units in every institution and at every level of the system. For example, each university (or whatever organization a citizen was associated with) had a party committee that advised the administration, organized meetings of students and employees to explain national policy and encourage everyone to work harder, and kept a weather eye on the general conduct and progress of the institution and its members. Each party unit elected representatives to the next highest party body, and the topmost group was the Central Committee, comprising several hundred leading party officials who elected the Politburo, or executive committee, which usually consisted of ten to fifteen members and, in effect, ran the country. CPSU members were expected to serve as exemplars of rectitude and diligence, and party officials and the secret police constantly scrutinized their conduct and activity. Consequently, some individuals chose not to enter the CPSU, although it was the chief avenue for advancement to the highest positions in almost all fields of endeavor.

A huge bureaucracy and managerial class ran day-to-day life in the Soviet Union. When the USSR adopted the 1936 constitution, the Soviet Union officially became a one-class proletarian society, although the state recognized subgroups of workers, collective and state farmers, and the toiling intelligentsia. In principle, the whole society owned the means of production, or all significant economic enterprise. In fact, the state, directed by the party, ran the economy, and the average citizen had no say in its operation. Collective farmers were permitted a small plot of private land and a few animals, and all citizens owned personal property, including, for the few who could afford it, an automobile. Public housing provided cramped quarters for a very low rent; education and medical care were free. By 1940, almost all Soviet citizens under age fifty were literate.

These basic features of Soviet life were established or consolidated under the Stalinist system. Because of incentive pay and the superior economic and political position of high state and party officials, the 1930s saw increasing social differentiation. Marxist critics even argued that the government and the party elite formed a "new class" of rulers determined to defend their privileges against the mass of the population.

A puzzling aspect of the Stalinist system was its increasing reliance on terror. Historians have advanced various explanations of this phenomenon, but none seems entirely satisfactory. Lenin and the early Bolsheviks had resorted to terror in the desperate days of the civil war and had not hesitated to use force to bloodily suppress the peasant uprisings and the Kronstadt rebellion in 1921. Yet it was never a regularized part of the early Soviet system. Political opponents were encouraged to emigrate or drop out of politics, the secret police existed but did not yet possess untrammeled authority, and the number of concentration camps was limited. Even Stalin in the late 1920s did not eliminate the rivals he defeated, sending a few, such as Trotsky, into exile and demoting others, such as Bukharin and Zinoviev. Between 1934 and 1938, however, all this changed with an escalating series of purges, arrests, banishments to forced labor camps (known as *gulags*), and, finally, mass terror against a large part of the population.

Attempts to explain this nightmarish period as Stalin's consolidation and reshaping of power, or the cleansing of the party as an evolving component of the Stalinist system somehow run amok, or as Stalin's coldly calculated effort to ready the country for war and ensure that he would have a free hand in foreign policy are, singly or even taken together, simply not convincing. Since Stalin destroyed both the records and most of the high officials involved, we will probably never know precisely what led to the purges and terror. Rational and policy considerations there undoubtedly were, but any persuasive explanation of this era must take account of Stalin's personality and outlook. Much of what occurred only makes sense if it stemmed in part from the disturbed mentality, pathological cruelty, and extreme paranoia of Stalin himself. Insecure despite having established a dictatorship over the party and the country, hostile and defensive when confronted with criticism of the excesses of collectivization and the sacrifices required by high-tempo industrialization, and deeply suspicious that past, present, and even yet-unknown future opponents were plotting against him, Stalin began in 1934 to act as a person beleaguered. He soon struck back wildly at enemies, real or imaginary. The atmosphere of uncertainty, fear, and denunciation spread rapidly through the Soviet system and soon began to feed on itself. Petty tyrants sprang up at all levels of the party and the bureaucracy, and soon almost the whole society was engulfed by recriminations, irrational punishments, and paralyzing terror.

Our account can only touch on what happened at the highest levels of the party and government, but readers are reminded that the terror reached into almost every Soviet family and that its victims suffered terribly in both psychological and physical terms (an unforgettable account is *Journey into the Whirlwind* by Eugenia Ginzburg). During 1933 and 1934, shortly after the Second Five-Year Plan started, considerable grumbling spread countrywide about the continuing rapid pace and intense pressure of the industrialization drive. This was reflected within the party, and just before and during the Seventeenth Party Congress, criticism of Stalin surfaced, which undoubtedly irked him. Sergei Kirov, head of the party organization in Leningrad (formerly Petrograd, renamed after Lenin's death in 1924), proved to be the most popular figure at the congress, and Stalin may have seen Kirov as a rival. Some months later, on December 1, 1934, an assassin, apparently with the complicity of the Leningrad secret police, murdered Kirov. Whether Stalin ordered the killing has never been proven, but he clearly benefited from the elimination of a political competitor for power.

In any case, the investigation of Kirov's murder touched off a widening offensive aimed at first at such 1920s opponents of Stalin as Lev Kamenev, Grigory Zinoviev, and several other Old Bolsheviks of Lenin's generation. In January 1935, this group was arrested and imprisoned, then accused a few months later of complicity in Kirov's murder. In the summer of 1936, Zinoviev, Kamenev, and fourteen others were publicly tried, the charges now including not only subversion of the party but treason to the Soviet state on the grounds that some of the alleged conspirators had connived with Trotsky, who was still in exile in Europe, and with Nazi agents. Further trials took place in 1937 and 1938. In these show trials, most of the defendants confessed to crimes they had not committed, probably as a consequence of intimidation (perhaps torture), drugs, and psychological brainwashing. Those not prepared to confess were generally shot without trial. Nikolai Bukharin, however, may have outwitted his persecutors, as the following excerpts from his initial plea and final statement at his trial reveal:

> I plead guilty to . . . the sum total of crimes committed by this counterrevolutionary organization, irrespective of whether or not I knew of, whether or not I took a direct part in, any particular act [his denial of guilt].[4]

> For when you ask yourself: "If you must die, what are you dying for?"—an absolutely black vacuity suddenly arises before you with startling vividness. There was nothing to die for, if one wanted to die unrepented. And, on the contrary, everything positive that glistens in the Soviet Union acquires new dimensions in a man's mind [his rejection of Stalinism].[5]

Stalin ordered Bukharin to be shot.

The terror reached its climax between 1936 and 1938. Its dimensions are hard to believe. Archival research has indicated that 1.6 million people were arrested, and up to 3.6 million individuals were in prisons, labor camps, and internal exile settlements. In 1937 and 1938 alone, 680,000 people were condemned to death for alleged crimes against the state and the revolution. But others were executed outside the Ministry of Internal Affairs (secret police) system, and several million prisoners died of deprivation in the forced labor camps. Thus, adding estimated purge deaths of 3 to 4 million to losses during collectivization and the 1932–1933 famine of 4 to 5 million, the victims of Stalinism up to World War II total 8 to 9 million. Stalin's blunders at the outset of the war in 1941 and 1942 cost several million more unwarranted deaths, making Stalin history's most terrible executioner.

The purges particularly targeted the CPSU itself, with 40 percent of its members arrested and its top leadership decimated. Almost 70 percent of the delegates to the Seventeenth Party Congress in 1934 were arrested, most of whom were shot. Of the 139 members of the 1934 Central Committee, 110 were killed or driven to suicide. The generation that had made the October Revolution and built the Soviet state was eliminated, with few exceptions. Their places were quickly filled by a rough, less educated, ambitious new generation willing to knuckle under to Stalin, among whom were two future leaders of the Soviet Union, Nikita Khrushchev and Leonid Brezhnev.

The army was decimated as well. Only a few years before Nazi Germany's attack on the Soviet Union, the Red Army lost to the purges three of its five highest-ranking officers (called marshals of the Soviet Union), thirteen of fifteen army group commanders, 90 percent of all generals, and 80 percent of all colonels. Other elites in Soviet society—members of the professions, economic managers, and writers and artists—were similarly destroyed. Even the secret police fell victim, as several of its chiefs were accused and executed. Finally, in early 1939, the purge wound down, perhaps because Stalin recognized that conflict with Germany was an imminent possibility. Throughout and after the purges, the official cult of Stalin continued to grow unabashedly. The monstrous crimes associated with the terror did nothing to temper the fulsome praise and repetitive flattery the Soviet press heaped on Stalin, tributes that he apparently craved and accepted as his due.

SOVIET CULTURE, 1917–1953

The conservatism, rigidity, and authoritarianism of the Stalinist system restricted and debased the arts. For a decade after the October Revolution, experimentation and daring marked much of the work in Soviet literature, theater, and the visual arts. In part a continuation of the modernism and avant-garde trends that characterized Soviet culture in the first years of the twentieth century, this artistic boldness also stemmed from a sense of responsibility to society and the glorious new order the revolution was to bring. Vladimir Mayakovsky, among many others, placed his talents at the service of the new Soviet state, designing posters, writing propaganda poems, and staging pageants and plays with revolutionary themes. A few artists, like Marc Chagall, felt uncomfortable bearing this burden of social commitment and moved to the West. But many others, like Vsevolod Meyerhold, an innovative theater producer, and the composer Sergei Prokofiev, while keeping in touch with artistic movements in the West, continued to develop bold new forms and themes within Soviet Russia and the successor Soviet Union. As a result, the 1920s were years of great artistic ferment and considerable achievement, with Soviet artists making significant contributions to world culture in such fields as music and the cinema. For example, Sergei Eisenstein, a creative film producer and director, helped to pioneer new techniques, and his major films remain classics today.

Much of this modernist art and experimental creativity was quite incomprehensible to the masses of Soviet society, many of whom were illiterate or barely educated. Consequently, some critics within the arts and within the party began to insist that Soviet culture should strive to achieve greater simplicity and directness and that it should instruct and uplift the average Soviet citizen. This point of view received a decisive boost when the "second revolution" began in 1928. Every aspect of Soviet life was to be conscripted to help drive the engine of industrialization, and the arts were soon assigned the role of instilling enthusiasm, patriotism, and a dedication to higher production goals among the Soviet public. Artists were called on to serve as "engineers of the soul." This new trend was officially confirmed in 1934, with the promulgation of the style of socialist realism, which remained the guiding principle of Soviet culture.

Socialist realism required the artist or writer to portray life not as it really was but as it ought to be. Individuals were to act positively, and events were expected to develop in ways that accorded with party policies and goals. Heroes should be clearly delineated and villains appropriately characterized. Happy endings were common, and although the charge that too often farm boy met girl but married tractor was exaggerated, many socialist realist stories and plays had a predictability and sameness that made them tedious if not downright boring. Socialist realist art, for example, did not intend to portray a "real" worker or peasant but rather a romanticized version of what they ought to look like.

Although a few creative artists, like the composer Dmitri Shostakovich and the poets Anna Akhmatova and Boris Pasternak, were able to continue to produce fine pieces even when criticized for not adhering to the guidelines of socialist realism, most Soviet literary and artistic works of the 1930s and 1940s were banal and uninteresting. How much they served their purpose of inculcating uplifting values and attitudes among the bulk of the population is difficult to tell, but certainly the vitality of Soviet intellectual and cultural life declined in this period. Science and technology, which had been given an influential role to play in industrialization, continued to advance, although even there, in certain fields, party orthodoxy intruded, as for example when Stalin endorsed the erroneous views of the agronomist Trofim Lysenko, mandating that all scientists adhere to them.

THE SOVIET UNION BEFORE AND DURING THE SECOND WORLD WAR, 1928–1946

During the late 1920s, the Soviet Union continued the two-track foreign policy it had begun as soon as the Soviet state was established: promotion of proletarian revolutions abroad and accommodation and trade with other nations. As had happened earlier, the pursuit of the former goal made the latter more difficult at various times, and in 1927, a "war scare" erupted in the Soviet Union, a fear that Great Britain, perhaps assisted by France, might attack the USSR, partly as a result of revelations of Soviet-sponsored subversive activity in Britain.

Stalin and Trotsky clashed over how much emphasis to give to inciting socialist revolutions in other countries, with Trotsky urging a more aggressive policy in this regard. But whichever line the Soviet Union took, it seemed to backfire. After Trotsky's expulsion from the party, Stalin pressured the small Chinese Communist movement to ally temporarily with the larger Nationalist forces led by Chiang Kai-shek. In 1927, however, Chiang turned on his Communist collaborators and destroyed all but a remnant of the Chinese Communist Party. On the other hand, Stalin advised the German Communists not to make common cause with the moderate Marxist party, the Social Democrats, against the nascent Nazi movement. Again, the result was disaster: the Communists fought the Social Democrats tooth and nail, thus making it easier for Hitler and the Nazis to come to power. Once firmly in control, Hitler crushed both the Communists and the Social Democrats.

After Benito Mussolini's Fascists came to power in Italy and Hitler's Nazis were gaining strength in Germany in the early 1930s, and since both fascism and Nazism made communism their chief foe, the USSR's Communists agitated vigorously in international meetings for general disarmament and the signing of nonaggression pacts. This effort met a fairly limited response, although the Soviet Union succeeded in completing nonaggression and mutual defense treaties with Poland in 1934 and with France and Czechoslovakia in 1935.

Beginning in 1933 to 1936, Stalin and his foreign policy advisors took a new tack. On the diplomatic front, they urged strengthening the League of Nations, to which the USSR was admitted in 1934, and espoused the doctrine of collective security. The latter was a call for nonfascist states, including both the Soviet Union and the Western democracies plus the latter's allies in eastern Europe, to band together against the menace posed by Fascist Italy and Nazi Germany, which were in the process of forming the Rome-Berlin Axis, which was later joined by militarist Japan. Meanwhile, in the domestic politics of nonfascist European countries, the CPSU instructed Communist parties to seek political alliances and coalitions with democratic (and occasionally even conservative) parties to ensure that local Fascist elements would not seize power. This new policy was called "the united front," or, in France, where such a Communist-democratic coalition came to power temporarily, the Popular Front.

In 1935 and early 1936, the strategy of collective security suffered two serious setbacks. Italy conquered Ethiopia, for which the League of Nations administered a slap on the wrist, and Britain and France did nothing to stop Germany from remilitarizing the Rhineland in defiance of the Versailles peace treaty. In the middle of 1936, General Francisco Franco led a conservative rebellion in Spain against the leftist antifascist government there. The resulting Spanish Civil War provided a major test of the collective security and united front policies, a test both policies failed, revealing fundamental weaknesses in each.

During the Spanish Civil War, Fascist Italy and Nazi Germany supplied financing, weapons, and even some troops to Franco's Nationalist forces. The Soviet Union eventually aided the existing government, known as the Loyalists, in the same fashion. But Great Britain and France adopted a stance of neutrality, arguing that it would be illegal to assist the Loyalists. Since collective security depended on the major antifascist powers' acting together, the Anglo-French position undercut the possibility of preventing or punishing Axis intervention in Spain and raised grave doubts in Stalin's mind about the Western democracies' reliability as partners in the struggle against Hitler. Moreover, within Spain, mutual suspicion and mistrust between the democratic parties and the Communists weakened the Loyalist war effort, and in the end, the Communists used the situation to destroy some of their political enemies on the left. This outcome naturally alarmed democratic elements in the rest of Europe about the Communists' real purposes in a united front.

By 1938, after Nazi Germany annexed Austria, German ambitions seemed boundless, and it was clear that Europe was moving toward war. The question was: Who would ally with whom? At the time, the most likely and natural alignment appeared to be the Soviet Union and Western democracies against the Axis. But since strong conservative and pro-fascist forces existed in France and, to a lesser extent, Britain, a combination of Germany-Italy with the Western countries against the Communist menace, so detested in Fascist and Nazi propaganda, was certainly a possibility, one that Stalin and his advisors greatly feared, given their Marxist distrust of capitalism. Least likely seemed a pairing of the USSR and the Axis, separated as they were by an immense ideological gulf. Yet that is just what happened.

Two developments in 1938 apparently led Stalin to decide to cast his lot with Hitler's Germany, as unlikely as this match seemed. The first was the outbreak in 1937 and 1938 of substantial armed clashes with Japan along the border between the Soviet Union and Japanese-occupied Manchuria. The Red Army acquitted itself well, but Stalin was concerned that if he became involved in a war with Hitler, Japan might seize the opportunity to attack Siberia, catching the USSR in the vise of a two-front war.

The second was a crisis over Czechoslovakia. Stalin saw that when Hitler brazenly threatened the Czechoslovak government, an important ally of both the Soviet Union and the Western powers, France and Britain reneged on their treaty obligations, backed down, and meekly handed parts of Czechoslovakia to Hitler at the Munich Conference in September 1938. What did this say about the Western powers' reliability as allies against Hitler? Did it not suggest that they hoped to see the Soviet Union embroiled with Germany, then stand aside?

The USSR had also pledged to aid Czechoslovakia and undertook some military preparations, but it remains unclear whether the Soviet Union would have made good on its commitment. The Soviet government said that it was prepared to do so, but since its promise was contingent on French support of Czechoslovakia, which did not materialize, the Soviet Union never had to act.

Regardless of Soviet intentions, the lesson Stalin drew from the whole affair was plain. In early 1939, the Soviet foreign minister who had espoused collective security, Maxim Litvinov, resigned, and in a March 10 speech, Stalin subtly suggested to the Germans the possibility of negotiations.

Secret talks got under way a few months later. Although Soviet diplomats concurrently continued to negotiate with the Western democracies about a possible alliance, neither side trusted the other, and those talks languished. On August 23, 1939, an astonished world learned of the conclusion of a nonaggression treaty between the Soviet Union and Nazi Germany. Hitler achieved his immediate aim, the neutralization of the Red Army, and within ten days, Germany launched the invasion of Poland that triggered World War II.

Tens of thousands of loyal Communists around the world, disillusioned by the Soviet Union's joining hands with communism's worst enemy, resigned from their parties because of the Nazi-Soviet pact. Stalin seems to have been unconcerned; he had achieved his objectives by this diplomatic coup. First, he had avoided getting entangled in a war with Hitler, especially at a time when the Red Army and Soviet industry were not fully prepared for such a major conflict. Second, he apparently hoped that, once Britain and France came into the war, the Western powers would check the Germans and the two sides would exhaust themselves in a long struggle. Finally, he had made the Soviet Union far more secure. A by-product of the pact was Soviet acquisition of eastern Poland under a secret protocol as well as Soviet domination of Estonia, Latvia, and Lithuania in the Baltic and of Bessarabia, which occupied parts of today's Moldova and Ukraine. The Soviet Union annexed all of these lands in the summer of 1940. Thus, Stalin gained considerable territory as a buffer between the Soviet Union and the West, a distance that in fact proved valuable when the Nazis invaded the USSR in 1941. In addition, there is some evidence that Stalin, shrewd as he usually was, genuinely believed he had made a deal with Hitler that might last for some time. In *Mein Kampf* and numerous speeches, Hitler had made it clear that eventually he intended to conquer the Soviet Union. Perhaps Stalin thought this was just brave talk and that, because Hitler must be a realist, as Stalin was, the German dictator would be content with the division of territory and influence in eastern Europe that the Nazi-Soviet treaty provided for.

Whatever the reasons, Stalin and his advisors acted as if the new alliance were a long-term arrangement. The Soviet government soon provoked a quarrel with Finland that led to the 1939–1940 Winter War in which the Finns fought courageously. Although they were far outnumbered, the Finns retained their independence, although they had to cede some territory to the USSR. Soviet leaders assumed that they had a free hand in the Balkans and even revived the old question of interest in the Turkish Straits, pressing the Turkish government for bases there. In the meantime, Germany invaded Norway in April 1940, the Low Countries of Belgium, Luxembourg, and the Netherlands as well as France in May and June 1940, and occupied much of the Balkans, including Greece and Yugoslavia, in the spring of 1941. The stage was now set for a June 1941 Axis invasion of the Soviet Union, which was code-named Operation Barbarossa.

When the Nazi armies rolled into the USSR on June 22, 1941, no one was surprised, except perhaps Stalin himself. Suspicious that the capitalist West was trying to push him into war with Germany, misled by disinformation planted by German intelligence, and sure that Germany would not be so foolish as to invade the Soviet Union when Great Britain on its other flank remained undefeated after the Battle of Britain, Stalin refused to believe warnings of the impending German attack from British intelligence, his own military authorities, and even Soviet agents abroad.

Caught unaware, the Red Army fell back, sometimes in good order, sometimes in disarray, with heavy losses and large numbers of prisoners taken (see Figure 12.1). For the first few days, the party and the Soviet government made no response, as Stalin momentarily panicked. He finally made a radio address to the Soviet people exhorting them to a patriotic defense of their socialist homeland, and he soon created a five-man defense committee to organize and direct the war effort. The British, who had been standing alone against Hitler for the past year, rallied to the Soviet cause, and an Anglo-Soviet treaty was signed in July 1941. After the United States entered the war in December 1941 following Japan's attack on Pearl Harbor, the so-called Grand Alliance of the Soviet Union, Great Britain, and the United States (later joined by Free France) was formed to fight Hitler and Mussolini.

In July 1941, the Germans made a decisive breakthrough on the central front, but decided not to throw all their strength at Moscow, turning instead to the south with its agricultural and mineral riches as well as the oil fields of the Caucasus. Nevertheless, by November and December 1941, Nazi forces had besieged Leningrad and were only a few miles from Moscow, where winter weather and Soviet resistance finally halted the German advance. Leningrad held out for two and a half years at a cost of seven hundred thousand dead,

FIGURE 12.1. Soviet prisoners captured during the German invasion in the summer of 1941.

and a Soviet counterattack eased the pressure on Moscow. During the summer of 1942, the Germans renewed their advance, making large gains in the south. At the end of 1942, in a brutal and devastating battle at the city of Stalingrad (now known as Volgograd), the Red Army, in house-to-house and sometimes hand-to-hand fighting, checked the German advance. Moreover, because Hitler refused to order a retreat, most of the German Seventh Army was captured there. The Soviet forces, however, failed to follow up their advantage, and a second major turning point in the war occurred at the Battle of Kursk in July 1943, the greatest tank battle in history. Soviet units, though suffering severe losses, finally routed a strong German force, starting a German retreat back across the USSR that ended with the Red Army's occupation of Berlin in April 1945 (see Map 12.1), in which hundreds of thousands of civilians and soldiers on both sides were killed. When fighting in the European theater ended in May 1945, at least twenty-five million Soviet citizens, including both military personnel and civilians, were dead. The physical, financial, and emotional damage to the Soviet Union and its population was colossal, and the impact of the Second World War, known as the Great Patriotic War, continues to be felt in Russia, Ukraine, and the other former Soviet republics to this day.

Besides their military mistakes in the Soviet Union, the Germans made a major political blunder. When Nazi forces first entered the USSR, many people, particularly Ukrainians, welcomed the Germans because they resented

MAP 12.1. The Eastern Front, World War II, 1939–1945.

Communist rule and exactions. If the Germans had treated the occupied population decently and met their basic demands, such as breaking up collective farms and reestablishing religion, they would have greatly weakened the Soviet people's will to resist and perhaps have won the war. But in part because Nazi ideology considered Slavic peoples as subhuman and in part because the Germans wanted to exploit the occupied territories economically, they instituted a reign of terror. Before long, the local population began to resist, and partisan bands did much to harass the Germans throughout the war. Moreover, word of what German rule was like spread behind the Soviet lines and stiffened the Soviet population's resistance.

Relations between the Soviet Union and its Western allies were far from smooth during the war. The United States provided $11 billion in lend-lease aid to the USSR, and both sides were committed to Hitler's total defeat, but prewar suspicions lingered. The major bone of contention was how soon the Western powers would open a second front against the Germans, thus relieving pressure on the Eastern Front. The Allies insisted they needed time to prepare, that it would be disastrous to launch an invasion of Nazi-occupied Europe prematurely, and that diversionary efforts, such as the campaigns in North Africa and the Allied landing in Italy, did in fact weaken the Nazis and draw forces away from the German-Soviet front. Soviet leaders kept pressing for an early invasion of Western Europe (it finally took place June 6, 1944); they feared that the Allies were deliberately holding back, hoping the Germans and the USSR would exhaust each other, thereby reducing Western casualties and preserving Allied strength as a way of ensuring Western domination of the postwar world.

Specific incidents also fueled bad feeling among the members of the Grand Alliance. For example, Western leaders allied with those Poles who had escaped from Poland and were still fighting Hitler were appalled by the Soviet attitude toward the discovery in eastern Poland of a mass grave of several thousand brutally murdered Polish officers. Despite strong indications that the perpetrators of this Katyn Forest massacre were Soviet forces (which later proved to be the case), the Soviet government refused to permit an independent investigation and blamed the Germans. Difficult diplomatic issues connected with the shape of the postwar world also evoked disagreements among the Allies.

CONCLUSION

After a belated Soviet entry into the war in the Pacific and a token invasion of Manchuria, Japan surrendered in August 1945. The Soviet Union suffered the greatest loss of life of any participant in World War II as well as extensive destruction of almost one-third of the country. Yet the Great Patriotic War acted as a psychological purge, removing the suspicion, tension, and uncertainty of the 1930s. The Soviet people and the CPSU gradually banded together in an all-out struggle to defend the country and repulse the Axis aggressors. By the end of the war, Soviet morale and prestige were high, buoyed not only by victory but by the wartime toleration of Orthodox religion and of greater intellectual freedom. Most citizens looked forward to a better life, and Soviet writers heralded the Soviet people as saviors of Western civilization from Nazism, just as Kievan Rus' had saved Europe from the Mongols in the thirteenth century and the Russian Empire had defeated Napoleon in 1812. Although, again, the USSR's vastness, assisted by Generals Winter and Mud, had helped the nation survive, Soviet patriotism could justifiably boast of the Red Army's triumphs and the people's total mobilization for the war effort. As a result, the Soviet Union emerged from World War II as one of two superpowers, along with the United States. These two large countries would dominate world affairs in the decades ahead.

At the same time, Soviet society was scarred and exhausted. Within a period of seventeen years, the population had experienced forced industrialization and modernization, the brutal reorganization of rural life, a chilling and inexplicable terror that killed millions of people, and a wearing, savage, and devastating modern war that lasted almost four years. Shell-shocked and bewildered, the people wondered what their sacrifices had meant and where they were headed. Would Stalin, whom, after some doubts, they had loyally followed in the fight for survival, at last turn out to be a benevolent leader? For Soviet citizens in 1945 and 1946, the future was open, and great hopes could be cherished.

FURTHER READING

Applebaum, Anne. *Gulag: A History.* New York: Doubleday, 2003.

Barber, John, and Mark Harrison. *The Soviet Home Front, 1941–1945: A Social and Economic History of the USSR in World War II.* New York: Longman, 1991.

Berkhoff, Karel C. *Motherland in Danger: Soviet Propaganda During World War II.* Cambridge, MA: Harvard University Press, 2012.

Brain, Stephen. *Song of the Forest: Russian Forestry and Stalinist Environmentalism, 1905–1953.* Pittsburgh: University of Pittsburgh Press, 2011.

Braithwaite, Rodric. *Moscow 1941: A City and Its People at War.* New York: Alfred A. Knopf, 2006.

Dolot, Miron. *Execution by Hunger: The Hidden Holocaust.* New York: W. W. Norton, 1987.

Figes, Orlando. *The Whisperers: Private Life in Stalin's Russia*. New York: Metropolitan Books, 2007.

Fitzpatrick, Sheila. *Everyday Stalinism: Soviet Russia in the 1930s*. New York: Oxford University Press, 1999.

Getty, J. Arch, and Oleg V. Naumov. *The Road to Terror: Stalin and the Self-Destruction of the Bolsheviks, 1932–1939*. Translations by Benjamin Sher. New Haven, CT: Yale University Press, 1999.

Ginzburg, Eugenia Semyonovna. *Journey into the Whirlwind*. Translated by Paul Stevenson and Max Hayward. New York: Harcourt Brace Javanovich, 1975.

Glantz, David M., and Jonathan M. House. *When Titans Clashed: How the Red Army Stopped Hitler*. Lawrence: University Press of Kansas, 1995.

Goldman, Wendy Z. *Women at the Gates: Gender and Industry in Stalin's Russia*. Cambridge, UK: Cambridge University Press, 2002.

Gregory, Paul R. *The Political Economy of Stalinism: Evidence from the Soviet Secret Archives*. Cambridge, UK: Cambridge University Press, 2004.

Hellbeck, Jochen. *Revolution on My Mind: Writing a Diary Under Stalin*. Cambridge, MA: Harvard University Press, 2006.

Hosking, Geoffrey. *Rulers and Victims: The Russians in the Soviet Union*. Cambridge, MA: Belknap Press of Harvard University Press, 2006.

Jones, Jeffrey. *Everyday Life and the "Reconstruction" of Soviet Russia During and After the Great Patriotic War, 1943–1948*. Bloomington, IN: Slavica Publishers, 2008.

Kaganovsky, Lilya. *How the Soviet Man Was Unmade: Cultural Fantasy and Male Subjectivity Under Stalin*. Pittsburgh: University of Pittsburgh Press, 2008.

Khlevniuk, Oleg V. *The History of the Gulag: From Collectivization to the Great Terror*. Translated by Vadim A. Staklo. New Haven, CT: Yale University Press, 2004.

———. *Master of the House: Stalin and His Inner Circle*. Translated by Nora Seligman Favorov. New Haven, CT: Yale University Press, 2009.

Kotkin, Stephen. *Magnetic Mountain: Stalinism as a Civilization*. Berkeley: University of California Press, 1995.

Lewin, Moshe. *Russian Peasants and Soviet Power: A Study of Collectivization*. Translated by Irene Nove. Evanston, IL: Northwestern University Press, 1968.

Merridale, Catherine. *Ivan's War: The Red Army, 1939–1945*. New York: Metropolitan Books, 2006.

Murav, Harriet, and Gennady Estraikh, eds. *Soviet Jews in World War II: Fighting, Witnessing, Remembering*. Boston: Academic Studies, 2014.

Naimark, Norman M. *Stalin's Genocides*. Princeton, NJ: Princeton University Press, 2010.

Pinkus, Benjamin. *The Jews of the Soviet Union: The History of a National Minority*. Cambridge, UK: Cambridge University Press, 1988.

Reid, Anna. *Leningrad: The Epic Siege of World War II, 1941–1944*. New York: Bloomsbury, 2011.

Roberts, Geoffrey. *Stalin's Wars: From World War to Cold War, 1939–1953*. New Haven, CT: Yale University Press, 2006.

Rossman, Jeffrey J. *Worker Resistance Under Stalin: Class and Revolution on the Shop Floor*. Cambridge, MA: Harvard University Press, 2009.

Scott, John. *Behind the Urals: An American Worker in Russia's City of Steel*. Enl. ed. Bloomington: Indiana University Press, 1989.

Service, Robert. *Stalin: A Biography*. Cambridge, MA: Belknap Press of Harvard University Press, 2005.

Snyder, Timothy. *Bloodlands: Europe Between Stalin and Hitler*. New York: Basic Books, 2010.

Tucker, Robert C. *Stalin in Power: The Revolution from Above, 1928–1941*. New York: W. W. Norton, 1990.

Ulam, Adam B. *Expansion and Coexistence: Soviet Foreign Policy, 1917–73*. 2nd ed. New York: Praeger, 1974.

Viola, Lynne. *Peasant Rebels Under Stalin: Collectivization and the Culture of Peasant Resistance*. New York: Oxford University Press, 1996.

THE SOVIET UNION DURING THE COLD WAR: SUPERPOWER, STABILITY, AND STAGNATION, 1946–1984

Despite the harrowing devastation of the struggle against Nazi Germany, Soviet society under Stalin and the CPSU's relentless discipline recovered physically from the war fairly quickly, although the emotional toll of the Great
Patriotic War lingered. The Soviet system remained rigid, inefficient, and unproductive, especially when compared to the surging economies of the West.
Moreover, the wartime alliance between the Soviet Union and the West soon
deteriorated into mutual suspicion and hostility. When Stalin died in 1953,
his successors, led by Nikita Khrushchev, modified Stalinism in an effort to
spark the economy and spur creativity. They also sought to avert the danger
of nuclear war by improving relations with the West. For a brief period in the
late 1950s, Soviet society appeared to blossom, but Khrushchev's reforms soon
foundered.

Senior party leaders critical of Khrushchev's policies ousted, but did not
purge, him in 1964 and set about restoring stability and building up Soviet military power. Although their efforts largely succeeded, economic growth slowed,
dissident intellectuals castigated the system, and a better-educated populace
became increasingly cynical and bitter about the inflexibility, arbitrariness,
and waste that characterized post-Stalin society. In the mid-1980s, a young,
energetic party chief, Mikhail Gorbachev, introduced sweeping changes that
eventually led to the collapse of the Soviet system.

AFTER THE WAR:
RECONSTRUCTION AND REPRESSION

Although triumphant over the Nazis, the Soviet people faced the monumental task of recovering from the staggering losses and devastation the war had brought. In the first two postwar years, they had to cope with minimum rations, a near famine in Ukraine, lack of housing, inadequate fuel and clothing, and wrenching social and psychological adjustments. Nevertheless, many citizens took up the challenge of recovery with considerable hope. They assumed that the relaxation of Stalinist orthodoxy during the war—the slight leeway given artistic and personal expression, the encouragement of the Orthodox religion, the resuscitation of Russian national heroes and traditions—would carry over into the postwar era as a reward for their devotion and courage, which had made victory possible. Some even believed that reconstruction would take place at a moderate pace, given their enormous sacrifices during the war and that the wartime allies of the USSR, particularly the United States, might help them recover.

The Soviet people did not have to wait long before these hopes were dashed. In a February 1946 speech, Stalin announced his harsh and forbidding program for the postwar Soviet Union. He called for sacrifice, superhuman work, and rigid conformity. He made clear that the Soviet government would rebuild the country by its own exertions, with minimal help from the West, whose capitalist system Stalin plainly distrusted. Stunned, Soviet citizens had no choice but to settle grimly to the task.

In 1946 and 1947, several developments underscored the completeness and severity of the renewed Stalinism imposed on the country. As soon as the war was over, the Soviet government made strenuous efforts to recover those citizens who had fallen into Western hands. Some of these were prisoners of war (POWs) captured by the Germans and liberated by the Allies; others were civilians whom the Germans had taken to Germany for forced labor or who had retreated from the USSR with the German armies rather than fall under Soviet rule again. In a tragic and terrible blunder, the Western governments at first cooperated with Soviet authorities in repatriating both POWs and civilians, many of whom strongly resisted going back. Once they were home, Stalin branded them as traitors and had many of them shot, imprisoned, or sentenced to forced labor.

At the end of the war, Stalin also persecuted several non-Russian nationalities. He snuffed out further expressions of nationalism and autonomy among the Caucasian peoples and the Ukrainians, who had been permitted during the stress of war to revive a sense of self-identity and traditional values as a means of encouraging them to make an all-out effort in the fight against Germany. In addition, the Soviet dictator accused some smaller national minorities of collaborating with the Germans. He abolished the autonomous territorial enclaves of the Volga Germans (who had immigrated to the Russian Empire in the late eighteenth century), the Crimean Tatars, the Chechens, and the Ingush (the latter two are peoples from the Caucasus Mountains). The state sent the leaders of these groups to forced labor camps and deported the rest of the populations to Siberia and Central Asia.

Stalin also became concerned about the attitudes of Soviet citizens who, during the war and postwar occupation of Germany and Eastern Europe, had come into close contact with Western cultures and values. The Soviet ruler recognized that hundreds of thousands of Red Army and government personnel abroad could compare, generally unfavorably, Soviet conditions with the standard of living that they observed in such countries as Romania, Hungary, and even war-torn Germany. To prevent such potential disaffection from spreading, Stalin sharply curtailed relations between the USSR and Europe and the United States. By imposing this "iron curtain," as Winston Churchill dubbed it, the state prevented Soviet citizens from traveling in the West and blocked the importation of Western visitors, materials, and ideas.

The USSR also instituted the Fourth Five-Year Plan, with high goals for total output and strong emphasis on heavy industry. Not only did this require substantial exertions by the population, but the slighting of housing and consumer industry meant that living conditions for the average citizen improved only slightly and slowly from the stringent wartime level. The Soviet people were expected to work hard but benefit little. Nevertheless, by the early 1950s, with the help of reparations from Germany, Eastern Europe, and Manchuria, the country's infrastructure was largely rebuilt, and production surpassed prewar levels.

THE COLD WAR

During the crusade against Fascist Italy and Nazi Germany, the capitalist West and the communist USSR joined in a common struggle for survival. For the moment, leaders of this Grand Alliance shelved, but did not abandon, their differing ideological principles. Stalin even agreed in 1942 to the Atlantic Charter, a vague statement of humanitarian and democratic war aims worked out by Franklin D. Roosevelt and Churchill. At the first major meeting among the allies, the Tehran Conference of November 1943, the Big Three (Stalin, Roosevelt, and Churchill) established cordial personal relationships. In 1944, they approved the creation after the war of a successor to the League of Nations, the United Nations (UN). They conceived this new international body, however, as a mechanism for extending great power control into the postwar world; the USSR, Britain, and the United States as well as later allies France and China each retained veto power over all important decisions of the UN's chief executive organ, the Security Council. The Soviet government also acknowledged its responsibility to repay American lend-lease aid, which eventually totaled $11 billion and whose trucks and logistical equipment were critical to the Soviet counteroffensives against Germany in 1943 and 1944 (in the end, the USSR repaid only part of the debt). Moreover, Stalin supported the idea of easing trade restrictions after the war, and he agreed to joint occupation and control of Germany following its defeat.

Beneath this atmosphere of allied cooperation, however, disagreements over political and diplomatic questions cropped up. These differences led to the disruption of the alliance and the beginning of a long, hostile relationship between the Soviet Union and the West known as the Cold War. Since the 1950s, historians have vigorously debated the origins of and blame for the Cold War. Revisionist scholars have attacked the dominant Western view that communist expansionist policies and the Soviet government's xenophobic refusal to cooperate with its former allies caused the break. Instead, they contend, economic and anticommunist considerations in US foreign policy spurred a drive for American dominance in Europe and the rest of the world designed to surround the socialist bloc and ensure Western control of vital resources and trade routes. In the face of this American-led "imperialism," they argue, the Soviet Union reacted defensively, taking steps to safeguard its security and its economic independence.

As with so many heated historical issues, elements of truth exist on both sides. Although we know little about how Stalin viewed the postwar world, a few clues suggest that he initially wished to continue cooperating with his wartime partners. He needed peace and stability so that the Soviet government could concentrate on the huge task of rebuilding the country. He also may have hoped that his wartime allies would aid Soviet reconstruction efforts. Yet at the same time he was suspicious of the Western nations, fearing that their capitalist ideology and leadership might drive them to constrain or even attack a weakened Soviet Union. Further, the Soviet dictator was determined to advance the security of his country. In particular, in the light of the historic record of attacks on the homeland from Europe, he sought to ensure that pro-Soviet governments ruled the nations of Eastern Europe, providing a buffer zone for the USSR's defense. Moreover, he could herald the establishment of communist regimes there as part of the inevitable advance of Marx's world socialist revolution.

Western leaders, for their part, saw Soviet efforts to dominate Eastern Europe as antidemocratic and expansionist, and they feared the revolutionary potential of strong communist parties in France, Italy, and several Asian countries. As a result, they adopted the policy of containment, designed to check the spread of Soviet power and communist revolution by establishing military bases and building "areas of strength" in countries surrounding the Soviet Union. Not surprisingly, Stalin and his colleagues viewed such efforts as a menacing "encirclement" of their nation and protested vigorously.

Each side was thus, to a considerable extent, imprisoned by its own perceptions and misconceptions. The breakdown of joint action and policy, the mutual recriminations, and the growing enmity between the Soviet Union and the West sprang from deep ideological mistrust, each party believing the other to be intrinsically committed to worldwide dominance. Marxism-Leninism taught that, as the capitalist system neared its death throes, it would do everything possible to crush socialism and thus stave off its inevitable defeat. Conversely, Western leaders believed that the communists were bent on world revolution and could be checked only by vigorous counteraction.

Two significant postwar issues reflected how these divergent worldviews played out in practice: the postwar division of Germany and the political alignment of Eastern Europe. After initial confusion within all the Allied governments, the Soviet Union, Britain, the United States, and France agreed at the February 1945 Yalta Conference and the July 1945 Potsdam Conference to control Germany jointly, even though each power had its own zone of occupation. The victorious nations also determined that Germany should pay substantial reparations, half of which would go to the Soviet Union because of its greater wartime losses. Stalin apparently favored a unitary German state under common supervision, recognizing that if Germany were split up, its richest regions would fall under Western influence. His economic planners, however, seem to have convinced him to treat Germany primarily as a resource for the restitution and recovery of the Soviet Union. The Western leaders, in contrast, wanted to permit gradual restoration of the German economy and polity so that the country would not become a drain on the postwar world.

Between 1945 and 1947 these different approaches led to escalating quarrels between the Soviet Union and the Western powers over the level and methods of Soviet transfers to the USSR of eastern German factories, goods, and equipment as part of Germany's reparations payments. Western officials concluded that the Soviet Union was "milking" Germany and expected the West to cover any resulting shortfalls. Soviet officials felt that they were only taking what they rightfully deserved. In addition, disagreements arose over de-Nazification, the reestablishment of German political parties, and economic relations among the four zones of occupation. In frustration, the British and US governments began to coordinate activities in their two zones of occupation and invited the French to join them. Alarmed that the Western Allies were creating a reunified western Germany that might later be armed against the USSR, the Soviet Union cut off land access to Berlin in June 1948. The city was under four-power joint control, but lay over one hundred miles inside the Soviet zone of occupation. Rejecting the use of force, the Western authorities responded to this blockade with an intensive airlift of supplies to their sectors of the city. They also made clear their determination to stay in Berlin. After eleven months of the Berlin Airlift, Stalin called off the blockade, but by the end of 1948, the de facto division of Germany was confirmed. Before long, two separate German states emerged: the German Democratic Republic (East Germany) under Soviet domination and the Federal Republic of Germany (West Germany) allied with the West.

Disagreements over Eastern Europe further poisoned Soviet-Western relations at the end of the war. At the February 1945 Yalta Conference, the Western powers obtained from the Soviet Union a promise to hold free elections in Poland and, by implication, in other nations of the region. Churchill and Roosevelt also agreed, albeit reluctantly, to the reimposition of Soviet control over the Baltic states of Estonia, Latvia, and Lithuania, part of eastern Poland, and Bessarabia (part of today's Moldova and Ukraine). Poland was compensated for territory lost in the east with land in the west taken from Germany and the German population in that region was forcibly deported.

Nevertheless, in the spring of 1945, Soviet operatives forced the creation of a communist-dominated government in Romania and postponed elections in Poland. Over the next three years, communist politicians, with indirect support from occupying Red Army forces, undercut coalition governments in most of Eastern Europe and set up regimes modeled on and subservient to the Soviet system. The climax of this process occurred in early 1948, when a communist-dominated government came to power in Czechoslovakia, and the respected Czechoslovak foreign minister, Jan Masaryk, committed suicide shortly afterward. The Western powers protested violations of the Yalta agreement, but they could do little. Some historians have suggested that the United States should have offered extensive economic aid to the USSR in exchange for political concessions in Eastern Europe, but it is unlikely that Congress would have supported such a gamble. Military intervention was out of the question since the Western countries had rapidly demobilized their forces after the war, while the Red Army remained on the ground in much of Eastern Europe. Why Stalin reneged on his Yalta promise is unclear, but zealous Soviet and Eastern European communists who wanted to spread the socialist revolution westward

MAP 13.1. Soviet territorial gains in Europe, 1939–1949.

may have convinced him that he could guarantee the USSR's security only if he established in Eastern Europe not just neutral but strongly pro-Soviet communist regimes (see Map 13.1).

Almost before it had been established, Soviet hegemony over Eastern Europe was broken by the defection of communist Yugoslavia under its wartime leader, Josip Broz, known as Tito. Yugoslav communists had come to power on their own as a result of a long guerrilla struggle against conservative opponents and the Germans, and Tito and his comrades had no intention of submitting to Soviet domination. Angered by Tito's resistance to Soviet orders, Stalin expelled Yugoslavia from the Cominform, the organization of communist parties that had replaced the Comintern, in 1948. Stalin reportedly said that he could wiggle his little finger and that would be the end of Tito. But Tito opposed Soviet subversion staunchly, and Stalin apparently decided that military occupation of Yugoslavia would be too costly.

The United States took the lead in responding to perceived Soviet revolutionary expansionism. In June 1947, to counter the growing strength of large communist parties in France and Italy, the US government launched the Marshall Plan, a program of extensive economic aid to Europe designed to buttress its reconstruction and economic stability. The Western European countries participated willingly, and Marshall Plan assistance contributed significantly to their economic rejuvenation in the postwar era as well as to the decline of communist influence in the region. Although several coalition governments in Eastern Europe expressed interest in the Marshall Plan, Soviet authorities, after brief hesitation, forbade their enlistment, accusing the United States of trying to insinuate imperialist control over Eastern Europe through the program.

A postwar communist revolution in Greece alarmed Western statesmen, who were unaware that Tito, not Stalin, was its chief supporter. Stalin's diplomatic pressure on Turkey to cede to the Soviet Union bases on or near the Turkish Straits, together with abortive Soviet efforts to annex a slice of northern Iran, further upset democratic leaders. As a result, American president Harry S. Truman announced in the spring of 1947 that the United States would provide economic and military support to Greece and Turkey and to any other country threatened by communism, a principle soon known as the Truman Doctrine. In practice, Western support facilitated the triumph of conservative Greek forces over communist rebels in a fierce, three-year civil war.

The height of the Cold War arrived in 1949 and 1950. In the former year, the Western powers banded together in a mutual assistance alliance known as the North Atlantic Treaty Organization (NATO). Before long, the Soviet Union responded by creating an Eastern alliance system, the Warsaw Pact.[1] Also in 1949, the Chinese communists came to power, winning a civil war waged off and on against the Chinese Nationalists since 1927 and intensively since 1945. Their Nationalist opponent, Chiang Kai-shek, was forced to retreat to Taiwan, and the Soviet Union gained a major ally in Asia.

The Korean Peninsula, like Germany, had been divided into two zones of occupation after Japan's defeat, a northern one under Soviet control and a southern one under American control. As the Cold War intensified, these two zones followed the German pattern, and the separate states of the Democratic People's Republic of Korea (North Korea) and the Republic of Korea (South Korea) emerged. In June 1950, a communist army from North Korea invaded South Korea. American forces under UN sponsorship rushed to the defense of the South Koreans. US leaders believed that Moscow had instigated the attack, but archival evidence indicates that Stalin acquiesced in the invasion and supplied equipment, arms, and high-level military advisors only after persistent North Korean appeals for Soviet assistance. He apparently feared that withholding support would drive the North Koreans into the arms of the Chinese. When North Korea neared defeat, the Soviet Union sent air-defense forces, including a few pilots, and encouraged the Chinese communists to intervene, which they did. Stalin may have hoped to see the Americans and Chinese tangled in a long ground war in Asia, but the latter withdrew after a military stalemate was reached, roughly along the line of division of the country before hostilities began.

Taken as a whole, Stalin's foreign policy after the Second World War achieved some important Soviet objectives. Except Greece, which aligned with the West, and Finland, which remained independent but was careful not to antagonize the Soviet Union, the whole belt of states in Eastern Europe lying between the Soviet Union and Western Europe became communist, although Yugoslavia and later Albania rejected Soviet direction and dominance. Through the Council of Mutual Economic Assistance, many countries in Eastern Europe, Asia, and the Caribbean were closely linked to the Soviet Union economically, usually on terms favorable to the latter.[2] East Germany was incorporated into the Soviet bloc, communist control was established in North Korea, and a communist revolution took place in China, albeit with minimal help from the Soviet Union.

On the other hand, Soviet actions in Eastern Europe and Germany and the invasion of South Korea provoked a strong reaction from the Western powers. Moreover, the Soviet Union, with the establishment of a pro-Western state in West Germany, lost any chance to extend its influence in Germany as a whole, and the position of communist parties in France and Italy weakened. The Soviet government faced continuing hostility from the West, and its prospects in the rest of the world did not seem bright. Still, the Soviet Union was secure and, in 1949, had developed its own atomic bomb.

THE FINAL YEARS OF STALINISM

As the Cold War intensified and Soviet citizens struggled to rebuild their nation, Stalin tightened his grip on the Soviet system. Although named generalissimo in the glow of victory, the Soviet dictator remained suspicious and secretive. He continued the loose administrative arrangements employed in the war, which permitted him to play ambitious subordinates off against each other. The Central Committee and the Politburo met irregularly, and he did not convene a party congress until seven years after the war. The Soviet dictator reestablished firm control over the armed forces and took harsh measures to reimpose communism in Estonia, Latvia, Lithuania, and western Ukraine. Overcoming guerrilla resistance in these areas, the government sent tens of thousands to labor camps or punishing exile in Siberia.

Stalin also launched a virulent ideological attack on capitalism abroad and on deviations from Stalinist orthodoxy at home. During the wartime Grand Alliance, Stalin and the Soviet government had played down the Marxist-Leninist view that the socialist and capitalist systems were inherently antagonistic, but in 1947, Stalin reaffirmed strongly that the world was divided into two camps, a peace-loving socialist one led by the Soviet Union and a warmongering, aggressive one led by the United States. He called on the Soviet people to make sacrifices to ready the Soviet Union for defense against threatened attacks by American imperialism, and he appealed to all "progressive" people in the world to rally to the Soviet cause.

The domestic implications of this ideological hardening were a crackdown in Soviet intellectual life and a new emphasis on Stalinist orthodoxy. A number of Soviet writers, composers, and artists were attacked for "bourgeois cosmopolitanism," that is, for not adhering closely enough to socialist realism in their work and to the Stalinist line generally in their attitudes. Since a large proportion of those castigated were Jews, an undertone of anti-Semitism permeated the campaign.

As he grew older, Stalin became increasingly suspicious, isolated, and irrational. He ruled virtually alone, acting through a personal secretariat and a set of party and government officials who were expected to carry out his orders unquestioningly and were too frightened to suggest alternative policies. Consequently, we know little about the motivations for Stalin's policies or what was occurring behind the scenes. In 1952, for reasons that are unclear, Stalin convened a party congress, the first since 1939. He also made some slight shifts in foreign policy. Whether these moves presaged a major change of direction and the initiation of new programs, as some have speculated, or whether they were simply the groundwork for a violent new purge, as others have concluded, is simply not known. Muddying the situation was the "Doctors' Plot": charges published a few weeks before Stalin died accused a group of mostly Jewish physicians, including several who worked in the Kremlin, the seat of the government and the party, of attempting to poison high officials. Whether this story was an omen of a new reign of terror with a strong anti-Semitic tone is not clear. After Stalin's death, the doctors were exonerated.

KHRUSHCHEV AND DE-STALINIZATION

On March 5, 1953, Stalin, then seventy-four years old, died from natural causes. With Stalin gone and no arrangements made for the succession, his close associates in the party appealed, in rather apprehensive tones, for the Soviet public to remain calm and to support "collective leadership," that is, rule by members of the Politburo (at that time called the Presidium). At the same time, they began jockeying for position, hoping to capture the supreme power that Stalin had wielded.

First, however, Stalin's successors decided to deal with the danger posed by Lavrentiy Beria, the head of the secret police, the KGB. Apparently, they feared not only the power that he derived from control over the country's internal security forces but also his ability to use the information about each of them that he had collected over the years. Moreover, Beria, from motives unknown, was espousing liberal reforms at home and concessions in foreign policy, ideas that frightened his insecure and conservative colleagues. At a dramatic meeting on June 28, 1953, they arrested the secret police chief, charging him with antiparty activities and treason. In December, Beria was secretly tried and executed.

The two main candidates to succeed Stalin were Georgy Malenkov, a colorless party stalwart who had seemed for a time in the early 1950s to be the heir apparent, and Nikita Khrushchev, an ebullient, dynamic, and versatile diamond in the rough who had apparently lost favor with Stalin in the dictator's last years. After Stalin's death, Malenkov became premier, and the party elite chose Khrushchev as first secretary of the party. Although Malenkov sought broad support by urging greater emphasis on consumer-goods production, Khrushchev gained the backing of influential military and economic officials by appearing to favor a continuing focus on heavy industry and by opposing proposed cuts in the defense budget. Effectively using his control of party affairs and key party appointments, Khrushchev gradually eclipsed his rival and, in February 1955, engineered Malenkov's demotion from premier to minister of electric power stations.

FIGURE 13.1. Nikita S. Khrushchev. (Courtesy of the Library of Congress, LC-USZ6–1382)

Hardly a commanding presence, the new leader of the Soviet Union was short, plump, and homely (see Figure 13.1). In the words of one of his personal secretaries, however,

> his broad face, his double chins, his enormous bald head, his large turned-up nose, and protruding ears could belong to any peasant from a central Russian village. . . . And only his eyes, his tiny, shrewd, gray-blue eyes that variously radiated kindness, imperiousness, and anger, only his eyes, I repeat, showed him to be a thoroughly political man who had gone through fire and water and was capable of making the most abrupt changes.[3]

His temperament and curiosity impelled Khrushchev to innovate and to propose significant changes in Soviet domestic and foreign policy. His training and experience kept him within the bounds of socialist orthodoxy and a one-party system. Born the son of a peasant turned coal miner in southern central Russia, Khrushchev received only primary schooling before becoming a machinist and fitter in the mines. Radicalized by Marxist literature as a teenager, he joined the Bolshevik Party and fought in the civil war. Afterward, he rose by grit and ambition through the party, which provided him with two years of education along the way. He directed party affairs in Moscow in the mid-1930s, including the construction of the Moscow subway system, and then served as party boss for Ukraine from 1938 to 1949. Spared from the purges, perhaps because Stalin admired his work in Moscow, Khrushchev had nevertheless acquiesced in the terrible purges of 1937. The new Soviet leader had also overseen the forcible incorporation of eastern Poland into the USSR in 1939 after the Nazi-Soviet pact and the reintegration of Ukraine into the Stalinist system after World War II, both processes involving suppression of anti-Soviet guerrillas and the shipping of hundreds of thousands of people to the forced labor camps. Later, when he denounced Stalin's crimes, Khrushchev hardly came to the subject with clean hands.

Khrushchev and his colleagues faced the considerable dilemma of how to reduce the rigidity and inefficiency of the Stalinist system without endangering the party's absolute control over the government and society. The Soviet economy had become increasingly wasteful and unproductive in Stalin's last years. The population as a whole was cowed by the threat of terror and exhausted by the continuing demands that Stalin had imposed upon them. Party officials and government bureaucrats had been paralyzed in making decisions or introducing new ideas because they were unsure of Stalin's views and opinions and because he might decree at any time a new orthodoxy or policy that would put them in the wrong; at a minimum, they would be demoted and disgraced and, at the worst, packed off to a forced labor camp. At the end of the Stalinist era, the system was creaking to a halt, with productivity, commitment, and progress all faltering.

First, Stalin's successors sought to reduce Stalinism's arbitrary terror. Thousands of political prisoners were released, and Soviet citizens were assured that random arrests were a thing of the past. The party emphasized "strict Leninist legality," which gave people a clear idea of where they stood and how far they could go in thought and action before running afoul of the regime. Intellectuals were encouraged to be more creative and to innovate to some extent. Managers and bureaucrats were instructed to think of new ideas and to participate more actively in economic decision making.

These measures improved the social and political climate of Soviet life, but Khrushchev shrewdly recognized that to spark the Soviet economy and society, to instill widespread initiative and commitment, the party would have to confront the repressive and conformist legacy of the old system more directly. Stalinism was out of date, and new methods were required if the Soviet Union were to function efficiently and have any hope of competing with the United States. Moreover, much like the situation Vladimir Lenin faced in 1921, the Soviet Union could not count on revolutionary help from abroad. Europe was recovering rapidly from the war, the Third World was busy achieving independence, and the chances of imminent world revolution were dim. Nor, given the suicidal danger of nuclear weapons, could the Soviet Union force the spread of communism as long as the United States was prepared to counter Soviet expansion. Consequently, the effort to improve Soviet life and move toward the ultimate goal of full communism would have to come from within.

In these circumstances, Khrushchev took a daring gamble. To rejuvenate Soviet society (and perhaps also to tarnish those political opponents closely associated with Stalin), Khrushchev decided to attack Stalinism and then to replace it with a reformed system. The risks of such a course were great. The Soviet power structure and foreign communist parties were filled with long-time Stalinists who would almost certainly resist a frontal assault on their recent hero and patron. Of even greater danger, criticism of Stalinism could logically lead to condemnation of the party itself and of the political monopoly through which it controlled Soviet society.

Of the top party leaders, only Khrushchev had the audacity to spearhead Stalin's debunking. He hit upon the clever idea of focusing his criticism not on the system as a whole but on Stalin himself. The party could thus be right, even though Stalin had been wrong.

Khrushchev launched the de-Stalinization campaign in February 1956 at the Twentieth Party Congress, to which he delivered a long, "secret" speech, castigating Stalin for a number of errors and crimes. The speech was secret only in the sense that it was not published and was intended primarily for party officials, but Western sources soon printed it, and Soviet citizens were shortly apprised of its gist by word of mouth. Khrushchev acknowledged Stalin's achievements in the party before 1934 and his success in industrializing the Soviet Union. But he went on to charge Stalin with having nurtured "a cult of personality" for his personal aggrandizement. This course had violated well-established party norms and led to grievous mistakes, including the murder of guilty and innocent alike in the purges, the failure to prepare the Soviet Union adequately for the German attack in 1941, poor military leadership during World War II, and repression and foreign policy errors in the postwar era.

Khrushchev also gave a chilling description of working with Stalin:

> Stalin was a very distrustful man, sickly suspicious. . . . He could look at a man and say: "Why are your eyes so shifty today?" or "Why are you turning so much today and avoiding to look me directly in the eyes?" The sickly suspicion created in him a general distrust even toward eminent party

workers whom he had known for years. Everywhere and in everything he saw "enemies," "two-facers," and "spies." Possessing unlimited power he indulged in great willfulness and choked a person morally and physically.[4]

Some of the individuals Stalin had falsely accused were rehabilitated in the speech itself. Others were restored to a place of Bolshevik honor in succeeding months; in particular, almost all the military leaders Stalin purged were subsequently vindicated. Most of the several million political prisoners in jail and in the camps were released in 1956 and 1957. The attack on Stalin was renewed at the Twenty-Second Congress in 1961, at which time his body was removed from Lenin's mausoleum on Red Square and places named after him were renamed.

Khrushchev's de-Stalinization campaign scored some successes at home. The party reined in the secret police and reduced arbitrary repression. Some energy and initiative were pumped back into the system. A loosening of rigid party controls over Soviet culture that had begun to develop shortly after Stalin's death, known as "the thaw" from the title of a 1954 novel by Ilya Ehrenburg, intensified after 1956, despite sporadic attempts to reimpose tight socialist orthodoxy. Vladimir Dudintsev's novel *Not by Bread Alone* scathingly castigated bureaucratic obscurantism in the system, and Yevgeny Yevtushenko's poems, which he read to large and enthusiastic audiences, called for honesty in public and private life and vigilance against a return to Stalinism. In November 1962, Khrushchev even personally approved publication of Aleksandr Solzhenitsyn's damning indictment of the forced labor camps and of the Stalinist system as a whole, the novel *One Day in the Life of Ivan Denisovich*.

At the same time, Khrushchev never fully trusted intellectuals and artists. In the fall of 1963, the Soviet leader viewed an exhibition of mildly abstract art. Disgusted and annoyed, he said of one still life that it was full of "messy yellow lines which looked, if you will excuse me, as though some child had done his business on the canvas when his mother was away and then spread it around with his hands." Moreover, he made sure that party control of cultural and intellectual life was maintained, despite a slight easing of restrictions and some encouragement of independent creativity among the intelligentsia.

PEACEFUL COEXISTENCE AND TROUBLES IN EASTERN EUROPE

As with his daring de-Stalinization campaign, Khrushchev proved innovative in the foreign policy arena. Before he died, Stalin had ordered a crash program to develop Soviet nuclear capabilities, but he had not reconsidered the overall position of the USSR in a world of two nuclear armed superpowers. Khrushchev and his colleagues soon tackled the issue. Given the enormous destructive power of atomic and hydrogen bombs, it was suicidal, the Soviet leaders realized, to predicate Soviet doctrine and external actions on the Leninist premise of a "frightful collision" between the socialist and capitalist systems. Instead, Khrushchev propounded an extension of the Leninist principle of peaceful coexistence, arguing that capitalism and socialism could live side by side until the time when socialism, by nonviolent means, such as economic example, political competition, and propaganda, would win over the world's peoples, and a global system of socialist states would be established. Or, to put it another way, for socialism to triumph, as it was bound to do according to the laws of history, war was not inevitable. The victory could come by peaceful means.

Soviet ideologists developed the new theory of the noninevitability of war during 1954 and 1955, and Khrushchev enunciated this doctrine at the Twentieth Party Congress in February 1956. Even earlier, however, Stalin's successors had begun to ameliorate the confrontational policies of the Cold War, and there is some evidence that Stalin himself was beginning to soften his foreign policies just before his death. In 1952 and 1953, Soviet authorities encouraged Chinese and North Korean acceptance of an armistice in the Korean War. In the civil war that had erupted in Vietnam after World War II, Khrushchev and his colleagues endorsed a ceasefire in 1954 and a partition of the country between forces of the communist revolutionary leader Ho Chi Minh and French-backed conservative elements in southern Vietnam. Also, the Soviet Union and the Western powers agreed in 1955 on a peace treaty with Austria that ended their postwar occupation of that country in exchange for an Austrian pledge of neutrality.

In 1958, Khrushchev reversed the closure of his nation that had existed since World War II and admitted Western tourists, scholars, and businesspeople to the USSR. He vigorously sought trade with the Western world and promoted cultural exchange agreements with the United States and other countries. Soviet performing arts groups, exhibits, students, and academicians came to the West and vice versa. Finally, the Soviet leader developed closer diplomatic, political, economic, and cultural ties with the countries of Asia, Africa, and Latin America and was delighted when Fidel Castro, the leader of a revolution in Cuba, declared in 1961 that he was a Marxist-Leninist and would establish a socialist system in Cuba.

Although the new policies associated with peaceful coexistence (or peaceful competition, as it should more accurately be called) did much to refurbish the Soviet image and enhance Soviet influence in the world, Soviet foreign policy also ran into marked setbacks in the 1950s and early 1960s, some within the socialist bloc itself and some in relations with the Western powers. Stalin had encouraged the view that international socialism was a monolithic movement wisely modeled on the Soviet experience and benevolently directed by the Soviet government. Many critics of the Soviet Union and most Western leaders unhesitatingly accepted this picture of socialist unity and Soviet control. Yet as early as 1948, the myth was shattered when the Yugoslav communists chose to pursue their own course free of Soviet dictation.

After Stalin's death, it became increasingly difficult to maintain unanimity within the bloc and direction by Moscow. As part of his de-Stalinization policies, Khrushchev relaxed the Soviet grip on Eastern Europe slightly, and some Eastern European leaders who had been persecuted in Stalinist times were rehabilitated. This was not enough, however, and in 1956, open opposition to Soviet domination erupted in Poland and Hungary. The Polish assertion of greater independence was spearheaded by Władysław Gomułka, a popular Polish communist, and other party leaders. In a dramatic showdown in Poland in October 1956, Gomułka and his colleagues reportedly told a visiting Soviet delegation headed by Khrushchev that if Moscow tried to enforce greater conformity on Poland, the Polish people, to the last man, woman, and child, would fight. The Soviet leaders backed down, and Gomułka was permitted to initiate reforms in state and party affairs in Poland.

Events in Hungary had a less benign outcome. For a number of months in 1956, there had been growing restiveness among Hungarian intellectuals and party members, but no individual or group emerged to focus and direct this discontent. Instead, the mood of disaffection spread to the general populace, and in October and November 1956, a popular rebellion broke out against the existing government and Soviet dominance in Hungary. Reformers under Imre Nagy struggled to control the situation, but dissatisfied rebels continued to attack Hungarian security and party institutions and personnel. At first, Khrushchev and his colleagues seemed willing to negotiate with the new Hungarian leaders.

In early November, however, as public pressure in Hungary for the removal of Soviet troops and the withdrawal of Hungary from the Warsaw Pact mounted, the Soviet leadership decided to act lest Hungary slide into the Western camp. They may also have feared the impact of Hungarian reformism on political and social stability at home. With sixty thousand troops, the Soviet army crushed the rebellion, killing or wounding more than four thousand Hungarians and subsequently executing three hundred rebels and imprisoning ten thousand more. Thousands of Hungarians fled to the West. Since almost everyone, including many people within the socialist bloc and the Soviet Union, knew that the rebels were just average citizens, not counterrevolutionaries and hooligans as the Soviet media charged, the suppression of the uprising gravely damaged the Soviet Union's image as a defender of the rights of the masses, and many communists in the West left the party at that time.

THE SINO-SOVIET SPLIT

In the late 1950s, Khrushchev encountered mounting difficulties in his relationship with Chinese communist leader Mao Zedong and in the Soviet Union's formal ties with China. The roots of the growing Sino-Soviet hostilities were deep, with multiple branches. After Stalin's advice to the Chinese communists in 1927 to cooperate with Chiang Kai-shek had resulted in their near destruction by Chiang, the communist revolutionary movement in China went its own way, fighting mainly on its own against the Nationalists and then, after the Japanese invasion of China in 1936, against the Japanese as well. Until near the end of World War II, the Soviet Union maintained rather distant relations with both Nationalist China and the communist Chinese in order not to offend Japan, with which it had signed a nonaggression treaty in 1941 designed to prevent the Red Army's having to fight a two-front war. Soviet entry into the war against Japan in the summer of 1945, after the defeat of Germany, made the Soviet government a cobelligerent with Nationalist China, and it reached an agreement with Chiang Kai-shek in August 1945. Because Stalin wanted to maintain this relationship and was not eager to see an independent communist movement come to power, the Soviet Union provided little direct support to Mao Zedong and his comrades as they battled to victory in China. Instead, Soviet authorities helped the Chinese communists indirectly by turning over Manchuria, which the Red Army had occupied in August 1945, as well as the Japanese war material captured there. They also provided some logistical support to the Chinese communist armies.

Nevertheless, the Chinese communists could justifiably feel that they had made their own revolution and were not beholden to anyone, least of all to Stalin and his Soviet comrades. Mao apparently resented the Soviets' meager assistance to his revolution, and these feelings were intensified when the Soviets limited their aid to the new communist Chinese government in 1950 and required repayment with interest. In addition, the Soviet government drove a hard bargain in the diplomatic and territorial arrangements that accompanied signing of a formal alliance between the two largest socialist countries. Finally, in what was clearly a personal affront, Stalin refused to treat Mao as an equal when the latter visited Moscow in December 1949.

Despite these inauspicious portents, relations between the USSR and the People's Republic of China were ostensibly close in the 1950s. From the Soviet point of view, it was important to keep the Chinese as allies during the Korean War, for which the Chinese supplied "volunteers," and while Moscow was having difficulties elsewhere in the socialist camp, notably in Yugoslavia, Poland, and Hungary. For their part, the Chinese modeled their system and pattern of rapid development on the Stalinist experience. Moreover, the new government needed Soviet economic and military assistance, no matter how limited, and it wanted Soviet diplomatic backing in its efforts to oust the nationalists from Taiwan and to win admission to the United Nations.

As the 1950s progressed, however, frictions increased. Mao was displeased with Khrushchev's de-Stalinization campaign, both because he had not been consulted about its advisability and because he thought it implied too soft a line in international affairs. After Stalin's death, Mao considered himself the senior communist leader and the chief Marxist theoretician in the world, yet Khrushchev treated him as a junior ally. Quarrels developed over the amount and quality of Soviet aid, and the Chinese bitterly resented the high-handed manner and methods of Soviet advisors and technical assistance personnel in China.

Lying beneath these surface irritants, however, were divisive territorial, political, and ideological issues. Ever since the seventeenth century, when imperial Russian expansion eastward reached the border of the Chinese empire, the regions lying between these two great countries and the exact boundaries between them had been in dispute. The Chinese believed that in the late nineteenth century and first half of the twentieth, when China was weak, the Russian state, whether imperial or Soviet, had taken advantage of China's relative decline in power to extract unfair territorial concessions. The Soviet authorities, on the other hand, argued that their position in the East Asia was historically justified and that, since 1949, they had been more than generous in trying to make boundary adjustments satisfactory to the Chinese.

The political and ideological questions centered in part on sibling rivalry within the international socialist movement. The Soviet leaders assumed they should head the movement, given their revolutionary seniority and greater power. The Chinese, historically sensitive on issues of precedence and ruling the largest communist country in the world, resented the Soviet Union's self-proclaimed role and, in any case, believed that the Soviet leaders often erred in their direction of the socialist bloc. Moreover, in Southeast and South Asia, the Soviet Union and the People's Republic of China competed for influence directly, the Soviet Union supporting the North Vietnamese against China and the Chinese backing Pakistan against the Soviet Union's friend India, for example.

The ideological dispute arose in part over Khrushchev's new doctrine of the noninevitability of war and his policy of peaceful coexistence. The Chinese insisted that these ideas violated true Leninism, making the Soviet leaders guilty of the serious ideological crime of "revisionism" (changing Marxist orthodoxy). The Chinese ideologists took a hard line, maintaining that the world communist movement should actively foment revolutions in the Third World and aggressively undermine world imperialism at every opportunity. They insisted that it was wishful thinking to believe socialism could be achieved peacefully and that coexistence was only an imperialist trap designed to lull the socialist states into passivity while the capitalist armies prepared to encircle and destroy them. In retort, the Soviet leaders accused the Chinese of adventurism and warmongering and of endangering the security of the socialist system in the nuclear age. By 1960, the differences between the Soviet Union and China had erupted into public denunciations and direct action. The Soviet side cut off aid to China and withdrew its advisors and technicians, including those who had been assisting the Chinese to develop nuclear technology.

SOVIET RELATIONS WITH THE WEST

Flare-ups of the Cold War broke through the calmer atmosphere of peaceful coexistence on occasion during the late 1950s and early 1960s. Germany remained a touchy issue between Moscow and Washington, with Soviet leaders charging that the West was rearming West Germany as a future aggressor against the USSR. In November 1958, Khrushchev suddenly announced that the Soviet Union would sign a unilateral peace treaty with the German Democratic Republic (East Germany) and give the East Germans control of the access routes to the Western sectors of Berlin unless the Western powers agreed within six months to withdraw their occupation forces from Berlin and recognize the city as an independent entity. The Soviet leader thought that he could pressure the West to recognize the German Democratic Republic as a Soviet satellite and relinquish Berlin. He apparently also hoped that a success over Berlin would quiet domestic critics of his recent cuts in Soviet ground forces and show the Chinese and their sympathizers in the world socialist movement that he could be tough on the imperialists. His calculations failed, however, when the Western powers rejected the ultimatum and reaffirmed their determination to stay in Berlin.

Khrushchev then sought broadened accommodation with the West, making a successful visit to the United States in September 1959 and unilaterally cutting Soviet troop strength in 1960. But the Soviet shooting down of an American U-2 spy plane torpedoed plans for a summit meeting in May 1960. Moreover, the nuclear buildup undertaken by the new US administration of John F. Kennedy in 1961 and the continued flight of talented East Germans to the West alarmed Khrushchev and his advisors. Once again, they stepped up pressure on Berlin. President Kennedy stood firm, and in angry response, Khrushchev agreed in August 1961 to East German leaders' plans to cut off the German Democratic Republic from West Germany by erecting a barrier between the two states. In Berlin, this barrier took the form of a twelve-foot-high concrete wall, which stood until 1989. In the fall of 1961, Khrushchev quietly eased the pressure on Berlin and agreed to negotiations on the issue, which dragged on until 1972. The Berlin Wall harmed the image of socialism and the Soviet Union, and his back-down over Berlin weakened Khrushchev's position at home.

The gravest crisis of this period, and indeed of the entire postwar era, occurred in October 1962. In the late 1950s, the Soviet Union had begun to reorient its military capability and its strategic doctrine around "rocket forces," that is, long-range ballistic missiles equipped with nuclear warheads. The United States, however, had substantial superiority over the Soviet Union both in missiles and in total numbers of nuclear weapons, including those delivered by planes and those launched from submarines. In a daring but foolhardy effort to overcome this inferiority before the United States knew what had happened, Khrushchev undertook to place medium-range Soviet missiles in Cuba, whence they could threaten the southeastern United States. American intelligence soon discovered this Soviet gambit, and President Kennedy, after several days' somber discussion with his advisors, ordered a blockade of Cuba to prevent further Soviet missile shipments to the island. He also asked the Soviet government to withdraw the missiles already in place.

It was a tense confrontation. If the Soviet Union refused to back down, the United States would have to invade Cuba, and a Soviet-American war, with the likelihood of devastating nuclear exchanges, could hardly be averted. At first, Soviet ships continued steaming toward the American naval forces stationed off Cuba, but at the last minute, they either turned back or, if they had no military cargo, submitted peacefully to being stopped and searched. Khrushchev communicated his willingness to withdraw the missiles in exchange for an American pledge not to invade the island and a secret US commitment to remove its largely obsolete missiles from Turkey. Kennedy agreed, and the American face-saving promises permitted Khrushchev to claim that he had thwarted the aggressive designs of American "imperialism." The Soviet leader failed, however, to convince his critics in the Politburo, and two years later, they used Khrushchev's back-down over Cuba as one of the reasons for ousting him from power.

The Cuban missile crisis sobered both sides in the East-West struggle, and in the following year, the Soviet Union and the Western powers signed a treaty banning all but underground tests of nuclear devices. The Soviet and American governments also agreed to establish a "hot line" of direct communications between Moscow and Washington, permitting the top leaders of each country to talk promptly and without intermediaries in the event of another major crisis.

KHRUSHCHEV: REFORMER OR REPAIRMAN?

Although his setbacks in foreign affairs provided ammunition for Khrushchev's opponents, failures on the domestic front led more directly to his downfall in 1964. Yet he accomplished a good deal, and the Soviet population clearly benefited from his efforts. Was Khrushchev a far-seeing reformer determined to recast Soviet socialism? Because he acted primarily as an energetic repairman, rushing here and there to apply patches to breakdowns in the system, the answer has to be no. Nevertheless, his domestic changes pushed Soviet society in new directions, and some of his policies foreshadowed the reforms Gorbachev would institute three decades later.

Neither doctrinaire ideologue nor innovative theorist, Khrushchev approached the problems of Soviet life pragmatically. Yet he sincerely sought improvement. Believing deeply in socialism's promise to provide a better life, he was convinced that citizens, if properly exhorted and rewarded, could be enlisted in the struggle to achieve that goal. Although Khrushchev never doubted the validity of the one-party system, the party, he believed, should guide and direct the people toward socialism without resorting to random terror. In 1961, he even promised that the Soviet Union could achieve communism "in the main" by 1980.

Many of his policies reflected these convictions. He strove to establish "socialist legality," that is, to ensure the rule of law and justice in people's civic and daily lives. As a result, individuals felt a much greater sense of personal security, for they knew that if they eschewed antiparty and anti-Soviet activities, the regime would not resort to arbitrary and illicit actions against them.

On coming to power, Khrushchev recognized that the Soviet economy was near crisis. He turned his attention first to the faltering agricultural sector, reducing taxes on the collective farmers' private plots and assisting collective farms with higher prices for their products and increased investment funds. In February 1954, he launched the daring Virgin Lands Campaign to bring under cultivation for the first time millions of acres in Kazakhstan and southwestern Siberia. This effort initially increased the Soviet annual grain yield from 82.5 million to 125 million tons, but uncertain rainfall and over-cultivation led to falling output in later years.

Khrushchev strove to improve industrial efficiency, increase housing, and strengthen planning. Reversing the position he had adopted during his power struggle with Malenkov, Khrushchev encouraged production of consumer goods and tried to curtail military expenditures. Moreover, he radically reorganized economic administration, dividing the nation into 107 regional economic councils called *sovnarkhozy*. He hoped to break the central bureaucracy's stranglehold on economic policy as well as to increase local participation in and supervision of decision making and production. This reform had some economic advantages as well as many drawbacks. Politically, however, it antagonized vested interests in the party who had been running the economy from Moscow. Their disgruntlement, plus growing doubts about the impact of de-Stalinization in Eastern Europe and the effectiveness of the policy of peaceful coexistence, led before long to a revolt of the party elite against Khrushchev's leadership.

In early summer of 1957, his opponents combined against him, although, unfortunately for them, they failed to develop a common or coherent platform. While the Soviet leader was away in Finland, the Presidium (Politburo) voted to remove him. Khrushchev, however, outmaneuvered his foes, calling a meeting of the party's Central Committee, in which he controlled a majority, to overrule the Presidium and denounce what he called the "Anti-Party Group" of his enemies. Unlike in the days of the purges or even more recently with Beria's fate, Khrushchev's opponents were not shot but merely demoted to minor positions or allowed to retire on pensions.

In the late 1950s and early 1960s, Khrushchev continued to seek ways to bolster the Soviet economy and had some early successes. On his visit to the United States in 1959, he declared jubilantly to his capitalist hosts, "We will bury you." He did not mean that socialism would literally conquer capitalism but rather that, with the gains he believed the Soviet Union was making, the day was not far off when it would outproduce the United States and thus win the rest of the world over to its socialist way of organizing modern industrial life.

For the Soviet people, Khrushchev improved housing and provided modest annual increases in their standard of living, while promising much more within twenty years. He markedly improved the lot of Soviet farmers and pensioners. The Soviet leader also accelerated the space program, which resulted in the launching of the first space satellite, *Sputnik*, in 1957. In ideology, he argued that the Soviet Union had now completed the phase of building socialism and was in "the transition to communism." Moreover, in a new party program adopted in 1961, Khrushchev abandoned earlier Soviet rhetoric about class struggle and the dictatorship of the proletariat, calling for collaborative efforts to create a "state of all the people." He espoused greater citizen involvement in public life and a concomitant reduction of the state's role. He harangued individuals throughout the country to work harder and to participate in grassroots efforts to improve the economy and social life. In addition, Khrushchev sought to broaden citizen participation in local and district soviets, and he established "comradely courts," in which fellow citizens judged minor offenders against public propriety and social order. At the same time, he strengthened the party's role in running the country and suppressed criticism of the party and of himself.

Juxtaposed to the record of improving Soviet citizens' lives, however, Khrushchev increased Russian domination over non-Russian groups in the Soviet Union. In 1962, he did not hesitate to authorize a bloody suppression of spontaneous workers' demonstrations in the city of Novocherkassk. He also cracked down on organized religions, forcing the closure of many churches and harassing clergy, bishops, and ordinary believers. Finally, Khrushchev did nothing to halt the continuing environmental degradation of the USSR begun in Stalinist times.

What had seemed in the late 1950s like a positive prognosis of socioeconomic development and an improving quality of life had considerably dimmed four or five years later. Moreover, in the early 1960s, Khrushchev introduced a major revamping of the CPSU structure, including term limits for holders of most party posts. The organizational changes in the party and, earlier, in the economy ruptured long-standing patron-client relationships and threatened the careers of many top bureaucrats and CPSU leaders. Unaware of his associates' increasing resentment and laboring under the burden of continuing economic problems at home and clear defeats abroad, Khrushchev found himself in October 1964 ousted from power in much the same fashion he had won it. A colleague, Leonid Brezhnev, rallied a majority of top party leaders against Khrushchev and then blocked his efforts to appeal to the party's Central Committee. Khrushchev was retired to a comfortable apartment in Moscow and a villa just outside the city, while his erstwhile comrades denounced him for reckless experimentation, attempting to establish a new "cult of personality" and "harebrained scheming."

In his almost ten years as dominant leader of the USSR, Khrushchev implemented de-Stalinization largely successfully, experimented brashly with limited results, and created for the outside world a new image of the Soviet Union as a dynamic society. Yet Khrushchev tinkered with the system rather than changing its structure or principles fundamentally. The Soviet Union was still a bureaucratic, authoritarian state dominated by one party run in turn by a handful of top leaders. Probably Khrushchev could not have gone further without endangering the party's monopoly of power. He had made unlikely a return to Stalinism, but he had not launched a more creative and responsive system. Yet his efforts helped inspire Gorbachev and the reformers of the 1980s.

STABILITY AND STAGNATION:
THE BREZHNEV YEARS

The succession after Khrushchev proceeded smoothly, despite some observers' predictions of intense political struggle and perhaps violence. Leonid Brezhnev (see Figure 13.2), who dominated Soviet politics for almost twenty years, from 1964 to 1982, was a worker's son who had become an engineer. He rose through the ranks of the party as a protégé of Khrushchev, serving in supervisory positions in industry, agriculture, and, during the war, the army. Stolid and cautious, he used his bureaucratic experience and his ties in the party to bolster his position. He pursued moderate, low-key policies and was careful not to rock the boat. For the first decade after Khrushchev's ouster, Brezhnev had to maneuver among potential rivals, emphasizing the collective nature of the party's rule and playing the role of first among equals. After 1975, he openly became the sole leader and even permitted a mini cult of personality to grow up around him.

At first Brezhnev and his colleagues largely continued Khrushchev's policies, although they dismantled some of his organizational experiments and ended his antireligious campaign. Under pressure from the armed forces, they soon began a major buildup of Soviet military capabilities, both in conventional weapons and in nuclear missiles and submarines. This program created a further strain on the Soviet economy, and Brezhnev wrestled unsuccessfully with the problems of increasing Soviet productivity and arresting the decline in the rate of Soviet economic growth, which dropped from 8 to 10 percent in the 1950s to 3 to 4 percent in the 1970s. Brezhnev struggled, also in vain, with the deficiencies of Soviet agriculture.

A prominent example of the dysfunction that characterized the Brezhnev years was the Baikal-Amur Mainline Railway (BAM), which Soviet propaganda proclaimed as the "Path to the Future." Covering more than two thousand miles across Siberia and the Soviet Far East, BAM was intended to showcase the unity, technology, and willpower of the postwar Soviet Union. Begun in 1974, BAM was officially announced as complete in 1984 but not actually finished until 2003. The railway was supposed to serve as a trade route to the Pacific and as an engine for the development of Siberia. Despite these lofty goals and the massive commitment of economic resources on its behalf, BAM proved to be an extraordinarily expensive boondoggle and a cruel joke to many Soviet citizens, as the railway suffered from a lack of quality materials and construction expertise, and was victimized by poor planning and an inferior workforce.

Early gains in the Soviet populace's standard of living leveled off by the mid-1970s, and Soviet citizens grew increasingly disillusioned with the party's

FIGURE 13.2. Leonid Brezhnev. (Courtesy of the Library of Congress, LC-USZ62–42178)

promises of a glorious socialist future. Goods shortages and inadequate consumer services were the rule. In an effort to make daily life more tolerable, almost everyone had to participate in the so-called second economy, which included activities that the regime tolerated but did not endorse: moonlighting in private jobs, pinching state equipment and supplies, buying and selling on the black market, and bribing storekeepers and head waiters to obtain scarce items and restaurant seats. Having to resort to these measures irked Soviet citizens and made them cynical about the regime and party. Nevertheless, the majority of the populace tacitly assented to an unwritten social contract with the regime: the government would guarantee them an orderly, stable society, lifetime employment at which they did not have to work too hard, and a reasonable standard of living. In return, the people would accept authoritarian, oligarchic rule and not press for social, economic, or political freedom.

Brezhnev abandoned Khrushchev's promises about the transition to communism, arguing instead that the Soviet Union had reached a stage of "developed socialism." Never entirely clear about what this entailed, Brezhnev seemed to have in mind a more efficient, technologically advanced, productive society. In 1977, Brezhnev proudly superintended ratification of a new Soviet constitution. The document made only minor changes to the 1936 constitution, updating and clarifying some legal provisions and reaffirming the leading role of the party in the Soviet state.

Brezhnev and his colleagues managed to calm the political waters roiled by Khrushchev's slapdash reorganizations and twists of policy. They slowed the pace of de-Stalinization while vetoing efforts to rehabilitate the tarnished dictator. They also proclaimed a new approach in party life, dubbed "trust in cadres," that is, reliance on the ability and wisdom of party leaders and stalwarts. The change produced political stability but also encouraged deal making among party, government, and economic officials at the local level. In addition, some regional party leaders became petty despots and slid into favoritism and corruption. Party officials' privileges in pay, housing, special stores, vacation retreats, and elite schools evoked widespread resentment among the population. Soviet citizens also bridled under the regime's bureaucratic, almost arrogant indifference to popular needs and aspirations.

DÉTENTE AND RENEWED COLD WAR

Brezhnev and his colleagues generally supported Khrushchev's inclination after the Cuban missile crisis to seek closer relations with the West. Surprisingly, US intervention against the communist revolution in Vietnam did not block closer US-Soviet relations, though it certainly strained ties between the two countries at times. After World War II, an indigenous revolutionary movement led by the communist Ho Chi Minh had sprung up in Indochina, which the French had colonized in the nineteenth century and the Japanese had occupied in 1941. Both nationalists and communists fought against the reestablishment of French rule in a broad-based movement that the Soviet government encouraged but directly aided only slightly, as we saw earlier. In 1954, the Soviet Union and the Western powers agreed to partition Vietnam into a northern communist-dominated zone and a southern anticommunist zone. At the end of the 1950s, the United States gradually assumed the responsibility of assisting South Vietnam in its civil war against communist insurgents, who received extensive assistance from North Vietnam. This commitment led finally to massive American armed intervention in Vietnam. Since North Vietnam was an ally of the Soviet Union and South Vietnam was an ally of the United States, the risk that Soviet support of Ho Chi Minh and his forces would severely damage Soviet-American relations grew. During the course of the war, however, both the Soviet and American governments, although highly critical of each other's stance in the Vietnam struggle, tried to minimize the deleterious impact of the war on their political relationship. Washington played down Soviet aid to the North Vietnamese, and Moscow conveniently overlooked the American military assault on its Indochinese ally.

In the summer of 1968, however, peaceful coexistence and Soviet foreign policy in general suffered a serious setback when a new crisis erupted inside the socialist camp. A group of communist reformers in Czechoslovakia led by Alexander Dubček began to introduce changes designed to "humanize" Czechoslovak socialism. The reforms were almost entirely related to internal party affairs and domestic policies, and Dubček and his followers were careful to stress that they had no intention of altering Czechoslovakia's adherence to the Warsaw Pact or its close alliance with the Soviet Union. Why these assurances failed to satisfy the Soviet leaders is not entirely clear. The most likely explanation is that they feared not only how far the Czechoslovak reformers might go and what impact this might have within the Soviet Union but also the possibility of growing pro–West German sentiment in the Czechoslovak party.

Led by the Red Army, Warsaw Pact forces (excluding Romania) invaded and occupied Czechoslovakia in August 1968. Unable to resist, the Czechoslovaks soon found themselves back under a communist government run by pro-Soviet hardliners. Yugoslav and Italian communist leaders protested the brutal repression of independent socialism in Czechoslovakia, as did Western statesmen, but Brezhnev was unfazed, announcing instead that the Soviet Union had the obligation to interfere in the affairs of communist societies that appeared to be "damaging either socialism in their own countries or the fundamental interests of the other socialist countries," a precept subsequently known as the Brezhnev Doctrine. The armed intervention in Czechoslovakia seriously harmed Soviet prestige worldwide and set back the evolving cooperation between the Soviet Union and the West after 1963. Brezhnev's repression of the Czechoslovak reformers also ignited protests among Soviet students and intellectuals and strengthened the growing dissident movement in the USSR.

In the early 1970s, the Soviet Union embarked on a new phase of coexistence, usually called détente. In international parlance, the word refers to a relaxation of tensions, but the Soviet leaders pushed it further in a consistent effort to reach agreements with the United States and the Western European nations on several important issues. The most significant by far was arms control. In the late 1950s and throughout the 1960s, both the United States and the Soviet Union had tacitly agreed to a nuclear stalemate. Each side made sure that it had enough nuclear weapons that could survive an attack by the other side to permit it to launch a devastating retaliatory strike. The certainty that retaliation would occur prevented, or deterred, the other side from attacking. This strategy of deterrence seemed to work, but it depended on neither side's getting too far ahead of the other in the arms race.

Soviet-American negotiations on arms control, begun in the 1960s, were suspended during the frigid Western reaction to the Soviet invasion of Czechoslovakia. In the early 1970s, progress was made, however, and in 1972, Brezhnev and President Richard Nixon signed an agreement banning antiballistic missile systems and a treaty limiting strategic weapons on both sides, the Strategic Arms Limitation Treaty, known as SALT I. To be sure, the treaty structured rather than curbed the arms race, as both the Soviet Union and the United States sought to improve the quality and survivability of their nuclear arsenals. A second agreement, SALT II, was signed in 1979; it was not ratified, but both countries informally abided by its provisions. From the Soviet point of view, the pursuit of arms-limitation accords had two important advantages. First, it helped reduce tension between the superpowers and presented the Soviet government as essentially peace-loving and accommodating. Second, it helped retard the Western military buildup and extension of the West's superiority in advanced technology and sophisticated military hardware.

Besides progress on arms control, détente helped produce a provisional settlement of the German question. Finally recognizing the reality of the division of Germany and the Western powers' determination to remain in Berlin, Soviet leaders agreed in 1970 and 1971 to a peace treaty with West Germany and to revised arrangements safeguarding the status of West Berlin. These accords paved the way for convocation of a European security conference in Helsinki, Finland, in the summer of 1975. After World War II, the Soviet Union and the Western powers had been unable to agree on peace treaties for Germany, Poland, and Czechoslovakia. Therefore, there was no formal recognition or international sanction of the new boundaries that had resulted from the war and the Soviet reorganization of Central Europe afterward (see Map 13.1). At the Helsinki meeting, the Western powers agreed to recognize the sensitive borders between Poland and East Germany and between Poland and the Soviet Union as well as other boundaries in the region in exchange for a Soviet promise to increase trade, cultural contacts, and the protection of human rights across all Europe. The Helsinki Accords and the earlier admission to the United Nations of both East and West Germany completed the process of legitimizing the postwar order and finally achieved a long-desired Soviet goal of gaining international recognition for the socialist regime in East Germany and for the Soviet position in Eastern Europe.

Although Brezhnev could point by the mid-1970s to a substantial buildup of Soviet military might and to some successes in the USSR's relationship with the West, he ran into difficulties in other parts of the world. Efforts to patch up the Sino-Soviet quarrel ran afoul of the internal radicalization of Chinese politics during Mao's Great Proletarian Cultural Revolution of the late 1960s. In March 1969, armed skirmishes broke out on the Soviet-Chinese border along the Amur River, and both sides threatened sterner action. By 1970, however, the crisis had cooled, and Brezhnev initiated negotiations with the Chinese, though these talks made little progress.

In the Middle East, Soviet policy encountered a major setback in 1967, when the Soviet Union's client states of Egypt, Jordan, and Syria suffered a humiliating defeat in the Six Day War against Israel. The USSR had to bear the heavy cost of replacing its allies' huge losses in arms and equipment. Moreover, in 1972, the Egyptian government, anticommunist in outlook and annoyed by Soviet meddling and dictation, rebuffed Soviet aid and expelled Soviet advisors. Finally, the Soviet Union was excluded from the peace process in the Middle East that resulted in the Egyptian-Israeli peace signed at Camp David in 1979.

From its apogee in the mid-1970s, détente rapidly eroded over the next decade. Three major trends drove this deterioration of Soviet-Western relations. First, neither side liked the weapons policy of the other, despite progress in negotiating SALT II. American strategists, on the one hand, feared a growing Soviet preponderance of heavy missiles with large warheads that might be used in a preemptive strike on the United States and objected to Soviet deployment of intermediate-range missiles that could reach targets in both Asia and Europe. Soviet leaders, on the other hand, condemned the placement of American cruise missiles in Europe and the proliferation of warheads on the United States' more accurate missiles. By the early 1980s, although both sides were abiding by the unratified SALT II agreement, the nuclear stalemate had grown tense, and each country was racing to develop more sophisticated weapons.

Second, human rights proved to be a thorny issue in Soviet-Western relations. Efforts by Brezhnev and Nixon in the early 1970s to expand trade greatly between the superpowers foundered on public and congressional criticism of Soviet restrictions on the emigration of dissatisfied Soviet Jews, who wished to leave the USSR for Israel or the West. After the 1976 elections, new president Jimmy Carter pressed the Soviet leaders to end the repression of intellectual and religious dissidents and to expand Jewish emigration. Brezhnev sharply rejected these American protests and clearly resented what he considered US interference in the Soviet Union's domestic affairs.

Finally, Brezhnev's continuing campaign to extend Soviet influence in the Third World alarmed anticommunists in Washington and other Western capitals. Although Soviet gains were in fact small, revolutionary activities in

Somalia, Ethiopia, Angola, and Nicaragua sparked calls for stern measures to stem the flood of communist expansion. In December 1979, the Soviet invasion of Afghanistan crystallized these apprehensions and ruptured détente for the next half decade.

The Soviet leaders blundered into Afghanistan partly because they misperceived the political situation there and partly because they greatly underestimated the Afghan people's grit and will to resist. Without Soviet assistance, a weak Marxist government came to power in Afghanistan in 1978. Because of popular opposition to its radical policies, this regime was on the verge of collapse in December 1979. Apparently, the Soviet leaders believed, quite erroneously, that the Marxist government would be replaced by an anti-Soviet, Islamic regime linked to the United States and China. To preserve the power of a friendly government in Afghanistan and enhance Soviet security by ensuring a pro-Soviet government on the USSR's southern border, Moscow ordered in the Red Army. The Soviet leaders obviously expected to overcome Afghan resistance and set up a puppet government in a matter of weeks.

The Afghan people, with a long history of opposition to British and imperial Russian interference in their country and with a fervent dedication to their land and their Islamic faith, fought a bitter, wasting guerrilla struggle for nine years, substantially assisted with arms, supplies, and money from the American and Chinese governments. The Soviet Union finally had more than one hundred thousand troops in Afghanistan, suffered substantial casualties, and bore most of the fiscal costs of the war. Afghanistan was devastated, hundreds of thousands of Afghan citizens were killed, and three to four million Afghans fled to Pakistan and Iran.

The war in Afghanistan tied up a considerable number of Soviet troops and equipment, drained the budget, and was unpopular at home. Despite some analogies to the futile American effort a decade earlier in Vietnam, there were important differences, among them that Afghanistan lay along the Soviet border, thereby posing a different sort of security problem, and that religion as well as nationalism played key roles in sparking the Afghans' struggle against the foreign invaders.

Undercut by the Soviet invasion of Afghanistan, détente suffered another blow in 1980 with the accession to office of a new American president, Ronald Reagan, who was committed to an expansive military buildup and global opposition to what he later called the Soviet "evil empire." Moreover, the crushing in 1981 of an independent Polish workers' movement, Solidarity, further strained Soviet-Western relations. Solidarity, which numbered ten million members, arose spontaneously in the summer of 1980 to protest economic inequities and government mismanagement and corruption in Poland. But when

Solidarity pressed for political control and threatened one-party socialist rule, General Wojciech Jaruzelski, under pressure from Moscow, declared martial law in December 1981 and banned the movement. Western leaders protested vigorously but could do nothing.

Détente collapsed in part because each side conceived the process differently. US leaders and the public believed that it meant not only a relaxation of tensions but positive and trusting cooperation. For their part, Brezhnev and his colleagues never assumed that détente signified a cessation of superpower competition in the world arena. They wanted to reduce tensions where possible and to strike deals of mutual self-interest but not to abandon their revolutionary prerogative of stirring up trouble for the imperialists wherever they could.

By the time of his death in 1982, Brezhnev's foreign policy lay in shambles. He had achieved nuclear parity with the United States and used military strength to expand Soviet influence in the Third World, but the collapse of détente and the war in Afghanistan placed heavy burdens on the Soviet Union. His successors faced a spiraling arms race, a continuing dispute with China, and expensive commitments abroad.

SOVIET SOCIETY IN FLUX

Brezhnev's emphasis on political stability masked deep-seated changes in Soviet society from the 1960s to the early 1980s. Soviet citizens became increasingly urbanized and more highly educated in that period. Two out of three people now lived in cities, ending the dominance of rural culture and outlooks in Russian and Soviet life. In 1981, over 10 percent of the Soviet population had completed higher education, compared to 1.5 percent in 1959; more than 70 percent had completed secondary school, against 12 percent in 1959. Most people were also more knowledgeable about the outside world and more skeptical about the regime's claims and record.

A generation gap had developed as well. By 1980, those under the age of fifty had only the dimmest memory of World War II, and those under forty-five had no adult experience with Stalinism. An aging leadership shaped by the Stalin era thus ruled a predominantly post-Stalin population. Younger people were increasingly critical of the deceptions, inefficiencies, restrictions, and failed promises of Soviet socialism. They came to believe that the system could do better, that basic changes were needed.

A handful of brave citizens turned their doubts into active opposition to the regime. A few fighters for religious freedom demanded autonomy for churches and congregations and an end to government interference in religion.

A small group of intellectuals espoused basic human rights, including freedom of expression and adherence to the law. Writers and artists resorted to *samizdat*, that is, the creation of works that would never receive official approval for publication but circulated privately among the intelligentsia. Dissidents published an underground journal, the *Chronicle of Current Events*, and formed committees for the defense of human rights. Prominent scientists like the renowned physicist Andrei Sakharov and authors like Aleksandr Solzhenitsyn joined the campaign. The dissidents among the intelligentsia, most of whom were atheists, nevertheless supported the religious dissenters. They also came to the defense of Jews who were being denied permission to emigrate (called *refuseniks*) and non-Russians who were protesting Moscow's suppression of ethnic minorities' autonomy and cultural integrity in the USSR.

Brezhnev and his colleagues treated the dissidents harshly, expelling them from their jobs and housing, imprisoning them, forcing them into exile abroad, and, horribly, confining them in mental hospitals. Solzhenitsyn was only one of many talented writers, musicians, ballet stars, and artists forced out of the country. Sakharov was confined to the provincial city of Gorky (now known by its traditional name of Nizhnii Novgorod) to cut off his contacts with Western scientists and journalists.

The dissidents, never more than a few thousand strong, had little influence on the mass of their fellow citizens and irritated rather than threatened the regime. Yet they sparked worldwide concern over human rights abuses in the USSR, served as a conscience for educated Soviet citizens, and kept alive the hope that alternatives to Soviet socialism might one day emerge among the Soviet peoples.

Apart from the dissident movement, a growing number of Soviet citizens rallied around the cause of environmentalism during the Brezhnev era. Imperial Russian and Soviet industrialization from the 1880s into the 1960s had polluted the country's air and water, exploited and wasted natural resources, and seriously degraded the environment in the Soviet Union. The regime suppressed information about environmental problems and covered up two major accidents resulting from the production of nuclear and biological weapons in the 1950s and 1960s. The government was unable, however, to stop the growth of a spontaneous citizens' movement formed in the 1960s to end the pollution of Lake Baikal in Siberia, the deepest lake in the world and the habitat of unique plants and fish. Other groups took up different environmental issues, sometimes with success, as when strong opposition forced the government to drop a plan known as Sibaral to divert several Siberian rivers to the Aral Sea in Central Asia. Citizens' associations also formed in pursuit of other interests, such as historical preservation and the revival of non-Russian traditional cultures. Moreover, the government itself relied from time to time on studies prepared by technical and other specialists in the intellectual community. Individuals involved in informal associations or specialized task forces frequently turned into strong supporters of reform in the Gorbachev era.

During the Brezhnev era, more citizens became aware that Soviet society suffered from major social problems, which the regime ignored or swept under the rug. Alcoholism pervaded Soviet life. Those under the influence of alcohol committed the majority of crimes, including rape, assault, and robbery. Heavy drinking also fostered spousal and child abuse and became the single most cited reason for divorce. Drunkenness led to substantial absenteeism and to poor performance and accidents on the job. Although alcoholism had been a problem in imperial times as well, Soviet authorities refused to recognize it as a disease. Moreover, because state revenues depended in part on the sale of vodka, the regime made no effort to curtail supplies. Although the Soviet government concealed most of the relevant data, such crimes as theft of state property and juvenile delinquency rose sharply. Poverty existed, with perhaps as much as 20 percent of the population having inadequate housing, food, and clothing.

Under Brezhnev, public health declined, and the health care system, which the regime consistently underfunded, fell behind its Western counterparts. Life expectancy for men dropped, and the infant mortality rate climbed. Except in a few specialized fields, Soviet medical techniques and facilities became increasingly outdated.

Rising divorce rates in these years had a direct connection to the shifting status of women, who shared in the social and attitudinal changes under Brezhnev. Making up 54 percent of the population at the end of the 1970s, many women benefited from the higher levels of education and somewhat improved standard of living since Stalin's death. In addition, women increasingly made independent choices about marriage, divorce, family size, and career path. Yet because of inadequate sex education and the shortage and poor quality of birth control devices, many Soviet women had four to six abortions, and some had as many as a dozen.

In the 1980s, almost 100 percent of non-Asian Soviet women of working age were either studying or held jobs, compared to about 75 percent in 1939. Women predominated in education, retailing, agriculture, and health care, but these careers paid little and had low status. Moreover, women seldom held the top posts and, overall, earned only 73 percent of the average male wage. Women were also poorly represented at the highest levels of the party and government, with only 4 percent of Central Committee members being women and no female ministers in the Soviet cabinet.

Finally, women continued to carry a heavy double burden, that is, to combine full-time employment with up to thirty hours a week of domestic responsibilities, including shopping, cooking, cleaning, washing, and caring for children. Although women had made some progress, Soviet society remained largely patriarchal in many ways, and the full equality promised by the socialist vision of 1917 remained out of reach.

The Brezhnev years saw a marked shift in the composition of the Soviet population as the proportion of ethnic Slavs declined, while the percentage of Central Asians climbed from 6 to 10 percent between 1959 and 1979. Party leaders' concern over this trend prompted the Brezhnev regime to adopt pro-natalist policies that encouraged Slavs and particularly ethnic Russians to have large families.

Although Brezhnev promised ethnic groups a continuation of Leninist policies that respected minority cultures, nationalism flourished among non-Russians as they became better educated and more urbanized along with the rest of the population. Study of indigenous language and literature expanded, and groups to advance local culture were established. Non-Russian intellectuals and elites increasingly resented Russian domination of the central institutions of the party and government and protested what they viewed as Moscow's economic exploitation of the local regions.

When Brezhnev died in 1982, Yuri Andropov, reputedly the ablest member of the ruling Politburo and head of the KGB since 1967, succeeded him. Although Andropov espoused greater efficiency and labor discipline and tentatively put forth some economic reforms, his poor health and early death in 1984 prevented him from making any substantial impact. Andropov's successor, Konstantin Chernenko, a nonentity in his mid-seventies, was in power for only a little over a year, dying in early 1985. Mikhail Gorbachev, who succeeded Chernenko, represented a different generation and soon began to develop radical reforms for the Soviet system.

CONCLUSION

Brezhnev and his immediate successors did little to build on the modest changes in the Soviet system initiated by Khrushchev or to renew his failed efforts to rejuvenate the economy and society. Instead, they opted for political continuity and the expansion of Soviet military power. But by the early 1980s, the Soviet Union faced a series of crises abroad as well as a stagnant economy and cynical, apathetic citizenry at home. At the same time, long-term subsurface changes in society and the patent inability of the aging leadership to keep up with the rapidly advancing nations of Europe and Asia prepared the ground for a major upheaval in a deceptively placid and stable society. The stage was set for Mikhail Gorbachev.

FURTHER READING

Andrews, James, and Asif Siddiqi, eds. *Into the Cosmos: Space Exploration and Soviet Culture*. Pittsburgh: University of Pittsburgh Press, 2011.

Bialer, Seweryn. *Stalin's Successors: Leadership, Stability, and Change in the Soviet Union*. New York: Cambridge University Press, 1980.

Boym, Svetlana. *Common Places: Mythologies of Everyday Life in Russia*. Cambridge, MA: Harvard University Press, 1994.

Cohen, Stephen F., Alexander Rabinowitch, and Robert Sharlet, eds. *The Soviet Union Since Stalin*. Bloomington: Indiana University Press, 1980.

Dobson, Miriam. *Khrushchev's Cold Summer: Gulag Returnees, Crime, and the Fate of Reform after Stalin*. Ithaca, NY: Cornell University Press, 2009.

Edmonds, Robin. *Soviet Foreign Policy: The Brezhnev Years*. New York: Oxford University Press, 1983.

Ellis, Jane. *The Russian Orthodox Church: A Contemporary History*. Bloomington: Indiana University Press, 1986.

Fursenko, Aleksandr, and Timothy Naftali. *Khrushchev's Cold War: The Inside Story of an American Adversary*. New York: Norton, 2006.

———. *One Hell of a Gamble: The Secret History of the Cuban Missile Crisis*. New York: Norton, 1997.

Garthoff, Raymond L. *Détente and Confrontation: American-Soviet Relations from Nixon to Reagan*. Washington, DC: Brookings Institution, 1985.

Harris, Jonathan. *The Split in Stalin's Secretariat, 1939–40*. Lanham, MD: 2008.

Holloway, David. *The Soviet Union and the Arms Race*. New Haven, CT: Yale University Press, 1983.

Jones, Jeffrey W. *Everyday Life and the "Reconstruction" of Soviet Russia During and After the Great Patriotic War, 1943–1948*. Bloomington: Indiana University Press, 2008.

Kagarlitsky, Boris. *The Thinking Reed: Intellectuals and the Soviet State, 1917 to the Present*. Translated by Brian Pearce. New York: Verso, 1989.

Khrushchev, Nikita. *Khrushchev Remembers*. 2 vols. Translated and edited by Strobe Talbott. Boston: Little, Brown, 1970, 1974.

Kotkin, Stephen. *Armageddon Averted: The Soviet Collapse, 1970–2000*. Oxford: Oxford University Press, 2008.

Luthi, Lorenz M. *The Sino-Soviet Split: Cold War in the Communist World*. Princeton, NJ: Princeton University Press, 2008.

Mastny, Vojtech. *The Cold War and Soviet Insecurity: The Stalin Years*. New York: Oxford University Press, 1996.

McCauley, Martin, ed. *Khrushchev and Khrushchevism*. Bloomington: Indiana University Press, 1987.

Raleigh, Donald J. *Soviet Baby Boomers: An Oral History of Russia's Cold War Generation*. Oxford: Oxford University Press, 2012.

Taubman, William. *Khrushchev: The Man and His Era*. New York: Norton, 2003.

Valenta, Jiri. *Soviet Intervention in Czechoslovakia, 1968: Anatomy of a Decision*. Baltimore: Johns Hopkins University Press, 1979.

Ward, Christopher J. *Brezhnev's Folly: The Building of BAM and Late Soviet Socialism*. Pittsburgh: University of Pittsburgh Press, 2009.

Zhuk, Sergei I. *Rock and Roll in the Rocket City: The West, Identity, and Ideology in Soviet Dniepropetrovsk, 1960–1985*. Washington, DC: Woodrow Wilson Center Press; Baltimore: Johns Hopkins University Press, 2010.

Zubok, Vladislav M. *A Failed Empire: The Soviet Union in the Cold War from Stalin to Gorbachev*. Chapel Hill: University of North Carolina Press, 2007.

CHAPTER 14

GORBACHEV AND THE COLLAPSE
OF THE SOVIET UNION, 1985–1991

On January 12, 1991, arguments, scuffles, and demonstrations swirled around the parliament building in Vilnius, the capital of Lithuania. Lithuanian nationalists confronted supporters of a newly formed "national salvation committee," who called for the dismissal of the Lithuanian parliament and the institution of emergency rule by Soviet president Mikhail Gorbachev. Lithuanian radio and television stations broadcast news and commentary backing the defenders of Lithuanian rights. At about two a.m. on January 13, reporters heard shots from the area around the main television transmission tower. Units from the local Red Army garrison were storming the tower. To overcome the token resistance of local guards and a handful of Lithuanian nationalists, the Soviet forces used tanks and machine gun fire. Fourteen people were killed as they were shot, beaten, or crushed under tank treads.

Only ten months earlier, the Lithuanians had asserted their right to independence and proclaimed their intention to withdraw from the Soviet Union. Gorbachev's conservative opponents viewed this act of defiance as symbolic of the political and moral disintegration of the nation caused by the reforms that the new Soviet leader had introduced upon coming to power in 1985. They determined to stop the Lithuanians at any cost. In the months preceding the January violence, elements from the army, the secret police, and the former Lithuanian Communist Party had harassed Lithuanian draft evaders, seized various public buildings and presses, and sent tanks rumbling by the Lithuanian parliament building as part of "military exercises." None of these activities had deterred the Lithuanians, and the killings at the tower only intensified their struggle for freedom from Soviet domination.

On January 13 and for days after, thousands of pro-independence Lithuanians rallied around their parliament building, erecting makeshift barricades. Others created a shrine near the television tower, to which hundreds brought flowers daily. Moscow authorities, including Gorbachev, insisted that the local Red Army commander had acted on his own and that they had known nothing about the attack until afterward. Reformers doubted this account and protested the violence. Although an uneasy calm prevailed in Lithuania for the rest of the winter, and Lithuanian and Soviet authorities renewed negotiations on the Baltic state's transition to independence, many observers concluded that the bloody January night in Vilnius symbolized the basic dilemma of the Gorbachev era: how to transform Soviet socialism without breaking up the USSR or precipitating civil conflict between reformers and conservatives. This chapter recounts Gorbachev's unsuccessful efforts to solve that dilemma.

THE ORIGINS OF THE GORBACHEV REFORMS

Mikhail Gorbachev seemed an unlikely individual to shake the Soviet system to its foundation. A party worker his entire life, he ascended into the circle of the CPSU elite by the late 1970s and faithfully served Leonid Brezhnev, Yuri Andropov, and Konstantin Chernenko in turn. His colleagues in the Politburo chose him as party leader in March 1985, partly for his dynamism and partly because his rivals for the post were mediocre. Yet his supporters also believed Gorbachev to be a loyal and dedicated communist, which indeed he was. Several circumstances, however, set Gorbachev apart and soon spurred him on the road to reform. He was younger than the other top leaders. Born in 1930, he had been too young for service in World War II and had missed most of the Stalin era.

As a university student, he had shared in the enthusiastic hopes for betterment generated by Nikita Khrushchev's halting reform efforts. Thus, Gorbachev represented a new generation tied neither to the Great Patriotic War nor to Stalinism. He and his cohorts wanted to rejuvenate socialism and improve Soviet life.

In addition, Gorbachev, unlike his predecessors, who were engineers and technocrats, had studied law and approached Soviet problems from a broad social and humanitarian perspective. Finally, both Gorbachev and his wife, Raisa, had become well acquainted with Western ideas and writings as students. In the 1960s, they had traveled in Western Europe, observing firsthand the growing disparity between Soviet and Western lifestyles and economies.

In jettisoning the comfortable continuity and safe mediocrity of the Brezhnev era and seeking to modernize and improve Soviet society, Gorbachev (see Figure 14.1) and his fellow reformers were reacting to profound changes that had taken place within the Soviet population in the four decades since World War II. Most people now enjoyed a relatively sophisticated life in the

FIGURE 14.1. Mikhail Gorbachev, General Secretary of the Central Committee of the CPSU and President of the Presidium of the USSR Supreme Soviet, addresses the United Nations General Assembly in 1988. (UN Photo / John Isaac)

city, not a brutal existence of isolation and privation in the peasant village and collective farm. People were much better educated than in Stalin's time and understood more about the outside world and their own society. They were not so pliable, and many had been chafing under the paternalistic domination and rigid tutelage of a narrow-minded oligarchy and gerontocracy. Some were beginning to want a say in where Soviet society was headed and how it was run. Many were critical of the continuing international tension and the lack of rights at home that accompanied the Brezhnev era.

Gorbachev possessed a general idea of where he wanted to lead the nation, but he certainly did not have a detailed blueprint for reform. He sought a better-off, more efficient, but still socialist society. The new Soviet leader wanted to modify, not recast, the faltering system he had inherited.

Gorbachev began by defining problems. As he sought solutions, however, one change led to another. Before he was fully aware of the cumulative impact of the reforms, he had torn apart much of the Soviet edifice, and the whole building was tottering. Nevertheless, almost from the beginning, Gorbachev recognized that his alterations embraced many aspects of Soviet life and were to some degree interrelated. In 1988, he described his reforms as including

> not only the economy but all other sides of social life: social relations, the political system, the spiritual and ideological sphere, the style and work methods of the Party and of all our cadres. Restructuring is a capacious word. I would equate restructuring with revolution . . . a genuine revolution in the minds and hearts of the people.[1]

Gorbachev and his supporters believed in the urgency of sweeping changes in part because they saw clearly how poorly the Soviet system was performing and how rapidly the continually advancing societies of Japan, the United States, and Western Europe were leaving it in the dust. Fundamental changes were necessary to maintain the great power position of the Soviet Union and to protect its security. In analyzing the Soviet system's difficulties, Gorbachev and his supporters focused on three major problems: inefficiency, backwardness, and poor morale. Although these were clearly interrelated, Gorbachev singled each out for special condemnation.

In regard to inefficiency, he faced up to the unpleasant fact that the Soviet economy's rate of growth had steadily declined since the 1960s and that in the early 1980s it was growing little, if at all. Given the needs of defense and the expanding demands of the Soviet population, this was an unacceptable situation.

In regard to backwardness, Gorbachev recognized that Soviet technology and techniques were behind the times. Soviet products were costly and shoddy, and the USSR's quality of life was clearly inferior to that of the highly industrialized societies of Japan and the West. Not only was the Soviet Union falling behind its chief competitors, but it seemed likely that before long the Soviet Union would sink into the second rank of the world's countries. Gorbachev himself summed up the Soviet Union's bleak circumstances:

> Analyzing the situation, we first discovered a slowing economic growth. . . . A country that was once quickly closing on the world's advanced nations began to lose one position after another. Moreover, the gap in the efficiency of production, quality of products, scientific and technological development, the production of advanced technology and the use of advanced techniques began to widen, and not to our advantage.[2]

On the issue of poor morale, Gorbachev attacked widespread apathy, sloth, corruption, cynicism, and alienation in Soviet society, a set of attitudes and behavior perhaps best summed up as a collapse of civic virtue:

A gradual erosion of the ideological and moral values of our people began. . . . Eulogizing and servility were encouraged; the needs and opinions of ordinary working people, of the public at large, were ignored. . . . The presentation of a "problem-free" reality backfired: a breach had formed between word and deed, which bred public passivity and disbelief in the slogans proclaimed. . . . Decay began in public morals. . . .

At some administrative levels there emerged a disrespect for the law and encouragement of eyewash and bribery, servility and glorification.[3]

In Gorbachev's view, all these deficiencies taken together—and he saw them as mutually reinforcing—seriously reduced the Soviet Union's military and political power in international affairs. Even worse, they made it unlikely that Soviet socialism could achieve the goals Gorbachev believed it should be able to attain. He insisted that a reformed Soviet Union could have a productive, efficient, technologically advanced economy, a rational and relatively humane society, and a peaceful, mutually beneficial relationship with the rest of the world. When these targets were reached, according to Gorbachev, Soviet society would be a shining exemplar of modern socialism and, as such, would soon win over to the socialist cause the majority of other nations. At the same time, Soviet citizens would enjoy a more secure, fruitful, and rewarding life.

PERESTROIKA AND ECONOMIC REFORMS

Shortly before and immediately after coming to power as the elected general secretary of the CPSU in March 1985, Gorbachev espoused a vague program of change. He urged economic decentralization, more self-government in institutions and society, increased public discussion of vital issues, and greater democracy in the party. He also made clear that he viewed the party as the chief instrument of reform. During his first two years in office, the new Soviet leader appointed a number of reformist advisors, replaced a number of senior and intermediate party leaders, and initiated a few steps to improve economic performance. The last included exhortations to accelerate production and improve efficiency as well as calls to link pay to quality of performance. Gorbachev even attacked alcoholism, primarily by restricting the sale of vodka, but this effort failed. He also pioneered a new leadership style, mingling with crowds on the street, listening to public complaints, and engaging in spirited exchanges with citizen critics of the existing situation.

When his early measures had little effect, the new Soviet leader called for *perestroika*, or restructuring, in Soviet society. Although the term is often applied to the entire package of Gorbachev's reforms, here we will use it to specify only those measures designed to rejuvenate the economy. Since Stalin's economic revolution of 1928 and 1929, with its emphasis on centralization and rapid industrialization, the Soviet economy had concentrated on quantity of output as its chief goal and its primary standard of effectiveness. Perestroika aimed to replace that criterion with new goals and measures: efficiency, rationality, high quality, and diversity of goods and services. At first, Gorbachev insisted that neither central planning of the economy nor state ownership of all major resources and productive capacities, the essentials of socialism, would be changed. By early 1990, however, under the pressures of a faltering economy and widespread popular grumbling, Gorbachev decided to permit private ownership of some enterprises.

Before this radical change of heart, Gorbachev had already altered the Soviet economy considerably with a complex set of reforms, five of which will be summarized here. One early reform, which had potential long-term benefits, was the effort to decentralize day-to-day economic decision making and to make factories and other individual economic units self-sufficient and profitable. Each unit's management was asked to decide for itself what to produce, how to produce it most efficiently and at the lowest cost, and where and how to sell the resulting product. Enterprises could also set wages and hire and fire workers. They would no longer receive financial subsidies from the state and would sink or swim on their own. Most of these changes were embodied in the Law on the State Enterprise, which went into effect on January 1, 1988.

A second area of reform, a corollary to decentralization, created a limited market mechanism through contracts for acquisitions and sales made by individual economic units. Economic reformers hoped that this change would lead to a rational allocation of goods, a selection of quality products, and rejection of shoddy merchandise.

Third, the government encouraged jointly owned or cooperative small businesses in services such as restaurants and repair shops and in light industry such as clothing and household articles. Even though the state heavily taxed these businesses, remaining profits were divided among members of the cooperative. Prices the cooperatives charged were not controlled and were consequently considerably higher than state prices for the same goods and services which, however, were often in short supply or simply unavailable.

A fourth reform was encouragement of foreign trade and foreign investment in the USSR. Gorbachev hoped both to acquire from abroad needed high-tech products, such as electronics, and to upgrade Soviet manufacturing methods through exposure to more advanced techniques from Japan and the West. The state ended its previous monopoly on foreign trade, and individual economic units were allowed to make their own arrangements with foreign suppliers and purchasers. Even joint ventures with foreign companies were permitted.

Finally, the reforms included several innovative steps to help the rural economy. The most important was permission given to families or other small groups on a state or collective farm to lease state land and arrange their agricultural work on a contract basis. Also, they were required to sell only part of their produce and livestock to the state; they could freely sell the remainder of their goods at higher prices on the open market.

During its first few years, perestroika's results were mixed at best. Some goods and services of better quality appeared, but many Soviet consumers considered their prices too high, and shortages of basic products continued and sometimes worsened. For example, in the fall of 1989, laundry detergent was simply not available, even in the two largest cities, Moscow and Leningrad. Soviet economic growth, after a brief spurt, slowed again and, by 1989, had not achieved even the levels of the 1970s. Soviet products were not able to compete internationally, and widespread inefficiency and waste continued to characterize the Soviet economy. Moreover, by early 1990, many citizens were highly critical of restructuring. The tangible and quick benefits they had expected had not materialized, and many citizens felt they were in fact worse off than before. This pessimism only exacerbated the economic situation: consumers rushed to hoard scarce items and showed little enthusiasm for working hard.

Although many factors explain perestroika's failure, a few were primary. First, perestroika was only a partial reform. Gorbachev wanted to retain key features of socialism while introducing some capitalist mechanisms. For example, because uncontrolled prices smacked of capitalist exploitation and because higher prices would provoke a strongly negative reaction among a population long accustomed to low, state-subsidized prices, Gorbachev was reluctant to open the market completely and to free most prices. As a result, managers of economic units were trying to make sensible decisions on costs and profit-and-loss calculations with totally unrealistic prices. Or, to take another example in the same area, Gorbachev and his advisors encouraged units to make their own decisions at the local level but left in place the central economic ministries in Moscow to provide overall plans and guidance. The result was interference from the central planners and ministry managers and inadequate independence and scope for the local managers—in short, a mishmash of a system and, not surprisingly, unsatisfactory results.

Bureaucratic inertia and resistance formed a second significant roadblock to economic reform. Both central planners and local administrators and producers were used to operating in the old ways. They were reluctant to change, and many who might lose their positions of power and influence if perestroika were to succeed actively opposed the reforms.

Finally, popular attitudes acted as a brake on restructuring. After years of not working too hard and enjoying a modest though predictable lifestyle, many Soviet citizens were unwilling to participate actively in perestroika's risks. Doing a good job and working effectively did not seem to promise much of a reward when there was little to buy or do. Moreover, rumors circulated that some might lose their jobs and that higher prices would soon become widespread. Higher and better-quality production depended in part, even under restructuring, on better work habits and different attitudes on the part of Soviet workers at all levels. Yet most people were slow to change, and by 1991, the economic situation deteriorated, and popular dissatisfaction with Gorbachev mounted.

NEW ATTITUDES IN SOVIET FOREIGN POLICY

Ironically, the area in which Gorbachev's reforms achieved the most, foreign affairs, brought him little credit at home, where Soviet citizens cared more about the worsening condition of their daily lives than diplomatic successes abroad. The Soviet leader's promotion of peace and improved relations with the outside world made him popular in Europe and America, but not in the USSR.

When he came to power in 1985, Gorbachev faced a dismal foreign policy scene. The Soviet Union's powerful position in world affairs had seriously eroded. Bogged down in a war in Afghanistan, deadlocked in a seemingly interminable quarrel with China, burdened with heavy subsidies to prop up communist economies in North Vietnam and Cuba, and confronted with an increasingly powerful North Atlantic Treaty Organization (NATO) and a nuclear arms and space race with the United States, the Soviet regime was clearly overcommitted and stymied. Gorbachev's first concern was to reduce these pressures so that he could concentrate on internal reform. But he also genuinely believed in international cooperation and felt that global peace would benefit everyone. Thus, early in his tenure in office, the new Soviet leader called for fresh approaches and innovative ideas in Soviet foreign policy, a process that he labeled "new thinking." Before long, he initiated changes that over the next five years revolutionized Soviet diplomacy, in the process ameliorating international tensions and markedly improving the Soviet Union's image in the world. Gorbachev helped to end the Cold War and shift the emphasis from the military and ideological struggle between capitalism and socialism to political accommodation and economic and cultural interaction.

Early in his rule, Gorbachev changed Soviet national security policy. Beginning near the end of Khrushchev's tenure in office and increasingly in the late 1960s and 1970s under Brezhnev, the Soviet leadership allocated extensive resources to enlarge the USSR's armed forces, both conventional and nuclear. This rearmament forced the nation to spend at least twice as much of its gross national product on defense as did the United States, a heavy burden for Soviet citizens and the faltering Soviet economy. The new Soviet leader stopped the military buildup and vigorously advanced arms control proposals. In doing so, he argued that Soviet security policy should be based on the idea of "reasonable sufficiency." Though a bit vague, this doctrine seemed to mean that the USSR should maintain only enough armed force to be reasonably sure that it could rebuff any threat to the security of the country. In other words, Gorbachev shifted the emphasis to defense and to limiting the Red Army's commitments outside the Soviet Union's borders.

Implementing this tenet, he first diplomatically and then militarily disengaged the USSR from Afghanistan in 1989 after a more than nine-year deployment. At the same time, the Soviet Union unilaterally reduced its armed forces, and scaled back its defense budget by several billion rubles. Finally, the USSR cut military assistance to Vietnam, Ethiopia, Cuba, and Nicaragua and made clear that it was not interested in any new military operations abroad.

The combination of Gorbachev's ideas of "new thinking" and "reasonable sufficiency" powerfully affected arms control issues between the Soviet Union and the West on three important levels. The first and most dramatic result was an agreement signed in December 1987, the Intermediate Nuclear Forces (INF) treaty, to remove from Europe and Asia missiles with a range between three hundred and thirty-four hundred miles. Under this pact, the Soviet Union eliminated twice as many intermediate-range missiles as the United States, but both sides kept short-range and battlefield nuclear weapons in Europe. West Germans and other Europeans were nonetheless delighted with the INF agreement because the missiles involved would have landed on them in the event of war between NATO and the Warsaw Pact powers.

A second result was the superpowers' decision in principle in 1988 and 1989 to cut long-range, or strategic, nuclear weapons by at least 50 percent. Subsequent negotiations resulted in the Strategic Arms Reduction Treaty (START I) embodying this decision. The US Congress and the new states of Russia, Belarus, and Kazakhstan that emerged after the Soviet Union's 1991 breakup adopted the treaty. Bilateral talks begun in the Gorbachev era resulted in 1992 in a new Russian-American agreement (START II) that further reduced nuclear arms, although the post-Soviet Russian parliament balked at ratifying this successor treaty.

A final outcome of the USSR's new security policy emerged in joint efforts among Gorbachev and Western leaders to reduce conventional forces in Europe. These negotiations were well advanced when rejection of socialist rule by the Eastern European nations and dissolution of the Warsaw Pact led to the phased withdrawal of the Red Army from Central and Eastern Europe.

Early in his tenure, the new Soviet leader instituted important changes in other areas of Soviet foreign policy, notably the USSR's relations with the developing world, the United Nations, China, and the West. After Stalin's death, Khrushchev and subsequent Soviet leaders sought to advance socialism in Asia, Africa, and Latin America through arms sales, economic assistance, and support of Marxist-Leninist revolutionary movements. The greatest impact of this endeavor had been to frighten anticommunists in the West; actual gains for socialism were small. In Cuba, for example, Fidel Castro's communist regime, hobbled by the nation's dependence on a single export, sugar, had mismanaged the economy and required hundreds of millions of dollars annually in Soviet assistance. Similarly, although the Vietnamese socialists had triumphed after a decades-long struggle against the French and then the Americans, their rule had been inefficient, and they too depended on massive Soviet aid. A socialist revolution succeeded in Nicaragua in the 1980s, and Marxist governments came to power in Angola and Ethiopia, with Soviet and Cuban assistance, yet these regimes were shaky, and the prospects for the advance of socialism elsewhere in the developing world appeared dim in the mid-1980s.

In his reevaluation of Soviet foreign policy, Gorbachev made clear that he was downgrading efforts to export revolution and that he did not expect any immediate victories for socialism in Asia, Africa, and Latin America. Instead of seeking influence or domination, Gorbachev said, the Soviet Union would not interfere in the internal affairs of such countries; rather, it would support their independent foreign policies and do what it could to assist them in development—on their own terms and with no strings attached. Gorbachev expressed hope that Soviet trade with the developing countries would substantially increase, and he forswore any intention of taking sides in regional or local conflicts in the developing world.

Together with this new general approach to the developing countries, Gorbachev took specific actions to ease tensions in Asia, Africa, and Latin America. He put pressure on Vietnam to withdraw its troops from Cambodia, which it finally did after a fourteen-year conflict. He cooperated in reaching a settlement designed to end the civil war in Angola and to ensure the independence of Namibia in southern Africa. Finally, he encouraged the revolutionary Sandinista government in Nicaragua to seek a political rather than a military solution to its struggle against US-backed Contra rebels.

At the same time that Gorbachev sought to regularize Soviet relations with states in the developing world, he initiated a more positive approach to the United Nations than his predecessors had adopted. He paid up almost all the USSR's obligations to that body and urged both large and small countries to support the UN's political and ancillary activities more fully. In an important speech to the UN on December 7, 1987, Gorbachev called for cooperation on such transnational issues as protection of the environment, management of developing nations' debts, and exploration of outer space.

Before Gorbachev came to power, the Soviet government began efforts to improve relations with China, but little progress was made. Gorbachev intensified the process of accommodation, but at first had little success. Chinese leaders insisted that, although they were happy to reestablish trade and economic relations with the Soviet Union, close political ties depended on four preconditions: the USSR had to reduce the number of troops and weapons positioned along the Chinese border, progress had to be made on the resolution of long-standing boundary issues, the Soviet Union had to see to it that Vietnam withdrew its troops from Cambodia, and the Red Army had to get out of Afghanistan. By 1989, Gorbachev had managed to fulfill all these conditions, and a major summit meeting convened in Beijing, the Chinese capital, in May 1989. Unfortunately, when Gorbachev arrived, Chinese students and workers were in the midst of public demonstrations and political protests that included occupation of Beijing's Tiananmen Square. This made the visit awkward, to say the least, and after Chinese leaders bloodily suppressed the student demonstrations a few weeks later, Gorbachev put the improvement of Sino-Soviet relations on the back burner.

Soviet policy in the rest of East Asia in the late 1980s was less successful. Japan remained critical of the Soviet Union, in part on ideological grounds and in part because of the Soviet refusal to return to Japan the Kurile Islands in the northern Pacific, which Soviet forces had occupied at the end of the Second World War. In Korea, Gorbachev urged the reclusive and oppressive socialist regime of Kim Il-sung in North Korea to seek closer relations with the newly democratic government of South Korea, but this advice was largely ignored.

Some of Gorbachev's greatest successes in applying "new thinking" in foreign policy came in the USSR's relations with Western Europe and the United States. The new Soviet leader determined to reverse the souring of détente that had occurred at the end of the 1970s and in the first half of the 1980s. In the fall of 1985, he held his first summit meeting with Ronald Reagan in Geneva. As Gorbachev hoped, he succeeded in charming the American president and locking the United States into serious arms control negotiations. Reagan began to support détente, soon agreed to the INF treaty, and endorsed further arms-control efforts. A meeting in October 1986 at Reykjavík, Iceland, strengthened the burgeoning cooperation between the superpowers' leaders. After George Bush succeeded Reagan in 1988, Soviet-American relations warmed still further. The new US president signed the START I arms-control accords and encouraged greater economic and cultural contacts between the two nations. Moreover, in 1990 and 1991, Gorbachev threw Soviet support behind the American-organized coalition against the regime of Saddam Hussein in Iraq, a former Soviet ally, although the USSR did not contribute troops to the Gulf War that followed. Gorbachev's encouragement of greater freedom of expression and religion within Soviet society and his approval of Jewish emigration largely eliminated the human rights issue between the two countries and contributed importantly to improving ties between Moscow and Washington.

Many Europeans were enthusiastic in welcoming the new Soviet leader's efforts to cut back arms and reduce tension. Gorbachev's visits to Western European capitals brought forth large crowds chanting, "Gorby, Gorby!" His policies greatly reduced many Europeans' fears of communist aggression and a possible NATO–Warsaw Pact war in Central Europe. For his part, Gorbachev called for a future "common European house" stretching from the Atlantic Ocean to the Ural Mountains, and espoused substantially increased trade with the more advanced European countries.

GLASNOST'

In reaching out to the rest of the world, Gorbachev strove to be more direct and open and displayed a willingness to listen to the concerns and opinions of others. This stance represented the foreign policy aspect of his domestic policy of *glasnost'*. Although the term is usually translated as "openness," no clear English equivalent exists, and in practice, the term had a more limited connotation. Gorbachev called it "openness in the interests of socialism." During the late 1980s, glasnost' meant the freedom, in fact the duty, to criticize and suggest innovations but within certain, if rather vaguely defined, limits. For example, glasnost' was not license to condemn Gorbachev, the CPSU as a whole, or the main principles on which the Soviet social and political system operated. Gorbachev was seeking fresh ideas, initiative, creativity, and originality, all to be applied to solving the country's massive economic and social problems. As a by-product, glasnost' supported accountability by encouraging criticism of poor performance, corruption, and idleness in the Soviet bureaucracy. Glasnost' did not, however, mean complete freedom of the press and of expression. Rather, Gorbachev wanted glasnost' to serve the positive purpose of encouraging new ideas, stimulating constructive attitudes and action, and raising the morale of the Soviet people as a whole and of the most creative group, the scientists, writers, engineers, and other university-educated specialists, in particular.

In April 1986, an environmental disaster at a Soviet nuclear power plant in Chernobyl in northern Ukraine near the border with Belarus provided a major stimulus to glasnost'. At first, government and party officials reacted to the accident in customary Soviet fashion, shrouding the affair in secrecy and displaying incompetence and confusion. Finally, after several weeks, Gorbachev acknowledged the seriousness of the meltdown and the resulting radiation, and during the summer of 1986, the Soviet press candidly discussed the Chernobyl disaster in detail. Moreover, in December 1986, the Soviet leader personally telephoned noted physicist and dissident Andrei Sakharov to invite him to return to Moscow from exile in the city of Gorky imposed by the KGB. Sakharov soon resumed his interrupted career and became an active supporter of democratic reforms until his death in 1990.

Glasnost' had an exhilarating effect on Soviet society in the second half of the 1980s. After sixty years of intellectual repression and conformity, people were astounded and delighted to be able to write and say pretty much what they pleased. Because the outer limits of permissible expression were quite broad, individuals could tackle almost any subject without fear of reprisal. This provided a great psychic lift for the educated elite of the Soviet Union and, as Gorbachev hoped, led to a flood of new ideas and constructive criticism.

In literature, works far removed from the dreary tenets of socialist realism were published, including interesting and revealing fiction and poetry by both established and emerging women writers, like Anna Akhmatova (see Chapter 12), Bella Akhmadulina, and Tatyana Shcherbina. Both Soviet and foreign authors had books published that had been banned for many years: for example, Anatoly Rybakov's *Children of the Arbat*, a novel about growing up under Stalinism, Boris Pasternak's *Doctor Zhivago*, a long-prohibited epic of the Russian Revolution, and George Orwell's *Animal Farm*, a satire of the Stalin era.

Radical new themes and approaches emerged in film, theater, and the fine arts. As in literature, both works long suppressed and new pieces appeared. Artists who had painted religious themes and in abstract styles but had never been able to show such works in public were now honored with exhibitions and brisk sales. Several popular movies attacked aspects of the Stalin era, and plays criticizing the bureaucracy and the problems of daily life were popular.

Newspapers, magazines, and television all expanded and diversified under glasnost'. The evening news on television, once the occasion of yawns, was now eagerly watched for the latest revelations. Issues of such radical publications as *Ogoniok* were snapped up at once and passed from hand to hand. Social problems such as crime, drugs, prostitution, and deviance, which had formerly been treated gingerly, if at all, were now discussed openly in the media. Even the KGB, the Soviet secret police, invited journalists to visit and ask questions.

Because history had been so greatly distorted under Stalin and because almost all Soviet citizens knew that what they had been taught about the past did not square with what had actually happened, glasnost' sparked great interest in revising the historical record. First, existing textbooks and courses in history were scrapped, followed by the establishment of a major commission on historical revision. Most historical personages in the Soviet past whom Stalin had purged or had written out of history were rehabilitated, although notably not Leon Trotsky. Formerly taboo subjects, such as the purges, collectivization, and the secret protocol of the Nazi-Soviet pact of 1939 under which Stalin and Hitler had divided Poland and Eastern Europe, were discussed. Moreover, Western authors whose historical works had previously been heavily criticized and banned were now given a royal welcome, and their books were translated and published in the Soviet Union.

Finally, glasnost' stimulated widespread public discourse on a range of topics from political and ethnic issues through social problems such as alcoholism and domestic violence to environmental and ecological questions. In several cases, public opposition blocked major projects that critics insisted would have deleterious effects on the environment, such as an effort to dam the Gulf of Finland near Leningrad. At the same time, thousands of public organizations sprang up to advance all sorts of social, recreational, and intellectual concerns. Some organizations were interested in historical preservation, some in enhancing the local environment, and some in health or religious questions. With a few exceptions, public meetings and demonstrations were tolerated, including rallies to support the building of a memorial to the victims of Stalin's oppression. Many Orthodox churches reopened, and the number of religious believers increased.

An interesting corollary of glasnost' was Gorbachev's decision to reverse his predecessors' policy regarding emigration from the Soviet Union. Earlier, Jews and others who wanted to leave had innumerable obstacles to overcome, but by 1988, Gorbachev had moved to a policy of virtually free emigration, and in 1989, some seventy thousand Jews left for Israel and the United States. This reflected greater openness and removed a major sore point in American-Soviet relations.

DEMOCRATIZATION

Like perestroika and glasnost', the term "democratization" can be misleading. Just as restructuring did not mean a total rejection of socialism, and openness did not signify a complete freedom of expression, democratization did not mean a fully representative and democratic system. Nevertheless, Gorbachev introduced substantial changes in the Soviet political system and, in early 1990, paved the way for adoption of a multiparty system. Gorbachev clearly had two chief goals in mind that he hoped democratization would accomplish. First, he wanted to use this set of reforms as a weapon against entrenched officialdom, whether in the party or the government. He saw democratization as a way of getting rid of bureaucrats who had old-fashioned ideas, were corrupt, or opposed his reform program. Second, he hoped democratization would unlock popular energies and initiatives and give people a stake in the system. He wanted to stimulate citizen participation in the new course he was setting and to provide individuals with a renewed sense of purpose and direction, attitudes that Stalin had squelched and that had been missing from Soviet society since the heady early days of revolution and the establishment of Soviet power against great odds. At first, however, Gorbachev retained and stoutly defended the basic Leninist concepts of one-party rule and of the party leadership's providing guidance and direction for the citizenry as a whole.

When Gorbachev introduced democratization, he proposed that citizens play a more active role in existing governmental and social organizations. He urged people to demand an accounting from officials, and he contended that directors, managers, and other executives should be elected rather than appointed. In addition to this pressure from below, the Soviet leader acted from above in the traditional way, ousting large numbers of old-line bureaucrats. In his first four years in office, he fired, retired, or transferred more than one-half of the senior officials in the party and government. Nevertheless, opponents of reform remained in the secret police and the armed forces, and many bureaucrats of the old stripe still existed in the middle and lower levels of the administration.

To accelerate democratization, Gorbachev called a special party conference in late June 1988. Over stiff opposition, he pushed through the adoption of political reforms in both the party and the government. These changes encouraged (but did not require) multicandidate elections and called for voting to new, representative governmental bodies at all levels. After the Soviet constitution had been amended to reflect the new arrangements, elections were held throughout the USSR in March 1989 to choose two-thirds of the members of the Congresses of People's Deputies for the Soviet Union and for each of its republics. The remaining one-third of the deputies were appointed by various organizations, including the CPSU, trade unions, and scientific groups. The national congress of twenty-two hundred representatives in turn elected a Supreme Soviet of almost five hundred deputies. Later changes eliminated the Congresses of People's Deputies except for one in Russia and one at the national level.

The elections were freely conducted and occasioned lively public interest and debate. Almost 90 percent of the electorate voted, and in three-quarters of the races, they had more than one candidate to choose from, unlike the old-style single-candidate elections. To the party's chagrin, the voters rejected some of its senior leaders, reflecting a popular mandate for change. Still, 87 percent of those elected to the national Congress of People's Deputies were CPSU members, and 65 percent were party or government officials.

During this period of political reform, Gorbachev had continued to insist on the CPSU's dominant role. During 1988 and 1989, however, the position and prestige of the party rapidly declined. Critics, both within and without the party, strongly attacked its monopoly of political power (enshrined in Article 6 of the Soviet constitution) not only in the media but in debates at the fall 1989 session of the new Supreme Soviet. Scandals regarding corruption and abuse of authority on the part of prominent party officials were aired in various regions of the country. Dissident party units in the Baltic region declared adoption of multiparty systems in their republics. Confronted with these pressures and with increasingly strident protests against party domination of the reform process and perhaps discouraged by the ineptness, conservatism, and insensitivity of many upper-level and district party officials, Gorbachev apparently decided in early 1990 to sacrifice the party's unique role in order to try to save the system and the country. He proposed abrogation of Article 6 and toleration of parties other than the CPSU, a recommendation that the chief policy-making body of the party, the Central Committee, adopted after intense debate.

GORBACHEV'S LATER REFORMS AND FALTERING CONTROL

Although the new Supreme Soviet elected Gorbachev as its head, making him president of the USSR, the Soviet leader began to lose ground politically in 1989. Several factors contributed to Gorbachev's eclipse and to the disintegration of the Soviet Union. Democratization unleashed political forces that Gorbachev could not control and that increasingly isolated him. Democratic reformers objected to his presidency on the grounds that the new president should be picked in a popular election, not by a limited parliament. They also attacked his ties to the party and the old guard and insisted that full democracy be instituted. In addition, radical economic reformers castigated the president for his hesitancy in moving to privatize the economy and establish a full, free-market system. The most prominent and popular leader of the democratic opposition was Boris Yeltsin, a former head of the Moscow CPSU organization who had rebelled against the party leadership in the fall of 1987 and resigned from the CPSU in 1990. A self-declared populist, Yeltsin railed against party privileges and demanded improvements in the average citizen's lot. In popular elections in the spring of 1991, voters chose him president of the Russian Republic within the USSR.

At the other end of the political spectrum, party stalwarts, military and police chiefs, Marxist ideologues, Russian nationalists, and conservative bureaucrats chastised Gorbachev for selling out socialism at home and abroad and for undermining the values and institutions that had made the Soviet system powerful and cohesive. As early as March 1988, a letter from a Leningrad educator, Nina Andreyeva, summing up conservative criticism of the Gorbachev reforms was published in the party press and widely discussed. In response to pressures from both the Right and the Left, Gorbachev temporized, sometimes seeming to endorse further reform, sometimes siding with the old guard. Walking a political tightrope, he was unable to find broad centrist support as articulate members of Soviet society became increasingly polarized and as the bulk of the population grew disgusted with the politicians' quarreling and outraged by their own deteriorating standard of living.

Indeed, the failure of his economic program doomed Gorbachev's efforts to construct political consensus. According to Western critics of perestroika, the Soviet leader made several fundamental errors. Unlike the Chinese economic reforms of the 1980s, which began with agriculture, Gorbachev's proposals left institutional and market arrangements on the farms unchanged. As a good communist, he did not want to abandon collectivization entirely and shift to private landownership and production. Moreover, Gorbachev also resisted all-out privatization of industry and the complete freeing of prices, measures essential to a full conversion to a market system. As a result, under the halfway measures of perestroika, confusion reigned, production lagged, the new semimarket worked only fitfully, agricultural output declined, and consumers faced shortages, long lines, and higher prices. Beginning in 1989, miners and other key workers launched a series of strikes and formed independent trade unions. Public complaints about the collapsing economy mushroomed, and Gorbachev's popularity plummeted even as he received high praise abroad.

Moreover, Gorbachev made little headway in changing many citizens' long-ingrained attitudes and behavior. Clinging to the egalitarian values of the revolutionary past, they resented that some individuals, viewed as profiteers, benefited financially from perestroika and that substantial differences in income and lifestyle between the average citizen and these immediate beneficiaries of reform had emerged. Few responded to Gorbachev's calls for hard work, quality output, and a willingness to sacrifice and participate. Most citizens preferred the Brezhnev-era "contract" that guaranteed a minimum living standard and halfhearted work in return for social and political docility.

The revelations of glasnost' also undercut Gorbachev's "revolution." As people learned how past Soviet regimes had distorted history, repressed the citizenry, stifled creativity, and consistently lied to everyone, indignation and disgust mounted. Many citizens questioned the legitimacy not only of the government but, more importantly, of the party, Marxism-Leninism, and even the 1917 Revolution. Socialism was discredited, and the values that had upheld the system for seventy years were shown to be false and baleful. Some citizens looked nostalgically to the Orthodox religion or to tsarist times and mores, while many young people uncritically adulated Western customs and culture. Most individuals, profoundly disillusioned and disoriented, were unsure where to turn. Gorbachev, tainted by his party tie and damned by his economic failures, fell completely out of popular favor.

Developments in Eastern Europe and on the periphery of the USSR sounded the death knell for Gorbachev's vision of reform. In Poland, the communist government installed after the suppression of Solidarity in 1981 had failed to undertake significant social and political reforms. Moreover, the Polish economy floundered, and the populace remained sullen and uncooperative. Harassed by widespread strikes in 1988, the government agreed with representatives of the original Solidarity leadership, including Lech Walesa, and with other opposition groups to hold partially free elections in the spring of 1989. The communists fared poorly, and a new coalition government headed by Solidarity promised democratic reforms and the installation of a market economy.

In response to these developments in Poland, Gorbachev reiterated his assertion on coming to power four years earlier that the Eastern European socialist states must find their own solutions to domestic problems. He also made clear that the Soviet Union would not attempt to impose its reform policies on other systems and that, despite the Brezhnev Doctrine, he would not interfere with or try to influence the changes taking place in Poland. Reassured by Gorbachev's commitment to nonintervention, Polish reformers abandoned socialism in the fall of 1989 and embarked on the road to a privatized economy and a representative political system.

The other states of Eastern Europe soon followed Poland's example. In November 1989, the socialist regime in East Germany collapsed in the face of mass public protests in major East German cities and the flight to the West of tens of thousands of East German citizens. The Berlin Wall, a symbol of the division of Europe between socialist and nonsocialist countries, was dismantled, and free passage between East and West Germany was permitted for the first time since 1948. During 1990 and 1991, Germany was reunified under leadership dominated by the former West Germany. The new German state abandoned socialism and adopted a democratic and free-market system. In addition, the Western allies admitted the unified German nation to NATO. In Czechoslovakia, relatively small public demonstrations led by students in December 1989 forced the resignation of the communist government. By early 1990, Czechoslovakia, too, had rejected socialism and within three years split into the independent states of the Czech Republic and Slovakia, while Hungary and Bulgaria soon followed in turning away from socialism. Only in Romania did the collapse of socialism lead to violence. In 1989, several days' fighting and some casualties accompanied a popular revolution against the repressive regime headed by Nicolae Ceauşescu.

Gorbachev acquiesced in these Central and Eastern European "revolutions," recognizing that he could do little to block them. Under pressure from the new nonsocialist governments, he dissolved the Warsaw Pact and initiated the phased withdrawal of all Soviet troops from Central and Eastern Europe. Although Western leaders and public opinion welcomed these developments and praised Gorbachev for his statesmanship and commitment to peace, conservative critics in the USSR were outraged by what they considered the craven surrender of the Soviet domination of Eastern Europe. They argued that accepting the downfall of socialism there gravely threatened Soviet security interests and would permit the encroachment of Western influence and pressure hundreds of miles eastward, to the USSR's own borders. Gorbachev attempted to appease such opponents by softening his domestic reform program, but this effort only further undercut his already precarious political position.

Last and perhaps most significantly, rising nationalism among the non-Russian groups living around the circumference of the country brought the political turmoil in the Soviet Union to a boil and led directly to Gorbachev's downfall. As early as 1986, violent riots erupted in Kazakhstan after the Soviet regime replaced an ethnic Kazakh with a Russian as head of the republic's party bureaucracy. The next year, serious ethnic tensions developed in the Caucasus between Armenians and Azerbaijanis over control of Nagorno-Karabakh, a region inhabited predominantly by Armenians but located in Azerbaijan. Troubles also arose in the Baltic republics. By the summer of 1989, the Lithuanians, Latvians, and Estonians were demanding full economic independence, with the aim of secession from the Soviet Union clearly the goal of more radical elements among them. Even in Ukraine, the second largest republic in the Soviet Union, many of its inhabitants began to press for greater autonomy and self-determination on the basis of their separate history prior to 1649 and their somewhat different cultural and intellectual traditions.

These nationalist fissures greatly complicated Gorbachev's reform efforts, and during his first four years in office, he was unable to develop any program or formula to satisfy the complaints of the non-Russian groups. In addition to their historic, religious, and cultural separateness, many non-Russian nationalities resented what they believed was ethnic Russian economic exploitation of their territory, and they opposed what they saw as Russian social and political domination of their lives. They took advantage of glasnost' and democratization to express their grievances and assert political and economic autonomy. Gorbachev's reluctance to recognize their claims only heightened their determination to throw off Moscow's yoke.

In the fall of 1988, the Lithuanians formed a nationalist popular front called Sąjūdis. Soon, similar movements sprang up in Latvia, Estonia, Georgia, and Moldavia (today's Moldova). As nationalist sentiment mounted, local communist leaders, in an effort to hang on to their influence, cooperated with or even joined these fronts, and in December 1989, the Lithuanian Communist Party declared its independence from the CPSU in Moscow. The Supreme Soviet of Lithuania declared in March 1990 its intention to seek independence for the nation, and the reactionary attempt to suppress Lithuanian nationalists in Vilnius in January 1991 only intensified the drive for a complete break from Moscow.

Similarly, police brutality against Georgian nationalists in April 1989 stimulated the formation of a Georgian independence movement, the Round Table for a Free Georgia. In the elections of October 1990, the Round Table won 54 percent of the vote. In March 1991, Georgians declared that they would seek independence and elected the nationalist Zviad Gamsakhurdia president. Lithuania moved toward full independence in the spring and summer of 1991, and republican governments in Ukraine and Russia asserted that they, not the central government, would control their resources and economies.

In March 1991, in a futile effort to stem the rising nationalist tide, Gorbachev submitted a proposed new treaty of union to a national referendum. Six restive republics—Georgia, Armenia, Moldavia, Estonia, Latvia, and Lithuania—refused to participate. Many of the voters in the remaining republics were unsure what they were voting for, but a majority endorsed the treaty. Its provisions, however, did not go far enough toward confederation to satisfy most of the non-Russian nationalists. As a result, Gorbachev made further concessions, and on July 24, he won tentative approval from leaders of the USSR's republics, except those that had abstained in the earlier referendum, for a new arrangement, to be called a "Union of Sovereign Republics." The signing of this treaty was set for August 20. To earlier accusations that he had weakened the party and "lost" Eastern Europe, Gorbachev's opponents added the charge that he was now wrecking the state itself, destroying the unitary structure that had brought the nation power and pride for more than seventy years. Despite ominous signs of discontent from conservative elements in the party, army, and secret police as well as warnings from liberals and the US government of a right-wing attempt to seize power, Gorbachev, apparently unperturbed, left Moscow for his customary August vacation on the Crimean Peninsula. He intended to return briefly to sign the treaty.

THE ATTEMPTED COUP OF AUGUST 1991

Late in the afternoon of Sunday, August 18, Gorbachev's security guards informed him that unexpected visitors from Moscow had arrived at his opulent *dacha* (seasonal residence) on the Black Sea coast and wanted to see him. Surprised and suspicious, the Soviet president tried his landline telephones and found that they were all dead. When he received the delegation, which included representatives of the army, the secret police, and conservative political forces as well as his formerly trusted personal chief of staff, they asked the Soviet president to endorse an emergency committee being formed to deal with the current crisis. Gorbachev refused and pointed out to the conspirators that no legal or constitutional authority had appointed the committee and that they were acting recklessly and treasonously. Leaving him under house arrest, the delegation returned to Moscow.

The next morning, Monday, August 19, radio stations began the day with solemn classical music, usually played on the death of a Soviet leader, followed by an announcement that eight leaders of the Soviet government had established the State Committee on the Emergency Situation to solve the country's urgent problems. They promised to repudiate the union treaty scheduled for signing the next day, to revive the collapsing economy, and to stamp out crime and profiteering. Members of the committee included the vice president, the minister of defense, the head of the KGB, and the minister of the interior, all of whom were Gorbachev appointees. The committee averred that it was acting in place of President Gorbachev, whom they claimed was incapacitated by ill health.

As tanks deployed in the streets of Moscow and other parts of the country and as civilian leaders not involved in the conspiracy tried to decide what to do, the average person was bewildered and wary. By afternoon, however, citizens had begun to engage troops in conversation, persuading them of the folly of using force against the population. Moreover, several leaders, notably Boris Yeltsin of the Russian Republic, whom the coup leaders had clumsily missed arresting that morning, and Anatoly Sobchak, the mayor of Leningrad, came out strongly against the coup. To dramatize his opposition, Yeltsin climbed on a tank outside the Russian Republic's headquarters, known as the White House, and harangued a small group of supporters, condemning the seizure of power as illegal and calling for civil disobedience against it. His defiance and the inept performance of the coup leaders at an early evening press conference galvanized opposition in Moscow and throughout the country. By nightfall on Monday, over fifty thousand citizens had gathered around the White House, building makeshift barricades and forming a human wall against potential attackers.

During the next twenty-four hours, opponents of the putsch managed to persuade army and air force officers designated to take over key installations and government offices, including the White House, that such action would risk thousands of lives and might touch off civil war. On Tuesday, August 20, the crowd around the White House grew to over one hundred thousand. Although three young Muscovites were inadvertently killed when an inexperienced tank crew panicked in the act of withdrawing and one person was shot in Lithuania, confrontation between the army and the coup's opponents was avoided. By Wednesday, August 21, the conspirators were in disarray, and their plot collapsed in the face of Yeltsin's courageous resistance, the military forces' unwillingness to fire on civilians, and growing popular opposition to the coup in Moscow and other parts of the country. Two conspirators committed suicide. The others were arrested but soon freed on bail, and in December 1993, two plotters were elected to the Russian parliamentary Duma. In March 1994, the Duma amnestied the others awaiting trial. Meanwhile, Gorbachev had been released on August 22 and flown back to Moscow to take up the reins of government.

But the failed coup had changed everything. What little authority Gorbachev and the Soviet government still retained slipped away from them in the fall of 1991 as the economic crisis deepened and the various republics went their own ways. Latvia, Estonia, Ukraine, Belarus, Azerbaijan, and Moldavia (now called Moldova) all asserted their independence in late August and September. In response, Gorbachev set up a state council of presidents of the republics, but other than approving independence for Estonia, Latvia, and Lithuania, the council accomplished little. In a referendum on December 1, 1991, Ukrainian voters reaffirmed their republic's separate status. On December 8, the leaders of Russia, Ukraine, and Belarus formed the Commonwealth of Independent States, ignoring the central Soviet government. The federal administration still existed in Moscow, but republican authorities paid little attention to it. With no country and no government over which to preside, Gorbachev finally resigned as Soviet president on December 25, 1991, and shortly afterward, the Soviet Union was formally dissolved. A dramatic era in modern history came to an end.

CONCLUSION

Irony marked Gorbachev's six-year rule. Determined to improve Soviet life, he began with a series of reforms intended to rejuvenate the CPSU, resurrect the economy, and refurbish the socialist system. But the changes that he introduced disrupted the economy, led to the CPSU's demise, and encouraged the discarding of Soviet-style socialism. Before long, change spiraled out of Gorbachev's or anyone else's control. Successes in openness and democratization undercut his own and the CPSU's authority, threw into question the values of Soviet socialism, and released long-repressed nationalist aspirations that could not be contained within the USSR's federal structure. At the same time, Gorbachev's inability to revamp the economy demolished potential popular support and made it impossible for him to master the processes he had unleashed.

Yet Gorbachev accomplished a great deal. He repudiated the Brezhnev-era legacy of mediocrity, corruption, and stagnation. He stimulated genuine participation in social and public affairs, thus laying the groundwork for the mostly unrealized possibility (except in Estonia, Latvia, and Lithuania) of democracy. He uncapped the creativity and energy of the educated and thoughtful elements in society and enlisted them in the search for a better system. He strengthened the rule of law, permitted Jewish emigration, and guaranteed, albeit not for an indefinite period, the freedom of religion for anyone who chose to practice it.

Additionally, Gorbachev replaced the Cold War with cooperative and friendly relations between the Soviet Union and the West. To the world's relief, he capped the arms race and initiated major steps to reduce nuclear stockpiles and conventional forces on both sides. He helped to settle controversies in the developing world, withdrew Soviet forces from Afghanistan, and established normal relations with China. He acquiesced in broad popular upheavals to replace Soviet-style socialism in Central and Eastern Europe with democratic and free-market regimes. And he accepted the reunification of Germany and the end of confrontation between East and West. The Soviet leader reduced the risk of nuclear Armageddon and moved the international climate toward calm and cooperation. Despite these successes, Gorbachev earned little credit at home, where to this day many leaders and average citizens alike condemn his actions in hastening the destruction of the Soviet Union.

In the end, Gorbachev's dream of a more humane, just, and efficient Soviet Union was dashed. He failed to realize that the CPSU, his chosen instrument of reform, was a flawed tool increasingly despised by the majority of the population. Too late, he accepted the need for a multiparty system, and also yielded his socialist principles far too slowly. Gorbachev delayed in implementing privatization and a free market, and he never fully understood the depth and significance of the resurgent national feeling among non-Russians that his reforms helped to unleash. The last leader of the Soviet Union could only watch as the tidal wave of national independence movements across the USSR swept aside the federal state that the Bolsheviks had built seventy years earlier. The Soviet Union was dead, and its successor states were left to face an uncertain future.

FURTHER READING

Beissinger, Mark R. *Nationalist Mobilization and the Collapse of the Soviet State.* Cambridge, UK: Cambridge University Press, 2002.

Breslauer, George W. *Gorbachev and Yeltsin as Leaders.* Cambridge, UK: Cambridge University Press, 2002.

Brown, Archie. *Seven Years That Changed the World: Perestroika in Perspective.* New York: Oxford University Press, 2007.

Buckley, Mary, ed. *Perestroika and Soviet Women.* Cambridge, UK: Cambridge University Press, 1992.

Duhamel, Luc. *The KGB Campaign Against Corruption in Moscow, 1982–1987.* Pittsburgh: University of Pittsburgh Press, 2010.

Feshbach, Murray, and Alfred Friendly Jr. *Ecocide in the USSR: Health and Nature Under Siege.* New York: Basic Books, 1992.

Graham, Loren R. *The Ghost of the Executed Engineer: Technology and the Fall of the Soviet Union.* Cambridge, MA: Harvard University Press, 1993.

Hosking, Geoffrey. *Rulers and Victims: The Russians in the Soviet Union.* Cambridge, MA: Belknap Press of Harvard University Press, 2006.

Kelly, Catriona. *Children's World: Growing Up in Russia, 1890–1991.* New Haven, CT: Yale University Press, 2007.

Kotkin, Stephen. *Armageddon Averted: The Soviet Collapse, 1970–2000.* New York: Oxford University Press, 2001.

McFaul, Michael. *Russia's Unfinished Revolution: Political Change from Gorbachev to Putin.* Ithaca, NY: Cornell University Press, 2001.

Remnick, David. *Lenin's Tomb: The Last Days of the Soviet Empire.* New York: 1993.

Rywkin, Michael. *Moscow's Muslim Challenge: Soviet Central Asia.* 2nd ed. Armonk, NY: M. E. Sharpe, 1990.

Smith, Hedrick. *The New Russians.* Reprint. New York: Harper Perennial, 1991.

Suny, Ronald Grigor. *The Revenge of the Past: Nationalism, Revolution, and the Collapse of the Soviet Union.* Stanford, CA: Stanford University Press, 1993.

Weiner, Douglas R. *A Little Corner of Freedom: Russian Nature Protection from Stalin to Gorbachev.* Berkeley: University of California Press, 1999.

CHAPTER 15

RUSSIA IN A POST-SOVIET WORLD, 1991–2000

As the last hours of December 31, 1999, ticked away, many Russian citizens, disillusioned with their lives in post-Soviet society, expressed little interest in the twentieth century's demise and cherished scant hope for the new millennium ahead. New Year's Eve found them at home, staring apathetically at their television screens, a usual nightly recreation. Some beneficiaries of the new order toasted their gains at upscale restaurants, posh night clubs, trendy bars, and private parties, while other, mostly younger citizens unenthusiastically wandered the streets in Moscow, St. Petersburg, and other cities, watching fireworks displays mounted by local officials. Those who stayed at home watched disinterestedly as a familiar face appeared on TV to convey New Year's greetings: their president, Boris Yeltsin, architect of the new order and Russia's leader for over seven years (see Figure 15.1). Heavily criticized at home and abroad, he nevertheless still represented for some citizens the "genuine" Russian person. Yeltsin, frequently in poor health, appeared drawn, depressed, and ashen as he addressed the nation. In a poignant talk, he announced his resignation as president, six months before his term's end, and apologized movingly for his failure to bring to the Russian people the good life promised when communism collapsed. Appealing for forgiveness, Yeltsin concluded sadly, "Not all our dreams came to fulfillment. . . . We thought we could jump from the gray, stagnant totalitarian past to a light, rich and civilized future in one leap. I believed that myself . . . but it took more than one jump."

Founder of the "new" Russia, Yeltsin presided over an erratic, messy, incomplete transition from the failing Soviet system to an entirely different society struggling to implement democratic and free-market reforms. Evaluations of his presidency among both Russian and Western observers diverged sharply. Some charged that, bewitched by inappropriate advice from outside specialists and inexperienced domestic economists, he pushed flawed policies

FIGURE 15.1. Boris Yeltsin, president of the independent Russian Republic and future Russian Federation. (REUTERS)

of headlong marketization and privatization that produced corruption, crime, and impoverishment; that he introduced a semi-authoritarian political system rampant with cronyism and inefficiency; and that he recklessly initiated a cruel and hopeless war against a small minority in the state, the Chechens of the northern Caucasus. Yeltsin's defenders pointed to the formidable obstacles he confronted in revamping Russia, to his facing down of obstructionists and reactionaries, to his maintenance of democratic forms, and to his success in keeping peace with Russia's near neighbors and strengthening friendly relations with Europe and the United States.

BORIS YELTSIN AND THE NEW RUSSIAN FEDERATION

From the ashes of Soviet communism arose the Russian Federation, surrounded on its western and southern borders by fourteen other states corresponding to the former constituent republics of the Union of Soviet Socialist Republics (USSR) (see Map 1.1). As these newly independent nations struggled to build a reordered life, Russia's size and extensive resources helped it to emerge as the dominant power and bellwether of change in the region. In its new incarnation, Russia benefited from several advantages. The new state commanded extensive assets, inheriting 51 percent of the former Soviet Union's population, 76 percent of its territory, and 61 percent of its gross national product. Russia also possessed most of the former Soviet Union's petroleum, timber, and mineral resources, and boasted a foreign trade surplus. No outside force threatened it; in fact, its former rivals, the Western powers, rushed to proffer advice, moral support, and economic assistance. Finally, its people were mainly ethnic Russians and, for the most part, well educated and skilled.

Yet the task ahead was overwhelming. Boris Yeltsin and his supporters set in motion one of the swiftest and most sweeping revolutions in modern history, equaling if not surpassing the 1789 French Revolution, the Bolsheviks' overthrow of the imperial autocracy in 1917, and even the Chinese Great Leap Forward of the 1950s. The new Russian leadership sought radically to transform the four most basic aspects of the entrenched Soviet system. First and foremost, their about-face encompassed replacing, almost overnight, a centralized, planned, state-owned economy with a free-market system, including unregulated prices and wages; private ownership of factories, businesses, and most resources; and all-out competition for profit. Second, the new leaders scrapped Marxist-Leninist ideology for the unfamiliar, novel values of individualism, responsible free choice, consumerism, and self-reliance. Third, rejecting the oligarchic, tightly controlled Soviet polity, Yeltsin confirmed the democratic changes begun under Mikhail Gorbachev and extended them to include fully free and broadly representative elections; freedom of speech, press, and assembly; and steps toward a functioning parliament and an impartial judiciary and legal system. Finally, instead of seeking the overthrow of the existing world system and brandishing hostility toward Western and other noncommunist nations, Russian foreign policy now advocated international cooperation, friendly relations with Europe and America, and peaceful intercourse with surrounding states, including former parts of the USSR.

Given the magnitude of what Yeltsin attempted, the wonder is not that the road was rough and painful or that his efforts often failed, but that society survived at all and emerged with a deformed but functioning market economy and fairly stable relations with its neighbors. Moreover, Russia's progress, however stunted, was achieved in the face of staggering obstacles. The economy the new leaders inherited was in a state of collapse. The Soviet infrastructure largely built after World War II was decaying and outmoded. Political and bureaucratic opponents of reform were well placed and intransigent. Regional self-interest often trumped national policy. The people as a whole were confused, dispirited, and apathetic. Attitudes and outlooks developed in Soviet times remained entrenched, undermining most reform efforts. Social problems, such as alcoholism, corruption, crime, and worsening health care, multiplied. Finally, although non–ethnic Russians made up only about 17 percent of the new state's population, several groups, notably the Volga Tatars and the Chechens, strongly resisted continued Russian hegemony.

ON THE ROAD TO CAPITALISM

As the Soviet Union fell apart in late 1991, Yeltsin and his advisors gave the highest priority to revolutionizing the top-down socialist economy of the Soviet period. In October 1991, they adopted a radical economic program based on "shock therapy," the premise that only rapid conversion to market mechanisms could successfully transform the socialist system. Yeltsin soon appointed a young economist, Yegor Gaidar, to oversee its implementation. The Gaidar team freed almost all prices in January and February 1992, a step that soon succeeded in restocking the empty stores with domestic and imported consumer goods, although often at prices out of most citizens' reach. The reformers also sought to control inflation, reduce the government's huge budget deficit, and make the ruble convertible to other currencies. This last goal was eventually achieved, but the other aims proved more elusive.

The first results of "shock therapy" were hardly encouraging. In 1992, Russian production, hobbled by deficiencies passed along from the larger Soviet system and floundering under the new ground rules, declined by an estimated 20 to 25 percent. Inflation reached 30 percent a month, budget deficits mounted, and trade with the former Soviet republics and the rest of the world plummeted. As prices skyrocketed, wage payments were delayed. With the former Soviet social safety net in disarray, the average citizen was forced to work at more than one job, to barter or sell personal possessions, and to rely on garden plots in order to survive. Pensioners, others with fixed incomes, and young women and unskilled workers (who were the first to lose their jobs) suffered especially. By some estimates, the poverty rate in Russia reached 40 percent. Yet despite widespread grumbling and discontent, the Russian population somehow survived the first two winters of reform, and few signs of social unrest surfaced.

In the following years, economic reform posted a spotty record, with more downs than ups. Reform policies were implemented inconsistently and erratically partly because of leadership failings, but chiefly because of an old-guard rejection of the new order. Widespread support for change existed, but the many opponents of "shock therapy" reform, primarily former communists, former economic bureaucrats, and factory and farm managers, insisted that markets and free prices be phased in and that the state still operate some sectors of the economy. The radical reformers, though acknowledging some short-term disruption and pain, countered that such costs would be far less than the drawn-out woes that a gradual transition would bring. The political and ideological resistance to economic reform often thwarted Yeltsin's full implementation of key changes or forced him to make concessions that undercut the transformative program's efficacy. Also, Yeltsin's deteriorating health, which was exacerbated by his alcoholism, weakened his determination and ability to advance reform at crucial periods.

Nevertheless, the overall pattern of change emerged in bold relief. The Soviet command economic system was scrapped in favor of open markets and private enterprise. The privatization program begun in 1992 and 1993 transferred ownership of most of the nonagricultural economy from state to private hands. In the process, a small elite (some of whom would come to dominate the state after Yeltsin's departure from power) seized control of many enterprises and natural resources, thus establishing an oligarchy. The new owners often stripped the assets of their properties and pocketed exorbitant profits. By 2002, an estimated 97 percent of small-scale businesses (including stores, restaurants, and service institutions) and 75 percent of large factories were privately owned. The state still controlled some defense industries, utilities, and energy companies, while state and collective ownership remained dominant in agriculture. Agricultural land could not be bought or sold through normal channels. Privatization was notably successful in housing: by the turn of the century, a majority of people owned their own dwelling space, and almost 40 percent of urban dwellers had a country cottage, or dacha. Little sentiment favored a return to state socialism, and many Russian citizens, especially young people, were reconciled to or even enthusiastic about their version of capitalism.

Besides privatization, the reformers could point to other achievements. In 1992 and 1993, inflation had reached peaks of 20 to 30 percent a month. By the early 2000s, it had been reduced to about 10 to 15 percent a year. The precipitous drop in industrial production dating from the late Soviet era was finally reversed in 1999, and the Russian economy grew steadily during the first decade of the twenty-first century.

SETBACKS AND PROBLEMS

The privatization of agriculture proved far more difficult, however. Yeltsin took few initiatives in this area, and less than 10 percent of farms were privately owned by 2001. Collective and state farmers remained reluctant to risk managing individual farmsteads; the government failed to support private farmers with needed credit, agricultural equipment, and technical assistance; and the managers of the existing agricultural system continued to press for substantial state subsidies and to resist reform. Consequently, agricultural output and productivity remained a weak spot in the economy, and rural Russia, in a familiar historical pattern, suffered poverty, backwardness, and despair.

Over the first post-Soviet decade, the reformers also suffered numerous setbacks. Political pressures and Yeltsin's vacillations often hindered efforts to maintain tight control of the money supply. Fiscal largesse distributed in the first half of 1996 to help Yeltsin win reelection to the presidency contributed to monetary instability and budget woes. In August 1998, weakened by a fiscal crisis in the East and Southeast Asian economies, the financial system collapsed. The Russian government defaulted on its bonds and devalued the ruble. Though painful and humiliating at the time, this crisis had some benefits. It sapped, at least temporarily, the economic and political power of the oligarchs, or tycoons, financiers and manipulators who had profited most in the early days of what some called Russia's "crony capitalism." The 1998 debacle also spurred a restructuring of Russia's substantial external debt. Finally, the cheaper ruble brought favorable terms of trade for Russian exports and made consumer goods produced at home cheaper than imports.

Despite the economy's improved performance after 1998, major problems remained. Entrenched Soviet-era beliefs in state control and government entitlements blocked new product development and entrepreneurial initiative. Apathy and disillusionment hampered creativity and productivity. In the late 1990s, extortion, at least in its violent and criminal forms, was substantially reduced, but bureaucratic interference and endemic corruption continued to cripple economic activity. In 2000, on an educational trip to Novgorod, police stopped the tourist bus coauthor John Thompson was on three times to demand a payoff from the driver, who explained that the travel company simply built such expenses into the cost of the tour. In 1999–2000, coauthor Christopher Ward was asked to pay bribes to police officers who stopped him in Moscow to check his travel documents. Inefficient monopolies, remnants of the Soviet era though now in private hands, dominated some industries and blocked innovation and diversification. Russian capital continued to flee abroad, while domestic and foreign investment in Russia remained abysmally low. As a result, the economic infrastructure—factories, equipment, transport, utilities, and buildings—remained outdated and crumbling. Too large a share of the economy depended on energy and other natural resource exploitation, leading some to compare Russia to a Third World country. Oil and natural gas, along with minerals and timber, dominated Russian exports and supplied the bulk of the country's foreign exchange earnings. Although the rise in world petroleum prices during the decade after 1999 greatly benefited the Russian exchequer, both Russian and Western specialists pointed out the urgent need for modernization of petroleum exploration and extraction in Russia.

CHALLENGES OF LIFE IN POST-SOVIET RUSSIA

Most Russian citizens, disillusioned with perestroika, had once looked to the post-1991 reforms as the vehicle to deliver the better life that their leaders had promised since 1985. When some citizens continued to suffer, many people turned against reform or lapsed into apathy. A few, like the talented Russian circus clown Yuri Nikulin, kept their sense of humor: "Where were Adam and Eve born? In Russia, of course. They had no home, were naked and had one apple between them; yet they thought they were in Paradise." A daily struggle to survive, frequent payoffs to get anything done, spreading crime, and fears of unemployment in addition to an uncertain future came to be viewed as normal. Intellectuals who were highly honored and well rewarded in Soviet times suffered a depressing decline in status and income. Widows, pensioners, veterans, laid-off state employees, and single parents felt the pinch particularly. The contrast with the security of the Soviet welfare state was stark. As a factory worker commented in 1994, "In the past I took life for granted and wouldn't think about what to do or how to live. Now we have to think about it all the time, just to scrape by."

As the gap between rich and poor widened, some Russian citizens profited from the transition to capitalism. Among those who soon began to amass rubles and dollars were former officials in industry and government; slick traders, including millions of shuttlers, who bought consumer goods in Turkey, China, and Europe for resale at home; some hardworking entrepreneurs; and assorted shady wheelers and dealers, extortionists, and criminal elements. These "new Russians" flaunted their wealth by building expensive country houses, spending lavishly on consumer goods, and traveling in grand style to Mediterranean resorts and other trendy destinations. At the same time, many young people saw and often seized opportunities in the new economic structure. In a 1997 poll, two-thirds of people under thirty-five thought life was getting better, whereas two-thirds of those over fifty-five concluded that conditions in Russia were getting worse.

In the 1990s, both investors and ordinary citizens deplored the spreading influence of organized gangs, dubbed "the Russian mafia." Racketeers seized control of some retail and service operations, gouging consumers, bribing officials, and muscling out or extorting payoffs from competitors. In the early 2000s, Yeltsin's successor, Vladimir Putin, managed to crack down on these elements, and their impact lessened. Nevertheless, crime rates remained quite high, while prostitution, gambling, and drug use flourished. As a result, many Russian citizens, accustomed to the staid security of the Soviet era, grew increasingly frightened and resentful. In addition, although unemployment rates were officially low, hidden unemployment and wage arrears created job insecurity, which further eroded people's confidence.

Moreover, the physical surroundings in which many Russian citizens lived decayed. Buildings, utilities, and public services were not well maintained. Air and water pollution and other environmental problems, a bitter legacy of Soviet socialism's emphasis on all-out industrial growth, persisted. Neither environmental activists nor the government commanded the resources to enforce conservation measures or to repair earlier devastation.

Health concerns also surfaced as a major social issue after 1991. As the state-supported health care system collapsed, the cash-strapped government struggled to maintain hospitals and other facilities, while citizens complained angrily about the shortage of medicines and the inequities of a growing fee-for-service medical practice. The rise in infant mortality that had started in the Soviet era continued, leveling off in 1994 and dropping slightly thereafter. Tuberculosis spread rapidly in the late 1990s, and drug addiction, particularly to heroin, spiked in the same period. By the turn of the century, Russia was confronting a looming AIDS catastrophe. In 2002, HIV-positive individuals were estimated at one million. The government responded feebly to this crisis, with insufficient treatment and little AIDS-prevention education. Drug addicts, prostitutes, and soldiers, the most heavily infected groups, increasingly spread the virus throughout the population.

AIDS-related deaths contributed to Russia's alarming demographic crisis, with the population shrinking by about six hundred thousand people a year. Not only were too many infants dying in post-Soviet times, but uncertainty about current and future conditions and a divorce rate approaching 70 percent led many people not to have children at all. By 2001, the fertility rate sank to 1.17 percent, far below what is needed to maintain a stable population level. Concurrently, the death rate rose, as alcoholism, widespread smoking, accidents, cancer, suicide, and cardiovascular disease took their toll, especially among Russian men. By the early 2000s, life expectancy had recovered from earlier lows but still remained at sixty-one for men and seventy-two for women (compared with seventy-four and eighty, respectively, for citizens of the European Union). Although in the 1990s tens of thousands of ethnic Russians from former Soviet republics immigrated to Russia each year, the gap between births and deaths meant that the total population shrank, dropping from nearly 150 million in 1991 to below 145 million in 2002. Some experts estimated that Russia might contain as few as 120 million people by 2030, with concomitant shortages of recruits for the army and workers for the economy. No industrialized country has ever experienced such a population calamity in peacetime.

The skewed gender and age structure of Russia's population only made this dismal picture bleaker. In 2001, Russia had 9.1 million more women than men. In addition to fewer husbands being available, educated Russian women often decided not to marry because they did not want to be trapped in a traditional patriarchal relationship or because so many men were heavy drinkers. The Russian population was also aging, with 38 percent above working age in 2001. Some continued to work, but the growing number of pensioners will be an increasing burden on the economy in the future.

The transition from socialism created particularly challenging obstacles for women. As homemakers, they not only continued to cope with traditional problems of spousal abuse and alcoholism but also now faced shrinking family income and skyrocketing prices, at least in the early 1990s, as well as the reduced availability of health and child care facilities. As workers, women were often the first laid off, making up 70 percent of the officially unemployed in 1995. When working, their average wage level reached only 60 percent of what men were paid. Moreover, few women reached senior executive positions in the new free-market enterprises or in the democratized government, where the Duma contained less than 10 percent female deputies. Finally, women in early post-Soviet Russia felt victimized by the spread of prostitution, pornography, and crime.

At the same time, several positive signs for the future position of women emerged, albeit for a limited period. Various feminist groups sprang up, some concerned with rape awareness and counseling for rape victims and others focused on helping women in business and the professions. An organization in Moscow even dared to take on the patriarchal Russian custom of sexual harassment in the workplace. Women played active roles in a range of grass-roots organizations working on social and environmental issues, and talented women succeeded in retail and other small businesses. They also served as key leaders in some regional administrations, and several women contributed importantly to legislation in the Duma. With growing prosperity, prospects for women in Russia appeared to brighten. Recent events (see Chapter 16), however, have made such hopes more remote.

CHANGING CULTURAL ATTITUDES

The years after 1991 proved to be a dispiriting time for many Russian citizens. Economic hardship, the repudiation of old values, generational tension between young and old, insecurity, and dismay at the blatant inequities and crudities of "Wild East" capitalism produced cynicism, fatalism, and, occasionally, despair. Despite considerable disorientation and bewilderment, many citizens seemed relieved to surrender such negative features of Soviet socialism as false and repetitive propaganda, petty party interference in their lives, and repression of individual and civil rights. As one friend told coauthor Thompson in 1993 after complaining bitterly about economic conditions and crime, "Still, the important thing is we are free!"

The diminution of Russia's world stature, some youngsters' repudiation of the Soviet-era patriotic cult surrounding World War II, and the indifference of many to the heroic achievements of the past proved particularly painful to veterans, military officers, and many former communists. They adopted a stance of injured pride and nationalism that at times fostered xenophobia and anti-Semitism, as some blamed the West and Jews for Russia's plight. Rumors that Western aid and commerce were part of a conspiracy to expropriate the country's resources and make Russia a vassal state were widely circulated— and believed by many. In addition, drawing on the egalitarian values of Russian and Soviet culture, many citizens found repugnant the materialism and consumerism of the new era, with its flashy Western imports, crassly commercial culture, and ostentatious displays of wealth. Finally, an ugly undertone of racism erupted as some Russian citizens denounced "the dark-skinned" or "people from the south," that is, Tatars, Central Asians, and inhabitants of the Caucasus, for crime, profiteering, and every imaginable ill. The wars against the Chechens on Russia's southern border in the mid-1990s and the early 2000s only intensified this prejudice.

Popular attitudes toward the horrors of Joseph Stalin's regime became another puzzling and disturbing psychological phenomenon of the post-Soviet era. Unlike Germany, where both government and society struggled successfully to confront and deal with their Nazi past, the vast majority of Russian citizens appeared unwilling even to acknowledge, let alone come to terms with, the murder of millions of their fellow citizens during the 1930s and 1940s. A few farsighted individuals banded together in the human rights organization Memorial, seeking to collect historical data about Stalin's repressions and to honor the victims by identifying them and erecting monuments and plaques in their memory. But the government most often ignored or hampered these efforts, and the public generally showed no interest or consciously turned a blind eye to Memorial's activities. One citizen, whose father, aunt, and uncle were all executed during Stalin's purges, explained Russian citizens' reluctance to deal with such past horrors: "It's our country's deep wound. You can forget about a wound if you don't touch it, but when you touch it, it bleeds again."

In their bewilderment after 1991, some ethnic Russians turned to the Orthodox religion, but the church suffered from weak leadership and was tarnished by revelations that several high clerics had collaborated with the KGB in the Soviet era. Orthodox prelates struggled to regain control of church lands and properties seized under communism and to reconstruct and refurbish damaged and decaying church buildings. Their interest in material matters alienated some younger Russian citizens. Moreover, Orthodox leaders faced aggressive competition from Protestant, Catholic, and sectarian missionaries. In 1997, church officials, after hard lobbying, secured a Duma law that imposed numerous requirements on religions other than Orthodoxy, Islam, Judaism, and Buddhism, but they failed to achieve their goal of an outright ban on Protestant, Catholic, and sectarian activity. Conservative in outlook and unresponsive to Russia's socioeconomic ills, the Orthodox leaders did little to provide new direction and inspiration for the country's floundering citizenry.

Some advocates of democracy expected a blossoming of Russian cultural life once the yoke of Soviet socialist conformity was lifted. Although a few creative individual artists and writers emerged amid the chaos of the post-1991 transition, most cultural institutions and much artistic activity suffered throughout the 1990s from diminished budgets, disinterested audiences, and dynamic competition from Western publications, television shows, and movies. The Russian film and publishing industries suffered particularly. Moreover, many "new Russians," with little sense of Russia's artistic tradition, used their ill-gotten rubles and dollars to foster clothing, décor, and architecture in the worst possible taste, a rush to vulgarity, garishness, and banality that blemished the cityscapes and environs of Moscow and St. Petersburg with ugly signs, billboards, and buildings.

Yet by the late 1990s, Russian culture had begun a notable revival. The Russian government's determination to abandon Soviet strictures and to refrain from interfering in artistic and cultural matters helped kick off a renaissance in Russian creativity. Although state-supported cultural institutions received miniscule subsidies compared to Soviet times, the government tried to maintain traditional organizations and buildings. The Ministry of Culture's budget grew by 25 percent in the early 2000s. In St. Petersburg, the government supported renovation of the Mariinsky Theater and the Russian State Museum as well as plans for a new performing arts center. In Moscow, restoration of the Moscow Conservatory and the Bolshoi Theater began, and the mayor and the Russian government supported film festivals and the Third International Theater Olympics in 2000.

Freedom for artists to create also meant freedom for audiences to choose, which some critics argued meant the dominance of lowbrow culture and trash.

But the new license also meant diversity, encouraging the founding of two new theaters and three new opera companies in Moscow as well as the opening of many small theaters, galleries, and clubs there and throughout the country. In the first years after the Soviet collapse, nineteenth-century Russian classics were most frequently performed at concerts, opera halls, and theaters, but by 2000, contemporary compositions and new plays had taken center stage. Moreover, traditional cultural giants, like the Kirov Opera and Ballet under the dynamic direction of Valery Gergiev and the Hermitage Museum in a loose partnership with the Guggenheim Museum, survived and grew stronger in the short term by revamping their repertoires and presentations.

The publishing industry, at first hit hard by the influx of Western books and periodicals, had perked up by the end of the 1990s, with a number of Russian authors racking up substantial sales thanks to Russian citizens' continuing passion for reading. Adventure stories, detective fiction, romances, and self-help books dominated the market, but critically acclaimed prose and poetry occupied a growing niche. Almost submerged at first by the tide of American and other imports, the film industry, though still struggling in 2000, turned out some twenty new productions a year, including several internationally recognized films. Some talented visual and performing artists decamped to the West after 1991, but those remaining in Russia continued to seek an authentic Russian voice in their particular media. On balance, Russian culture entered the twenty-first century more vibrant and flourishing than at any time since the imposition of Stalinist conformity seventy years earlier. This vibrancy, as we will see, did not last long.

INCOMPLETE DEMOCRACY IN THE YELTSIN ERA

For the first two years after 1991, discontent over economic conditions, concern about social disintegration, unreformed Communists' ideological aversion to capitalism, and nationalists' resentment of the collapse of the Soviet empire and Russia's weakened world position all fueled mounting opposition to Yeltsin's regime, even though most citizens were relieved that Soviet conformity and authoritarianism had been swept away. During the fall of 1991, Yeltsin concentrated on protecting Russia's interests as the USSR disintegrated. His first priority was to establish Russia's predominant position in whatever different structure emerged among the former components of the Soviet Union. Although declaring his republic's full sovereignty and supporting the symbolic step of adopting a new Russian flag based on the pre-1917 imperial flag, Yeltsin also strove to create a confederation among the former Soviet republics.

When Ukrainians voted for independence on December 1, 1991, the Russian president decided to abandon Gorbachev and any hope for a revamped Soviet Union. Asserting the independence of Russia, he cooperated with leaders from several other former republics to set up the Commonwealth of Independent States (CIS), a loose association that ignored the old federal structure. (The CIS is discussed more fully later in this chapter.) Yeltsin then accepted the USSR's demise and turned to domestic challenges.

Because of Yeltsin's absorption in the issues surrounding the Soviet Union's collapse, and because he apparently did not realize how much popular support he had garnered in defeating the August 1991 coup, in the following months he failed to push through the political reforms and constitutional changes needed to underpin genuine democracy in the new Russia. Instead of acting swiftly to rid himself of the old Soviet-era political institutions—the Russian Congress of Deputies elected in March 1989 and the Russian Supreme Soviet chosen by that congress, both of which contained a number of Communist Party holdovers and other conservatives—Yeltsin sought to cooperate with the politicians and structure in place. This effort sputtered along with declining success for the next two years as the president and his opponents in the soviet tussled over economic policies.

Conflict between the central government in Moscow and the republic's districts and regions generated additional political opposition to Yeltsin. Pressure for autonomy on the part of almost thirty million non-Russian citizens of the new state exacerbated the struggle for power between Moscow and the periphery. By granting non–ethnic Russians some local self-rule and making extra concessions to the Tatars living along the Volga River, the government managed to avert ethnic violence, with the notable exception of the Chechen region in the northern Caucasus, where bitter warfare raged between 1994 and 1996 and again from 1999 to 2006. Elsewhere, local authorities, taking advantage of the political infighting between the president and his conservative opponents in the Supreme Soviet, finagled financial subsidies from each side and resisted Yeltsin's efforts to control regional appointments and policies. Officials outside Moscow husbanded local resources and unilaterally reduced the share of taxes sent to the capital. In the mid-1990s, the state established the Federation Council, which represented the eighty-nine regions of the Russian Republic, and elections at the local level that generally produced popularly controlled governors and other officials who helped stabilize relations with the central government. As Yeltsin's grasp on power began to slip in the late 1990s, the regions once again asserted their authority, and Moscow-periphery tensions escalated.

In Moscow, the conflict between Yeltsin and his critics sharpened during 1993. Both sides resorted to tactics of dubious legality. The president often tried to govern by decree, bypassing the legislative process. In turn, the soviet regularly introduced constitutional amendments designed to constrict the president's power and legislation that undercut the government's economic policies. Yeltsin survived threats to impeach him but had to sacrifice his economic reform point man, Gaidar, who was replaced as prime minister by Viktor Chernomyrdin, a Soviet-era industrial manager and more moderate figure. In a popular referendum in April 1993, 58 percent of voters supported the president, and 53 percent backed his economic program, despite its meager results to that point.

Taking advantage of this victory, Yeltsin convened a constitutional convention, urging it to adopt the government's draft constitution, which provided for a strong presidency. His opponents objected, and by September, no agreement had been reached. Moreover, legislative recalcitrance had stalled the president's reform program. Increasingly frustrated, the Russian leader dissolved the soviet on September 21, 1993, and called for elections to a new and differently structured parliament in December. This decisive action soon led to a major political crisis. The opposition convened a rump session of the soviet that rejected the president's dissolution decree as unconstitutional, ousted Yeltsin, and installed Alexander Rutskoi, an Afghan war veteran, as acting president. About two hundred soviet deputies, plus assorted hangers-on, staged a sit-in at the soviet's headquarters, the same White House that had been the scene of Yeltsin's bold rebuff to the attempted putsch in August 1991.

The government cut off services to the White House and tried to negotiate with its occupiers during the succeeding week. No solution was found before events spiraled tragically out of control. On Sunday, October 3, several thousand ardent supporters of the soviet broke through the government forces' cordon around the White House. Opposition leaders, exhausted from the long siege and out of touch with the political reality in Moscow, deluded themselves that this sortie represented the start of a popular uprising against Yeltsin in the city. At their urging, the mob attempted to seize city hall and the main television station, and fighting broke out. Facing armed action against his government, Yeltsin called in local troops whose units shelled the White House the following morning, causing over a hundred casualties and major damage to the building. The holdouts inside surrendered and were placed under arrest (though most received amnesty later).

Observers inside and outside of Russia were appalled by the violence and loss of life, but no mass support for the rebels materialized. Calm was quickly restored in Moscow, while other cities and regions remained quiet. Despite deep resentment of the continuing economic hardships, many citizens were fed up with the political squabbling and cared as little for the oppositionists as for the government. Yeltsin accelerated arrangements for the already announced parliamentary elections in December and ordered that a final draft of the new constitution be submitted to voters at the same time. As election-eering began, the moderates split over the pace of reform and who should lead the nascent political parties. Yeltsin mistakenly stood above the electoral fray, sticking by an earlier refusal to form his own political party. One group, Russia's Choice, was clearly pro-Yeltsin, but others were critical of the government in varying degrees. With the liberals and centrists in disarray and public dis-may over economic conditions mounting, extremists on both the Left and the Right campaigned vigorously against the existing regime.

Despite fears of widespread public apathy, 54.8 percent of 106 million reg-istered voters participated in the December 1993 elections. Of those voting, 58 percent approved the presidential constitution, which gave Yeltsin the power to appoint the prime minister and cabinet and largely to determine domestic and foreign policy, while reserving some fiscal authority to the new parliamentary lower house, the Duma. Under special and not very demanding conditions, the president also had the right to dissolve the Duma, to order popular referenda, and to rule by decree. No clear winner emerged in the parliamentary elec-tions. Conservative and ex-communist groups garnered 38 percent of the seats, with the result that Yeltsin's opponents outmatched the 36 percent of deputies elected from the pro-reform parties. But the opposition often failed to act in concert and proved more a hindrance than a complete block to the govern-ment's continuing reform efforts.

With the elections behind them and a new constitution and legislature in place, Russian citizens settled into what appeared to be a more stable sys-tem. Although the bulk of the population remained politically apathetic or cynical, most citizens valued their right to choose and their ability to criticize the government and other authorities without fear of Soviet-style retribution. The rights of free speech and freedom of the press were vigorously asserted, particularly as newspaper and television commentators, politicians, and many individual citizens regularly and pointedly lambasted the Yeltsin regime over economic malaise, crime, and cronyism (the undue influence of Russia's rich-est businessmen in government and the economy). The lack of effective po-litical parties proved, however, a major weakness of the fledgling democracy. The Duma parties operated as personal factions, and none, except possibly the ex-communists, had a broad base in the electorate or a viable national orga-nization. Thus, personalities dominated, programs were shifting and unclear, and voters had no sense of identification with a well-defined political organi-zation or purpose.

Party ineffectiveness only magnified the constitutionally endorsed pre-ponderant power of the presidency in the Russian system. Yeltsin frequently appeared to act erratically and arbitrarily, bypassing the Duma and evoking taunts of "Tsar Boris." At the same time, the president had to take account of public opinion and the continuing legislative opposition to much of his program. Often Russia appeared to have reached a political stalemate. Yeltsin's deteriorating health, made worse by alcoholism, further complicated the picture. The president had serious heart attacks in the summer and fall of 1995 and was able to work only intermittently. Nevertheless, the Russian leader pushed ahead with prosecution of a military campaign against Chechen rebels and with preparations for parliamentary elections in December 1995 and a presidential ballot in June 1996.

As during the first Duma campaign in 1993, the moderates could not coalesce around a single party in preparing for the 1995 elections. At the same time, the government's opponents were divided and often at odds with each other. Consequently, although dissatisfaction with the meager results of reform remained widespread, pro-government candidates did not fare as badly as might have been expected. The overall results returned a Duma quite like the 1993–1995 body, with reformers and sympathetic independents winning about 30 percent of the seats, communists 33 percent, and the nationalists slipping to about 12 percent. Clearly, many in the electorate had vented their frustration with living conditions by supporting the communists, a familiar party and one that promised better times. But the voters had not swung to the far right, and the decline of nationalist strength reflected the waning influence of chauvinist slogans among a younger body politic. The Communist leader, Gennady Zyuganov, early made clear that he intended to criticize the government heavily but would not use his bloc of votes to obstruct all parliamentary business or to bring the government down. So for the next four years, the Yeltsin regime and the Duma coexisted in an often tense but not entirely unproductive relationship.

The presidential elections of 1996 now loomed large over the country. Despite recurring heart troubles and bouts of passivity earlier that year, Yeltsin made clear that he wanted a second term. At first trailing Communist candidate Zyuganov in the polls, Yeltsin rallied and stumped energetically in the run-up to the June balloting. In addition, Russia's big businessmen, who had at first shown little interest in the election, began to pour money and media support into the president's campaign once they realized that Zyuganov would be the alternative to Yeltsin. Finally, Western organizations provided experienced electoral strategists and expert campaign organizers to advise the Yeltsin reelection effort.

Despite this assistance, Yeltsin barely prevailed in the first round of voting in mid-June 1996, winning 35 percent of the vote to Zyuganov's 32 percent, with recently retired General Alexander Lebed, who had campaigned as a tough-guy maverick, drawing almost 15 percent, and the liberals' hope, Grigory Yavlinsky, garnering just over 7 percent. The electoral share of the nationalists and the extreme Right dipped even lower than in the 1995 Duma elections, falling to 5.8 percent of the ballots. In the runoff round in July, the two top candidates would compete, and even assuming that most of the liberal vote would swing to the president, Yeltsin and his handlers could see that he might have difficulty achieving the majority needed for reelection. Seeking to attract some of Lebed's law-and-order supporters, Yeltsin persuaded the general to support him in return for Lebed's appointment as national security advisor. Although renewed heart trouble sidelined the president for several weeks before the runoff, his final campaign profited from a heavily financed television blitz and openhanded promises of "goodies" for regions, groups, and institutions. In addition, the president wielded the bogey of communism, insisting that he represented the chief bulwark against a return to the bad old days. Yeltsin won handily, with 53.7 percent of the vote, while Zyuganov lagged at 40.2 percent. Voter turnout neared 70 percent, surpassing the 65 percent of balloters in the 1995 Duma elections. Russia had thus managed several national elections, two parliamentary and one presidential. Critics pointed out obvious flaws: big-money interests possessed too much influence, the president wielded too much power, and parties were weak and disparate. Yet for a country that had not known open voting since 1917, these three elections indicated that most citizens relished the opportunity for choice at the ballot box.

Yeltsin's performance in his second term was decidedly mixed. In November 1996, the president underwent major heart surgery and was unable to direct the government actively for months. From 1997 to 1999, his health and drinking problems recurred, and his conduct of public affairs became increasingly erratic. Although Yeltsin managed after some months to fire the outspoken and ambitious Lebed, and he continued to support the overall reform program, his subordinates, including Prime Minister Chernomyrdin, proved mediocre and ineffective leaders. Critics asserted that the Russian ship of state was without a firm hand at the helm and that Yeltsin's family and a coterie of unsavory behind-the-scenes advisors were in fact the real rulers of the country—and not always in the public interest. Yeltsin responded lethargically to the major financial crisis of August 1998, and he fired and hired prime ministers at will until choosing Vladimir Putin in August 1999. Nevertheless, Yeltsin remained on good terms with US president Bill Clinton and with other Western and world leaders. He continued relatively benign relations with Russia's neighbors, including former Soviet republics, and he cooperated with the United States on arms control and denuclearization.

Some critics of Yeltsin's eight years in office insist that he acted undemocratically, tolerated cronyism and corruption, botched the transition to a market economy, and callously ignored the hardships his policies visited on the Russian people. His defenders point to successful institutionalization of the Duma and local governmental organs, free and fair elections, the installation of a free enterprise system (even if at considerable cost), and a restrained and positive foreign policy. But both detractors and supporters agree that Yeltsin badly mishandled the brewing trouble in Chechnya.

TERRORISM AND WAR IN THE CAUCASUS

The Chechen ethnic group of the northern Caucasus has a long history of opposition to established authorities, dating back to its resistance to the imposition of imperial Russian rule in the first half of the 1800s and including its banishment to Central Asia by Stalin during World War II. Many Chechens returned to their homeland during Nikita Khrushchev's rule, and in 1991, nationalist leaders declared independence even though the tiny region of Chechnya, with about one million inhabitants, was isolated and landlocked on the southeastern edge of the Russian state. In the fall of 1992, a complicated struggle over land and indigenous rights among Russian Cossacks, Chechens, and other local peoples in Chechnya ended in rioting and pillaging, with several hundred deaths and much property damage before three thousand Russian troops restored order. During 1993 and 1994, Chechen chieftains reaffirmed their earlier claim to separate status and established local rule in some areas. After clumsy Russian attempts to subvert this inchoate and poorly organized breakaway movement, Defense Minister Pavel Grachev and hardline advisors to Yeltsin persuaded the president to launch a military offensive against the Chechen rebels in December 1994. Following a bungled attack that caused several thousand civilian and military casualties, Russian forces finally occupied the Chechen capital, Grozny, in January 1995. Western leaders as well as Islamic states sympathetic to the Muslim Chechens condemned the government's brutal use of force against a handful of rebels. Nationalists in Moscow mostly backed Yeltsin's actions, while centrist, democratic, and even communist elements were critical, belittling the president's claim that he had been forced to act to hold the Russian Republic together.

In 1995, despite overwhelming superiority in troops and weapons, the Russian army, its largely conscript soldiers demoralized and its generals incompetent, proved incapable of quelling the Chechen rebellion in the countryside. Extremist demands from both sides stymied efforts to reach a political settlement to the dispute. The Russian occupiers had little success forming a viable pro-Moscow government in Grozny. Chechens themselves could not agree on what future they sought, opinions running from full independence to limited autonomy. Uniformly anti-Russian, Chechen rebel forces were a ragtag lot of idealistic nationalists, Islamic radicals, and opportunists, including bandits and extortionists, some of whom were former "freedom fighters" trained and equipped by the Central Intelligence Agency to undermine Soviet rule in Afghanistan a decade earlier. As tens of thousands of Chechen warriors took to the mountains to launch guerrilla warfare against the Russian army, casualties and criticism mounted. The Chechen war also bled the Russian treasury at a time when the government was struggling to control the budget. Despite a nominal ceasefire in July 1995, sporadic fighting and off-and-on peace negotiations continued into mid-1996.

After Chechen rebels retook Grozny in August 1996, General Lebed, newly appointed as Yeltsin's national security advisor, secured a shaky settlement to the conflict. Although the Russian government proclaimed that it had prevented a precedent of unilateral secession, the Chechens could well claim victory. The peace deal provided for withdrawal of almost all Russian forces, establishment of an interim government of moderate Chechen nationalists to have "special status" within the Russian Federation, and a referendum on independence after five years. With upward of ten thousand dead and wounded plus some one hundred thousand Chechen casualties, military and civilian, Yeltsin reluctantly signed off on these terms and promised a fresh start for Chechnya.

The 1996 settlement lasted only a little over two years, however. Russian officials' reluctance to consider complete independence for Chechnya and political disarray among the Chechens blocked progress toward a permanent resolution of Chechnya's status. In Chechnya, the situation deteriorated. Despite Russian promises, reconstruction, relief, and economic development lagged; the Russian-backed government was largely ineffective; and disorder, banditry, and rebel activity predominated in the rural areas. Moreover, Islamic fundamentalism and rebellion appeared to be spreading into other areas of the northern Caucasus. During the summer of 1999, bands of Chechen separatists began operating in Dagestan, a region next door to Chechnya. In September, bomb blasts of unknown origin destroyed several apartment houses in Moscow and in the southern town of Volgodonsk, killing several hundred people. Vladimir Putin, whom Yeltsin had named prime minister the preceding month, quickly blamed Chechen rebels for these attacks, though neither at the time nor subsequently did the Russian government present convincing evidence of Chechen complicity. Nevertheless, the Russian public, terrified and angered by this terrorism, responded enthusiastically to Putin's tough stance.

In October, amid fervent exhortations from Putin and President Yeltsin, whose term would expire in June 2000, the Russian army plunged once more into the Chechen quagmire.

POST-SOVIET RUSSIAN FOREIGN POLICY

Amid the debris of Soviet socialism's demise, President Yeltsin faced two urgent foreign policy issues. First, he had to craft new relationships with the new state's closest neighbors, the fourteen other former republics of the Soviet Union, soon called Russia's "near abroad." These smaller nations surrounded Russia to the west, south, and southeast, leaving only Finland to the northwest and Mongolia and China to the east as previously established states sharing extensive borders with Russia (see Map 1.1). Second, Yeltsin needed to maintain and expand the good relations with the West developed by Gorbachev. In particular, the Russian president aimed to enhance Russian security by ensuring that the United States and its European allies would not take advantage of Russia's weakness and by working with these same states as well as Ukraine, Belarus, and Kazakhstan to control and reduce the huge arsenal of nuclear weapons left behind by the Cold War. Also, Yeltsin desperately sought economic and technical assistance from capitalist countries as he tried to wrench his society onto the unfamiliar path of open markets and free enterprise.

Relations with Russia's Neighbors

At the outset, it appeared that establishing good relations with the "near abroad" would be the most challenging task. In December 1991, the Russian president cooperated with the leaders of Ukraine and Belarus to declare the Soviet Union formally dissolved and to found the Commonwealth of Independent States (CIS), intended as a loose confederation of the former Soviet republics. All these new states, except Georgia, which was embroiled in civil strife, and the Baltic countries, which were pursuing an independent path, adhered to the CIS on December 21, 1991. From its birth, the CIS encountered major obstacles. The other CIS members feared Russian domination of the new body, and agreement on thorny issues of trade, economic cooperation, territory, and minority rights proved elusive among so many disparate members. Individual governments resorted to making bilateral arrangements with their neighbors, often undercutting CIS efforts. Each successor nation acted independently in foreign affairs, and the major global powers soon recognized the new states. The United Nations admitted them all, with Russia assuming the Soviet Union's permanent Security Council seat. Despite several attempts to strengthen the CIS, it never evolved into a working confederation and remained a convenient forum to discuss common issues and a place to work out lower-level facilitating agreements among the members.

Apart from the CIS framework, Russia pursued bilateral relations with its nearest neighbors during the first decade of independence. A number of prickly issues arose, but by 2000, most had been peacefully resolved. During the Soviet era, particularly after World War II, many ethnic Russians had moved to the USSR's non-Russian republics, where they played important economic and political roles. The demise of the Soviet Union resulted in some twenty-three million ethnic Russians now living in these border countries, with the largest groups in eastern Ukraine, the Baltic states, and northern Kazakhstan. During the 1990s, almost four million of these displaced people moved to the new Russian Federation. The remainder, however, now a minority in the new non-Russian states, urged the Yeltsin administration to help protect their rights. Particularly in the Baltic states of Estonia, Latvia, and Lithuania, many Russian speakers were aggrieved by citizenship requirements, which often included learning the difficult local language.

Some also felt discriminated against economically. Under pressure from Russia, Scandinavian countries, the European Union, and the United States, the Baltic governments and their Russian populations gradually worked out compromises on citizenship, language, and minority rights. By 2002, Russian minorities were benefiting from the Baltic economies' considerable progress, and their discontent became increasingly muted.

Another issue revolved around the removal of military units and bases. In Estonia and Georgia particularly, Yeltsin's government used the presence of Russian troops to pressure the new states. Only after several years were all Russian forces withdrawn from Estonia. Some Russian units remained, however, in Georgia and Tajikistan. A related problem entailed the responsibility for and cost of environmentally cleaning former Soviet military sites. A third point of friction centered on adjusting borders, which Stalin had often set arbitrarily. The most troubling potential dispute arose between Russia and Ukraine. In 1954, to mark the three hundredth anniversary of Ukraine's accession to Russia, the USSR transferred control of the Crimean Peninsula from the Russian to the Ukrainian Soviet Republic. Although substantial Ukrainian and Tatar minorities inhabited the Crimea in the 1990s, ethnic Russians made up a majority of the population, and Russia claimed the former Soviet Black Sea naval fleet and its base port at Sevastopol. Resisting nationalist pressure to recover the Crimea for Russia, Yeltsin managed to reach a settlement in May 1997 that guaranteed the territorial integrity of Ukraine's borders and a Russian lease on

Sevastopol for twenty years. However, the issue of Crimea would return to the forefront, and in March 2014 Russia annexed the peninsula.

For the time being, though, Russian-Ukrainian relations proved friendlier than expected, given many nationalist Ukrainians' detestation of three centuries of Russian rule. Both sides worked hard to resolve difficult economic issues surrounding trade and Ukrainian arrears in paying for energy imported from Russia. Ukraine found itself in a weak bargaining position as its leaders moved sluggishly to implement reform and its economy floundered during the 1990s and early 2000s. Nevertheless, the two governments cooperated with each other and the United States on military and security issues, including the transfer of former Soviet troops to the Ukrainian armed forces and the dismantling of all nuclear weapons on Ukrainian soil, the last a crucial task completed in 1996.

The enlargement of the North Atlantic Treaty Organization (NATO), the defensive alliance led by the United States, emerged as a sticking point in Russia's relations both with the Baltic states and Ukraine and with the West. Arguing that NATO was essentially directed against Russia, the Yeltsin and Putin administrations criticized the inclusion of Hungary, Poland, and the Czech Republic (which occurred in 1999) and strongly opposed plans to add Ukraine and the Baltic states (Estonia, Latvia, and Lithuania joined NATO in 2004). The European powers and the United States countered this hostility first by carving out a special position for Russia within NATO itself, permitting Russia to sit on the NATO Council for most deliberations, though not those regarding future expansion and certain military matters. Second, the Western nations redefined NATO's mission to make the alliance broadly responsible for European security, including that of Russia and Eastern Europe, and for protecting its interests in nearby regions.

Yeltsin found the new failed state of Belarus, just to Russia's west, a minor irritant. Some Russian nationalists and a few Belarusian politicians beat the drums for a merger of Russia and Belarus, but the Russian president managed to finesse these efforts by establishing a token union and making the conditions for genuine union unacceptable to both groups. Russian leaders generally agreed that Belarus's disastrous and unreformed economy and political authoritarianism could only become an added burden for reform-minded Russia.

Russia's relations with newly founded states in the Caucasus and Central Asia followed a complicated, sometimes tortuous course. In Kazakhstan, with a Russian population of more than six million, Yeltsin and Kazakh president Nursultan Nazarbayev cooperated to ease emigration for those ethnic Russians who wished to leave and to control friction between those remaining and the local population. Elsewhere, Russian policy focused on security threats from the south, especially the spread of Islamic fundamentalism from Afghanistan and Iran, and on maintaining Russian economic and political influence in the region. In Georgia, Russian military leaders backed anti-Georgian secessionist efforts of the minority Abkhaz people and obtained the right to station troops in Georgia and to maintain bases along Georgia's Turkish frontier. In Armenia and Azerbaijan, Russia asserted its military presence and commercial interests in the development of the latter's extensive oil reserves in and around the Caspian Sea.

In Central Asia, Russian troops intervened in a long-running civil war in Tajikistan, partly for humanitarian reasons and partly to ensure the security of Tajikistan's long border with Afghanistan. In other states, Russia asserted some influence and broadened commercial ties but respected the Central Asian states' independence, including their Islamic basis and slow pace of economic and political reform after 1991.

Further east, Yeltsin successfully bolstered Russia's relations with China and India. In Southeast Asia, Russia received high marks for promising to turn over the former Soviet base at Cam Ranh Bay to the Vietnamese government. Regarding Japan, fishing rights in nearby seas were clarified, and the Japanese promised support for Russian development of a new natural gas field in Siberia and construction of a pipeline to Russia's Pacific coast. No agreement could be found, however, on the festering dispute over ownership of the Kurile Islands seized by the Soviet Union after World War II.

Russia, the United States, and Europe

Apart from stabilizing ties with the "near abroad," the main focus of Russian foreign policy during the first post-Soviet decade continued to be relations with the West, particularly the United States. To be sure, Russia, weak economically and militarily, had little choice but to seek reconciliation with the United States. The new state urgently needed Western support and friendship as it ventured into a new era. Yet Yeltsin had to fend off nationalist critics at home who blamed the United States, especially the CIA, for Russia's loss of great-power status and demanded that Russia reassert its dominance in Eastern Europe and surrounding regions. Yeltsin's presidency coincided with that of Bill Clinton, and the two established a congenial and effective working relationship. Their most impressive achievement came from a joint commitment to continue the process of nuclear disarmament begun under Gorbachev. Going beyond the first Strategic Arms Reduction Treaty (START I) of July 1991, the United States and Russia agreed in START II to reduce nuclear arms on each side to a level of 3,000 to 3,500 weapons. Presidents George W. Bush and Vladimir Putin signed a pact on May 25, 2002, setting an even lower figure of no more than 2,200 warheads by 2012, with Russia hoping for 1,500 and U.S. military specialists targeting about 1,750. Although certainly both a desirable objective and a cost-saving measure for both sides, the treaty still left each country with weapons totals that could vaporize the entire world.

Earlier, the two countries had succeeded in enhancing nuclear security by persuading Kazakhstan, Belarus, and Ukraine to surrender for dismantling former Soviet nuclear missiles on their territory, a process completed by the end of 1996. The United States also provided funds for the inspection, supervision, and defusing of weapons on both sides, for much improved security at remaining Russian nuclear sites, and for the employment of Russian atomic scientists who might otherwise have been tempted to work for aspiring nuclear states such as Iraq, Iran, and North Korea.

Western aid proved quite a different story. Although emergency relief assistance was effectively delivered to Russia in the difficult winters of 1991 to 1992 and 1992 to 1993, Russian leaders clearly hoped that substantial economic help would be the reward for their cooperative attitude. Indeed, the Western powers and Japan earmarked some $40 billion for assistance to Russia in the first half of the 1990s, but only a small portion of this sum was actually delivered because of delays in setting specific targets for the aid. Moreover, according to critics, the help that did arrive was often misspent, was siphoned into the pockets of rich tycoons, or simply disappeared. Much Western economic assistance was channeled through the International Monetary Fund, whose strict budgetary and fiscal requirements Russia greatly resented. Unilateral American aid, both governmental and private, amounted to some $5 billion in the 1990s. Its effect was disputed, with critics claiming that most of it was wasted and defenders arguing that it successfully targeted specific needs, including technical assistance and support for key civic and grassroots organizations. By the early 2000s, with the Russian budget and economy healthy, Western aid had tapered off. Despite the Western powers' willingness to help, their inclusion of Russia in key economic summits, and their support of eventual Russian entry into the World Trade Organization, many Russian citizens complained that the West had not only done too little but had in fact used aid to undermine or control the economy.

Russia and the United States disagreed over developments in the former Yugoslavia. When the Yugoslav state first began to dissolve in the late 1980s and early 1990s, Russia supported the position of the Serbs, who were fellow Slavs and Orthodox Christians, and criticized Western interference in the region. In 1994, however, Russian leaders helped broker a compromise with the Bosnian Serbs and sent Russian units to participate in peacekeeping efforts in

Bosnia. Nonetheless, tensions between Russia and the West again intensified in 1999 after NATO forces intervened in Serbia, whose government Moscow supported, to aid separatist forces in the ethnic Albanian and predominantly Muslim enclave of Kosovo.

CONCLUSION

In reviewing the record of new Russia's first decade, observers were divided, some seeing the glass half full, others depicting it as half empty. Certainly, the cataclysmic transition from a doctrinaire, authoritarian, totally regulated system to a democratic society proved difficult to achieve. Many Russians suffered economically, socially, and psychologically.

In the process of reform, mistakes were certainly made, and negative features surfaced. At times, the economy appeared near meltdown, and a small elite profited unjustifiably from the chaos and the sale of state assets. Environmental damage from the Soviet era remained unrepaired. Political conflict between reformers and conservatives led to a brief but violent confrontation in October 1993 and to later periods of near governmental paralysis. Under the new constitution, the president possessed too much power. Crime, corruption, deteriorating public health care and other social services, growing drug and AIDS problems, and skyrocketing divorce rates created social conditions that made life difficult for many. Materialism, selfishness, apathy, and despair all flourished.

On the other hand, by 2000, the economy was growing markedly in output though slowly in productivity, and the percentage of the population living in poverty dropped. Although rural life remained bleak, an increasing number of city dwellers began to taste the benefits of reform. Elections, a working legislature, regional autonomy, and a partially free press undergirded Russian democracy. Revamped educational institutions opened a number of opportunities, particularly for younger Russian citizens. Although cheap Western imports flooded into Russia, cultural life and creativity rebounded. Russia's stature in the world, though clearly diminished from its days as the Soviet superpower, had solidified. Despite outsiders' fear of a renewed Russian imperialism, Yeltsin established generally good relations with the newly independent states on Russia's borders, exerting influence but not domination there, and with Russia's neighbors in Asia. Both the United States and the European powers allotted Russia a significant role in European security and international affairs, and relations with the West remained friendly and cooperative. For all his failings and occasionally erratic policies, Boris Yeltsin, Russia's first-ever elected leader, provided a substantial foundation on which a new Russia could be built. What form this new Russia would take, however, would lie largely in the hands of Yeltsin's successor, Vladimir Putin. Putin's vision for Russia would take the nation in a new and more contentious direction.

FURTHER READING

Åslund, Anders, ed. *Russia's Economic Transformation in the 1990s*. Washington, DC: Pinter, 1997.

Blasi, Joseph R., Maya Kroumira, and Douglas Kruse. *Kremlin Capitalism: Privatizing the Russian Economy*. Ithaca, NY: ILR, 1999.

Colton, Timothy J. *Yeltsin: A Life*. New York: Basic Books, 2008.

Colton, Timothy J., and Michael McFaul. *Popular Choice and Managed Democracy: The Russian Elections of 1999 and 2000*. Washington, DC: Brookings Institution Press, 2003.

Condee, Nancy. *The Imperial Trace: Recent Russian Cinema*. Oxford: Oxford University Press, 2009.

Davis, Nathaniel. *A Long Walk to Church: A Contemporary History of Russian Orthodoxy*. 2nd ed. Boulder, CO: Westview, 2003.

Dawisha, Karen, and Bruce Parrott. *Russia and the New States of Eurasia: The Politics of Upheaval*. New York: Cambridge University Press, 1994.

Denisova, Liubov. *Rural Women in the Soviet Union and Post-Soviet Russia*. Edited and Translated by Irina Mukhina. New York: Routledge, 2010.

Ellison, Herbert J. *Boris Yeltsin and Russia's Democratic Transformation*. Toronto: University of Toronto Press, 2006.

Gustafson, Thane. *Capitalism Russian-Style*. Cambridge, UK: Cambridge University Press, 1999.

Henry, Laura A. *Red to Green: Environmental Activism in Post-Soviet Russia*. Ithaca, NY: Cornell University Press, 2010.

McFaul, Michael, and Sergei Markov. *The Troubled Birth of Russian Democracy: Parties, Personalities, and Programs*. Stanford, CA: Hoover Institution Press, 1993.

Millar, James R., and Sharon L. Wolchik, eds. *The Social Legacy of Communism*. Washington, DC: Woodrow Wilson Center Press; Cambridge, UK: Cambridge University Press, 1994.

Remnick, David. *Resurrection: The Struggle for a New Russia*. New York: Random House, 1997.

Shevtsova, Lilia. *Yeltsin's Russia: Myths and Reality*. Washington, DC: Carnegie Endowment for International Peace / Brookings Institution Press, 1999.

Stella, Francesca. *Lesbian Lives in Soviet and Post-Soviet Russia: Post/Socialism and Gendered Sexualities.* New York: Palgrave Macmillan, 2015.

White, Anne. *Small-Town Russia: Postcommunist Livelihoods and Identities—A Portrait of the Intelligentsia in Achit, Bednodemyanovsk and Zubtsov, 1999–2000.* New York: RoutledgeCurzon, 2004.

Yeltsin, Boris. *The Struggle for Russia.* Translated by Catherine A. Fitzpatrick. New York: Times Books, 1994.

CHAPTER 16

THE PUTIN ERA: RUSSIA IN THE TWENTY-FIRST CENTURY

Parents in Beslan, a quiet, provincial town in North Ossetia, not far from Chechnya, were busy in the early morning of September 1, 2004, preparing for the festive opening day of school. They were helping their children dress, boys in freshly ironed white shirts and girls in new dresses with white bows in their hair. Parents and students then walked together to School Number 1, a two-story brick building near the center of town. Bouquets of flowers, flags, and balloons provided colorful decoration for the occasion. Just as the program began, popping noises were heard, and several adults testified later that they thought the sounds came from balloons bursting.

Almost immediately, however, heavily armed men, some of them masked and all in dark or camouflage clothing, ran into the courtyard and ordered everyone into the large, recently renovated gymnasium. In the ensuing panic and confusion, the terrorists shot several adults and children. Soon, almost twelve hundred hostages huddled on the gym floor. Their captors killed several more individuals for not keeping the terrified students quiet. The gunmen announced that their captives would be freed only when Russia withdrew all its troops from Chechnya—occupied since 1995 as a result of the Chechen rebellion. The hostage takers then busied themselves with hanging strings of bombs on wires stretching from one basketball hoop to the other. Later, they also mined the windows. During the first day only, the terrorists permitted hostages to go to the bathroom and to drink water.

Local authorities were too stunned to develop a plan of action, and the Russian government reacted slowly and deceitfully. Television and radio channels claimed that there were only three hundred hostages, which angered the terrorists and the students' relatives. President Vladimir Putin made no response at first; then, as his advisors remained divided over whether to negotiate or storm the school, steps were taken to implement both courses of action.

On the siege's second day, the terrorists permitted a negotiator to enter the school. He persuaded the hostage takers to release nursing mothers and their infants, some twenty-five people in all, but he also reported the rapidly deteriorating condition of the remaining hostages. The terrorists had cut off water to the captives, and some children had resorted to drinking urine captured in their shoes. In oppressive heat and with no food, a number of individuals had grown weak and were nearly delirious.

Meanwhile, Russian special forces deployed to Beslan surrounded the school. Hundreds of local militia and armed fathers milled about as well. In this volatile situation, when a terrorist bomb exploded accidentally shortly after noon on September 4, pandemonium ensued. People inside and outside the school started shooting. At one point, the terrorists even appealed for a cease-fire, but the authorities could not control events. After four hours of mayhem, all but one of the thirty-two terrorists, as well as almost three hundred innocent children, parents, and teachers, lay dead.

The Beslan tragedy markedly scarred the early years of Putin's presidency. His government's falsifying of news about the hostage taking, his belated and limited response, and his blaming local corruption and incompetence for what had happened all seemed a throwback to Soviet times and foreshadowed his later antidemocratic policies. Most significantly, in a speech and press conference after Beslan, Putin stressed xenophobic and anti-Western themes that, in succeeding years, would recur frequently in Russian domestic and foreign policy. He lamented the collapse of the Soviet Union and Russia's resulting weakness. He pictured the West as trying to keep Russia down, angrily rejected Western pressure for a political settlement of the Chechen war, and blamed Boris Yeltsin and foreign forces for the crisis there. The shame of the Beslan massacre strengthened Putin's authoritarian tendencies.

THE RISE OF VLADIMIR PUTIN

The first of many paradoxes about Putin, who has served as Russia's president from 2000 to 2008, prime minister from 2008 to 2012, and president again beginning in 2012, is the contrast between the obscurity of his early, undistinguished career as a civil servant and the dominant role he played as the authoritarian ruler of his country in the first two decades of the twenty-first century. His rapid ascension to power and his ruthless exercise of it during his presidency testify to his intelligence, determination, competence, and political skill. Putin brought Russia much-needed stability, rapid economic growth, and a revived sense of national pride. However, the Putin years have also been

FIGURE 16.1. Vladimir Putin. (bibiphoto / Shutterstock.com)

characterized by the erosion of democratic governance, the spread of corruption and coercion, the continuing collapse of infrastructure, the recurring harassment of Russia's neighbors and Western institutions such as the European Union and NATO, the annexation of Crimea, and military and economic support for separatists in the Donbas civil war in eastern Ukraine.

Putin is the first recent Russian leader with no direct memory of World War II or Stalinism. Born in Leningrad (now St. Petersburg) in 1952 of working-class parents, he was a tough, reserved boy, seemingly anxious to defy authority and convention. Not very big, he was nevertheless often involved in youthful scuffles and fights, which whetted a burgeoning appetite for sports, especially boxing and judo. His passion for the latter, at which he excelled in citywide competitions, probably rescued him from hooliganism or worse. Bright in school, Putin became fascinated as a teenager with books, movies, and TV shows about adventure and espionage. He came to admire the exploits of secret policemen and, as a senior in secondary school, sought employment with the KGB in Leningrad. Told that he was too young and needed higher education, Putin soon enrolled in Leningrad State University.

On completing a degree in law, he went to work for the KGB in 1975. After several years keeping tabs on dissidents and foreign academic visitors to Leningrad (probably including this book's coauthor, John Thompson), Putin, who had studied German in school and university, was posted to Dresden, East Germany, in 1985. He spent five years in this backwater, apparently engaged in both agent recruitment and low-level collection and analysis of mostly non-confidential information. In January 1990, Putin was transferred back to Leningrad. At this point in his career, he appeared to be an unremarkable agent and civil servant. Superiors did not single him out, and he received no special awards or commendations.

As the Soviet system began to unravel in 1990 and 1991, Putin became increasingly restive in the routine KGB assignments given to him on his return from a now reunified Germany. He worked for a time in the president's office at Leningrad State University and then took a job with a former law professor and prominent liberal reformer, Anatoly Sobchak, who headed the Leningrad City Council. Putin offered to resign from the KGB, but Sobchak said that he did not mind if Putin continued to work for them, and the KGB declared that the future president should stay on in the "active reserve." During the abortive August 1991 coup, Putin supported Sobchak in staunchly opposing the plotters and backing Boris Yeltsin. When Sobchak was elected mayor of Leningrad (soon renamed St. Petersburg) shortly afterward, Putin quit the KGB and took a job in the new city administration, rising to become a deputy mayor. He helped promote foreign investment in the city and region and survived a minor scandal over contract awards.

In 1996, when Sobchak lost his reelection bid, Putin resigned from city government but was soon offered a job in Moscow working in the office managing Kremlin property and assets. He then moved to the position of deputy chief of staff in Yeltsin's presidential administration. Capable and self-effacing, Putin endeared himself to Yeltsin, who, in 1998, made this rising star head of the domestic counterintelligence agency, the Federal Security Bureau. Yeltsin, who was constitutionally required to step down in 2000 after two terms, had run through four different prime ministers during 1998 and the first half of 1999. According to his memoirs, the Russian president decided in August 1999 to make Putin prime minister because the young civil servant had the backbone, ambition, and talent to succeed to the presidency in the June 2000 elections. Yeltsin's appointment of an almost-unknown bureaucrat and former KGB agent stunned and bewildered many Russian and Western observers. But Yeltsin must have been delighted with his protégé's resumption of war against the Chechens a month later and with the public acclaim this brought the new leader. As Yeltsin's health and ability to govern deteriorated noticeably during the fall of 1999, he decided to step down early to give Putin a better run at the presidency, announcing his resignation on New Year's Eve 1999. Coauthor Christopher Ward watched Yeltsin's resignation speech on television from his

Moscow apartment that evening and wondered, like many others, what kind of leader the unknown Vladimir Putin would be.

Although Putin began his prime ministership in Yeltsin's shadow, his firmness, confidence, and considerable competence soon won over Yeltsin's supporters, some moderates, and the broad public. Young, fit, imperturbable, and determined, he presented a reassuring figure in a time of uncertainty. Many Russians vested their hopes for stability, security, and better times in him. By the time Putin became acting president in January 2000, he was immensely popular and the overwhelming favorite for the upcoming presidential elections. The government's victory in the December 1999 Duma elections, in which almost 62 percent of the electorate had voted, bolstered his position. A new government-linked party, Unity, won 16.6 percent of the vote, which together with the 15.5 percent of a new center-right grouping, the Fatherland, plus the support of a number of nonparty deputies, provided the Yeltsin-Putin regime with a bare but working majority in the new Duma. The ex-communists slipped slightly to about a quarter of the vote, with the democratic Left at 11 percent and the extreme Right trailing at 4 percent.

Constitutional provisions for an election within three months after a president's resignation moved the presidential balloting up from June to March 2000. With a bland, all-encompassing platform that promised continued reform and economic improvement as well as running against weak opposition, Putin coasted to victory with 53 percent of the vote. His main opponent, the ex-communist Gennady Zyuganov, lost some ground compared to the 1996 elections but still polled almost 30 percent of the ballots. By 2001, Putin had weakened the communist deputies' position in the Duma, which the president now dominated. The pressing question was what the young, vigorous new leader would do with his electoral mandate.

ECONOMIC GROWTH AND CONTRACTION

Putin's first and continuing priority was to bring prosperity, order, and stability to Russia. Benefiting from a devalued ruble after the financial collapse of 1998, the Russian economy had recovered moderately even before Putin took office. Bolstered by increased energy production and skyrocketing revenue as oil and natural gas prices rose precipitously in the first years of the twenty-first century, the nation's economy grew by almost one-third from 2001 to 2008 at 6 percent per year. After a brief downturn in the 2008–2010 world recession, the economy rebounded to increases of 4 or 5 percent in 2011 and 2012. In most years, Putin was able to run substantial budget surpluses. He also set up a stabilization and rainy-day fund from energy income and paid off Russia's foreign debt. Major Russian cities became boom towns, as garish, modernistic buildings proliferated in city centers and ostentatious, oversized McDachas (country mansions) crowded the surrounding countryside. Big department stores, fancy boutiques, fast food outlets, trendy restaurants, sushi bars, and a variety of retail outlets sprang up in Moscow and other major metropolises (see Figure 16.2). Foreign exchange surpluses allowed Putin to bring pension payments up to date and to maintain fairly cheap utilities and transportation. According to World Bank figures, Russians' real disposable income surged by 11.2 percent per year from 2002 to 2006 and continued to increase modestly from 2010 to 2012. Urban citizens in particular enjoyed a markedly better standard of living, with a wide range of goods and services available to them. Between 1992 and 2010, the percentage of the population living below the poverty level dropped from 34 to 13 percent, just below the US rate. Inflation was controlled, and unemployment fell. Most young city dwellers had a range of educational and job opportunities.

At first, conditions in the countryside were not as promising, with many farmers struggling and widespread pockets of rural poverty. Although private

FIGURE 16.2. The new and the old: modern Moscow ads with a Stalin-era skyscraper in the background. (Courtesy of Dr. Daniel Wood)

farming was legalized, most agricultural output remained on former state or collective farms. In the mid-2000s, however, Putin energized farming output by making credit easily available through regional agricultural banks, supporting grain prices, lowering taxes, and providing state-subsidized leasing of modern agricultural machinery. As a result, output soared, livestock herds began to be rebuilt, and Russia became again a grain exporter (though still importing meat and other foods).

The overall record of the Russian economy in the first decade of the twenty-first century was quite impressive. But bad news existed as well. Here, we run into the second paradox of Putin's presidency. He came to power with an avowed goal of creating a modern, efficient, diversified, and globalized economy in Russia, yet the rush to cash in on high oil and gas prices made Russia too dependent on a single economic sector: energy. In 2010, energy products accounted for almost one-third of Russia's gross domestic product, one half of government revenues, and two-thirds of export earnings. Russia came close to fitting the model of a colonial or Third World country, relying on raw material exports to sustain the economy. The significant fall in world energy prices that began in 2014 had a damaging effect on the country. Meanwhile, with a few exceptions, Russian factories were neither efficient nor technologically advanced, and Russian products seldom had the quality or appeal to compete on the world market.

Moreover, Russia's economic booms of 2001–2008 and 2010–2014 produced glaring inequalities. Moscow, and to a lesser degree St. Petersburg, profited most from the good times, and this opened an enormous gap between that city and the rest of the country. Moscow in 2006 provided 25 percent of the nation's gross domestic product and attracted 40 percent of foreign investment. Moreover, larger cities and towns benefited much more economically than rural areas. This disparity, common throughout Russian history, seemed more glaring because of modern communication and transportation, which made the contrasts visible to all Russian citizens. Last, the good times created sharp differences in income. In mid-2008, Russia boasted eighty-seven billionaires, most of them in Moscow. Another one to two hundred thousand individuals were considered truly wealthy, and the numbers of relatively affluent middle-class Russians swelled into the millions. But some twenty-five million citizens struggled to survive, and many others got along on modest incomes. Moreover, those in the bottom ranks suffered disproportionately from the collapse of the Soviet safety net, which had provided free medical services and education, extremely cheap housing and utilities, and controlled prices on necessities. The costs of secondary and higher education and of health care plus rising prices for food and other necessities overwhelmed many Russian families. Pensioners, veterans, single mothers, and many women workers did not fare well amid the growing prosperity, and the economic downturns of recent years have hurt these groups even more.

Another downside to the economic upturn that ended in 2014 was that small businesses did not grow as quickly as the rest of the economy. Individual entrepreneurs faced a range of obstacles: limited access to credit, volatile prices, bureaucratic red tape, murky property rights, and extensive corruption. Although Putin set as a major objective the simplifying of procedures for starting a small business, and some progress was made on this score, by 2006, fifty or more permissions and licenses were still required to open a store, restaurant, or other small enterprise. The president also promised to attack widespread bribery and extortion, no longer by armed mafia as in the 1990s but by local and central government officials; however, Russia continues to rank among the most corrupt nations in the world.

Moreover, Russia's halting economic progress until 2014 contributed little to improving the deplorable environmental conditions in most of the country. Relatively little effort went either to remedying the degradation and pollution left over from the Soviet era or to installing new safeguards and technologies that would improve Russia's air, water, and natural resources.

A glaring failure to address Russia's infrastructure crisis also marred Putin's economic record. Not only was little done to repair crumbling roads, bridges, rail lines, and buildings, but almost no new construction for economic purposes was undertaken. For example, between 2005 and 2010, the Russian government did not build a single major modern highway, while the Chinese were creating a high-speed rail network and five thousand kilometers of new roads. At the same time, Putin's partially successful efforts to improve the economy and raise Russians' standard of living produced a third major paradox of his presidency. He repeatedly stressed his faith in a market system, rejecting any return to Soviet-style state socialism. Yet his policies steadily increased government control over the economy and state ownership of key industries, especially in energy. Moreover, by 2008, the distinction between government and business was badly blurred, with some state officials also serving as company executives and business leaders taking positions in government. Except for the retail and services sector, the Russian economy, rather than turning into a free-enterprise system, seemed almost a state corporation.

As a member of the Yeltsin administration, Putin had witnessed firsthand the strong influence wielded by Russia's biggest businessmen, the so-called oligarchs, on the former president's policies and decisions. He also knew that, during the 1996 election, they had manipulated the media in Yeltsin's favor and contributed major sums to his successful reelection bid. Putin, however, did not feel beholden to any of them, and on taking office, he apparently decided that a major objective of his presidency would be to rein in these powerful tycoons and establish firm state control over the economy. Eschewing direct confrontation with them at first, Putin cleverly circumscribed their economic and political influence, using the threat of investigation and indictment to force two of the most powerful into exile. In addition, he warned these dominant businessmen several times that they were not to meddle in politics. As long as they stuck to moneymaking, the government would leave them alone.

Most of the oligarchs heeded this admonition, but not billionaire Mikhail Khodorkovsky, head of the giant oil conglomerate Yukos, whose ambitions included becoming both a major philanthropist and a powerful politician. He hoped to buy off Duma deputies and institute a parliamentary government with himself as prime minister. Despite the clear signal given by the arrest of a senior Yukos official in the summer of 2003, Khodorkovsky strongly resisted Putin-backed tax changes and loudly criticized other government policies. That fall he was seized on charges of tax evasion and embezzlement. After a sham trial, Khodorkovsky was sent to prison for eight years. Huge claims for back taxes against Yukos were used to force its breakup and the sale of its assets, which passed to government-controlled firms, thus firmly establishing the Putin administration's control over Russia's vast energy resources and trade. In 2010, with Khodorkovsky due to be released on the eve of the 2012 presidential election, the government tried the oil magnate again on new charges of stealing and illegally selling oil when still head of Yukos. After receiving a pardon from Putin, Khodorkovsky was finally released from prison in 2013 and moved to Switzerland.

Another significant paradox of Putin's tenure emerged in his treatment of foreign investment in Russia. On ascending to the presidency, he had deplored the low level of such investment, pointing out that China and several developing nations received a larger share of international funds than Russia. He promised to increase investment from abroad substantially. Yet he ended by squeezing out any large outside ownership of Russian industry. Initially, the president had some success in enticing foreign investors, but many potential funders remained wary, citing still incomplete tax reforms; a corrupt, interfering bureaucracy, particularly at local levels; and, most unsettling of all, weakly developed laws protecting property and contracts. Western firms heavily penetrated the consumer market, but few successfully established production facilities. Russia badly needed Western technology and know-how, particularly to help raise productivity in old oil fields and to assist in exploiting new ones in the Far East and the Arctic. Yet the government reneged on agreements with British Petroleum for energy development on Sakhalin Island off

Russia's Pacific coast. Moreover, harassment and threats continually marred its relationship with British Petroleum, which had shares in a Russian energy firm. It is clear that foreign oil firms can play only a limited role in the future development of Russian energy, an economic sector Putin steadfastly keeps under tight government control.

A final puzzle of the economic policies of the Putin era was that both he and his colleague and one-time president Dmitry Medvedev spoke often and forcefully about the urgent necessity to modernize and diversify the Russian economy. The latter even promised to establish a center for technology and innovation, a "Silicon Valley" area where the latest techniques and inventions could be hatched and tested.

Nevertheless, despite all the rhetoric and Russia's patent need in this area, almost nothing was accomplished between 2000 and 2012. Again, the contrast with China was markedly to Russia's disadvantage. Both economic systems are based on state capitalism, but China is ahead in modernizing and diversifying its economy despite recent economic reversals. Russia remains heavily dependent on arms exports and its energy sector, and keeps falling further behind in technology and innovation despite massive governmental spending on defense. Moreover, Russia's entry into the World Trade Organization (WTO) in 2012 posed new challenges to the economy, as the government has resisted pressure to comply with WTO regulations and standards in its international economic relations.

Recent times have brought new strains to the Russian economy, culminating in the economic crisis the nation currently faces. A combination of factors, most notably sanctions imposed on Russia by the international community (particularly the United States and the European Union) because of Russia's role in the Donbas War in eastern Ukraine (discussed later in this chapter), coupled with persistently low oil and gas prices and weakening demand for other raw material exports, has reduced the value of the central government's currency and gold reserves. In response to the sanctions, Russia has banned the importation of many foreign products, which has resulted in economic hardship for some sectors of the domestic economy. While it was intended to be an exemplar of Russia's return to world prominence, the 2014 Winter Olympics in the city of Sochi along Russia's Black Sea coast was marred by accusations of cost overruns, worries about the safety of LGBTQ athletes, environmental degradation, doping on a massive scale by Russian participants, and even a cover-up of the deaths of foreign venue construction workers. Finally, the high cost of supporting Ukrainian separatists in the Donbas and the massive financial burden of Russia's intervention in war-torn Syria (also discussed later in this chapter) appear to indicate that the difficulties faced by the Russian economy will continue for the foreseeable future.

THE PUTIN-MEDVEDEV ADMINISTRATION

The new values and attitudes described in preceding sections facilitated corrosive changes that Putin carried out in politics and governance. The term "sovereign democracy," coined by one of Putin's advisors, remained ill-defined but reflected growing political authoritarianism. In another major paradox of his era, Putin reaffirmed on numerous occasions his commitment to democracy and civil freedoms in Russia but then regularly and blatantly curtailed and undermined those principles and structures. Whether in accord with a master plan or more pragmatically, he reshaped and took control of every institution or power center capable of challenging the president's authority. Under his aegis, the Russian political system has become highly centralized and authoritarian.

As we saw earlier, Putin first undercut and then dismantled the economic and political clout of the oligarchs. At the same time, he has forced closure of nearly all independent media outlets, substituting state ownership and control. When Putin worked in Yeltsin's presidential administration, he observed what a crucial role the media played in promulgating official policy, undermining opponents, and influencing voters. Apparently resolving after that experience to ensure a pro-government flow of information, in April 2001 the new president shut down NTV, a station that exposed corruption, investigated social problems, and criticized the Chechen war. Two successor television stations were forced to close in the next two years, partly because of government harassment and partly because of quarrels among the owners and fiscal mismanagement. As a result, from 2003, the state owned and dictated the content of all major television channels, establishing a monopoly over the main method by which most Russians obtained information. Small independent newspapers and radio stations still existed but reached a miniscule audience of under two hundred thousand, while an estimated thirty-five million Russians dutifully watched government newscasts on television each day. A few independent journalists remained, but several of these were murdered, and the rest practiced self-censorship. Questioning the president or calling the government to account in any meaningful way was dangerous. As one observer commented, "Freedom of speech exists in Russia as long as it's not a threat to the authorities." With only a few exceptions, the media in contemporary Russia is subservient to the will of the state.

In a third move to establish unchallenged central government authority, Putin restructured relations between Moscow and Russia's regions and local governments. Under Yeltsin, who often granted aid and made concessions to the eighty-nine regions, some had become virtually autonomous. In the early

2000s, Putin weakened the regional governors' position in the upper legislative body, the Federation Council, won authority to remove elected governors if necessary, and established seven large jurisdictions, or provinces, run by his appointees to supervise activity in the regions. After the Beslan massacre, on the pretext of increasing security at the local level, he ended the election of governors. Henceforth, the president appointed both the eighty-nine governors and the "supergovernors" of the seven large provinces as well as most mayors, regional police chiefs, and prosecutors.

Another significant control measure developed when Putin ensured that, despite some beneficial changes in the judicial system, the federal courts would serve his political purposes as the executive branch of the Russian government exercised de facto control over the judiciary, as in the trials of Khodorkovsky. In addition, criticizing the activities of foreign-linked nongovernmental organizations working in such fields as the environment, health, welfare, and education, he established restrictive regulations governing their activities.

Finally, Putin turned the electoral system into a farce. First, he manipulated the December 2003 election of Duma deputies, resulting in a huge pro-government majority that remains completely subservient to the president. He also rigged the March 2004 presidential balloting to ensure his overwhelming reelection with 71 percent of the vote and the 2008 presidential vote that made Dmitry Medvedev, his aide, president from 2008 to 2012. Putin returned as president after the 2012 presidential elections, which were criticized by some international observers for irregularities. During his first term, he had fulfilled, at least in part, his promise to bring order, stability, and prosperity to Russia, and his popularity ratings remained in the 70 to 80 percent range despite the war in Chechnya that began in the fall of 1999 and dragged on until 2005. He successfully courted a wide range of constituents, ranging from the Orthodox faithful (Putin's mother secretly baptized him at birth) to the military and the nationalist Right to civil servants and even some intelligentsia. No other politician has the standing or backing to mount a significant challenge to Putin, who faces near certain reelection to a fourth term as president in 2018.

Putin's minions in the Kremlin began early in 2003 to stage-manage the upcoming Duma and presidential election campaigns. First, United Russia, an openly pro-Putin party, was reshaped and bolstered, while a new party, Rodina (Motherland), ostensibly independent but in fact pro-government, was formed. Then, to discredit the liberal parties and the Communists, press and television campaigning harped on the ties of those parties and their leaders to the oligarchs and to the confusion and corruption of the Yeltsin years. Contributing to their own demise, liberal leaders quarreled among themselves and failed to present voters with a persuasive and coherent platform. As a result, the liberal parties failed to reach the 5 percent of the vote necessary to seat their deputies in the Duma. United Russia and Motherland ended up with almost three-quarters of the deputies and chaired all the Duma committees. Communist representation fell, becoming only a token opposition in the new Duma. Both parliamentary democracy and organized opposition to the government were virtually eliminated in the "free," but definitely not fair, elections of 2004, 2008, and 2012.

Both Russian and Western observers puzzled over why Putin, with a totally compliant Duma and strong backing in the country, failed to embark on major structural and policy reforms, particularly tackling corruption, cleaning up the army, and improving health and education. Instead, further efforts to control the economy, the media, and the political process have marked the Putin-Medvedev years. Although a number of former intelligence, security, and military officials (sometimes called the *siloviki*) served in the Putin central administration and key regional posts, they did not form a coherent bloc with an agreed agenda. Moreover, the president also appointed a number of businessmen and former civilian colleagues from St. Petersburg to top positions in the government. Thus, he ensured that no individual or group could accumulate much power and kept the reins of government in his hands and in those of his closest Kremlin advisors.

Putin pushed hard for a major overhaul of the armed forces, designed both to make the military more modern and efficient and to eliminate widespread corruption and abuse in the system. Despite a few minor improvements, basically nothing changed, and the loss of the submarine *Kursk* in 2000 after a torpedo exploded inside the vessel revealed a lack of training and maintenance in the Russian Navy. The Russian Army also remained poorly trained, equipped, and led. The two-year conscription system remained in place, inducting primarily those who were too poor or lacking in influence to escape the draft. Recruits continued to be hazed, beaten, and forced to engage in illegal activities. Desertion was common, and accidents, abuse, murder, and suicide resulted in over a thousand noncombat deaths a year. The army had too many officers and too few trained enlisted personnel, and the former often engaged in abusive, illegal, and corrupt behavior. Putin's inability to alter this situation demonstrated that, even in an authoritarian system, it is difficult to overcome entrenched pockets of graft, inefficiency, and indifference.

In early 2005, largely spontaneous street protests by pensioners forced Putin to modify recently enacted changes in the system of pensions and benefits, suggesting popular pressure could still affect government policy. In the spring of 2007, a loosely organized opposition group, Other Russia, helped promote small protest demonstrations in Moscow and St. Petersburg. In both cities, riot police intervened, hassling many demonstrators, including former world chess champion Gary Kasparov and former prime minister Mikhail Kasyanov, beating dozens of others, and arresting hundreds. The government's purpose was unclear since the bad publicity far outweighed any danger the few protesters posed. Possibly, this show of force signaled Putin's determination to keep tight control of the political process as the December 2007 Duma elections and the March 2008 presidential balloting approached.

The Russian constitution limited individuals to two consecutive terms as president. Putin steadfastly turned aside suggestions that the constitution be amended to permit him to run for a third term in 2012, but he agreed to lead the campaign of the pro-government United Russia Party during the run-up to the 2007 Duma elections. His popularity, state control of the media, officials' pressure for a large turnout, and a weak opposition ensured that United Russia and its affiliates won more than two-thirds of the seats in the new Duma. Shortly afterward, on December 10, 2007, President Putin made clear that he favored Dmitry Medvedev, his legal advisor and first deputy prime minister, as United Russia's candidate for president in the March 2008 election. Dutifully, Medvedev suggested the following day that, should he become president, he would ask Putin to serve as his prime minister. Thus, the stage was set for Putin to continue to play a leading role in Russia's political life after his term as president expired, just as he had been promising for some time.

When Putin anointed Medvedev as his successor, many observers speculated that the latter might represent a breath of fresh air in the stagnation creeping over Russia under Putin's rule. Part of this false optimism stemmed from Dmitry Medvedev's different background. Almost thirteen years younger, he grew up in an academic family and had no ties to the military or the security services. Studious and soft spoken, Medvedev had finished law school at Leningrad State University and had taught there in the late 1980s and early 1990s. He spoke English well and was an avowed fan of Western rock music, especially the heavy metal band Deep Purple. He and Putin met when both worked for the mayoralty administration of their law professor, Anatoly Sobchak. When Putin became prime minister in late 1999, he brought Medvedev to Moscow to serve on the Kremlin staff and then appointed him to run Putin's 2000 campaign for president. Medvedev subsequently held a number of responsible jobs under Putin, ending up as deputy prime minister. A warning sign about Medvedev's potential should have been his mediocre performance in two important assignments Putin gave him. As head of the giant energy firm Gazprom, Medvedev did little to improve efficiency or productivity, and as chairman of national task forces to improve education, housing, and health care, he accomplished little.

Medvedev's rhetoric also raised false hopes. In speeches both before and after becoming president, he attacked the "legal nihilism" existing in Russia, called for modernization and innovation in the Russian economy, and insisted that Russia could progress only under a democratic, free enterprise system. Many commentators in the West and some in Russia saw Medvedev as a clear alternative to Putin and waited expectantly for him to chart an independent course.

But Medvedev's actions soon belied his fine words and implied promises. His appointment of Putin as prime minister made clear that a tandem ruled Russia and that Medvedev would not do anything to upset the system Putin had so carefully constructed during the previous eight years. In his own four years as president, Medvedev undertook no major initiatives or policy changes. And while the Western and Russian press speculated about whether Medvedev would run for president in 2012 (he did not), and both Putin and Medvedev dropped hints to bolster these guesses, Medvedev revealed in September 2011 what some had suspected all along: that Medvedev was primarily a placeholder for Putin and that they had agreed as far back as 2008 that Putin would run for president in 2012 and, after the election, would appoint Medvedev prime minister. Moreover, during his presidency, Medvedev had pushed through a constitutional change extending presidential terms to six years. The blatant chicanery of the whole Medvedev-Putin swap angered many urban and educated Russians, who felt treated as fools, and contributed to the protests known as the Bolotnaya Square Movement (named after a location in Moscow), which was part of the abortive "Snow Revolution" of 2011 to 2013.

The main trigger of the protests was the obvious and somewhat desperate rigging of the December 4, 2011, elections to the Duma. During the late summer and early fall, polls and attitudinal surveys indicated that many citizens were apathetic and disinterested in another sham vote. Putin as prime minister began active electioneering, posing at times as a motorcyclist, arm wrestler, and scuba diver and forming a populist organization, the All-Russian Popular Front, to lure voters into supporting the government party, United Russia. As in earlier elections, extreme pressure was applied to local and regional officials to turn out the maximum vote for United Russia. Pro-government propaganda dominated all major media outlets. Yet as the election approached, polls showed that United Russia was running well behind its previous margins of victory. Consequently, in some precincts, patent ballot-box stuffing and falsifying the vote count were resorted to. Unfortunately for the government, cell phone cameras captured several blatant examples of such election fraud, and the photos were widely shown on the Internet. Despite the government's frantic efforts, official results showed that United Russia secured only a slim majority of Duma deputies, instead of the two-thirds representation hoped for, and 49 percent of the vote, 15 percent lower than the previous election. Some observers concluded an accurate tally would have given only about a third of the vote to United Russia. Clearly, portions of the Russian electorate were displaying growing disenchantment with the Putin regime.

Other signs indicated the same trend. On November 20, during the election campaign, the audience at a martial arts bout booed when Putin entered the arena. At subsequent public events, substitutes for Putin were also booed. On election night, some five thousand people in Moscow protested the rigged results, calling United Russia a party of "crooks and thieves," a slogan popularized by a well-known blogger. Then and during a second protest on December 6, some protesters were arrested and sentenced.

Putin called the protesters "monkeys" and labeled the white ribbons they wore "condoms." Using social media, various groups and individuals organized a mass demonstration at Bolotnaya Square on December 10, 2011, attended by some fifty thousand people, with smaller protests in a number of other cities. The authorities, apparently anxious not to antagonize the citizenry, issued a permit for the Moscow meeting, provided a polite police presence, arrested no one, and allowed state television to cover the event. The protesters appeared to be mainly middle-class citizens. They had no common agenda or organization, and their speeches chiefly complained about the fraudulent election and about general bribery and corruption. Similar protests occurred in Moscow on December 24, 2011, and February 5, 2012. In later, more polite comments, Putin refused the protesters' demand for new elections but offered to put TV cameras in polling stations for the March presidential election, fired a chief Kremlin ideologue, and offered minor concessions concerning the choosing of governors.

Amid the heavy presence of tanks, troops, and security service agents, the March 2012 presidential vote went off without major incident, with Putin officially garnering 64 percent of the vote against weak opposition. Voter rolls were padded, and special buses shuttled among polling stations to facilitate multiple voting. Yet in Moscow, Putin won only 50 percent of the votes. During the week following the election, citizen protests occurred in Moscow and other cities, but both the numbers and the enthusiasm were reduced. The protesters had no special organization or alternative platform.

By the early summer of 2012, Putin had given little indication of what his renewed presidency would entail. Clearly the protests sparked by the 2011 Duma and 2012 presidential elections reflected the frustration of Russia's growing middle class with a corrupt, arbitrary, and unrepresentative system. A possible reform might be a partial devolution of political power to regions and cities, which would probably produce a patchwork of populist, democratic, and authoritarian governance at the local level. Or Putin and his cronies might seek to engineer controlled changes in the direction of greater transparency and accountability. In either case, the stability and continuing prosperity of Russia is far from guaranteed.

Since 2000, Putin's policies have clearly pushed Russia toward authoritarianism. Putin also often spoke of wanting to establish "a dictatorship of law," and in his emphasis on law and order for Russia, some observers felt that the president gave greatest weight to the last word in that slogan. Most disturbingly for many doubters, Putin consistently showed little toleration for criticism, blaming his predecessor and Western interference for Russia's problems. His government also harassed and sometimes beat up human rights proponents, critical journalists, and opposition politicians. Instances of police brutality and intimidation were common.

The Russian legislative election to the State Duma, which was held in September 2016, and the next Russian presidential election, which is scheduled for March 2018, will reveal the path that Russia will take in the coming years. The 2016 legislative elections witnessed a significantly lower turnout than the 2011 elections. Nevertheless, they saw Putin's United Russia Party, under the leadership of Prime Minister Medvedev, increase its majority in the State Duma, which it has enjoyed since 2003. Regarding the 2018 elections, as we have seen, Putin now has obtained the right to run for a fourth term. Unless there is dramatic change in the Russian political landscape, the most likely scenario is that Putin will win the election and ensure his position as leader until at least 2024.

NEW CHALLENGES IN THE CAUCASUS

In the early 2000s, Putin had to deal with the ongoing insurgency in Chechnya, a running sore that pushed his domestic policies toward authoritarianism and gave his foreign policy a xenophobic and anti-Western tone. Later, he confronted a mutually hostile relationship with Georgia that deteriorated in 2008 into a brief war. Finally, continued unrest and sporadic violence in the North Caucasus remained a major problem as Russia entered the second decade of the twenty-first century.

The start of the second Chechen war in the fall of 1999 helped catapult Putin to power, but the struggle's dragged-out nature provided a persistent irritant during both his terms as president. When hostilities were renewed in 1999, Putin and his advisors expected a quick victory. Despite claims of better-trained troops, improved equipment, and more reliable intelligence, however, the Russians again proved incapable of defeating the Chechen insurrection. They succeeded eventually in controlling the main cities and towns, but even after Russian generals had declared the war over several times in 2001 and 2002, rebels continued to shoot down Russian helicopters, harass Russian garrisons, and control the Chechen countryside. Moreover, as had been rumored during the first Chechen war, Russian forces were accused of grave human rights violations, including the torture and murder of innocent civilians. And as independent observers noted, both sides in the savage struggle resorted to kidnappings, extortion, and illegal arms and drug sales to enrich themselves.

After the September 2001 terrorist attacks in the United States, the Russian president at once joined the American government's "war against terrorism," hastening to link the Chechen rebels with Al-Qaeda and portraying Russian actions in Chechnya as simply another front in that war. Grateful for Putin's prompt and thorough cooperation in their fall 2001 attack on Afghanistan, American and Western European leaders muted their criticism of Russia's Chechen policy.

By the fall of 2002, Putin appeared to recognize that military poultices were unlikely to heal the festering crisis in Chechnya. Moreover, polls indicated that public support for the Chechen war, which had helped bring Putin to power, was waning, with almost half the populace leaning toward a peaceful solution. Rumors of secret negotiations between the two sides surfaced. However, in late October 2002, forty-one Chechen commandos seized a Moscow theater and its more than eight hundred patrons, threatening to blow up the building and kill the hostages unless the Russian army withdrew from Chechnya. After several days' hesitation, Putin ordered special forces to end the takeover. Using an opiate-based gas, they immobilized and then killed all the hostage takers. At the same time, most of the hostages were also gassed, with 120 dying, in part, critics said, because the Russian government refused to tell medical personnel treating the stricken exactly what sort of gas it was. Yet public opinion in Russia overwhelmingly supported Putin's course of action. The hostage taking and resulting deaths hardened popular and governmental attitudes toward Chechens' demands for independence, but Putin went ahead with a promised 2003 referendum in Chechnya on its future status and a later presidential election there.

The rigged balloting produced overwhelming support for a new constitution that maintained Chechnya as part of Russia but also promised extensive autonomy. Later in 2003, voters dutifully elected a Russian-backed president, but Chechen rebels retreated to the mountains to continue the fight, while Chechen suicide bombers blew themselves up in subways and destroyed two Russian airliners. Terrorists also seized innocent children, teachers, and parents in Beslan, as we saw at the start of the chapter. The new Chechen president, Akhmad Kadyrov, a former religious leader in the region and a rebel supporter in the first war, began slowly to restore order, in large part by organizing a personal militia that didn't hesitate to use force in support of his government. In May 2004, however, the president was assassinated, and Putin's policy of "Chechenization," that is, of putting Chechens in charge of the province, suffered a setback. A pliant stand-in president was chosen, but real power remained in the hands of the slain president's son, Ramzan Kadyrov, then age twenty-seven, who headed the family militia. Acting like an old-fashioned warlord, he ruled arbitrarily and often cruelly but brought stability to Chechnya. In 2007, when he turned thirty, the constitutional age for the presidency, he was sworn in as leader of the province. Occasional guerrilla attacks continued, but the young president made notable progress in rebuilding the war-ravaged region. Moscow supplied 90 percent of his budget, a burden that some Russians complained of, and Kadyrov turned out a near 100 percent vote for United Russia in elections, but he remained an independent and high-handed subaltern.

The Chechen wars scarred Russian society. The cost lay not only in the ten to twelve thousand Russian soldiers and some hundred thousand Chechen fighters and civilians dead but in the brutalization of young Russians serving there; the displacement of tens of thousands of innocent Chechens; the sordid record of abuse, crime, and corruption; and the irrational fears and xenophobia brewed among the Russian populace as a whole.

While Russia retained good relations with Azerbaijan and Armenia, the third post-1991 independent country in the Caucasus, Georgia, presented Moscow with two bothersome issues. First, after a young, American-educated Georgian, Mikheil Saakashvili, came to power in 2004 in a popular uprising dubbed the Rose Revolution, he soon sought to exert Georgian authority over secessionist rebels in the autonomous regions of Abkhazia and South Ossetia. With many Russians living in these enclaves, Putin protested vigorously and insisted on maintaining a Russian military presence there. Putin made clear that Russia expected to wield preponderant influence over its neighbors in the "near abroad." Second, a number of American conservatives, led by Senator John McCain, saw the young Georgian president, despite his occasional fits of arbitrariness, as the bellwether of democracy and a counterweight to Russia in the region. Saakashvili curried American favor by contributing a respectable contingent of troops to the Iraq war effort. In spring 2008, American officials talked about expanding military assistance to Georgia and including Georgia and Ukraine in NATO.

To Putin, all this smacked of US interference in Russia's backyard and another step in a Western encirclement of Russia begun when the Baltic states were admitted to NATO. In March 2008, at a summit meeting in Sochi, Russia, Putin warned President Bush not to proceed with NATO membership for Georgia and Ukraine. On a visit to Georgia in July, American secretary of state Condoleezza Rice in private talks strongly advised the Georgian president not to provoke Russia, but in public remarks indicated that the United States favored Georgia's admission to NATO. Apparently counting on American backing and angered by border clashes and Russian troop movements in the preceding few days, Saakashvili ordered Georgian troops to advance and occupy the South Ossetian capital during the night of August 7. The Russian forces, which had been reinforcing their units all spring and summer, mounted a massive counterattack on August 8 and soon overwhelmed the Georgian troops and, within the next five days, occupied almost a third of Georgia. European leaders' frantic diplomatic efforts resulted in a cease-fire brokered by French president Nicolas Sarkozy. Unfortunately, the Russians interpreted its vague terms as suited them and never did withdraw their forces to prewar lines, as called for by the armistice. Russia quickly recognized the independence of Abkhazia and South Ossetia, although almost no other country did. In response to strong Western criticism, Putin made clear that if the West was going to recognize the independence of Kosovo (see following section), Russia had every right to do the same for Abkhazia and South Ossetia. Although the United States and the International Monetary Fund made up its financial losses, Georgia lost territory and prestige. Talk of Georgia joining NATO was dropped, and Putin claimed victory.

During his years in power, Putin confronted and failed to solve a third perplexing issue in the Caucasus. Neighbors of Chechnya in southern Russia, Ingushetia, Dagestan, and North Ossetia all had majority Muslim populations and a long history of restiveness under Russian rule dating back to the early 1800s. After 1991, currents of Islamic fundamentalism permeated this area, and waves of rebelliousness from Chechnya lapped over into the rest of the north Caucasus. Unemployment was high, and lawlessness spread. Instead of trying to provide assistance, religious toleration, and autonomy to this region, post-1991 Russian governments pursued a policy of repression, rejection, and arbitrariness. Bribery, corruption, torture, and murder were commonplace. Local officials were not held accountable, and near-anarchy reigned in some localities. Moreover, some young radicals, both men and women, resorted to terrorism and violence, carrying out attacks on buildings and suicide bombings of planes and the Moscow metro.

These assaults only fed Russians' racist views of the Muslim southerners, or "dark people," and stiffened the government's hard-line policy in the region. Putin remained adamant in refusing to grant some autonomy and local control of the police and security forces to the north Caucasus, and the future of the region appeared bleak.

RUSSIAN FOREIGN POLICY IN THE TWENTY-FIRST CENTURY

In managing Russia's relations with the rest of the world, Putin steadfastly pursued three aims: to restore international respect for Russia as a major power, to guarantee Russian influence with Russia's neighbors in Europe and at international organizations, and to counterbalance what he saw as America's striving for world dominance. On taking office in 2000, he maintained that he intended to pursue and extend Yeltsin's policy of working closely with Europe and the United States. At first, he acted accordingly, playing down concerns about NATO expansion in Eastern Europe and the Baltic region as well as overlooking American plans to build a missile defense system in Europe and US president George W. Bush's unilateral abrogation of the long-standing Anti-Ballistic Missile Treaty that barred such defenses. Beginning in 2002, however, as the United States lumbered toward war with Iraq, Putin's tone and policies gradually changed. He became increasingly critical of the West, bullied some of Russia's small neighbors, and opposed a number of American initiatives. Yet he continued to participate in Group of Eight (G8) summit meetings of the leading industrial nations, to maintain Russia's special relationship with NATO and its membership in a range of international organizations, and to meet privately with Bush and other Western leaders. Putin's earlier avowals that Russia's future lay in closer integration with the West and his continued cooperation with Western countries on some issues contrasted sharply with his increasingly anti-Western rhetoric.

Relations with the United States

His relationship with the United States had a promising start. In June 2001, Bush and Putin, two new presidents, met in Slovenia. Though they accomplished little of substance, the two leaders established warm personal relations. Putin liked Bush's down-to-earth manner, while the American president famously and inaccurately described his Russian counterpart as "an honest, straightforward man." Three months later, when terrorists attacked New York and Washington, DC, on September 11, 2001, Putin was the first world leader to call President Bush with assurances of sympathy and support. Within weeks, he delivered concrete help, sharing with the United States vital intelligence about and contacts in Afghanistan, providing over-flight rights for American aircraft, and facilitating the establishment of US bases in Tajikistan and Uzbekistan from which to launch the invasion of Afghanistan. Moreover, as described earlier, the Russian president was quick to enlist in "the war on terror," asserting that Russia was doing its part by battling Islamic terrorists in Chechnya.

In 2002, after lengthy negotiations, Russia and the United States agreed to additional sharp reductions in their arsenals of nuclear warheads, with the goal of cutting the number to between seventeen and twenty-two hundred. Even though US-Russian relations had soured considerably over the Iraq war (discussed below), Putin responded positively to an overture by newly elected American president Barack Obama to reduce further the nuclear arsenals on each side. In May 2010, a new Strategic Arms Reduction Treaty was signed; its terms mandated that, by 2017, each country retain only fifteen hundred deployed warheads and seven hundred delivery systems. Obama indicated that his eventual goal was for the two largest nuclear powers to lead the way to worldwide nuclear disarmament.

Apart from the new arms limitation agreement, President Obama's offer at the start of his term in January 2009 to "reset" relations with Russia had limited results. Progress was made on some minor issues, such as civilian nuclear energy cooperation, American support for Russia's admission to the World Trade Organization, and better trade relations. Yet major disagreements from an earlier time persisted. During 2002, Putin and his advisors became annoyed that Russia's strong support of the United States after September 11 had brought little tangible reward. They were also increasingly skeptical of Bush's determination to topple the Iraqi dictator Saddam Hussein. Although Russia had backed the 1991 Gulf War to liberate Kuwait, in the fall of 2002, Putin opposed American efforts to secure UN approval of the invasion of Iraq, favoring instead a strengthened weapons inspection program. Shortly after war broke out, he called it "a big political mistake," and endorsed German and French criticism of the war.

Other issues in the Middle East besides the Iraq War strained Russo-American relations. The United States opposed, but Russia encouraged, militant Islamic groups, such as Hamas in the Palestinian territories and Hezbollah in Lebanon. While the United States was critical of Syria's repressive regime, Russia has strengthened its relations with Syria by establishing military bases and sending more than four thousand troops to Syria since the civil war began there in 2011. When popular protests against the Syrian government erupted in 2011 and 2012, Russia and China blocked Western and Arab League efforts in the United Nations to impose harsh sanctions on Syria. Putin warned in particular against any outside military intervention, arguing that it would lead to civil war and was, in any case, illegal interference in the internal affairs of another country. Putin took such a hard line over Syria partly because he felt the United States and European powers had deliberately misled Russia over international handling of the rebellion against the Libyan dictator Muammar Gaddafi. In the Libyan case, Russia had agreed, under Western pressure, to UN sanctions and to limited assistance to the rebels. But when the United States and its NATO allies provided Gaddafi's opponents not just humanitarian aid but weapons, logistical and communications support, and aerial bombing, the Russians felt deceived.

Iran's rapidly developing nuclear program posed another Middle Eastern dilemma for Russia and the United States. Although neither country wanted to see Iran develop nuclear weapons, Russia and America struggled to find a common policy to deal with this possibility. In the early 2000s, the Russians promised the Iranians help in building a nuclear reactor, whose declared purpose was the peaceful generation of nuclear energy. In 2006, the Russians, hoping to head off Iranian efforts to develop their own enrichment capabilities, offered to supply the Iranians with highly enriched uranium for peaceful uses, but they were turned down. Although the Russians agreed in June 2010 to fairly stiff UN sanctions against Iran and canceled scheduled weapons deliveries to Iran, Putin also strongly criticized any suggestion that America or Israel might have to use military force against Iran if negotiations failed.

Moreover, throughout the Putin era, Russia strongly opposed an Iran-related project sponsored by the United States. Arguing that if Iran developed nuclear weapons, medium-range missiles with nuclear warheads could reach into Central and Eastern Europe, both Presidents George W. Bush and Barack Obama proposed setting up a missile defense system in Europe designed to thwart that danger. Originally, the United States wanted to erect this barrier in Poland and the Czech Republic. Russia objected vehemently, claiming that the system could easily be directed against Russia's own nuclear deterrent. Eventually, the Czechs lost interest, and plans were made to install the necessary radars and interceptors in Poland and Romania. Putin still attacked the whole idea, though he offered at one point an outdated Russian base as part of the missile defense system. Strenuous European and American efforts to enlist Russian cooperation in the project came to naught. The Russians, somewhat irrationally, brushed aside American explanations that the system obviously was not directed against Russia since the number and sophistication of the Russian missiles would overwhelm it. In 2011 and 2012, the United States proposed modifying the project by placing some of the defenses on naval vessels, but the Russian response was still *nyet*. Nonetheless, in May 2016 the United States activated an

$800 million missile defense shield in Romania, which it claims will help defend Europe from an attack from Iran (should that state develop nuclear weapons, despite the 2015 nuclear deal brokered by both Russia and the United States in which Iran agreed to eliminate or significantly reduce several key areas of its nuclear weapons program) but which Russia views as an aggressive NATO provocation near its own border. The United States also accused Russia of cyber espionage involving interfering with the 2016 United States presidential election when, according to third-party sources, Russian hackers stole and disclosed Democratic National Committee emails. With the election of Donald Trump, allegations that Russia might have interfered in the US presidential election intensified during 2017. The "Russiagate" scandal that followed elicited Russian denials of any collusion, while the Kremlin and the Russian media accused the domestic and Western critics alike of creating a phantom conspiracy.

Relations with the "Near Abroad"

Yeltsin had managed relations with Russia's closest neighbors reasonably well, working out issues with Ukraine and the Baltic states. In the Putin era, Russia consistently sought to extend its influence in these nations and, in 2008, briefly warred with Georgia, as described above. At other times, Russia resorted to intimidation and economic pressure. The most egregious case was Estonia. Russia had acquiesced reluctantly to the Baltic states' joining NATO, often expressed some resentment or jealousy at these little countries' remarkable economic progress after 1991, and complained sporadically about the treatment of Russian minorities in their territories. In May 2007, Putin and leading Russians reacted with outrage when, in preparation for the annual celebration of Germany's defeat in World War II and without much warning to the Russians, the Estonian government moved a statue commemorating the Red Army's role in liberating Estonia from the Nazis out of the center of the capital city, Tallinn, to a Soviet war cemetery on the outskirts of town. Russian agents stirred up rioting among ethnic Russians in the Estonian capital. Kremlin-backed youths in Moscow attacked the Estonian embassy and jostled the Estonian ambassador. Russian computers launched a cyberwar against many state and some private websites in Estonia, shutting them down for days at a time. This brief tempest blew over quickly, but it alarmed the Baltic peoples and their European supporters, reminding everyone that these tiny states lived in the shadow of a grumpy and temperamental Russian bear.

On Russia's western border, Putin twice enforced a substantial gas-price hike on Belarus. In 2011, Russia proposed a customs union with Belarus and Kazakhstan, but otherwise Putin largely ignored Belarus's authoritarian regime.

After some trade quarrels and brief Russian resentment of Poland's close ties to the West, Putin oversaw much-improved Russo-Polish relations in 2010. He reversed the long-standing Russian assertion that the Nazis had been responsible for killing thousands of Polish army officers at Katyn Forest in September 1939, admitting that Stalin's secret police were the murderers. Moreover, when the Polish president died in a plane crash en route to a joint Polish-Russian memorial service at the site of the massacre, Putin and many Russians expressed genuine grief and sympathized publicly with the Poles. To the southwest, the Russian president supported semi-independent Transnistria despite European efforts to see it reintegrated in the neighboring state of Moldova.

Relations with Ukraine, directly to Russia's south, proved rocky. In Ukrainian presidential elections in 2005, Putin openly supported a pro-Russian candidate, who appeared to have lost. Ukrainian officials' attempt to overturn this result sparked a popular uprising centered in the capital of Kiev in what came to be known as the Orange Revolution. After several weeks of demonstrations by protesters camped out in the city center, the Ukrainian government called for new elections in which a pro-Western candidate bested his Putin-backed rival. Putin's intervention appeared clumsy and ill-timed, but Russian commentators blamed the West, insisting that European organizations had supported and manipulated the demonstrators. The new Ukrainian government proved largely ineffective and, in 2006, could do little when Russia pressured it by unilaterally raising the price of natural gas Russia supplied to it. After rancorous negotiations, the dispute was settled, but Russia's neighbors and European countries both noted nervously that their dependence on Russia-provided energy left them open to political pressure from Moscow.

Relations with Asia

Putin and his advisors succeeded in extending Russian influence in the new Central Asian states, and farther east, they established good relations with China, signing a twenty-year treaty of friendship and cooperation on July 16, 2001. In addition, minor border disputes were resolved, joint military exercises were held in 2005, trade and arms sales were expanded, and scientific and technical exchanges were broadened. Russia and China joined in two Asian treaty organizations, but their effectiveness seemed limited. At the same time, many Russians were concerned about China's rising economic and military power. Chinese goods widely penetrated Russian markets, and some two million Chinese were living, working, and trading in Russia's easternmost territories.

In the early 2000s, North Korea's development of a few nuclear bombs led to Russia reasserting its traditional national interest in the Far East. After some hesitation, Russian diplomats participated willingly and effectively in lengthy negotiations among China, Japan, the United States, Russia, South Korea, and North Korea. These protracted talks ended with vague agreements in 2007 and 2011 that North Korea would give up its nuclear militarization in exchange for substantial financial, food, energy, and technological assistance from the other participants in the six-power negotiations. Details were never nailed down, and in 2012 Russia remained watchful as the young successor Kim Jong-un took power in North Korea and continued his country's nuclear weapons program while cracking down on perceived internal dissent to the point that he ordered the murder of his own uncle.

Relations with the European Union

Russia's relations with the European Union (EU) hit some rough patches in the late 2000s. EU members individually sought to work out terms with Russia that would better guarantee Europe's energy supplies and lower the risk of Russia's cutting off natural gas as a form of political intimidation. Collectively, however, the EU failed to agree on a coordinated energy security policy. Meanwhile, Gazprom, the Russian energy giant, extended its ownership and control of gas pipelines and contracted with Kazakhstan and Turkmenistan for their supplies of natural gas, leaving Europe heavily dependent on Russia for this vital commodity. However, as noted earlier, if Russia cut off gas to Europe, its own export revenues and economy would suffer grievously. Moreover, since half of Russia's foreign trade as a whole was with Europe, both sides had reason to stay on good terms.

Russia and the EU also wrangled over the extension of a treaty setting guidelines for the deployment of conventional military forces in Europe and over Russian demands that their citizens be accorded visa-free travel to Europe. Prolonged negotiations over terms of a partnership and cooperation agreement between the EU and Europe dragged on. Europeans responded tepidly to a Russian proposal for a new European-wide security agreement, which would presumably replace NATO.

A major irritant in Russian-Western relations centered on the status of Kosovo, a province of post-Yugoslav Serbia and the site of major Serb repression of the region's Albanian majority during the Balkan wars of the 1990s. After American airpower ended Serb rule in Kosovo, UN peacekeepers and a European governor had managed the affairs of the province beginning in 1999. In 2006 and 2007, a plan supported by the EU and the United States that provided for virtual independence for Kosovo in the near future aroused strong opposition from the Russian-backed Serbian government. Moscow's objections stemmed not from economic, political, or strategic interests in the region but rather largely from sentiment and exaggerated nationalism. Under the banner of Pan-Slavism (see Chapter 9), Russia had supported the Balkan Slavs in the late 1800s, and during the run-up to World War I, Russia had championed the Serbs against Austria-Hungary (see Chapter 10). Now, as Putin sought to restore Russia's self-respect and to reclaim Russia's position as a great power in Europe, it appealed to him and other Russian nationalists to pose as defenders of brother Slavs, the downtrodden and beleaguered Serbs. In addition, the Russians argued that giving Kosovo independence without Serbia's sanction would encourage separatists around the world to rupture many states' territorial integrity. In 2009, Kosovo unilaterally declared independence, and official EU and US recognition soon followed. Russia protested vigorously but also used the example of Kosovo to justify independence for Abkhazia and South Ossetia after its war with Georgia.

Overall, Putin's foreign policy record during the first fifteen years of his presidency was mixed and contradictory. Despite media allegations of a resumption of the Cold War, the new Russia, particularly its economy and culture, was in fact closely tied to the West. Putin sporadically renewed the pledge he made upon assuming office to work cooperatively on the international scene and with Europe and the United States. Many of Russia's actions, such as participating in negotiations over North Korea's nuclear weapons, working with the Europeans and the United States to deal with the danger of Iran creating a nuclear bomb, and working out details for joining the World Trade Organization, made good on that promise. However, by 2007, it was clear that long-simmering and deep-seated resentment about NATO expansion to Russia's borders, a nationalistic drive to gain respect and demonstrate Russia's position as a great power, and a perverse sense of strength derived from criticizing and opposing the United States on some issues had all led Putin and his advisors to pursue assertive foreign policies that at times bullied Russia's neighbors, irritated the Europeans, and deeply annoyed the Americans.

New Points of Contention in Foreign Relations

Recent tumultuous events in neighboring Ukraine have ushered in a more aggressive era of Russian policy and more contentious relations with NATO, the United States, the EU, and the Middle East that some have termed Cold War II or Cold War 2.0. In February 2014, the government of Ukrainian president Viktor Yanukovych rejected a pending association agreement with the European Union that would have brought Ukraine closer to the West and lessened its dependence on trade with Russia. This decision touched off protests in Kiev's Maidan Square (which came to be known as the Euromaidan Movement) and elsewhere in pro-Western areas of Western Ukraine, while counterdemonstrations that supported Yanukovych broke out in pro-Russian areas in eastern and southern Ukraine. In the face of intense domestic pressure and the possibility of civil war, Yanukovych abdicated his position and sought refuge in Russia, where he had received support from the Putin regime since his election in 2010. Russia's reaction to the Euromaidan protests and the possibility that Ukraine would cooperate with NATO, the EU, and the United States more closely was to denounce the Euromaidan movement as an illegal usurpation of the democratically elected Yanukovych. Simultaneously, Russia added military support to its preexisting political support of the ethnic Russian majority in eastern Ukraine, many of whom feared that their rights, Russian identity, and language would be trampled by the post-Yanukovych government in Kiev.

The resulting Donbas War (referring to one of the areas in eastern Ukraine that has seceded from the rest of Ukraine) began in April 2014 and continues to rage at the time of this writing. Pro-Russian and anti-Ukrainian government separatist forces took power in the Donetsk and Luhansk regions with the assistance of Russian military equipment and Russian "volunteers," who Moscow claimed had traveled to the restive regions of their own accord but who according to most international observers were actually active-duty Russian Army personnel in nondescript uniforms. Fighting consumed a number of cities in eastern Ukraine, an estimated two thousand civilians and ninety-five hundred military personnel have been killed, and over a million people have been internally displaced in what Russia officially terms an internal Ukrainian affair. Compounding the controversy over Russia's involvement in the Donbas War was the shooting down in July 2014 of an Amsterdam to Kuala Lumpur Malaysian Airlines aircraft flying over the combat area with the loss of all 298 passengers and crew. Although Moscow blamed Kiev for the incident, independent investigators have concluded that a missile fired by separatists brought down the aircraft. Whether the weapon was provided by Russia or was captured from Ukrainian government forces by the pro-Russian separatists remains a hotly contested issue between Russia and the West.

In March 2014, using the threat of violence against ethnic Russians living in the area as a pretext, a combination of pro-Moscow separatist forces and Russian military personnel occupied Crimea, which had been a part of the Ukrainian Soviet Republic from 1954 to 1991 and then of independent Ukraine since the collapse of the Soviet Union. A widely condemned referendum was held on the Russian annexation of Crimea that month, in which over 95 percent of voters approved Crimea's joining the Russian Federation. Ignoring international protests, Putin lauded the addition of Crimea to the state and suggested that majority ethnic Russian areas of eastern Ukraine might also wish to join Russia.

In an effort to stymie what Moscow perceives as an increase of NATO and EU influence in areas Russia has traditionally controlled or had a significant interest in, the Eurasian Economic Union (EEU) came into existence in January 2015. Consisting of Armenia, Belarus, Kazakhstan, Kyrgyzstan, and Russia, the EEU's intent is to create a customs union that will ultimately include all of the post-Soviet states, excluding the NATO and EU member nations of Estonia, Latvia, and Lithuania. While some of the Central Asian states, notably Tajikistan, have expressed interest in joining the EEU, others—such as Uzbekistan—remain hesitant. In addition, while Georgia, Moldova, and Ukraine have all been offered EEU membership, the governments of all three nations currently prefer to seek admission to the EU. Whether the EEU will serve as a viable alternative to the impotent Commonwealth of Independent States remains unknown.

Recently, Russia has also asserted itself outside of Europe in a way not seen since the Soviet Union's decade-long intervention in Afghanistan. In the aftermath of the 2011 Arab Spring, protests in a number of authoritarian regimes in North Africa and the Middle East either brought down or seriously challenged existing systems. Sectarian and antigovernment violence broke out in Syria and metastasized into a civil war that has killed nearly five hundred thousand and displaced over ten million people in the Middle East and Europe. Under the leadership since 2000 of Russia's ally President Bashar al-Assad, Syria's government launched attacks against various opposition factions in March 2011. Assad's violence against antigovernment forces, both Islamist and secular, has destabilized the entire region and is partially responsible for the rise of the Islamic State of Iraq and Syria (ISIS/ISIL) in the area. In September 2015, claiming that the Assad government requested its assistance, Russian forces began to attack various opposition groups in Syria, including ISIS, but mostly other antigovernment factions that posed more of a threat to Assad than ISIS. Intense international criticism has followed Russia's decision to intervene in Syria. Whether Russian assistance to the Assad government will help it to win the grinding Syrian civil war is yet to be seen, but the impact of Russian airstrikes against Assad's enemies, many of whom are supported by the United States and other powers, has been to strengthen the Syrian portion of the ISIS/ISIL self-proclaimed caliphate.

CONCLUSION

As it is still in progress, the Putin presidency is difficult to summarize and evaluate from a historical perspective. However, to many outsiders, his contradictory actions once appeared to produce a stable, orderly, and more prosperous society. Yet he has implemented his policies in a highly authoritarian and per-sonalized way. For a time, democracy and civic freedom were maintained in-stitutionally, but these elements have been ignored in practice for many years. Though an occasionally responsible member of the world community, Rus-sian behavior in foreign affairs recently has become consistently more abrasive and irritating to the United States, the European Union, and occasionally even Russia's erstwhile ally China.

For many Russians, however, Putin's rule represents a welcome respite from the turmoil of the Gorbachev and Yeltsin years, and as long as oil and pe-troleum prices remained high, his regime provided a decent standard of living. The Gorbachev and Yeltsin eras included years of revolutionary change, hard-ship, uncertainty, quixotic leadership, and loss of Russia's great power status. Many Russians welcomed the stability, economic growth (although it was not consistent), strong rule, and increased national pride that the twenty-first cen-tury brought. Security, well-being, and prospects for an even brighter future meant a great deal to most individuals. Dimly aware that Russia's burgeoning prosperity depended rather too heavily on energy and other raw material ex-ports, that almost one-fifth of the population still lived at or near the poverty level, and that a declining population and a looming health crisis compounded by alcoholism, AIDS, and environmental degradation posed long-term threats, Russians focused instead on the return of their country to prominence on the world stage.

Although the Bolotnaya Square protests about rigged elections erupted from 2011 to 2013 and broad resentment against corruption, lawlessness, and police brutality spread among the urban classes, many Russians remain ap-athetic to bribery, influence peddling, and bureaucratic arbitrariness. When reminded of these problems as well as demoralized and corrupt armed forces, shoddy health services, inadequate welfare provisions, and atavistic patriar-chal attitudes toward women, most individuals prefer to look the other way.

What of the future? Most Russians hope for continued security and prog-ress. As one delegate to the United Russia party congress put it sycophantically, "Vladimir Vladimirovich [Putin], you are lucky! And while you are the pres-ident, the luck accompanies Russia. You have become a talisman for tens of millions of people, a symbol of the successful development of the country. . . . I want you to stay with us, with Russia."

However, as more young people enter the professions and continue to ob-serve and comment on events both at home and abroad on social media, they may yet become more active politically, partly to ensure their economic inter-ests and partly to confront a number of pressing social, environmental, and health issues that need to be remedied if their country is to prosper. Bound to

Europe through culture and education, many younger, especially urban Russians may not want to give up those ties and might seek better relations with the West than their country has had in recent years. Moreover, with a long history of struggle for a better and more just life, many Russians still want economic prosperity and social stability, perhaps strongly enough to demand change from their government, whether it is ultimately led by Putin or someone else.

FURTHER READING

Agyeman, Julian, and Yelena Ogneva-Himmelberger, eds. *Environmental Justice and Sustainability in the Former Soviet Union.* Cambridge, MA: MIT Press, 2009.

Baker, Peter, and Susan Glasser. *Kremlin Rising: Vladimir Putin's Russia and the End of Revolution.* New York: Scribner, 2005.

Donaldson, Robert H., and Joseph L. Nogee. *The Foreign Policy of Russia: Changing Systems, Enduring Interests.* 5th ed. Armonk, NY: M. E. Sharpe, 2014.

Eichler, Maya. *Militarizing Men: Gender, Conscription, and War in Post-Soviet Russia.* Stanford, CA: Stanford University Press, 2012.

Fish, M. Steven. *Democracy Derailed in Russia: The Failure of Open Politics.* New York: Cambridge University Press, 2005.

Goldman, Marshall I. *Petrostate: Putin, Power, and the New Russia.* New York: Oxford University Press, 2008.

Hahn, Gordon M. *Russia's Islamic Threat.* New Haven, CT: Yale University Press, 2007.

Henry, Laura A. *Red to Green: Environmental Activism in Post-Soviet Russia.* Ithaca, NY: Cornell University Press, 2010.

Humphrey, Caroline. *The Unmaking of Soviet Life: Everyday Economies After Socialism.* Ithaca, NY: Cornell University Press, 2002.

Jack, Andrew. *Inside Putin's Russia: Can There Be Reform Without Democracy?* New York: Oxford University Press, 2004.

Ledeneva, Alena V. *How Russia Really Works: The Informal Practices That Shaped Post-Soviet Politics and Business.* Ithaca, NY: Cornell University Press, 2006.

Mankoff, Jeffrey. *Russia's Foreign Policy: The Return of Great Power Politics.* Lanham, MD: Rowman & Littlefield, 2009.

Meier, Andrew. *Black Earth: A Journey Through Russia After the Fall.* New York: Norton, 2003.

———. *Chechnya: To the Heart of a Conflict.* New York: Norton, 2005.

Politkovskaya, Anna. *Putin's Russia.* Translated by Arch Tait. London: Harvill, 2004.

Rose, Richard, William Moshler, and Neil Munro. *Popular Support for an Undemocratic Regime: The Changing Views of Russians*. New York: Cambridge University Press, 2011.

Sakwa, Richard. *The Crisis of Russian Democracy: The Dual State, Factionalism and the Medvedev Succession*. Cambridge, UK: Cambridge University Press, 2011.

———. *Putin: Russia's Choice*. 2nd ed. Abingdon, UK: Routledge, 2008.

Service, Robert. *Russia: Experiment with a People*. Cambridge, MA: Harvard University Press, 2003.

Tsygankov, Andrei. *Russia's Foreign Policy: Change and Continuity in National Identity*. 4th ed. Lanham, MD: Rowman & Littlefield, 2016.

Wegren, Stephen K. *Agriculture and the State in Soviet and Post-Soviet Russia*. Pittsburgh: University of Pittsburgh Press, 1998.

———, ed. *Putin's Russia: Past Imperfect, Future Uncertain*. 6th ed. Lanham, MD: Rowman & Littlefield, 2016.

White, Stephen, ed. *Politics and the Ruling Group in Putin's Russia*. New York: Palgrave Macmillan, 2008.

NOTES

CHAPTER 1: INTRODUCTION: ANCIENT RUSSIA AND KIEVAN RUS'

1. In addition to Russia, the other post-Soviet states are Armenia, Azerbaijan, Belarus, Estonia, Georgia, Kazakhstan, Kyrgyzstan, Latvia, Lithuania, Moldova, Tajikistan, Turkmenistan, Ukraine, and Uzbekistan.

2. Slavic peoples. The term "Slavic" is linguistic and refers to a group of people, Slavs, who speak one or more related languages. The word "Slav" probably comes from the term *slovo*, meaning "word," suggesting that the Slavs at one time spoke a common language. Today, more than twenty Slavic languages are spoken in the Balkans, Central and Eastern Europe, and many of the post-Soviet states. By about the year 600, references by Gothic, Byzantine, and Arab authors make it clear that Slavic tribes formed a considerable part of the population north of the Black Sea. Putting the written and archeological evidence together, we know that these early Slavs had well-developed agriculture, raised cattle and bees, fished and hunted, and knew how to weave and make pottery.

3. Basil Dmytryshyn, *Medieval Russia: A Source Book, 850–1700*, 3rd ed. (Fort Worth, TX: Holt, Rinehart and Winston, 1991), 74.

4. Samuel H. Cross and Olgerd P. Sherbowitz-Wetzer, trans. and eds., *The Russian Primary Chronicle* (Cambridge, MA: Medieval Academy of America, 2012), 84.

CHAPTER 2: KIEVAN RUS' IN CRISIS AND THE MONGOL CONTACT, 1054–1462

1. Basil Dmytryshyn, *Medieval Russia: A Source Book, 850–1700*, 3rd ed. (Fort Worth, TX: Holt, Rinehart and Winston, 1991), 129.

2. Frank Trippet, *The Emergence of Man: The First Horsemen* (New York: Time-Life, 1974), 139.

3. L. S. Stavrianos, *The Epic of Man to 1500: A Collection of Readings* (Englewood Cliffs, NJ: Prentice Hall, 1970), 241.

CHAPTER 3: THE RISE OF MOSCOW, 1328–1533

1. Basil Dmytryshyn, *Medieval Russia: A Source Book, 850–1700*, 3rd ed. (Fort Worth, TX: Holt, Rinehart and Winston, 1991), 134–135.

2. Ibid., 155–156.

Chapter 4: Ivan the Terrible and the Time of Troubles, 1533–1618

1. J. L. I. Fennell, trans. and ed., *The Correspondence between Prince A. M. Kurbsky and Tsar Ivan IV of Russia, 1564–1579* (Cambridge, UK: Cambridge University Press, 1955), 73–75.

2. Basil Dmytryshyn, *Medieval Russia: A Source Book, 850–1700*, 3rd ed. (Fort Worth, TX: Holt, Rinehart and Winston, 1991), 224.

Chapter 5: The Molding of Imperial Russian Society, 1613–1689

1. Joseph T. Fuhrmann, *Tsar Alexis: His Reign and His Russia* (Gulf Breeze, FL: Academic International, 1981), 149.

2. Paul Miliukov, *Outlines of Russian Culture*, Part I: *Religion and the Church* (Philadelphia: University of Pennsylvania Press, 1942), 38.

Chapter 6: Peter the Great and the Conundrum of Westernization, 1689–1725

1. Robert K. Massie, *Peter the Great* (New York: Random House, 1980), 142.

2. R. M. Hatton, *Charles XII of Sweden* (New York: Weidenfeld; 1968), 299–300.

3. George Vernadsky, ed., *A Source Book for Russian History from Early Times to 1917*, vol. 2 (New Haven, CT: Yale University Press, 1972), 349.

Chapter 7: Change and Continuity, 1725–1801

1. Isabel de Madariaga, *Russia in the Age of Catherine the Great* (New Haven, CT: Yale University Press, 1982), 1.

2. Warren B. Walsh, ed., *Readings in Russian History*, vol. 1, 4th ed. (Syracuse, NY: Syracuse University Press, 1963), 225–226.

Chapter 8: Autocracy, Dissent, and Ferment, 1801–1855

1. This vignette of the Decembrist uprising is based largely on material found in George Vernadsky, ed., *A Source Book for Russian History from Early Times to 1917*, vol. 2, *Peter the Great to Nicholas I* (New Haven, CT: Yale University Press, 1971), 524–530.

2. Ibid., 552.

Chapter 9: Reform, Reaction, and Modernization, 1855–1904

1. This account of the assassination is based on information found in W. Bruce Lincoln, *The Romanovs: Autocrats of All the Russias* (New York: Anchor Books, 1981), 443–447.

2. Thomas Riha, ed., *Readings in Russian Civilization*, vol. 2, *Imperial Russia, 1700–1917*, 2nd ed. (Chicago: University of Chicago Press, 1969), 375.

3. George Vernadsky, ed., *A Source Book for Russian History from Early Times to 1917*, vol. 3, *Alexander II to the February Revolution* (New Haven, CT: Yale University Press, 1972), 664.

4. Riha, *Readings in Russian Civilization*, 410, 413.

CHAPTER 10: REVOLUTION, REFORM, AND WAR, 1904–1917

1. Based on an account found in Howard D. Mehlinger and John M. Thompson, *Count Witte and the Tsarist Government in the 1905 Revolution* (Bloomington: Indiana University Press, 1972), 40–45.

2. Sir John Maynard, *Russia in Flux* (New York: Macmillan, 1948), 42–43.

3. Adapted from the version in Basil Dmytryshyn, ed., *Imperial Russia: A Source Book, 1700–1917* (Gulf Breeze, FL: Academic International, 1999), 309–313.

4. Mehlinger and Thompson, *Count Witte and the Tsarist Government*, 336.

5. Vladimir Mayakovsky, *The Bedbug and Selected Poetry* (Bloomington: Indiana University Press, 1975), 75.

6. Allan K. Wildman, *The End of the Russian Imperial Army: The Old Army and the Soldiers' Revolt (March–April, 1917)* (1980; reprint, Princeton, NJ: Princeton University Press, 2014), 89.

CHAPTER 11: REVOLUTION, CIVIL WAR, AND THE FOUNDING OF THE SOVIET STATE, 1917–1928

1. St. Petersburg was renamed Petrograd in 1914, renamed Leningrad in 1924, and returned to its original name in 1991.

2. This description of events on March 10 and 11, 1917, is based on W. Bruce Lincoln, *The Romanovs: Autocrats of All the Russias* (New York: Anchor Books, 1981), 717–722, as well as on other accounts.

3. Existing in its original form from 1917 to 1922, the Russian Soviet Federative Socialist Republic (RSFSR), commonly known as Bolshevik Russia or Soviet Russia, became one of the republics of the Soviet Union (USSR) in 1922.

4. Leonard Schapiro, *The Origin of the Communist Autocracy: Political Opposition in the Soviet State, First Phase, 1917–1922* (Cambridge, MA: Harvard University Press, 1955), 301.

5. Robert C. Tucker, *Stalin as Revolutionary, 1879–1929: A Study in History and Personality*, vol. 1 (New York: W. W. Norton, 1973), 270–271.

CHAPTER 12: THE STALIN REVOLUTION AND WORLD WAR II, 1928–1946

1. Warren B. Walsh, ed., *Readings in Russian History*, vol. 3, 4th ed. rev. (Syracuse, NY: Syracuse University Press, 1963), 761. Reprinted by permission of the publisher.

2. Joseph V. Stalin, *Works*, vol. 13, *July 1930–January 1934* (Moscow: Foreign Languages Publishing House, 1955), 40–41.

3. Feodor Gladkov, *Cement* (London: Martin Lawrence, 1929), 302–304.

4. Stephen F. Cohen, *Bukharin and the Bolshevik Revolution: A Political Biography, 1888–1938* (Oxford: Oxford University Press, 1980), 377.

5. Walsh, *Readings in Russian History*, 770–771.

CHAPTER 13: THE SOVIET UNION DURING THE COLD WAR: SUPERPOWER, STABILITY, AND STAGNATION, 1946–1984

1. Lasting from 1955 to 1991, the Warsaw Pact included Albania (until 1968), Bulgaria, Czechoslovakia, East Germany (until 1990), Hungary, Poland, Romania, and the Soviet Union.

2. Existing from 1949 to 1991, the Council of Mutual Economic Assistance (commonly known as COMECON), included Albania (until 1961), Bulgaria, Cuba, Czechoslovakia, East Germany, Hungary, Mongolia, Poland, Romania, the Soviet Union, and Vietnam.

3. Fedor Burlatskii, "A Political Portrait of Khrushchev," in *Soviet Historians and Perestroika: The First Phase*, ed. Donald J. Raleigh (Armonk, NY: M. E. Sharpe, 1989), 232–233.

4. Basil Dmytryshyn, *USSR: A Concise History*, 4th ed. (New York: Scribner, 1984), 544.

CHAPTER 14: GORBACHEV AND THE COLLAPSE OF THE SOVIET UNION, 1985–1991

1. Quoted in Seweryn Bialer, ed., *Politics, Society and Nationality Inside Gorbachev's Russia* (Boulder, CO: Westview, 1989), 122.

2. Mikhail Gorbachev, *Perestroika: New Thinking for Our Country and the World* (New York: HarperCollins, 1987), 19.

3. Ibid., 21–23.

INDEX